Praise for
The Round Barn, Volume One

"This is an intimate, endearing portrait of the Dougans, a remarkable American farm family guided by a set of principles painted on the silo inside their round barn. The book is a mosaic of beautifully written stories grounded in Jacqueline Dougan Jackson's personal memories, family traditions, oral-history interviews, and solid historical research. Jackson's stories—full of warmth, humor, and charm—give readers a fascinating insider's view of life on a pre-industrial dairy farm."

Robert E. Warren, Illinois State Museum, Director of
Oral History of Illinois Agriculture Project

"Jackie Jackson's *Round Barn* is a delight. The legendary creative writing teacher at the University of Illinois-Springfield has woven a rich and revealing tapestry of American farm life in its halcyon days. *The Round Barn* is so much more than a collection of stories. Think of it as a memoir of a Wisconsin dairy, one that links that farm to the wider world, lovingly crafted to pull the reader into a rich and wonderful world."

Mark R. DePue, Ph.D., Director of Oral History at the
Abraham Lincoln Presidential Library

"*The Round Barn*—with its example of a family farm run with decency and devotion to meaningful labor, and its layering of details about 20th-century farming and milk marketing—seems tailor-made for lovers of Wisconsin and Midwest history. The book is so complete a compendium of one farm's life that it seems difficult to categorize at first. Included are encyclopedic entries that document farm life. There are oral histories that derive from interviews with people who worked on the farm in the decades when Jackie Jackson was a child, and before. There are also maps, diagrams, and photos covering the span of the book. And there are profound nonfiction stories that open the inner lives of the family members like a pleated fan. Readers will finish this book with a genuine affection for members of the family, who come alive in its pages."

Anne-Marie Cusac
Wisconsin Book Festival, 2012

VOLUME TWO

THE
ROUND
BARN

A BIOGRAPHY
OF AN AMERICAN FARM

JACQUELINE DOUGAN JACKSON

Beloit
City
BC PRESS

Beloit City Press
Springfield, Illinois

www.roundbarnstories.com
www.jacqueline-jackson.com

First published 2012
Manufactured in the United States of America
ISBN: 978-1-881480-10-5

Design by Jeremy Schmidt
Artwork and cover by Megan Trever Ryan

Cover photos: The big house and the front of the round barn;
Esther with a calf.

Wesson Joseph Dougan, Wisconsin Farmer

Again, to Grampa

In Fulfillment of a Promise

CONTENTS
VOLUME TWO

A visiting school class checks out life on the other side of the fence.

TO THE READERS OF
THE ROUND BARN, VOLUME TWO

This is the second of three volumes about the Dougan Farm near Beloit, Wisconsin. Volume One, already published, is divided into three books organized around the milk business aspects of the farm: the cows and barns, milk processing, distribution. It contains stories, accounts, and history. This Volume Two continues with general farming aspects: crops, hired help, life in the big farm house and the little house, the development of hybrid seed corn, and the start of artificial insemination. Volume Three details two more farms, and relations with neighbors, Turtle Township, Beloit, Rock County, the state of Wisconsin, and the world. It contains a history of the farm's role in the development of artificial insemination and American Breeders Service, and the ending of this small but significant family farm and business.

The material is told through the eyes of Jackie, myself, who lived through much of this period. It is a collective biography, not a memoir. The entire work chronicles a way of life that in this land has waned and is now either vastly changed, or ended.

There is a wealth of stories connected with this farm through its years of activity—from W.J.'s buying of the farm in 1906, to his son's retirement from the milk business in 1967 and the seed business in 1972. Material has come from hundreds of sources. Some of the stories have already been published in *Stories from the Round Barn* (1997) and *More Stories from the Round Barn* (2002), both Northwestern University Press; these were originally part of *The Round Barn*, and have now been reunited with the parent work. They join many more stories, histories, oral histories, biographies, autobiographies, letters, diaries, essays, magazine and newspaper articles, school assignments, science and technology, scribbled notes, and what I call "accounts," with the stories forming the glue for the informational material—though that material often has stories within it. And everything bears on the telling of the farm's overall history.

Our farm was unusual in that my grandfather had a philosophy that he

Hilda with a helper hangs out wash on the Big House lawn. These volumes will hang out wash of the whole Dougan farm.

painted on his silo, and lived by. Over the years he, and my father after him, hired a diversity of help—local people (often Turtle Township neighbors), university students, men found by advertising in *Hoard's Dairyman*, and a number of foreign workers. These latter escalated in post World War II years, when two Scandinavians were on the farm every six months, through the American-Scandinavian Foundation. There were also handicapped workers. W.J.'s deafness gave him a special feel for the handicapped, and my father followed that lead as a natural course. In the teen years of the century the farm was on the cutting edge of alfalfa development, and then hybrid corn and artificial insemination in the thirties and forties. Both my grandfather and father stayed in close touch with the University of Wisconsin, and methods of scientific farming.

Over the seventy years of the farm's history it produced many documents. These have come from a variety of places: the attics and spare rooms of my parents' and grandparents' houses, also relatives' papers, books, photographs, and furniture had a way of accumulating at the farm. My Uncle Trever, my cousin Jerry, and my brother Craig contributed many documents. Papers, including ledgers, also came from my parents' home offices, the dairy office, business files, even the round barn itself. My grandparents' letters to their sons at college were mixed in with kids' drawings. No one had looked over these materials until my mother alerted me to their existence. When I continued to search, I found more valuable stuff stashed in boxes, photo albums, scrapbooks, work baskets, the backs (and cracks) of drawers, behind pictures, on closet shelves, or merely loose in peculiar places. I'm grateful that so many, however unlikely, have been preserved.

Readers may wonder why there is so much. I suggest several reasons. Ours was a literate family. Grampa and Grama were both college graduates at a time when the terminal degree was eighth grade. This was true also of my maternal grandparents. Both my parents had college degrees. Everyone was a reader and letter writer. Grampa and Grama wrote voluminously to their sons in college, worrying over spending and moral development, but also recounting news of farm and family. And because of Grampa's deafness, many things were written to him that would ordinarily have been spoken and lost. Grampa himself often wrote out what he wanted to discuss with his son the next day. And obviously, we were all inveterate savers. Much also was preserved by chance.

In addition, meticulous files were kept in the business. Every cow was documented, every milk route, all plantings. Business transactions were filed, and government correspondence.

To add to this vastness, since 1967 I sought out people who were willing to relate their experiences on the farm. My parents were vital in these oral histories, and partners in talking with others. It enriched their old age. I'm sorry I didn't get to certain key people before they died. Many had died before I was born, or old enough, savvy enough, to know what I was wanting to do.

Everything in these pages is directly connected with the farm. And everything is as accurate as I have been able to make it. I would say this book is true, but with these qualifications: memory is always in the present. Memories are fickle, including my own, and mutate from year to year. I've had different sources who don't agree on the same set of "facts"; in these cases I've taken the most likely or, if equally so, the most interesting. When there are gaps that have needed filling, I've supplied what would have been most likely, given the people and the times. The "accounts" are as factual as I've been able to make them, including the history, science, technology, and people. These have been aided by actual documents of the time. Though I have included much on many subjects, volumes have had to be left out.

When it comes to the actual stories, I have been more free. They fit the genre of creative non-fiction. Many are "true" all the way through, sometimes even to the major conversation. Mostly, details and conversation have been added, but always within a framework of actuality. Every story has its basis in a real occurrence. The interpretation of a situation is sometimes that of my source, but is often my own, and could well be wrong and is certainly only a partial picture. I've tried not to give in too often to my raconteur father's lifelong advice, "Never ruin a good story for the facts."

My mother is not adequately depicted in these pages. Her influence on everything, especially on the people herein, was tremendous. She was my grandfather's confidante and often his secretary. But mainly she was busy with her work in the music world, and raising her children to be musicians and dancers and artists and writers and scholars, as well as honorable people. Stories involving her are plentiful, but most not directly connected with farm activities.

With Volume Three yet to be finished, I am trusting my father's prediction is still premature. He had been supplying material, and reading and critiquing this work over many, many years. When it appeared the book was to be published, he (at age 90) asked me, "Now just how soon will it be out?"

—Jackie: "Well, I haven't finished it yet, and that'll take at least a year, and then it will take at least a year to edit and publish it—"

—Ron, shaking his head ruefully: "I'm afraid it's going to be a posthumous book."

—Jackie: "Oh, come on, Dad, you can manage to live a few more years!"

—Ron, quick as a flash: "I didn't mean me!"

This second volume is the next step toward proving him wrong.

"What's coming?"

FURTHER ABOUT THE NOW

In Volume One, I wrote a page about current agriculture. Here, I'll revisit that topic.

When my dad, Ron, was 21 and considering joining his father on the dairy, he listed both positive aspects and problems. He ended a letter, "But first I must fall in love with my cows!" That he did. But can a modern farmer fall in love with his cows?

Recently, at the 2012 International Dairy Expo, I talked with a farmer who lives north of Madison, Wisconsin. "I have a niece," I said, "who loves cows. She'd like to be a dairy farmer; what's she up against?" David's response was that today, no young person can afford to farm unless she inherits land or has a sponsor. Land prices have so skyrocketed, equipment continually more expensive, production costs high and rising, that one has to enter farming for keeps, with extreme ambition and desire. In order to feed the world farmers must use modern technology, acquire vast acreage, and mostly practice monoculture. "We're having to produce more, with less workers," David said. As to boots on soil, or hand on flank, a farmer truly up to date can run his business almost entirely by computer, using robot machines for milking, plowing, harvesting. David admitted that he is still using 1980s equipment—he can't afford to upgrade, with the small size of his operation. He added that most farmers have now leased their land to large corporations, or are lucky to be part of a corporate family farm—three or four sons joined in business, who can farm on a massive scale.

I ponder "feeding the world." Our farm was dedicated to feeding a small bit of that world, with the most nutritious food possible. A recent statistic states that global population is now estimated equal to the total of all peoples who have lived through recorded history. How are we to feed our increasing numbers? The fields around my central Illinois city, cultivated when I moved here, are now subdivisions that engulf nearby villages. A bumper sticker, "No Farms, No Food," underscores this growing loss of arable land. Our own family farm, the subject of this book, succumbed with nearly the whole township to I-90, its concrete and cloverleafs.

I could continue with overwhelming threats to food production: climate change, which we are party to, with troubles in our waters and watertables, our soils and air. The vital food chain is being disrupted, from lowly plankton through bats, bees, frogs, and at the top, ourselves. I fear the results of patented seed, and genetic modification — both new under the sun, both here, but neither sufficiently studied (if even possible) to foresee future consequences.

Is there hope? My grandfather gave talks countering "The Big Gloom." What would he say today? I think he'd cite the burgeoning farmers' markets, support of local foods, the growth of small organic farms, the slow food movement, backyard and community gardens, concern about what's both on and omitted from labels. He'd note that he'd always practiced "sustainable" agriculture and "biodiversity," now familiar words. He'd nod gravely at wind power. He'd approve the movement to restore carefully controlled raw milk (as was his), along with pasteurization. He'd be reading books by serious thinkers — Jared Diamond, Michael Pollan. He'd visit my university's Emiquon project which is returning to marshland farm fields along the Illinois River. He'd be astonished at "fat-free half-and-half," and show some gloom, I think, in having to search for farm animals in clover and sunshine.

As I've worked on this farm biography, I have learned and relearned lessons about food and values and cooperation and respect and integrity and, most important, stewardship. The story of the round barn is more than a look back: it's a touchstone for a different kind of agriculture that could offer hope for the future. A future where we may again fall in love with our cows.

ACKNOWLEDGMENTS

I wish to thank the many people who have helped me over the years, sharing their knowledge about the farm and the people who participated in its life. Many contributed pictures, clippings and other materials. A number have died since the collecting of material was begun. Some, like my Dougan grandparents, died before this work was begun in this form, but their contributions, and their lives, are the foundation of *The Round Barn*. A number of the living, and those who, like my parents, died while this work was in progress, have critiqued parts of the manuscript, including their own sections, thus keeping a brake on any tendency to fictionalize. There are surely contributors I've missed in this listing. I am grateful to all who have so generously helped me put together this work.

The family comes first: Eunice and Wesson Dougan, Ronald and Vera Dougan, Trever and Bernice Dougan, Jerry Dougan, Joan Dougan Schmidt, Karl Schmidt, Jeremy Schmidt, Pat Dougan Dalvit, Lewis Dalvit, Craig Dougan, Jackie Dalvit Guthrie, Stephanie Dalvit McPhillips, Damaris Jackson, Megan Jackson Ryan, Gillian Jackson Ferranto, Elspeth Jackson DeBow, Paul Campagna, and June Campagna Schaffer. Eloise Marston Schnaitter has been the richest non-family source, and supplied many details of Esther's story.

Others who participated in the stories or have told their own stories include Walter Abbott, Allen Adams, Arthur Adams, Hugh Alberts, Pat and Ralph Anderson, Lyall Bacon, Bob Babcock, Anthony Bannister, David Bartlett, Ada Beadle, Bill Behling, Oscar and Marian Berg, Theodore Booth-Clibborn, Al Bowen, Quentin Bowen, Earl and Geneva Bown, Floyd Brewer, Phyllis Bruyere, Helen Burnette, Fred Buschner, Anna Marie Calland, Ernie Capps, Georgia Clary, David Collins, Scottie Cook, Al Cox, Mrs. Gustave Dahlstrom, Jean Maxworthy Davis, Mathias Dietrick, Robert Fey, Ralph Flagler, Erv and Olive Fonda, Ron and Georgie Freitag, Bob and Evelyn George, Alfred Gerue, Gulbrand and Solveig Gjestvang, Dan Goldsmith, Lowrey Greenburg, Copeland Greene, Amos and Isabelle Grundahl, Russell and

Mary Adair Gunderson, Benny Harder, Robert Hart, Dorothy Bach Haugan, Paul Herreid, Phil Higley, John Holmes, Jean and Phil Holmes, Red and Loretta Holmes, Sally Holmes, Julia Hornbostel, Lloyd Hornbostel, Jim Howard, Jesse Hunt, Margaret Wieland Ikeman, Rodney Jennings, Florence and Justin Johnson, Howard Johnson, Raymond and Berniece Jorgenson, Bernard and Grace Kassilke, Charles Kellor, Mark Kellor, Jr., Dan Kelley, Glen Kinderman, Don King, Marie Knilans, Richard Knilans, Harlan Koch, Milton Koenecke, Omer Koopman, John Kopp, Marge Kopp, Lawrence Langklotz, Nils Lang-Ree, Lester L. Larson, George Lentell, C.E. Loomis, Dorothy Kirk Lueken, Neil Manley, Clair Mathews, Homer Mathews, Bob Maxworthy, Dolores McCormick, Polly Kirk Mersky, Howard Milner, Norman Neal, Roscoe Ocker, Stanley Otis, David Orlin, Sandy Parker, Norman Peebles, Ed Pfaff, Jerry Pfaff, Dick Post, Orland Potts, Larry Raymer, Cleo Reinfeldt, Lester Richardson, Katie Wieland Russell, Fay Sims, Oscar Skogen, Lester and Mildred Stam, Irene Sommers, John Sullivan, Helen Tapp, George and Elsie Tscharner, Russel Ullius, Fannie Veihman, Fred Veihman, Harry Vogts, Otto Waggershauser, Gary Wallace, Betty Beadle Wallace, Bridget Walsh, Jim Walsh, Dick Walsh, Robert Walton, Robert Wieland, Harry Wellnitz, Harlan Whitmore, Helen Wallace Wildermuth.

I owe thanks to many people for sharing their technical expertise; these are listed in Volume One. Also listed there are those many who have supported and critiqued during the writing and editing process, who have transcribed tapes, prepared photographs, and proofread the text. I must add to that list the recent proofing by my grandchildren: Mark, Miles, and Jay Ryan, and Rachel DeBow; also Katrin Fletcher, Marissa DeWeese, and Sue Reagan.

Continued thanks go to Mitch Hopper for his handling of my website *www.jacqueline-jackson.com* ; also to my daughter Megan for graphics, photography enhancement, and art work. She has also designed a website for the Round Barn books, which can be found at *www.roundbarnstories.com*.

A thank-you is due to my grandparents and parents for creating documents, letters, photographs, and other source material, and never throwing anything out. I'm also grateful for their colorful lives. I'm indebted to my brother Craig Dougan for his excellent memory and for the diaries he kept throughout his teens, and to my first cousin Jerry Dougan for all his assistance in supplying and critiquing family materials. Thanks go to Ed Grutzner who in his memoir, *Tell Me a Story, Grandpa* (2003), devoted a chapter to working on the Dougan farm. From it I have lifted valuable details.

A number of these stories were first published in the *Beloit Daily News* at the invitation of editor Bill Behling, associate editor Larry Raymer, and Minnie Mills Enking. Others have appeared in *Brainchild*, *At the Edges of Our Comfort*, *American Farm Youth*, *The Alchemist Review*, *The Writer's Barbeque*, *FOCUS/midwest*, *TriQuarterly*, and *TriQuarterlyOnline*. *Stories from the Round Barn* was read over Wisconsin Public Radio's Chapter A Day by Karl Schmidt, and *More Stories* by Jim Fleming. *Stories* has been read onto disk for the visually impaired by the Milwaukee (Wisconsin) Public Library, and used by CTB McGraw-Hill. Thanks go to Steven A. Larson, editor of *Hoard's Dairyman*, for permission to reprint material originally published in that magazine.

I appreciate my alma mater, Beloit College, for sponsoring Volume One through The Beloit College Press; plus Jason Hughes, Tim McKearn, and Ron Nief who facilitated publication of that volume. Again, my appreciation goes always to my writing mentors: Professor Chad Walsh of Beloit College, Professor Roy Cowden, Director of the Hopwood Program, University of Michigan, and Professor William Perlmutter, Academic Vice President of St. John's University, Minnesota.

For these *Round Barn* volumes, I have been rich in experienced editors. Mitch Hopper has been my technical editor, and Megan Jackson Ryan my graphics artist and editor. Rodd Whelpley, former editor at *Illinois Issues* (University of Illinois Springfield) contributed valuable preliminary work on the text. Roland Klose, former editor of *Illinois Times*, now an editor for *The Commercial Appeal*, Memphis, has worked extensively with me on the text. Freelance editor and author of prize-winning books, Jeremy Schmidt (who, being family, takes a personal as well as professional interest), has designed the books, has done further careful editing, and has guided the series into production. Professor Tom McBride has been my Beloit College Press editor. Overseeing the entire project, and never giving up on it, is the one who first accepted *The Round Barn*, my unequalled editor Reginald Gibbons of Northwestern University. I am grateful to you all.

XVIII

PROLOGUE

Every story has a beginning, and this one needs to start again from the same place. This prologue is therefore the same for this book, as for the previous volume and the volume to come.

There is the land. In the center of the land are the farm buildings. In the center of the buildings is the round barn. In the center of the barn rises a tall concrete silo. On the side of the silo are printed these words:

> The Aims of This Farm
> 1. Good Crops
> 2. Proper Storage
> 3. Profitable Live Stock
> 4. A Stable Market
> 5. Life as well as a Living
>
> W.J. Dougan

The inside silo of the round barn, showing W.J. Dougan's "The Aims of This Farm."

Jackie could read these words before she could read. She said, "What do they say?" and her older sisters read them to her, or a hired man, or whoever was there. She learned them by heart without trying. She did not ask what the words meant.

W.J. Dougan is Grampa. He had the words lettered there, inside the barn

Jackie Dougan, twelve, helping with the haying.

on the silo, when he had just built the round barn. That was 1911, when Daddy was nine years old. Jackie sees these words every day. Sometimes twenty times, on a day when she and Craig and the others are playing hide-and-seek in the barn. Sometimes not for several days in a row. But add up the times she has seen them, and the days of her life, and they will come out even.

———

Jackie is fifteen. She sits on the arm of Grampa's easy chair. She rumples his thinning hair and shapes it into a kewpie-doll twist. This is a ritual, with all the grandchildren, ever since they were little. Grampa laughs with his stomach, silently.

An idea strikes Jackie. She takes a pencil and paper. These are always near Grampa, for Grampa is deaf. They are always near Jackie, too, for Jackie writes things down. Maybe she has this habit from writing for Grampa all her life. Being his ears. She writes, "Grampa, I am going to write you a book. I am going to call it 'The Round Barn.'"

Grampa studies the paper. He takes a long time to ponder it. Then he nods slowly. "The Round Barn," he says. "Yes, the round barn will have a lot to say." He crinkles all over his face and laughs silently. He is pleased, she can tell.

"I can write," says Jackie to herself, "what the round barn sees. Not just what I know it sees. But what Grampa knows it sees. And Daddy. The milkmen. The cows. All of us! For the round barn is in the middle of us all, and it sees everything. It is the center."

Jackie thinks, here are the circles of the book. She draws a picture, starting with the silo and going out to the barn, and beyond.

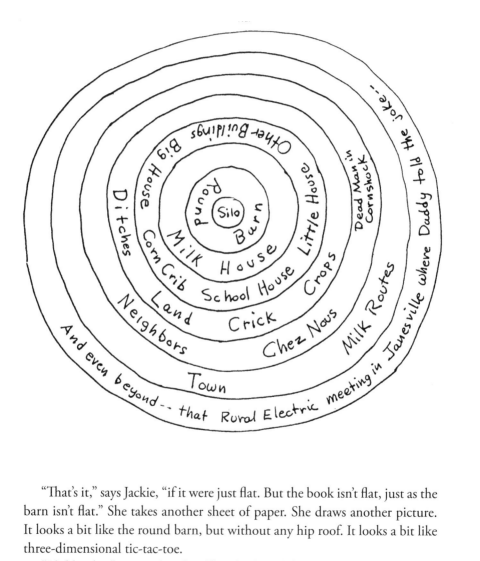

"That's it," says Jackie, "if it were just flat. But the book isn't flat, just as the barn isn't flat." She takes another sheet of paper. She draws another picture. It looks a bit like the round barn, but without any hip roof. It looks a bit like three-dimensional tic-tac-toe.

"It's like this," says Jackie. "We'll go back and forth in time, and wherever we are, it's the present. Here is when Grampa is young."

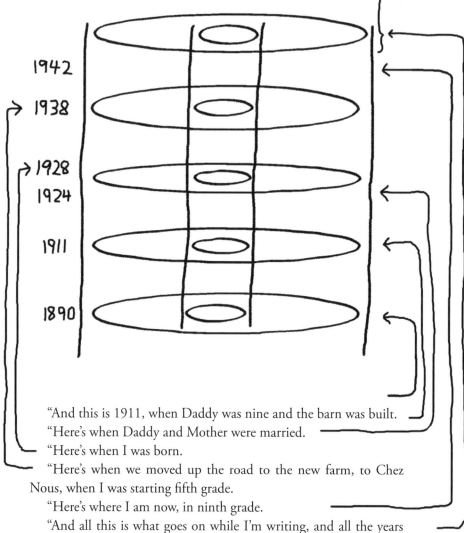

1942

1938

1928
1924

1911

1890

"And this is 1911, when Daddy was nine and the barn was built.

"Here's when Daddy and Mother were married.

"Here's when I was born.

"Here's when we moved up the road to the new farm, to Chez Nous, when I was starting fifth grade.

"Here's where I am now, in ninth grade.

"And all this is what goes on while I'm writing, and all the years after."

For the circles go out, concentric, in space. But they also go up and down in time. Like an onion. But not like an onion completely, for onion parts are too cleanly separated. They pop apart. It's more like elm wood. Elm logs can hardly be split, for the fibers interpenetrate, ring from ring, and bind all the circles together.

The story, the farm, Jackie decides, is like a log of elm wood. Everything, in all directions, in all dimensions, is bound together.

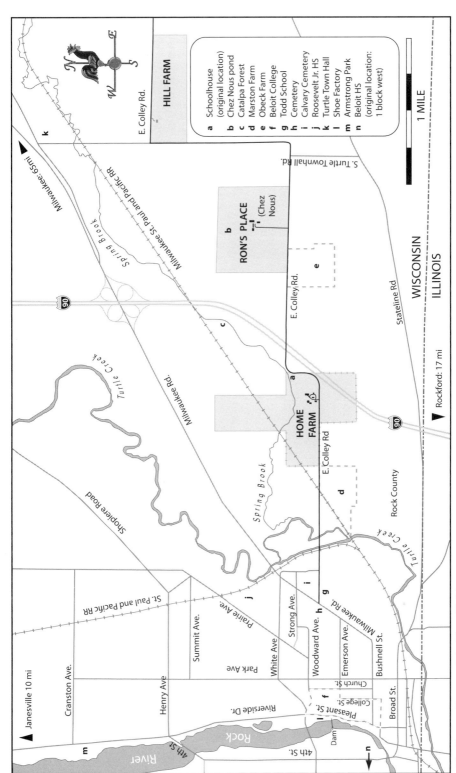

HILL FARM

a Schoolhouse (original location)
b Chez Nous pond
c Catalpa Forest
d Marston Farm
e Obeck Farm
f Beloit College
g Todd School
h Cemetery
i Calvary Cemetery
j Roosevelt Jr. HS
k Turtle Town Hall
l Shoe Factory
m Armstrong Park
n Beloit HS (original location: 1 block west)

1 MILE

RON'S PLACE

b (Chez Nous)

E. Colley Rd.

E. Colley Rd.

S. Turtle Townhall Rd.

WISCONSIN
ILLINOIS

Stateline Rd.

▶ Rockford: 17 mi

HOME FARM

E. Colley Rd

Rock County

Spring Brook

Turtle Creek

Milwaukee Rd.

Shopiere Road

Tutle Creek

St. Paul and Pacific RR

Milwaukee St. and Pacific RR

Spring Brook

▲ Milwaukee: 65mi

E. Colley Rd.

▲ Janesville 10 mi

Cranston Ave.

Henry Ave

Summit Ave.

Park Ave

Prairie Ave.

White Ave

Strong Ave.

Woodward Ave.

Emerson Ave.

Bushnell St.

Milwaukee Rd.

Church St.

College St.

Pleasant St.

Riverside Dr.

Broad St.

4th St.

Dam

ROCK RIVER

j
i
g
h
f
e
c
a
d
m
n

The Dougan Farms and the City of Beloit.

The Dougan Dairy Farm as it appeared by 1960.

Megan Trever Ryan

Chez Nous, the home farm of Ronald and Vera, who remodelled the old farmhouse and moved here in 1938.

Megan Trever Ryan

FAMILY

Here is the family you'll meet in these pages.

Grampa: Wesson Joseph Dougan, 1868-1949

Grampa was generally called "Daddy Dougan" by farm people and the community. He began his career as a Methodist minister but left because of deafness. At fourteen he took over the work of the family farm — his father was injured — so he was unable to start high school till his father's death and the sale of the farm in 1887. He attended Wayland Academy in Beaver Dam and the University of Wisconsin. In 1906 he bought the Colley farm, began peddling milk in Beloit in 1907, and built the round barn in 1911. His mother, Delcyetta, bore him when she was forty-five. He had three older sisters, Della (of Mason City, Iowa), Ida, and Lillian. Ida married James Croft and lived in Beloit; they adopted a daughter, Hazel. After James's death, Lillian moved in with Ida. Grampa also had second cousins, Jennie and Nelly Needham, as well as a niece and nephew, the Bosworths — the "rich relatives" of Elgin, Illinois. The youngest of their four daughters was Betsy.

Grama: Eunice Trever Dougan, 1869-1959

Eunice came from England at six months, with eight siblings; two more were born in Wisconsin. She graduated from Lawrence College and taught for two years before marriage. Her oldest brother, George, was a conservative Methodist minister of some distinction; her youngest, Albert Augustus, became a beloved professor at Lawrence, wrote an ancient history textbook still in use, and has had a hall named after him. Uncle Bert was the Dougan kids' and grandkids' favorite, and Grama's sister Ria, nine when she came to the States, was the favorite aunt. Rose, the youngest, was epileptic and probably mildly retarded. Eunice was called "Mother Dougan" by the help who lived at the Big House.

Wesson and Eunice's Children

The first child, Esther (1900) bled to death at a botched birth (the drunk doctor cut the cord too close to the body). They had two sons, Ronald (1902-96) and Trever (1904-83). Esther (1909-76) was a foster daughter. All three attended the District 12 school (with occasional stints at a town school) and Beloit High School. Ronald went to Northwestern for three years; spent a year in France and married (in 1924) Vera Wardner (1895-1988) of Chicago, who was in France doing the same type of social work; returned to Beloit and took his senior year at Beloit College. He then went into business with his father. Trever attended the University of Wisconsin, married Bernice (Binney) Marion (1905-94), worked for United Airlines for many years, and eventually owned a Chicago blueprint firm.

Ronald and Vera's Children

Ronald and Vera had four children. Joan (1925) married Karl Schmidt and they produced Peter, Jeremy, Katie, Dan, and Tom. Patricia (1926) married Lewis Dalvit and had Jackie Jo and Stephanie. Jacqueline (1928) married Robert Jackson. They had four daughters: Damaris, Megan, Gillian, and Elspeth. Craig (1930) married Carol Glad who had two sons; Craig fathered Cynthia Sue and Trever. After Carol's death he married Barbara McDonald who had three children, thus making a family of seven children.

Trever and Binney's Children

Trever and Binney had two children. Jerry (1932) married Deborah Greabell and had Scott, Patrick, and Dan. Karla (1937) married John Pendexter and had Leslie, Jay, and Geoff.

Esther's Child

Esther had one son, Russell, born in 1926. He was killed in the Korean War, 1951. Russell married and had a son, Rusty.

BOOK FOUR
THE BIG HOUSE

The Big House, side barn, and round barn, about 1913.

1 ⚹ BERTHA ZIMMERMAN

Bertha Zimmerman is a handsome woman with a beautiful voice. She lives in Beloit with her husband Frank and son Charles, and gives singing lessons. She knows Mother through Treble Clef music club. She knows Daddy because they went to high school together, and because she's a Dougan customer. The two families are friends.

Jackie, a senior in high school, is in the car one Saturday when Daddy stops to leave a pint of cream for the Zimmermans.

"Oh, Ron," calls Bertha, "can you come in a minute? The other day I was going through some old papers of my grandmother's and came across a letter you'll be interested in."

"What hath she to do with me?" Daddy asks.

"Well, you knew my mother was living on the Colley farm at the time your father bought the place," Bertha says. "My father was the tenant farmer."

Daddy didn't know at all.

"And I was born there," adds Bertha, "upstairs in the big room on the southwest corner."

Daddy shakes his head in further astonishment. "That was my room," he says, "and later Esther's. I didn't know we had so much in common."

Jackie calculates the southwest corner. It was the guest room before Grama and Grampa moved to town. She'd often slept there, in the huge bed with the ornate, towering headboard that grazed the ceiling and seemed to lean over you so that you felt uncomfortably that it might crash down on you in the night. It seems odd that such intimate Dougan territory was ever shared with Bertha Zimmerman.

Frank Zimmerman looks up from his paper when they come into the living room.

"I hear your wife entered this world in my bedroom," Daddy says. "It's news to me."

"Not to me," Frank says. "Every time we drive out Colley Road and past

The Big House when W.J. and Eunice bought the farm in 1906.

the Dougan house, Bertha makes me tip my hat in deference to her place of birth."

Bertha finds the letter in her desk. "It's from my mother Mattie — Mrs. B.E. Thomas — and it's dated 'Beloit, Wisconsin, July 14, '01.' There's a lot about me as a baby, but I'll just read you the part about the farm and the weather."

She reads aloud:

> We are having awful weather now, one day this week the thermometer went up to 114 and the wind blew a perfect gale and so hot it felt like it came from an oven. Then just at noon the hayfield between us and town caught fire and burned 25 acres and the wind blew it toward us and our rye field caught fire and commenced burning, and burned about an acre but was just a trifle green to burn good. If it had burned, our buildings would have gone sure for the rye field comes up to the barns. Neighbors fought the fire for an hour and a half in that awful hot dry wind blowing right toward the buildings. I gave up all hope of their saving them. It was as near a burning out as I want to see. Bert said, if the wind didn't change, to take the children and walk up the road to the neighbors.
>
> Three weeks ago we had the biggest hail storm that the folks who got it ever saw. It was just a little streak, did not hail in town nor beyond a mile

north or south of us. Don't know how far east it extended but it pelted us good for about 15 minutes: wind blew very hard, hail stones as big as hickory nuts, the ground just white with them, and such a roar. Bert's folks near Manchester never got a bit of it, it cut off our rye and oat heads so there will be about half a crop. Pastures are as brown as can be, it's so dry corn is rolling up, have to feed the stock same as in winter.

"There, Ron — what do you think of that?"

"Absolutely fascinating," Daddy agrees, and takes the letter and reads the whole thing again, even the parts about baby Bertha having the croup.

He and Jackie discuss the Zimmermans all the way out Colley Road.

"Bertha and her sister were willowy glamour girls in high school," Daddy says, "and they liked to dance. I envied all my suave friends who took them out. But I was too shy and shrimpy to ask for a date with the popular Thomas girls, or with anybody for that matter." He tells Jackie how Grama and Grampa disapproved of dancing, but he learned to dance, secretly, out behind the horse barn. One of the hired men taught him.

As they approach the dairy Jackie says, "That's the field that caught on fire. Do you suppose it was spontaneous combustion in the terribly dry and hot hay? And the neighbors must have been old Mr. and Mrs. Smith, and the Marstons."

"No, they weren't there yet; I don't know who was there," says Daddy. "But people would have come from all up and down the road. With the fire heading east in gale winds, if they hadn't managed to stop it, it would surely have got the house and the barn — the side barn, of course — and the granary, Grampa moved it to build the round barn — and then the horse barn just behind that. He wouldn't have bought the place if all those buildings had been gone."

Jackie muses. "So us Dougans being here depended on a field of green rye back in 1901. Isn't it funny how — "

"Shh!" interrupts Daddy. He takes off his hat and holds it over his heart. Driving with one hand he speeds past the dairy buildings on the way up to Chez Nous. He replaces his hat. "Now go on. I just wanted to observe a moment of respect out of reverence for the natal place of Bertha Zimmerman."

2 ❧ BAREFOOT

I t is early October 1914. It's suppertime. Grampa sits midway on one side
of the dining-room table. Grama is at the end. Ronald and Trever and the
hired men are in their places. The men have showered, slicked back their hair,
and donned clean shirts and trousers. Fried potatoes steam in a dish on the
snowy tablecloth. There are pitchers of milk, slices of cold meat, bread and
butter, fresh applesauce, creamed carrots.

Grampa has said the blessing: "Bless the Lord, O my soul, and all that is
within me, bless His holy name. Bless the Lord, O my soul, and forget not
all His benefits."

The food is passed. People begin to eat.

Grampa looks around the table. He says, "I saw a sight today I have never
seen before, and I hope I shall never see again."

Everyone pauses to pay attention to Daddy Dougan.

"I went over to Tiffany very early this morning, to buy a cow," Grampa
says.

Everyone nods. They know where Grampa went, and that he returned
with a cow.

"It was still dark when I got there," says Grampa, "and I saw a light in
the barn. I went in, and saw a lantern way down at the end of the row of
cows. Someone was milking there, so I walked down to see who. And as I got
close, I saw it was a little lad, and he seemed to be milking in an odd sort of
manner."

Grampa has everyone's complete attention.

"It was chilly this morning," says Grampa. "There was frost."

Everyone nods.

"The little lad was barefoot," Grampa says, "and when I got up to him I
saw that he was balancing himself on the milking stool with one foot, and
holding the other one over the bucket"—Grampa pushes back his chair and
demonstrates—"and milking the stream of warm milk onto that dirty little

foot! And when that foot was warm, he put it down on the stall floor and raised his other dirty little foot and milked onto that one!"

The gathering is thunderstruck. Grampa looks at their stunned faces and laughs silently. His eyes disappear.

Then everyone explodes into laughter. When the hubbub dies down, Grama shakes her head in disbelief. "Wesson, that can't be true!"

Wesson assures her it is.

Ronald shouts into his father's ear trumpet. "Did you say anything to anybody? Did you tell his father or mother?"

Grampa laughs and shakes his head no. "The wife asked me in for a cup of coffee and some coffeecake," Grampa says. He adds, "I drank the coffee black."

Grampa bought a cow.

3 ⋊ THE GHOST OF BOB

The first dog at the Big House Jackie knows anything about is Bob. This is because there are two pictures of Daddy, when he's about fourteen, with a large black and white collie. In both pictures Daddy is sitting cross-legged on the incline that leads to the loft of the round barn, and Bob is beside him. In one picture there's also a calf. Bob looks to be a happy, loving dog; both he and her father are laughing. The pictures are full of sunshine and vitality.

Jackie hears two stories about Bob, though, and these dim the sunshine. The first one Moo-Moo tells her. Moo-Moo is the route man Lester Stam's wife Mildred; she and Lester, as a young couple, lived in the apartment over the milkhouse.

For many years Bob had been an excellent cowherd. Mornings and evenings he helped round up the cows from the pasture and bring them to the barnyard. But when Moo-Moo comes to the farm in 1922, Bob is very old. He no longer fetches cows. He no longer chases a stick when someone throws it. No one throws for him anymore, anyway—Ronald is away at Northwestern and Trever is a busy high school senior. Bob spends most of his time lying on the rug in the front room, beside Grampa's desk. It's Bob's spot. When Grampa works there he sometimes rubs Bob with his foot, or drops his hand and caresses an ear, and says, "Good old Bob." Bob rolls his eyes upward and thumps his tail.

Moo-Moo goes for walks around the farm buildings, and on Colley Road. When Bob is outside, he gets up stiffly and goes along. She walks slowly to make it easy for him. One day he sees her starting out. He rises, whimpers. He takes a few steps, sits down, and fairly cries.

"Bobbie," says Moo-Moo, "you don't always have to come. Go lie down in the shade and just rest yourself."

Bob gives her a grateful look and lies down again.

"He seemed so thankful I'd excused him from my walk," Moo-Moo tells Jackie. "It was as if he understood every word I said."

A few days later one of the hired men, George Hotton, brings a small dog to the farm. It's young and silly, and makes the men laugh. George brings it into the Big House when Moo-Moo and Grama are in the front room. It leaps and jumps at them, then runs to Grampa at his desk. It licks and barks. It pays no attention to Bob lying on his usual spot on the rug. Bob seems to cringe into himself.

"Hi!" says Grampa. "Where did this foolish pup come from?"

"Somebody gave him to me, but he seems to like you best," George says, and writes this to Grampa. He adds, "You can have him."

Grampa looks down at miserable Bob. "What would I do with Bob here?"

"I guess you'll just have to shoot him," says George as he writes it.

Old Bob struggles to his feet and gives Grampa a long look of anguish. Then he hobbles to the door to be let out.

"Such an expression!" cries Moo-Moo in dismay.

Grama says, "I do declare that dog knows what you said, George!"

"Fiddlesticks," laughs George, and goes out with his frisky pup.

It's a busy time, and for a day or so no one notices that Bob is missing. Then Grama begins to fret. "Where's Bobbie? I haven't seen him. Who's seen Bobbie?"

Nobody has seen Bobbie.

The following day the carpenters come to tear the porch and bay window off the front room. They will build a more spacious porch for the Big House. As they start tearing down the old structure, they come on Bob's body.

Bob, Ronald, and a calf, on the ramp before the loft doors.

Grama is upset. "He did hear!" she accuses George. "Just like I said, he thought you were going to shoot him, and he crawled in there to die!"

"Bobbie always could understand like a human," agrees Moo-Moo.

"Fiddlesticks!" says George.

George's pup gets himself run over within the week, and he's not replaced. For several years the Big House is dogless.

Then comes the second episode about old Bob, which Jim Howard, a former herdsman, tells Jackie when he visits the farm years later.

"Do you believe in ghosts?" he asks. "Do you believe a dog can see ghosts?"

Jackie is doubtful.

"You've never heard the story of old Bob?" Jim is incredulous. "Well, when I was working here Daddy Dougan got a young white collie to help with the cattle. The first night, they let him into the front room. That dog came running in, and the strangest thing, he stopped short of a certain spot, kind of crouched down, and barked and snarled. They tried to get his attention away from it, but he kept turning back, and going around it, and carrying on. He wouldn't cross it, no, he wouldn't cross it! Just circled and snarled. Nobody knew what in the world was the matter with that dog!

"Ronald dropped over, and we thought maybe the dog was hearing something downstairs, so we went to the cellar. Nothing was there, no rat, nothing on the ceiling above. So we came up again, and Ron looked at that white collie still crouching and snarling, and he said suddenly, 'He's seeing Bob!'

"'What?' I said, and Ron said, 'Bob's ghost!'

"Then they explained to me that W.J. used to have his desk just beyond that place on the carpet, and that for years Bob had lain there beside the desk. It was Bob's spot.

"'He can't be smelling Bob!' cried Mother Dougan. 'We've changed that rug since Bob died, and this new one's been cleaned, oh, several times! And of course it's vacuumed every week!'

"'Well,' said Ron, 'that proves it, it must be Bob's ghost. The collie senses something in Bob's spot.'

"And do you know?" Jim finishes. "That dog never did walk over that place! He'd always scout around it. What do you make of that?"

Jackie is willing to believe. "What ever happened to the white collie? I never knew about a white collie."

"It only stayed six months or so, and then ran off," says Jim. "Maybe Bob scared it away. Who knows? Maybe Bob's ghost is lying there yet."

"We'll need a dog to tell," Jackie says.

4 ⋇ I LOVE YOU, GRAMA

Patsy is four. Jackie is almost three. Grama's back is to them; she's bending into a chest upstairs in the Big House.

"I love you, Grama," Patsy says.

Grama doesn't even look around. She says, "What've you been up to now?"

Patsy on a fence. The Big House is beyond.

5 ⋈ AEROPLANE

It's the end of August, 1911. Trever, seven, is squirming on the hard board of a grandstand seat at the Beloit Fair. Ronald, nine, is beside him, reading. Trever is infinitely bored. Many of the people in the grandstand are bored, too, and restless. Well, they should be. This is the big moment they've all been waiting for, but the moment stretches on and on, and has not yet come. Maybe it won't come at all. Trever heaves a heavy sigh.

"It shouldn't be long now, Trever," says his mother. She doesn't sound convinced.

He looks down the field before the grandstand to its end, where the special hangar has been built to house the first aeroplane ever to fly in Beloit. The plane is inside, last night's paper said, shipped up by train from Chicago, along with its mechanics. The Shooting Star. But the doors are shut, and the people loitering outside don't look ready to open them. There's nobody he can spot who looks like the famous pilot, Jimmie Ward, whose picture has been all over the paper for the past week.

The people running the fair have given up trying to entertain the crowd. There have been horse races and carriage races and foot races. A juggler performed, and even a fire eater. Now there is just nothing, not even the man with the megaphone shouting that it will not be long now, folks.

Trever watches whenever a few boys spill out of the grandstand for a game of tag, wishing he were with them, but they always get shooed right back up. Earlier, he and Ronald had wandered all over the fair, noting the blue ribbons on the cattle and swine and poultry, wishing they had money for tickets to throw balls at ten pins or to fish for a prize in the miniature fishpond. They each did have enough money for one treat, cotton candy. Then they'd met their parents at the grandstand for hard boiled eggs and chicken drumsticks and apples and milk, rather than be allowed to buy from the many mouthwatering food booths.

Trever thinks back to all he and Ronald had read about the fair. "Mama,"

Shooting Star: an early Curtiss aeroplane.

he says, "the paper said they wouldn't let anyone in 'of a questionable nature.' But there are thousands of people here. How can they tell the bad ones?"

"Oh, I suppose if a drunk tries to come in," says Eunice, "or some vagrant, they'll stop him at the gate. And there's no gambling to attract gamblers."

"And the paper said they weren't allowing any shady shows that would flim-flam the public. What sort of shows do that? What does 'flim-flam' mean?"

"Never you mind," says his mother. "Now try to settle down — it can't be long now."

Trever sighs again, and thinks back to a week ago, when he and Ronald were sprawled on the living room floor, the many-paged supplement to the *Beloit Daily News* open in front of them. They are reading aloud the serial story.

There is always a continued story in the paper, and Trever and Ronald read them regularly. But this one is specially timed to what is going on in Beloit. It's been placed in the aeroplane supplement that tells all about the big air show coming next week, and is called "My Aeroplane Adventures." There's an illustration of a worried pilot in his leather cap; his eyeballs through the goggles are white marbles looking downward between the struts of his flimsy-looking craft. Under the picture are the words, "Had anything failed there would have been no alternative but a backward drop to awful destruction!" Today's episode is called "Fighting Fear in Cloudland."

"See?" says Trever, at the last paragraph. "He lives, even though his plane is wrecked in the storm, because they can't stop the story this soon."

"But lots of pilots really do die," Ronald says, and they turn back to study a column they've already scanned, "Aviation's Toll of Death." It lists world-wide deaths and their causes, from 1908: one death, a lieutenant flying with Orville Wright; through 1909, with four deaths, all in France and Italy caused by "an aeroplane turned turtle," "machine collapsed," "wing broke," and "motor exploded while in air;" to the many deaths in the previous year of 1910.

"Thirty-two," breathes Ronald, counting down the column.

"This one was making a turn against a high wind," whispers Trever, who can read almost as well as his brother.

"Here's falling into harbor," Ronald points, "and 'colliding with pylons marking course.' He must have been in a race."

Trever says, "Listen to this: 'While making flight in machine of own invention!'"

They read on down in hushed tones—both from the grimness of the subject, but mainly because their mother might not approve of their reading about such terrible fates. Maybe she'll decide it's not wise to go to the air show, to perhaps see the pilot plummet from a plane turned turtle. Along with deaths caused by falls, there are those where the pilot lost control, where motors stopped suddenly, where struts or wires broke, or where a pilot failed at making a spiral dip. Treacherous air currents are the cause of several fatal

Jimmie Ward in the cockpit, enjoying the company of an admirer.

accidents. A canvas ripped out on one plane, and threw the machine back-wards. And one aeroplane vanished over the English Channel. Only two en-tries say "cause unknown." When ages are given, all the men are young. One is only seventeen.

Trever and Ronald are apprehensive. Both are uneasy for Jimmie Ward. They've already read and reread many details. He's flown in air shows all over the country. He's at the International Aviation Meet in Chicago right now, and just landed his plane after the propeller disintegrated in mid-flight. He cut his engine and glided back to the ground without crashing. His picture, and one of his Curtiss plane, cover the supplement's entire front page.

"Shooting Star," murmurs Trever. The plane's very name sparks magic.

Jimmie Ward will make two flights each day of the fair. Trever and Ronald have been promised that they'll see the very first flight.

The Beloit Fair isn't really in Beloit, but just outside South Beloit, in Il-linois. It's close to the farm, on the other side of the State Line Road, before Turtle Creek. The paper describes how the grounds have been spruced up, the bleachers scrubbed, the tracks leveled. All the concession stand allotments are contracted, all the pig stalls rented. So many cattle are coming to be judged that the barns on the grounds are full, and many cows will be stabled in town. They are expecting five thousand people the first day, and at least twice that number the next.

The paper also includes an absorbing column about world records, with top altitude 9,714 feet, and top speed 67.86 miles per hour. There's even an article about the courage of women flyers, called aeronauts. The headline is, "Ladybirds Who Soar on Wings of Modern Magic," with a drawing of one flying serenely; she holds a control stick in either hand. But Trever hadn't bothered to study that article.

Now, a week later, he wishes he had that story with him, had the whole supplement with him. He gives Ronald a poke. His brother grunts and goes on reading.

Suddenly there's a stirring in the crowd. Trever looks down the field. The hangar doors are opening! The spectators' voices rise to a shout, people are standing. Ronald closes his book.

"It's starting, boys," says their father, pulling out his pocket watch. Eunice says, "Well, it's about time!"

All necks crane as men wheel the plane out.

"It looks just like the pictures," Trever says. "Like a big box kite."

The aeroplane, being pulled into some kind of position, is largely air — thin wings above and below, held together by poles and wires, bicycle wheels in a triangle underneath, a propeller in front, a tail with an upright tag on it, a mechanical clump in the middle which must be the engine, and in front of it, a place for the pilot to sit. One of the men must be Jimmie Ward!

"How does anyone dare entrust his life to that contraption?" says Eunice. "It wouldn't hold a fly!"

One man is indeed Jimmie Ward is in a jacket and the familiar helmet. He waves to the crowd, which is settling back onto their seats. He does something around the engine till it starts to roar, steps to the propeller— it must be a new one—gives it a mighty swing till it's spinning, then climbs up into the plane. He adjusts himself on the seat.

With another wave to the now silent crowd, he taxis down the field, speeding up. Trever holds his breath.

And then, right in front of the center grandstand, the little craft lifts off. It's airborne! The crowd cheers. The plane rises, circles the field, circles the fair, then heads east in the direction of Turtle Township and the farm. It dwindles to a speck, disappears. The crowd waits, murmuring.

The speck reappears, grows, and the plane is back. It swoops low over the field, people gasp and duck. Trever ducks too, though he knows the aeroplane is not dangerously near. It climbs again, higher and higher. Trever holds his breath again, hoping for, yet fearing, a spiral dip. His fingers are white grasping the grandstand seat. But Jimmie Ward does not attempt any daredevil feats. He heads east again, returns, circles the crowd several more times, then settles into a smooth landing. The plane bumps over the turf, the propeller slows, the engine sputters to a stop.

"He's been in the air twelve minutes," says Wesson, consulting his watch. "It's now 5:37."

Jimmie Ward waves, and jumps to the ground. A number of official-looking men advance to meet him, reaching to grab his hand. But the crowd cannot be held back. People surge onto the field.

"Wait, boys!" cries Eunice, but Trever and Ronald are among the first. They squirm through those ahead till they are close to the fragile double-strutted wings, and can hear the newspaper reporter shouting questions. Trever drinks in every detail of the aeroplane, from its propeller blades to the taut, guy-wired tail.

Jimmie Ward stands at ease, chatting affably with the reporter, consenting for his picture to be taken with the officials. Answering questions from the crowd.

Trever is dazzled. When Jimmie Ward is facing the other way, he darts forward and tentatively touches a wire near the tail. Shooting Star! Jimmie turns in time to see him and Trever jumps back, his face flaming. But the famous man steps over and ruffles Trever's hair. "That's all right, sonny!" he says. "Did you enjoy the show?"

Trever nods dumbly.

"You're going to be a pilot some day, aren't you?"

"Oh, yes!" blurts Trever, and his ears ring.

"Good boy," says Jimmie Ward. "Here's something to remember this day." He reaches into his jacket pocket and hands Trever a small brass medallion. He then turns back to the officials.

Trever is too overcome to say thank-you. He turns the medallion over and over in his hand. It's about the size of a nickel and has an imprint of an aeroplane on one side. On the other is "International Aviation Meet, Chicago 1911."

"What did he say? What is it? Let's see it," says Ronald, from a circle of close-pressed boys. He holds out his hand.

Trever backs away. "I'll show you all later. Maybe."

After a few more minutes the crowd is herded from the plane. Then Jimmie walks beside it as the mechanics wheel the craft back to the hangar. Trever watches as it disappears inside and the big doors close.

He holds the medallion tight in his hand, and his hand tight in his pocket. He hears his mother calling impatiently, "Come along, boys! There can't be a second flight today! We're leaving!"

Finally he turns and joins his family. He climbs in the buggy and rides home. On the way, his father speaks of the marvels of modern technology. Ronald maintains an accusing silence. But Trever is hearing only the roar of the engine in his ears, feeling only wind in his face. Smoothing the little medallion with the finger that touched the Shooting Star.

He will fly, like Jimmie Ward! He will fly! He has never been surer of anything. He has lost his heart to the skies.

6 ⚹ GRAMPA'S WORK PLANS

Grampa is a record keeper. He keeps track of every penny, every laborer, every cow. He keeps track of every customer, until Daddy joins him and takes over that aspect of the business. Grampa's records are kept in various ledgers, large and small, or notebooks, or in cubbyholes of his roll-top desk. One vital record, in a medium-size three-ring notebook, is the daily plan for the work of the farm.

Each day has its page; he writes the date at the top. He then lists, in pencil, the jobs that are to be done that day. The list isn't exhaustive, it's in the range of necessity and possibility. Sometimes, under Miscellaneous, abbreviated to "Miscl," there are suggested extras, if these jobs can be fitted in. Sundays the page is different. It heads up the beginning of the work week and lists the tasks to be accomplished in the next six days.

Grampa usually fills in this daily record in the evening. First he makes large checks before the items of the day just ended, what was managed. If a job is not undertaken or not completed, he makes a zero before the listing. He notes the weather in small script in the upper left corner. Looking back, he'll be able to remember the conditions that affected that day's labor. Then, on the next page, he writes the date for the morrow, and the jobs to be done, both the work and the farmhands he plans to have do it. He includes himself among the farmhands. At the end of the year, he bundles up all the pages for reference and storage, and starts afresh.

The notebooks are interesting to peruse, even to marvel at, as the variety of work unfolds in regular rhythm. For most readers they tend to be somewhat tedious, unless one knows the farm and circumstances well, for Grampa only occasionally enlivens his text by details or commentary to himself. A story-account is a rarity.

Examination of a few pages from late June 1942, shows a busy time. The previous week the farm has been mainly occupied with silo filling. That accomplished, it is now onto haying and cultivating. Grampa's spare list doesn't say whether the hay-loader is used, or how the cut hay is turned into wind-rows. He doesn't name particular machinery, or anything about tractor versus horses, unless this information is pertinent to the project at hand. He knows, and if the men don't he will tell them. It's enough for his record to indicate the general job.

> Clear, hot Saturday 6/26
> Work Today
>   Cultivating Hill Farm—18 acres, Mr. Beadle & Red
>   Haying
>   A.M.
>   a. putting up new rope Round barn
>   b. unloading 3 loads clover
>   c. hauling 7 big loads from field 2b. Milton T (excellent hay)
>   d. cutting field 2b Mr. G, WJD, Don, Sam, Geo H
>   Miscl: vaccinating 94 pigs 6:30 a.m. Mr. B, Red, Sam, Mr. G, Dr. Knilans.

The next page, 6/27, is a Sunday ("hot"), where Grampa writes, "Outline of Week Work."

> Regular chores.
>   Haying: As weather permits we must push haying with extreme vigor.
>   To this end,
>   a. Finish field 2b quickly as possible (Monday)   (Tues)
>   b. cut and cock Field 4 while No. 2B is curing in windrows (Weds)
>   c. Cut a good piece on No. 2 (We must aim to cut some everyday if
>   possible.)
>   Corn—Cultivating and Hoeing
>   Miscl.
>   a. Fix cow passage under culvert (as far as poss until it dries) (Mon)
>   b. Fix pasture fences (Tues)
>   c. Cut thistles and docks

At the end of this page, Grampa has come back and written in ink, "In spite of the Sunday night rain we very closely followed the above outline. Accomplished a little more than planned. WJD."

A perusal of this following week shows that rain had halted the haying on Monday, except for Mr. Griffith's afternoon turning of the windrow hay. The time was devoted to shipping cattle and hogs by Mr. B., George, and barn men; fence repair by Mr. G. and Dan; the passage under the culvert worked on by WJD, Red, and Sam, and in the afternoon, Mr. B. gathered corn from corn dealers. Tuesday is a return to haying with the cutting of alfalfa, and 6 loads of dried hay were hauled in from Field 2. It was too wet to cultivate, but not to hoe the garden and sweet corn. Dan poisoned the potato bugs. (We do not learn what poison was used: 2-4D is mentioned elsewhere; DDT is not yet on the horizon.) George hauled manure and Red fixed the pasture fence at the culvert.

By Wednesday the corn could be cultivated, five loads of hay brought in from Field 2, finishing it, ten acres raked on another field and the garden hoed some more. And so the week goes. Grampa notes that he is short on help, Sam was called home, and Dan took his vacation. Henry was off all week. But he has filled in with route men. Ockie Berg and Milner are familiar delivery names.

The summer continues with more haying and cultivating, and various chores—getting a chicken house from Brodhead, and then the chicks, repairing trucks, fixing a chute in the round barn, fixing a hog lot fence, cutting weeds and thistles, getting the machinery ready to cut grain. Tending the garden, cleaning the cow yard.

And by mid-July, corn detasseling has begun.

By the first week of December, the men are binding hemp—raised for rope during the War, at the Government's bidding. All the help pitches in on this. Later it is shocked. (The late June pages do not mention hemp care—it is flourishing unaided by then, hemp needs little encouragement. Its planting, in early May, is recorded, however.) Next comes husking corn—Grampa enlists all the help again, and the milkmen too when they finish their routes. After the husking is shelling. This is finished by mid-month and the sheller stowed. A truckload of corncobs is driven to a neighbor's farm. Storm windows go up at the office and elsewhere. The barnyard water tanks on all three farms have their heaters overhauled; in addition the tanks are banked around with straw.

Early in the month Grampa and Mr. Beadle select cattle for shipping; they also cull hogs. Dr. Knilans comes down and inspects the heifers and cows for pregnancy. He trims the bulls' feet. This latter takes the help of not only Grampa and Mr. Beadle, but Ronald and Red Richardson. With the ground not frozen yet, Red does some early plowing for the spring season.

In early December heifers are dehorned, and the next day, Grampa writes,

Preparing a field for planting.

"Care of dehorned heifers," giving himself that responsibility. Dehorning can kill an animal if it is a bleeder, or gets an infection.

There is no end of work to do. Hay is hauled for the horses, straw hauled for bedding. A load of coke is fetched and poured in a bin for the milkhouse boiler.

The seasonal work is different (except for "regular chores" which must include the daily milking and barn routine, and the milkhouse work—this latter mostly Ron's responsibility) but there continues to be plenty of work for everyone. None of the regular workers are laid off, even in January or February. And when spring comes, with planting and seed corn deliveries, work only intensifies.

On December 18, however, a Friday, there is a story: the end of the page is labeled "Emergency."

> Fire in walls of cooler room discovered at 4:30 a.m. Department called. Firemen control at 7:00. Damage to roof and bathroom of flat. And ceiling of washroom lost. 40 gal vat of whole milk, 350# also.
>
> Mr. G. and myself spent ¾ day each in cleaning up and getting fire out deep down in insulation.

The Saturday work that is on the following page, 12/18, (clear, mild):

I. Repair Fire Damage—Mr. G, WJD, partly done
II. Haul manure—Freeman, Red (after hauling milk)
   Harry Vogts finished at Hill Farm
III. Miscl
  a. Get feed at Clinton
  b. Move cows—Beadle, Ruben

The Sunday page is brief:

Difficult day with chores. Rufus and Davis sick, also George B
We got a late start with milking—Red had to haul—and help with chores
  and milking
Beadle away after morning feeding of hogs and calves

There will be cold days coming, and the emergencies of blizzards and floods. Then will come milder days (perhaps a freak snowstorm in April) and all the planting work, the farrowing, and the beginnings of the new growing season.

There will also be other days in other years where significant events are known to have happened. These might be interesting to look up in Grampa's day book, to note whether there is commentary. If so, it will likely be brief and lacking emotion.

To get Grampa's thoughts and feelings, his admonitions and reflections, to know his heart, you need to go to his writings and letters—or to have been privileged to walk with him as you grew up.

7 ❧ WHAT IS A FARMER?

O n January 30, 1914, Wesson Dougan gives the major address for that day at the Farmers' Course Division of The Country Life Conference sponsored by the University of Wisconsin. It is printed verbatim the next day in the *Beloit Daily Free Press*, with the headline, "Beloit Dairy Man Gives Strong Address on Farm Problems at Conference." It's reprinted elsewhere, and ends up in the July 3 issue of *Hoard's Dairyman*, the international dairy magazine. The talk is titled "The Farmer and His Help." Wesson concentrates first on the farmer:

> What is a farmer? How can we define him? Is he the owner of the large es- tablishment who runs over a few thousand acres, milks a few hundred cows, and hires help in gangs? The December "World's Work" describes three such places in illustration of how to solve the farm's help problem. It does not touch our problem in Wisconsin, because our farmers are not of this class. Someone has defined the farmer as the man who makes his money in the country and spends it in the city as against the agriculturalist who makes his money in the city and spends it in the country. These agriculturalists have their mission and the real farmer may profit by their shipwrecks. But they are not real farmers. How would this do as a definition of a farmer? One who tills the soil, conserving its fertility; builds real farm homes; and enhances rural community life.
>
> Thus the real farmer has a mission larger and nobler than just buying land to raise corn to feed more hogs to get more money to buy still more land to raise still more corn to feed still more hogs to get more money to buy all the land that adjoins him. On the contrary his mission is social and philan- thropic. He must develop the soil to its highest efficiency and pass it on to posterity undiminished in fertility. He must build real homes. A house may be an elegant castle and yet not house a home. The farmer must develop his "living-plant" in all possible convenience and beauty, bringing into it art,

literature, and congenial guests to beautify and enrich character. He must give of himself to the home, in love, in genial and jovial spirit, in sympathy and hospitality. Nor does his mission end at his doorstep. He must maintain a community life. "No man liveth unto himself." Not if he really lives. The school, the church, all social and civic movements demand his cooperation. His mission is to make the farm the best place to live in all of God's beautiful world — to eclipse, in the minds of all country folk, the city, the resorts of leisure, the palaces of wealth, the allurements of commerce and manufacture. He must accomplish all this that the music of the country, its life and largeness, its repose and security, may be satisfying to this and to all succeeding generations. This is no small task.

At this point, W.J. gets to the second half of his title:

It is evident that this many-sided task must have its help problem. Labor in manufacture and construction is a definite quantity. The contractor knows how many man-hours it takes to accomplish his work. The manufacturer knows how many pieces can be turned out in an hour. So definite is this that wages in many of the great shops are largely based upon the piece-work plan. The farm is being put upon the factory basis, but we are slow to apply the principle of man-hours to our manufacture of farm products. We have yet to learn that laws govern farm work as well as other labor. Universally we are running our farms with short labor. Consequently work piles up, we push and sweat and fume. We work one man to death, hang his hide on the fence and hire another. By working the land with short labor we are thwarting all of our highest ambitions as farmers. We deplete the soil; retard development; impoverish the home-life; break our own lives; discourage the young and drive them from the soil, thus increasing the ranks of the consumers and decreasing and weakening the ranks of producers. The help problem stands at the very threshold of all agricultural progress.

Farm labor must be fitted to the task. What are the requisites of a good farmhand, what are his duties? He works with delicate and expensive machinery; the sensitive herd; the intelligent and faithful beast of burden; the responsive soil; and the almost talking, feeling plant life. To rightly understand and manipulate all these varying conditions he must be a man of intellect, sensibility, and high moral character. This latter requisite is of moment to all consumers of farm products. Cleanliness and purity is a crying need. The farmer touches the food at its fountain. Contaminated there, it goes on

Dougan help. W.J. stands on right, Trever (short pants) is midway; Ron (plaid cap) is on left. The herdsman, Art Kassilke, squats on the ground.

to the consumer ever increasing in danger to health and decreasing in food value. The farmhand must produce food upon honor. He must be a man of clean mind and healthy body. I have gone into a barbershop to get shaved and after observing the pictures on the wall have left without the shave. If a man's mind is dirty his hands are not apt to be clean. We must have help of pure minds and clean bodies because they touch the food supply at its source.

The Wisconsin farmer wants congenial help. The manager and his hired man largely work together. The men are a part of the family circle and influence the joys of the home life. At one time, a doctor friend of mine was buying a horse. He wanted me to drive it on a try-out. I did so for a day in my pastoral work. The horse was sound and a good traveler, but was of a disagreeable disposition. He minded the word to the letter. But he would take the bit in his teeth, lay back his ears and seem to say: "I will go — I will go like the dickens. But I hate to." If I put out my hand to caress him, his response was a frown and a leer. I told my friend he did not want that horse. He must associate with it too closely to be hitched behind such a brute. Thus with our hired help; we must associate with them so closely that their ideals, habits, and very moods have an influence upon every member of the home. We need congenial help as well as intelligent, sensitive, and clean minded, sound bodied men.

Where are we to find such men? The world is full of them. I am seldom without several applicants who measure up to this ideal. Our university and agricultural school are turning out a fine grist every year; many are men of the highest type. The trend back to the soil is calling some of the strongest, finest blood from the city ranks to the rural life. Many of these young men combine two of the largest factors in a successful man. They want to learn, are willing to bring the body under, curb appetite, regulate habits, and control the whole life to this end. They want to work and work hard. They strive to do better work each day. Occasionally, when a visitor sees my group of six clean, clear cut, high minded men, and when they are informed that not one of them uses tobacco or liquor in any form, not even swears at the cows, they want to know if I cannot direct them to such help. Can I? I might, if—if they themselves are worthy of such help. Hiring a man is something like proposing marriage. You must have something to offer. It is as preposterous for a low-minded, thriftless man, steeped in evil habits and profane tongue, to ask a clean souled, high minded, ambitious young man to work with him as it is for such a one to ask a sweet young woman to associate with him in the high work of home-making. If we are to have the right help, we ourselves must first be right. We must have a clean companionship to offer clean men. We must also have opportunity to offer these young men. Opportunity to follow something of the ideals held up in our colleges. Opportunity to work with thrifty flocks and herds. Opportunity to use good horses and up-to-date machinery. Put ourselves and our farms on this level and help of right quality will come without seeking.

Pay is another phase of the problem. What should be the wage scale? The tendency is to pay all men the "Going Wage." This puts down all ambition and encourages incompetency. If the going wage is $35 per month, there are men whose services are worth three times that, and others who are expensive help at one-half that amount. Can we discriminate in this matter on the same farm yet keep contented help? I regulate my payroll on two principles. The first, pay as generously as the income can possibly stand, and increase this pay as my business increases. The second, to distribute this pay among the men according to experience, ability, and length of continuous service on the farm. I pay as low as $10 per month and expect the ten dollar man to put in as many hours and to get as tired as the best paid man. In other words, I pay on quality of work and not quantity only.

One of the largest factors in the help problem is the treatment of farm-hands. What principles should we follow to hold men of the right quality to the soil? Can we stand over them as taskmasters demanding everything and giving only a paltry wage in return? Can we be indifferent to their food, housing, recreation, social, religious, and educational advantages? Whether or not these principles can successfully hold in manufacture, I do not know, but I do know they cannot hold on the farm. The farmhand is necessarily an independent worker. He must take a job and carry it through to completion. We cannot have a half dozen foremen to every farmhand. Therefore we must have responsible help. The manufacturer's home is not influenced by his help. The house and shop are separate. But the farmer's home is part of his shop. His labor is in his home. Therefore his home influences his help and is in turn influenced by them. In view of these two facts, what principle is wisest in our treatment of farmhands? It seems to me this is the briefest and clearest statement of the truth. "Live and let live." Our own lives should be enriched, enlivened, and freed from eternal drudgery. We should make the farm yield a life, and time to live, as well as provide a living. These advantages of education, society, religion, and recreation should be extended to all our help. I heard a highly progressive farmer say he did not see how it was possible to get regular weekly rest and recreation for all. This is a problem, especially on a dairy farm where milk is delivered for direct consumption.

For several years I have been working on the problem of obeying the fourth commandment on a dairy farm. The commandment is not only for the farmer to rest but for his sons and daughters, his man servants and maid servants, even the stranger within his gates. How can the dairy farmer secure this beneficent weekly rest for all? My first effort to this end was to have a day-man come on Saturday to help with the weekend work so the help could be in better shape to get a part of Sunday for rest. This plan helped some but was not a solution. I next tried giving each man a half-day off during the week. With all helping with the chores on Sunday each could get some time for rest on that day.

It was understood the manager was to have the whole Sunday to himself. This plan worked fairly well but told badly on the work accomplished for the year. There was one fault in the plan. I would let the men off as I could, during the week, when there seemed an opening. Unfortunately we might come to the last day of the week with none off. Then I must sacrifice either the work or the men. If the men, I allowed them extra for the half holiday. When Sunday came if the men had not been off I did not wish to claim my time and let the men do all the work, so the whole purpose of the half day was frustrated. It was a failure from every point viewed. It neither gave myself or the help regular rest, it added confusion and uncertainty of work, put us

"What principles should we follow to hold men of the right quality to the soil?"

back, and cost more to do the work. But why should it fail? Is the commandment not necessary today?

God's laws are given not merely to please an arbitrary deity. If this law of rest was necessary to the children of Israel, with their slow and plodding caravans and happy-go-easy camp life, how much more necessary is it to this age with its whirl of machinery, rapid transit, and yesterday's doings of the world discussed at our breakfast table? Why then, I asked, should my first efforts prove a failure? The answer was clear. Lack of system. Just as nine-tenths of our income, with the tithe systematically and conscientiously given to God's work of redeeming and bettering the world, will go farther, buy more happiness and success than the ten-tenths of our income selfishly kept. It is through no divine intervention that the nine-tenths does more. It is by applying a system to determine the tithe honestly, and open hearted interest in humanity in spending it, that blesses the nine-tenths. Just so in getting the one-seventh part of the time for rest. Thus I discovered the need for stricter system in my plan. I applied it.

For the past three years each man has had his regular half day. Burr takes Monday afternoon, Joe Tuesday, and so on through the week. They know when their day comes; anticipation helps its enjoyment. From noon until four o'clock the next morning they are their own man. They write their love letters, read, keep their notes or accounts, visit other farms or shops or go to town for pleasure. Never have I had a man abuse this privilege by simply loafing or bumming. Sundays the two men whose duty is in the farm work during the week turn in and help with the herd and dairy work. This lightens the work for all so each man has about one-half day rest on Sunday. All can go to church either morning or evening.

The plan is that the manager take the place of the man who is off each day, thus putting him in closer touch with the operation of each line of work. On Sunday the manager has his entire time with his family. I get up when I please and put on my Sunday clothes. There is some culture and a little religion in this. I spend the morning with my family in reading and leisure. If I go to church the horse is hitched up for me and when I come home it is taken at the door. Thus the day becomes a day of rest, a day with the family. The whole plan is in keeping with the spirit and purpose of the command, "Remember the Sabbath to keep it Holy." By this, the dairy farmer is enabled to keep the day of rest, recreation, and worship in as good a sense as his city brother of the store, office, or shop. After these years of experience, I am confident that the sincere endeavor to obey this command on any farm will go a long way toward solving the help problem. It will attract intelligent, ambitious, self-respecting men of good habits. It will inspire loyal and honorable service, the factors most desirable in our help. Adopted by any large proportion of any community it will rebuild the rural church society, encourage education, and help all social service endeavor, because the community will have time for these things. That the plan is also a financial success is shown in my gradually decreasing cost of labor in proportion to total income, and yet I am paying better wages and securing better help.

8 ⁂ BOUNCE

A dog Jackie knows well lives at the Big House. Grama sent away for him before Jackie was born. She wanted a trained dog to rid the farm of vermin. To her satisfaction she received a fully grown, experienced rat terrier — Bounce.

Bounce is aptly named. He's a small, short-haired, compact canine, rather like a bullet mounted on four wiry legs. He's brown with a stub tail. Jackie's earliest memories include Bounce, and from the very start he seems old and crotchety. He's a no-nonsense animal, undeterred by anything. There's no play in him, no affection. He never sidles up for a pat or warm word. He feels no need to keep you company. He's Grama's dog, and maybe he gets affection from her, but not to notice.

He does get food. Whenever Grama makes pies, any dough left over she spreads on a small pie tin and bakes with the rest. The browned crust is "Bounce's pie." Jackie, Patsy, Joan, and Craig learn early to drop by Grama's kitchen on baking days and beat Bounce to his pie. If you get there soon enough you can even make Bounce's pie yourself, rolling and rolling it out with the floury rolling pin on the marble slab table top and finally laying it, quite grey, in its pan as Grama urges, "Come along, now; all the rest are in." Then you quickly shake sugar and cinnamon on it, and put it in the huge wood-burning stove.

Similar is "Bounce's pancake." For some reason Jackie has never been able to fathom, the first pancake off any griddle is inferior. It simply isn't as light and fluffy as those to follow, the color isn't the same. That first pancake Grama always flips into Bounce's dish; it's "Bounce's pancake." But if one of the four is hovering in the kitchen, she or he can intercept the pancake and spread it with butter and jam. Years later, when the four are grown and away, they discover that each others' children all refer to leftover crust and the first pancake as "Bounce's pie," and "Bounce's pancake," without the faintest idea why.

What Bounce lacks in agreeable personality he makes up for in interest.

Santa delivers a pony to Joan, Patsy and Jackie while Bounce looks on.

It's Bounce who steps up to Grama's visiting sister, Aunt Ria, and piddles on her leg. It's Bounce who bites Joan on the chin when she tries to lift him.

But most of all, Bounce bounces. And he bounces on cue. If Jackie and Craig are on the Big House lawn and Bounce ambles by, they'll suddenly cry in excited tones, "Sic 'em, Bounce! Sic 'em, Bounce!" and start to run in circles. Immediately Bounce will run in circles too, emitting short staccato barks, nose down, looking for the rat he thinks has caused the commotion. Craig and Jackie sic louder, Bounce runs faster, and finally in a frenzy of frustration he'll rush to a certain elm tree, swarm up the trunk, and, at the peak of his leap, tear at the bark with his teeth and drop back to the ground. He'll bounce and tear till he's exhausted.

Even more satisfying is to stir Bounce up in the Big House. He'll be asleep. At a low, intense, "Sic 'em, Bounce!" he'll jump to his feet and growl. At another "Sic 'em!" he'll start running in circles, yipping and barking. His inciters race with him, around and around the dining room table, shouting louder and faster, "Sic 'em, Bounce! Sic 'em, Bounce!" When Bounce has been lathered to the height of agitated rage, someone will fling open the cellar door, at the corner of the dining room. Bounce will hurtle down the steps into the main cellar and throw himself on one of the posts that supports the floor above. At the top of his leap he'll grab, and drop down with a mouthful of splintered, shredded wood. Again and again he'll assault the post, keeping up a din of outraged barking while the delighted spectators keep shouting,

"Sic 'em, Bounce!" The sport ends when Grama yells downstairs to stop the hubbub. It's always the same post that Bounce viciously shreds, and over the years it comes to have such a deeply concave surface that one wonders how a beaver got into the cellar, and fears for the post's ability to provide any sort of support. To those who remember Bounce, it's still a source of wonder that a dog could have made such an indentation at such a height. When Jackie is grown she takes her children on a pilgrimage to see Bounce's post in the Big House cellar. They are gratifyingly impressed.

Jackie never knew Bounce to catch a rat. In fact, she's never even seen a rat on the farm. When she asks Daddy about it, he says Bounce was why, until he died, and they turned to Warfarin rat poison.

"When we'd tear up the floor of an old shed or corncrib, Bounce would be there with feet bouncing and jaws snapping. Rats to the left of him, rats to the right! He'd grab 'em and throw 'em over his shoulder. Blood to his elbows! And he never missed a one. He earned his keep, all right. Too bad you weren't at the right place at the right time. It was quite a sight."

Jackie shudders. It must have been boggling, but she guesses she'd prefer to have a rat terrier climb an elm or cellar post when she cries, "Sic 'em, Bounce! Sic 'em, sic 'em!"

Bounce ignores Grama and Aunt Laoda.

9 ❧ FEEDING HELP ON THE DAIRY FARM

Whenever an improvement is made to the farm or farm buildings, W.J. matches it with something for the Big House, to advance the quality of the home. Hence electricity, a dishwasher, an up-to-date stove to augment the wood-burning range. A vacuum cleaner that has outlets for plugging the hose into floorboards and a huge vacuum bag in the cellar, tucked up under the floor. (This contraption is dismantled when the persistent presence of clothes moths is finally traced to wool fluff vacuumed from rugs into the never-emptied vacuum bag.)

W.J. mentions his "equal attention to farm and home" philosophy in an article for *Hoard's Dairyman* in December, 1916. It's noted by the editor, who asks Eunice to write something about this aspect of life on the Dougan farm. When she agrees, A.J. Glover responds with pleasure, that her choice of subject and title are agreeable, and that they will bear the expense of photos.

"Feeding Help on the Dairy Farm," well illustrated, is published in December, 1917:

> The feeding of help is a perplexing question in dairy farm management for the dairy farm requires a larger amount of help and this help must be constant and contented. It must be taken largely from the ranks of young men, and for the most part, board must be provided by the farm. This is necessary because there is no permanent farm labor class in this country. Young men are seeking farm employment as a stepping stone to proprietorship. Therefore, as soon as they gain experience and a small capital they depart from the employed ranks to become employers. It is neither possible nor practicable to secure married men in sufficient numbers to do all the work.
>
> Many young men who seek employment have come from good farm homes, and have been accustomed to good home surroundings. The work is strenuous and requires men to be at their best. If it is essential that an army be well fed it is equally important that the men who shoulder the farm work,

and keep up the regularity and faithful service necessary in dairying, be well fed.

The table has a direct bearing to the financial success of the farm. While it must keep the men satisfied and well supplied with energy, it must be managed economically. A housewife could put the farm's whole income on the table. It is these factors that make the food question a large concern on the dairy farm.

Feeding help is managed in various ways. Some farms provide and supply a boarding house, and hire a woman to run it. Some provide the house and equipment and pay a family a stated amount per week for each man. Some pay the married men a stated amount to board the single men. Others take the help into the home and feed them at the same table with their families. It is this latter method that will be discussed here.

This method has its advantages as well as its inconveniences. It is always cheaper to feed one family, however large, than to divide them up into several homes. It places the employer in close relation with his men resulting in a better mutual understanding. It enables the employer to give more of himself and his influence to his men as an integral part of his own family. It enlarges the circle of friendships. Most of these employees later go out into active homemaking for themselves. They carry with them the memory of the kindly interest and helpful contact of their employer and his family. Thus the employer soon has many warm friends settled in many sections of the country.

The principal objection to this method is that it breaks into the family's privacy. Mealtime is the hour that most families anticipate, when its members can be alone. It is also a time when a mother can bring in little lessons of culture. The early evening is the children's hour, but with others in the home the parents cannot use it as they might, were they alone with their brood.

For the past ten years the method under discussion has been followed on "The Dougan Guernsey Farm." We keep from six to eight men throughout the year. Our room and kitchen requirements have been developed to meet their needs. We have a convenient sewer and water system, electric lights, and power. I mention this to preface the statement that we feed this number of men besides our own family of five with the help of one good assistant in the house.

It has always been our object to give our boys life as well as a living. During their noon hour or in the evening, they have a chance to enter the living room and enjoy the family circle with its books, papers, or music. There is more to the problem of caring for men than merely feeding them. These

A meal on the Big House lawn. Ron is standing, Trever squinting, W.J. is beside Trever, then Esther.

young men need the home life as an incentive to their best work. When a man can anticipate the meal hour, and knows he will be welcome in a comfortable home and will sit down to a well cooked, appetizing meal, it puts zest and spirit into his entire service.

To be sure, this method imposes a burden of careful management upon the housewife. She must prepare meals that will be well balanced and tasty but not too expensive. She must be regular both as to the time and character of her meals. She must not have feast one day and famine the next. There must always be plenty of well-cooked food.

Whatever may be my outside duties and however good an assistant I have, it has always been my policy to supervise the planning of the meals. Our general procedure for the three meals is this: Since it is not possible on a dairy farm for all to sit down to breakfast at the same time, we begin serving at 6 a.m. and continue until about half past seven. My assistant usually prepares the breakfast while I am preparing some part of the dinner.

We regularly have oatmeal, using about two parts oatmeal to one part sterilized bran. This is steamed from one to two hours. Besides this we often serve some prepared cereal such as corn flakes. With the breakfast foods we furnish plenty of whole milk and sugar, with good bread and butter or toast. Often some kind of warm bread is served such as graham gems, johnny cake, or buns.

The second part of breakfast is potatoes with eggs in season. When eggs are scarce we use dried beef gravy on toast or with potatoes, or sometimes French toast or pancakes with syrup. We serve coffee or cocoa for those who desire it; and we also aim to have plenty of fresh skim milk. Experts tell us there is more protein in skim than in whole milk. The protein for our families, as well as for our herds, is the expensive part of our ration. We get an abundance of fats in our food without the fat in our drinking milk. The taste of fat in whole milk is only a matter of habit. Skim milk is appetizing when one becomes educated to it. We use gallons of wholesome skim for drinking and cooking, and farmers and consumers alike who fail to take advantage of it are missing a valuable and economical food. We often serve fresh fruit in season or canned fruits and jams.

For dinner I always have meat or a good substitute such as baked beans, macaroni and cheese, or salmon loaf. I buy a pot roast for one day and there is always some left over. I do not use this for supper or breakfast but make another dinner from it. There are many ways to do this and the second day dinner may be enjoyed even more than the first. For example: Cut the meat into small pieces and put it in a granite pan. Fry some onions and add sliced or canned tomatoes, thicken a little, season to taste, and pour over the meat. Sprinkle this with buttered crumbs, and bake it in the oven. Another variety is a goulash. Cut the meat in small pieces and boil a few minutes. Into this

"The boys have a chance to enter the living room and enjoy the family circle with its books, papers, or music."

slice suitable vegetables and add a can of peas. Still another recipe is to grind the meat, season it with salt, pepper, and a little leftover gravy and perhaps some onion. Pile boiled rice around and over it and bake about half an hour. Serve on a platter with tomato sauce. A most simple way is to grind the meat and make a milk gravy with it. This with baked potatoes, good vegetables, and dessert, (plus bread and butter and milk) is plenty for one dinner.

It is my practice with a left-over meat dinner to serve plenty of vegetables and a substantial dessert. Whatever the dinner I always serve dessert, light or heavy, depending on the character of the meat course. Baked apples or jello with whipped cream make a good, light dessert, while pie, suet pudding, or apple dumplings make a good, heavy one.

We serve one or more vegetables for dinner fitted to the character of the meal. In vegetable season we often serve both cooked and raw at one dinner. A favorite way of preparing lettuce is to spread it with a dressing made from one half pint of whipped cream with a tablespoonful of salad dressing, as "The Yacht Club" and a little salt and sugar. The above is my dressing for salads of all kinds. For fruit salads I use a little more sugar and not so much salad dressing. I speak of the use of cream for I believe dairy farmers cannot feed more economically than to use freely of their own product. We have had many a summer meal for a family of sixteen or more where every item was taken from the farm except the flour, sugar, and salt. Here is an example of one such meal: chicken, new potatoes and gravy, lettuce salad, green peas, plenty of bread and homemade butter, and milk; and for dessert, strawberry short cake.

For supper I have potatoes and one other article, such as codfish, macaroni and cheese, or tomatoes, escalloped corn or salmon, or soup. Besides this we have sauce, cake or cookies, bread, butter, and plenty of milk when possible. With all these meals there is a chance for variety, and besides the substantials mentioned, relishes, pickles, and jams are used.

After breakfast I plan the dinner, make the dessert, and help with the cleaning while my assistant is busy with dishes, making beds, cleaning the dining room and kitchen, and preparing vegetables. In planning meals I try to have a balanced ration. It is no small task to furnish these ten hundred and ninety-five meals a year and give the variety and change demanded by human nature.

We have a great deal of company, especially during the summer months. Many times we entertain societies and classes. For afternoon company we serve a cafeteria lunch or lap supper. In these we provide plenty of sandwiches, baked beans, and escalloped potatoes for substantials, and other things as cakes, cookies, pickles, or fruits. We feed the farm help with the rest of the company so there is little extra work. I sometimes serve cafeteria when we have no company but are into extra chores such as housecleaning. With a few oven dishes, cottage cheese, and plenty of sandwiches, this is easily done and a pleasant change.

During the early summer I have practiced serving our evening meal outside; especially in strawberry season. We usually have a supply of cream and milk at this time also. With strawberries and cream, sandwiches, cottage cheese, and potato salad and milk, the meal is easily prepared, and all enjoy the out-of-doors.

After supper the men lie on the lawn or play ball or other sports. We frequently invite young people in for lunch and to spend a pleasant evening with music, reading, and games.

In this way, for ten years, we have managed to keep a high class of young men. We follow them with interest as they go out into larger activities, and it is gratifying to receive occasional visits or messages of remembrance. Twelve of our boys are now serving in the ranks; and as they are scattered over the different camps they write home to "daddy" and "mother" keeping us informed of their whereabouts. This is worth all the extra work and the inconveniences of having the men in the family. We believe our method has been rewarded with abundant success.

Hoard's illustrates the article lavishly. There's a medallion photo of Eunice at the start, and one showing the Big House, side barn and round barn, "The Home of the Dougans." Nine hired men, plus 15-year-old Ronald and Bob the dog, are pictured in an easy pose, lined up on the ramp to the upper barn: "Part of the Farm Family Mrs. Dougan Fed During the Summer of 1917." Inside the house the men seem stiff and self-conscious. One shot shows them gathered around a table, reading. Ronald and Trever, also reading, sprawl awkwardly on the floor. This photo quotes from the article about the boys having "a chance to enter the living room and enjoy the family circle with its books, papers, or music." In another photo the men are gathered at the piano. One has his hands resting on the keys; the others seem dubiously contemplating singing. The caption reads, "Time spent in song is not wasted when it makes young hearts beat warmer and is a part of the home life that leads the twelve 'Dougan boys' now serving Uncle Sam to write home to 'mother' and 'daddy.' The fact that these boys remember to write to 'mother' leads Mrs. Dougan to say, as mothers have a wont of saying, 'This is worth all the extra work and inconvenience of having the men in the family.'"

Not pictured are rows of pies, or mounds of vegetables on the kitchen table, or the extended family at meal time—Eunice says dinner and supper are always sit-down-together affairs in the dining room, with tablecloth and serving dishes. Grace and Bible readings would have been harder to portray.

In January Mr. Glover writes, "We have received many letters commenting upon the simple, direct way in which you treat your subject and the sensible manner you follow in the feeding of farmhands. We received what we consider a very high compliment from such a one who wrote, 'That woman certainly knows how to fix up grub for a hungry hired man.' It is a great accomplishment to know how to effectively appeal to a man and from the tone of your article, it is evident that you possess this quality." He adds, " I put this in writing that you may show this letter to Mr. Dougan, should he for a moment happen to think he is the larger part of the Dougan family. I was with him yesterday but did not venture anything about your article for I wanted to give you the opportunity of letting him know how it has been received."

Over the years Eunice has an occasional article written exclusively about her. Her "Master Homemaker" honor from the University of Wisconsin in 1926 prompts a three page interview in the 1927 *Armour's Farmer's Almanac*, "The Farm Woman and Better Agriculture," complete with biography, and in 1928 *The Farmer's Wife* publishes a well-illustrated feature, "Turning Handicaps to Gold." Eunice is almost always given a prominent paragraph in any article about W.J. She travels with him when he's on a speaking circuit, and is frequently part of the package. In Grampa's radio series over WLS a broadcast is allotted to her. But so far as Jackie knows, the *Hoard's* article is the only published one that Grama herself ever writes.

10 ⚹ THE WEDDING

Ronald is in the third grade. His teacher, Helen Gillette, rooms at the farm. She takes her meals at the big table in the dining room with Grama and Grampa, Ronald and Trever, and all the hired men.

For Ronald, the sun rises and sets on Miss Gillette. He goes across the field with her early in the morning, carrying both lunch buckets. He helps her open the schoolhouse, get the fire going, carry in wood, fill the water pail. After school he washes the blackboard and claps the erasers on the outside of the school building so vigorously that the clouds of chalk dust make him sneeze. He helps sweep out and tidy up. Then he walks back across the field with her, carrying both lunch buckets, now empty. Trever, in first grade, likes Miss Gillette too, but he can't be bothered coming early and staying late.

Miss Gillette is fond of both boys, but she's concerned about Ronald, for as soon as he gets home from school he curls up with a book. Except for his chores, he reads till suppertime. After supper he settles down again and reads till bedtime. It pleases Miss Gillette that Ronald likes reading so much, but she worries that he doesn't get enough exercise, doesn't play outdoors. All he does is read. She makes a bargain with him. She will read to him every evening after supper for an hour, if he will play outdoors after school till suppertime. Ronald agrees. He loves reading, but even more he loves being read to, especially if the reader is Miss Gillette.

There is plenty to do outside. He and Trever go down to the crick and repair the dam that makes their swimming hole. There are still hot days in September, and any day is good for the waterwheels they construct along the banks where the current flows fastest.

They have races in the field across from the house, starting with the big tree, and each following the fence in the opposite direction, passing each other on the far side of the field, then running on around and back to the tree. When Ronald gets a stitch in his side he stops quickly and spits under a stone. This is a sure cure. Though Ronald is older and taller, Trever always wins the

Ronald and a rabbit, the age he was at Miss Gillette's wedding.

races. Only once does Ronald outrun him. He's mad at Trever, chasing him, and his brother runs for the horse barn. Ronald has in his hand an old, large turkey egg he has found. He throws it at Trever just as Trever reaches the horse barn entrance. It misses, hits the top of the door just ahead of him, splatters back, and in the confusion of wiping egg from his eyes, Trever falters. Ronald overtakes him. Trever whirls, and a nasty fight ensues. Ronald wins because he's stronger and can pound Trever's head on the ground. But they are both covered with rotten egg.

They have another sort of contest. In the icehouse above the granary they each keep hidden a metal cocoa can, the brand with the picture on its side of the lady in the long dress holding a cup of Baker's Cocoa. The contest is to fill your can with pee before your brother does. They'll be down at the crick, or some other outpost, and Ronald will notice Trever edging away from him. Realizing what's up, he'll break into a run just as Trever does. Panting and gasping they'll reach the ladder to the icehouse and scramble up it. They'll dig their cans out of the sawdust, pry off the lids, fumble with their trousers, and start to pee. Such have been their exertions, however, that they are trembling. They piddle on the sawdust, piddle on their clothes, piddle on their hands. Precious little pee goes into the cans. They conduct this contest honorably. Neither one would dream of sneaking up to pee alone, or pour pee from the other's can.

Out in the horse barn they gather horse apples and keep them in special spots. Ronald's cache is in an unused horse manger. When cold weather comes, they don't have to wait for snow for snowballs; the horse apples freeze solid and they have horse apple fights. Ronald is usually the victor in a horse apple fight.

They find an old umbrella in the farm dump, and make bows and arrows to play Indian. The long spokes form the bows; they tie bowstrings to arch them. The short spokes are the arrows. They hold the arrows to the grindstone and pump the treadle. The grindstone whirls. Sparks fly from the spoke. They grind until the spoke becomes needle sharp. Trever shoots an arrow and hits Ronald in the eye. They rush him to the hospital. The arrow has pierced only the white part, so he won't lose his sight. But he wears a patch for a month. Their father confiscates the bows and arrows.

And every night Miss Gillette reads aloud, from *St. Nicholas* magazine, or Dickens, or *The Little Shepherd of Kingdom Come*. Trever, and Ronald with his patch on, curl up on either side of her. Grama listens and knits. Sometimes Grama plays a game of chess with Grampa during the reading, for though he's glad it's going on, he can't hear it.

On some nights, however, Miss Gillette doesn't read. She has a beau, whose name is Red Beaumeister. He has fiery red hair. He comes out to the farm and carries Miss Gillette away in his buggy. Ronald watches them go, and feels twinges of jealousy. He wishes he were old enough to be Miss Gillette's beau.

Miss Gillette ready to do a little cultivating.

Miss Gillette clowning with two of the hired men.

Spring comes. Ronald pokes a bar of metal from the dump through a bob wire fence. He turns it over and over, winding up the two strands of wire till they are taut as a spring and will turn no further. Then he lets go. The spring unwinds in a flash, spinning the bar of metal faster than the vanes on the windmill in a high gale. At the end the bar spins right out of the fence and strikes Trever on the chin. They rush Trever to the hospital. He has to have seven stitches.

Ronald learns that Miss Gillette is going to marry Red Beaumeister. The wedding will be on the lawn, as soon as school is out. The spirea bushes and Grama's roses will be the background. Grampa will be the minister. Grama will bake the cake and handle the reception. Everyone is invited: Ronald and Trever, the hired men, the schoolchildren and their families, people from town. It will be a gala event.

Although Ronald is sorry he can't marry Miss Gillette, he accepts the fate that has made such a difference in their ages, and pitches vigorously into the wedding preparations. He helps Grama with the kitchen work, keeping the woodbox full for the baking. He peels chicken off the bones of boiled hens for the chicken salad. He helps the hired men groom the lawn, he helps Miss Gillette pick flowers to put around the house. He hangs over his father's shoulder while Grampa refreshes himself on the wedding service.

On the morning of the great day he helps carry all the chairs from the house to the front yard and arrange them in rows. Then he helps the hired men build trestles of planks laid across milk cases, for the overflow guests. When there's nothing more for him to do he goes and scrubs up thoroughly. He gets dressed in his Sunday suit, a white shirt and tie, his long black stockings and his best shoes. He wanders into the kitchen.

His mother exclaims when she sees him. "My goodness, Ronald! It's still an hour and a half till the wedding! Don't get dirty, now!"

Ronald moseys around, keeping clean. Everybody else is still busy. He takes a book he's begun, *A Connecticut Yankee in King Arthur's Court*, and goes up to his room. He settles on his bed and starts to read.

He's already learned how the Yankee is transported back to King Arthur's time, and how he saves himself from death at the stake by predicting the exact time of an eclipse of the sun. Now Ronald reads how it feels to joust, in a ludicrously hot and heavy suit of armor, and worse yet, have a fly invade your helmet. He reads and reads, lost in the magic of Camelot. He finally reaches the last line, finishes it, and takes a moment to return to reality. The sun slants through the window.

Suddenly he remembers. The wedding! He sits up, transfixed. Things are strangely silent. He leaps off his bed, flings open the door, races downstairs through the empty house out onto the lawn. He stops dead.

Some hired men are carrying the trestles away. Out on the road, Trever is throwing a stick for Bob to chase. There's no sign of his parents, the bride, the groom. Not a guest is in sight. Ronald stands stricken. The wedding and the reception are long over.

He crawls into the middle of the lilac bush where no one can see him, and cries.

11 ❧ ESTHER, PART 1

It is May 1915. Wesson and Eunice are on their way to town to take the train to Sparta, where the Wisconsin Home for Dependent and Neglected Children is located. As they leave, they stop at Marstons', their closest neighbors down the road. Lura Marston, and her mother, Mrs. Smith, are the only ones in whom Eunice has confided about the many miscarriages she has had since Trever's birth, eleven years ago. Eunice says to the Marstons' only child, "Oh, Eloise, we're going to get you a little playmate, just your age."

Eunice and Wesson have longed for a daughter ever since their own first child died within a few hours of birth. At Sparta they sign indenture papers for a beautiful almost-six-year-old girl. She has light brown curly hair and a sweet face. Her most striking feature is her eyes, unusually large and blue. Eunice and Wesson are charmed. Her name is Agnes Groose. The papers state that Agnes is to stay with the Dougans until she is eighteen, at which time they must provide her with "two suits of good clothes" and fifty dollars, and she will be on her own. The papers also instruct that she be taught a trade at which she will be able to earn a living.

Agnes has sisters and brothers at the orphanage, but Wesson and Eunice take only her. They are not told anything about Agnes's parents.

They return on the train. At the farm Agnes meets her new brothers, Ronald and Trever, and

Esther at seven or eight, by the round barn.

they show her all over the house and barns. She is quiet and shy. She has her own room upstairs. Eunice arranges her few possessions in a drawer.

That night Eunice holds Agnes on her lap before bedtime. Agnes cuddles against her. Eunice says to her, "We've wanted a little girl for so long! Ever since our own baby died. We're going to change your name to Esther, after that baby, and after Esther in the Bible."

Agnes's body goes stiff. She draws away from Eunice. She will not cuddle anymore. Hurt and upset, Eunice puts Esther to bed.

Ronald and Trever with their new sister.

A few days later, Eloise Marston is invited to a tea party. She arrives, all dressed up. Esther is dressed up, too. Eunice introduces the girls and brings in the tea.

There is a small table and chairs and a cloth on the table. There is a small china tea set with a little teapot and diminutive cups. There are small sandwiches on a plate.

Esther presides at the teapot. "Won't you have some tea?" she asks politely. "Oh, pardon me," she says frequently, even when there isn't any need. Eloise is disappointed. Esther is so proper, so exaggerated. What sort of fun can she be?

When the party is over, Eloise says, "Goodbye, Esther."

Esther leans forward, her eyes suddenly hot and angry. "My name isn't Esther!" she hisses. "It's Agnes, the name my mother named me!"

The weeks go by, and Esther turns out to be fun to play with after all. She loses her formality. Eloise decides that that first day was the result of the new situation and the training of the orphanage.

Trever is delighted with a little sister. After all these years, he now has someone who will look up to him and listen to him, and Esther is an avid listener. He sits on the flour box in the kitchen and tells her stories while she fills the wood box for him. She follows him around and admires his ability in running and throwing and shooting pigeons with his air rifle. Ronald is glad enough to have a sister, too, but he's thirteen and busy with other things. Esther's coming doesn't particularly affect him.

On her sewing machine, Eunice stitches sturdy play clothes for her new daughter. She makes her a dress for church, and enrolls her in Eloise's primary class at Sunday School. She shows off her pretty little girl to all the other mothers. Esther smiles shyly at the attention.

Esther's new father takes her with him to see the piglets and to watch the calves being fed. At night, he sometimes holds her in his lap and they look at a picture book together.

Esther settles so well into life on the farm that it isn't long before it seems as though she has always lived there. She and Eloise are best friends and share a desk at school.

When Christmas comes, Esther receives a large and beautiful doll from her foster parents.

She names the doll Agnes.

She also receives, from Wesson's sister Lillian, a little silver spoon with AGNES GROOSE engraved on it. Neither Lillian nor anybody has been told Esther's former name, but Aunt Lillian rummaged through her brother's private papers and ferreted it out. The spoon is her way to remind Esther that she is not really a Dougan. Grama and Grampa are furious; Grama confiscates the spoon and hides it away in her own dresser drawer. "'Agnes!'" she exclaims as she crumples the tissue paper around the slender object and shoves it underneath her handkerchiefs.

Esther and Eloise are chums during their childhood. They play dress up together. Eloise's Grandmother Smith keeps, on an old iron bedstead in the attic, a number of basic hat forms of both felt and straw and one of velvet. At each change of season, she selects a suitable form from the "hat bed," buys ribbon or feathers or flowers or a little veil, and decorates her hat. The girls take the old ribbons and feathers and flowers and veils and decorate hats for dress up. Eunice lets Esther have her old hats for play, too, and long dresses, purses, and gloves. They keep Cracker Jack prizes and other small treasures in the purses.

The girls make elegant mud pies. Ronald and Trever made mud pies when they were younger, but theirs were rude affairs compared to the girls' confections. They carry down from the barn buckets of ground grain and make golden fillings for their chocolate layer cakes. They sprinkle white lime from the slack lime bin for frosting. They decorate cookies with fat brown velvet-weed seeds for raisins, and whole corn kernels. They carry off so much oil meal that the herdsman, passing them, says, "Hey, how much of that cattle feed are you using here, anyway?" But when Wesson passes he pauses, laughs till his eyes crinkle, admires the cakes, pats the playmates on their heads, and exclaims to the world in general, "Little gellies having fun!" "Gellies" is the way he always pronounces "girlies." The gellies smile up at him but don't speak.

The two listen in on club meetings in the living room of the Big House, or at the Marston house, and form their own club, the Cicero Club. Its elegant name comes from the writer whom Ronald is translating in his Latin class. Esther is president, and Eloise keeps the minutes.

The girls continue to attend school together, in the one-room district schoolhouse on the edge of the Dougan East Twenty. They go to Sunday School together and are in Mrs. Frey's class. When Mrs. Frey passes the collection basket Eloise usually puts in three cents. Sometimes, if she's lucky, it's a nickel. The other children also put in small amounts. All except Esther Dougan. Esther usually puts in fifty cents. Mrs. Frey exclaims, "Oh, look, children, what Esther has put in! Fifty cents to go to the missionaries! Isn't that splendid, children? Esther, dear, you must save all your money, you have so much to give. What a generous girl! Don't you think so, children?"

Esther smiles and blushes. "I get paid for my chores," she says.

At one point Mrs. Frey says to Eloise, "Don't feel bad, Eloise. Esther's a Dougan, and she can afford it." But Eloise is aware of Daddy Dougan's desk and the cashbox. W.J.'s office is at the end of the living room, a large roll-top desk against the north wall. The cashbox is on a shelf in a drawer. When the drawer opens, the cashbox can be swung out. Every day the milkmen come in after noon dinner and check in from their routes. They have lots of change in their change makers, for many people pay for their milk by leaving pennies and nickels and dimes in the returning empty bottles. The route men count their money and put it in the cashbox.

W.J. isn't careful about the cashbox. When there's a sudden call, an emergency in the barn or field or milkhouse, he leaps up as if he's killing snakes and is off running, leaving the cashbox unlocked, and sometimes even open. Eloise has seen this happen several times. She knows Esther has, too. And she knows that Esther sometimes helps her father stack the pennies, the nickels, and the dimes and slide the stacks into little dusky rose or green or blue sleeves, making fat heavy cylinders to take to the bank.

When the wartime flu epidemic strikes, the farm is hard hit. Eunice is ill; the help are ill; Ronald and Trever are ill. Aunt Lillian moves out from town, and she and her brother, W.J., put in twenty-hour days doing all the barn and milkhouse work alone. Esther, who doesn't become ill, is shipped to town. She lives at Aunt Ida's and goes to Strong School across the street for several months.

Albert Marston, Eloise's father, is returning with his team and wagon from the grist mill on the west side of town one day when he spots Esther wandering through a vacant lot several blocks from Strong School. It's during class hours. Esther spots him, too, and immediately drops into the tall weeds where she can't be seen. Albert stops and calls to her, but she doesn't respond. He tells his wife; Lura reports the incident to W.J. and Eunice. She feels they ought to know, to nip such behavior in the bud. Her

Eloise and Esther playing dressup.

parents ask Esther about her truancy. She is entirely innocent. She was in school the whole day. Mr. Marston couldn't have seen her. They believe Esther. They don't check with the school. Eunice tells Lura in the Marston kitchen that Albert is wrong, that he must have mistaken some other little girl for Esther. But Albert knows whom he saw. Thereafter, whenever Eloise tells her parents of Esther's deceptions, they don't tell the Dougans and instruct Eloise to stay quiet. "Her folks believe Esther in preference to anyone else," says Lura. Albert says, "We won't get mixed up in it again."

They try not to get mixed up in other ways. Esther often wants Eloise to stay overnight, but Eloise is reluctant. Esther has to get up very early; she's on the job by 5:30. Eloise feels uncomfortable staying in bed while her friend is working. She always gets up and helps, too.

"Then don't stay over," her grandmother Smith advises. "Say you're needed at home. That's true enough." She adds, "The Dougans are too hard on Esther. They order her about."

Lura mimics Eunice Dougan's sharp voice. "'Esta—get Ronald some more milk.' 'Esta—Trever hasn't had his pie yet.' 'Esta!' 'Esta!' 'Esta!'"

"I don't think Wesson realizes how hard Eunice is on Esther," Mrs. Smith says. "He can't hear."

Lura sniffs. "He has eyes, hasn't he?"

"Eyes can't smell trouble," Mrs. Smith replies.

12 ⚹ DIGNITY

Grama's oldest brother, the eldest of the twelve Trevers, is George Trever, PhD, DD, President of Gammon Theological Seminary in Atlanta, Georgia, and Professor of New Testament, Exegesis, and Christian Doctrine there. He is the officiant at Grama and Grampa's wedding, and the one who graced the pulpit of the Beloit Methodist Church for a few years where he purportedly said, when expostulating a point so vigorously that he expelled his teeth into the lap of a front row parishioner, "Would Mrs. Stenshaw please pass the plate?" Grama as a high schooler comes to Beloit for those few years and lives with her brother and his wife, Ada.

Every summer George and Ada come north, to be near family and friends, and for George to attend his home Methodist Conference. He fills his time with teaching, camp meetings, and guest preaching.

In August 1913, Ada dies from a fall in a bathtub. Grama and Grampa can't attend the funeral in Appleton. The day after the service George writes them pages of his sorrow, including that he plans to spend the weekend visiting places where Ada and he had so many happy times. "The hardest thing is to come when I have to go back alone to my desolate home. I shall return to Atlanta this year but have no plans beyond that. It seems impossible without Ada for you know wherever I was she was not far away."

In February 1914, George writes his sister a newsy letter. He gives details of the birth of his grandchild, Erna's baby, his son Arthur's transfer to a submarine. He then says:

> Well, the year is wearing away and I shall soon be going north again. Little did I think a year ago that my darling Ada would not be with me. But she is at home and better off, I'm sure. It has been pretty hard on me. We were so happy it seems too bad she had to be taken so early. Yet we had 30 happy years together, besides our courtship. It has been pretty lonesome sometimes, though I have kept busy.

He gives a lengthy list of where he has spoken all over the country, says he's studied and written quite a little, has had a fine boarding place, and that all the folks have been very kind. "So all in all I have managed to pull through so far pretty well. Considering. But what of the future? It does not seem I can go on this way indefinitely." His letter continues with all the family he intends to visit, then says, "You must count on boarding me awhile this summer. Tell Wess to have some old shoes, overalls and 'womas' ready and lots of work." He relates that Mrs. Fancelt is poorly and told him that Ada is better off not to live to be so old and helpless. "Yes, but what about me? Pray that when the time comes you and Wess may go somewhere near together."

"Well," says Eunice tartly, referring back to the family members' list, "I notice his plans don't include going to see Rose!"

Rose is the youngest Trever sister, a mildly retarded epileptic who has always had sheltered care. Currently she is in the Rock County Home, financially and emotionally supported almost entirely by Wesson and Eunice.

"We will take him to see her," says Wesson.

Summer comes, and true to his word, George includes a visit to his sister and brother-in-law. Times at the farm are being eventful. It gets electricity. It hosts open houses for customers, entertains church groups, and gives not one but two area-wide alfalfa parties with experts from the university down to lecture on the innovative crop. A hired man, Alan Turnbull, is a university student, writing his thesis about the farm. This demands attention and cooperation from everybody. Eunice takes a ten-day trip north, to the Methodist meeting ground, Camp Byron, and visits also a number of Trever siblings.

Wesson is modestly proud of the article published in the July 3 *Hoard's Dairyman*. It was his first substantial breakthrough into print other than newspapers. He reads it aloud to his visiting brother-in-law. The article gives Wesson's definition of a farmer as one who tills the soil, conserving its fertility; builds real farm homes; and en-

Uncle George at the farm, dignified.

hances rural community life. The real farmer has a mission that is larger and nobler than just making money.

George, who in his teens left a busy English Midlands town to come with his parents to a rocky Wisconsin farm, responds with scant enthusiasm. "Well, I could write an article that would show there's another side to farm life." Before George leaves, Alan Turnbull takes some photos of him in his farm garb, and he clowns before the camera.

In November, George writes from the south:

> Dear Sister Eunice,
> Your letter with pictures received and account noted. All right. Enclosed find a check for $1.00 and a stamp. The pictures certainly are well taken. Tell Alan he did a good job. But really, Eunice, I do not quite understand your remark as to my "playing farmer" and "idiot." Your letter sounds as if you and Wess were offended because I had them taken in that way. But you know that the whole matter was fun and so did the boys. If I remember aright you were present when they were taken and laughed as heartily as anybody when I stood that way. Who said I was playing "farmer?" Do you think that I make fun of farmers as though they are fools? Did I ever treat you and Wess as though I thought you inferior beings because you have a farm? Did you ever hear me make fun of farmers as such as though they lacked intelligence? Had it been some of the Trever girls who had taken offense at those pictures as though I was making out farmers to be fools I should not have been surprised but I must say I was surprised at you taking that attitude. You ought to know me better than that. Am I a snob setting myself up to be some superior being? Eunice, you do know me better than that and you do know that I was not making fun of farmers as such. I was simply showing what a difference a man might make in himself by wearing rough clothes and changing his usual demeanor. Really I cannot understand the tone of your remarks about the pictures. I was simply making fun of myself amongst my own folk. I supposed you knew that perfectly well.
> But I inferred from a hint dropped in a letter from Erna that I had offended your household by saying that I could write an article giving the other side of life on the farm. Wess certainly is enthusiastic about his business. That is why he succeeds in it. He has a right to like it too if he wants to and it suits his taste. So has anybody else. But must everybody else like it because he does? Must everybody else think that life on the farm is ideal because some folks like it? I simply could not endure it long, neither could I endure

my son-in-law's business. But is that saying anything against the business? Wess and Dick probably would not like mine, either. Every man to his own job, but don't insist that everybody must like your job. If I remember aright Eunice has not loved it overmuch herself. It is not because I think it an inferior employment that I do not want it, but simply because it does not suit my particular taste. That's all. Is there anything very bad about that? And I should not have made the remarks I did had not Wess read me his exceedingly rose-colored article about life on the farm. There is another side to it, as you yourself know, and so there is to all creation. Why did your household then think

Uncle George at the farm, undignified.

that I was running down the farm simply because I said that there are two sides to farm life? Let those that like it stick to it, but don't say that everybody ought to like it. I never did like the Chilton farm five minutes except to visit occasionally, and I have liked it at your house because you and Wess are you and Wess.

But it seems my last visit at your home was unusually unfortunate, or else you were unusually critical. I offended you about the pictures, it seems; I offended you about what I said regarding the farm, and I "lacked dignity" in speaking of Mrs. Graff and my relation with her. Really Eunice I do not understand what you mean by that. At Byron I told you as a beloved sister in the most serious and confidential way about it and when I was at your home it was seldom mentioned. It may be I did joke with you a little, but must I always wear a poker in my back at your house? As to being undignified anywhere else about so sacred a matter, I am sure I cannot understand you. At Erna's I never mentioned the matter at all until Dick began to joke about it and I never joked about it there except in reply to him. Erna knows that very well and will acknowledge it and once or twice I had a heart-to-heart talk with her about it. Professor Nelson and Mr. Roos themselves asked me about it at Conference and so did Dr. Plantz and in response I quietly told them,

"Yes. I was waiting on a lady," with not the least joke about it. They said they were very glad and Mrs. Roos urged me to bring Frances up there the evening of the wedding and they would invite a party of our dearest friends to welcome her. So I cannot understand your remarks about being undignified etc. Of course I am naturally free and jolly. Perhaps I would have made a happier home for my departed Ada and my children had I always been "solemn and holy" and everlastingly ministerial, never unbending but always stiff and starched. But dear Ada did not think so, neither do my children. And I guess I have been fairly popular in the best homes in Chicago and all over Wisconsin, in spite of my lack of dignity. My Conference seems to think a little of me, for it has sent me to three General Conferences and a reserve delegate to a fourth which has not been done to another preacher in it for 52 years. I can go and be welcomed to the best homes in any town where I ever preached, with all my lack of "dignity." And if I do say it, not many ministers had more friends on their charge than I generally had. What then is the matter now? Why did not my lack of "dignity" ruin my ministry?

But I am glad that you like my Frances. She certainly is a beautiful woman and in every way adapted to make me a happy home. I do love her dearly, and though I did not easily win her, she is devoted with all her noble heart to me now. We are to be married January 2nd in the evening by her brother. You will no doubt hear more about it, if you care to. She and I will take care of the "dignity" all right. Erna has taken the whole matter in the most daughterly way. Arthur and Bess write most sensibly and beautifully about it and said that if my mind was made up nothing would be gained by waiting. Let anybody see how I live here and I think few sensible people would say, "wait." My best friends here are glad that I shall not return alone after the holidays. Not one man in a thousand could have lived as I have for a year and 4 months and not go stark crazy. Most men when bereaved have somebody to keep house for them but I have nobody. Here alone day after day. If you think it fun try it. But I should never have married again had I not met such a lady as Frances Graff. She is the only one I ever saw that I could even look at. But she captured my heart sure enough without knowing she was doing it and we shall be married Jan. 2. I am to preach at the big Milwaukee gathering Dec. 31st.

Well, Eunice dear, this is not the kind of letter I generally write to you but your letter and the hint that Erna dropped did hurt me a little, I confess. But forget it. I hope your new help will turn out well. You will hear more about the wedding later.

Give my regards to Wess and the boys and tell them to stick to the farm if they like it.

Your loving brother, George.

Next time maybe I can make my visit more agreeable than the last one seems to have been. I'll try.

Jackie, who, after Grama's death, has found George's injured, angry, and defiant letter saved in Grama's letter box, can only conjecture what sort of bomb burst in the Big House when it arrived. Daddy, who would have been thirteen, doesn't remember. He does know he always loved Uncle Bert's visits, but not much Uncle George's. Perhaps Eunice was prudent and didn't show it to W.J., or anybody, but prudence was never one of Grama's virtues. Jackie pictures Grampa poring long hours over the letter — but if so, where are the annotations he always makes on the papers he pores over? On the other hand, Grampa had known his brother-in-law for well over fifteen years, long enough to have formed his own assessment of George's character. And it's only been a little while since the pecan grove.

At any rate, no permanent rift appears to have marred the family. Frances is indeed a jewel. It's doubtful that George ever again puts on old shoes, overalls and "womas." And nine years later, in 1923, he writes to his sister:

Bert tells us that Ronald is in France. That is a great experience for him, if he comes through all the temptation clean and strong. Of course any boy raised in a Christian home has to pass under the fire when he goes out into the world. Bert said that you are at home again, but not well. We are sorry and hope that you will be your old self one of these good days. But as we grow older we can hardly hope for that, though I am pretty vigorous yet. I am kept busy every minute preaching, conducting prayer meetings, delivering special addresses, weddings, funerals, etc., besides studying and writing a good deal.

Enclosed find a check for Rose. Say, I never have been told exactly what the rest are paying. I would really like to know. I want to do my share, but would like to know how my share compares with that of the others.

Uncle George, Jackie decides, is certainly still his old self.

13 ✻ FORD

It's 1922. Supper is over at the Big House but the family and hired men do not yet take their plates to the kitchen. Every night after supper Grampa reads aloud a passage from the Bible, and then, from a commentary, he reads various thoughts about that passage. Usually the men are content to listen respectfully to Daddy Dougan. It's part of being a family member.

Tonight, though, they are anxious to be away from the table. Jim has bought a new car, a Model T Ford, and all day they've been looking forward to tinkering with the engine, polishing the fenders, and taking the car for a spin. Their faces don't betray their impatience, but they exchange glances as they settle in for the lesson.

Grampa reads about Jesus and John the Baptist and the River Jordan. The selection isn't long. The men exchange glances again as Grampa closes the Bible and picks up the heavy commentary. He starts to read. The exegesis embroiders on the passage like a needle binding a button hole, over and under, before and behind. The men shift a bit in their chairs. The lesson is going on and on and Daddy Dougan seems nowhere near tying the knot and biting off the thread. They begin to squirm. Their thoughts are far from Jordan's banks. All thoughts are outside, parked beside the milkhouse. The men are yearning for the new black car.

Then Grampa reads, "And John said, 'Let us gather at the ford—'"

The men sit suddenly straight, electrified. Jim lets out a snort and tries quickly to smother it. But he can't, nor can the others, and in a moment all the hired men are braying uncontrollably.

Grampa senses the stir and looks up, puzzled. The laughter is catching and he begins to laugh, too, shaking his head. Finally he says, "I guess that's enough reading for tonight, boys," and closes the commentary.

The men grab up their dishes and rush from the table. Grampa sits alone, going back over the commentary, trying to find what was so funny.

Esther, coming from the kitchen to clear the serving dishes, reminds her father about Jim's new car outside, and explains the pun. She points out the line, the word. Grampa studies the passage, then laughs silently.

"I am glad," he says finally, "that these lads find our Bible sessions so applicable to their daily lives! Come along, gellie!"

He carries his own dishes to the kitchen, then he and Esther go to join the gathering at the Ford.

The American farmer, according to a 1920s Ford Motor Company advertisement, was "the happy and proud possessor of more than half the Ford cars in existence." Here, a Model T truck is loaded with dairy cows.

14 ⚹ GRAMPA DRESSES

At the Big House, Grampa and Grama have separate bedrooms. Grampa's is the larger, right off the hall, while Grama's adjoins his. There's a small cot in Grampa's room and sometimes Jackie sleeps there for her nap, or occasionally overnight. She likes to lie facing the wall and pick the ivy wallpaper off, to reveal bit by bit the rose pattern beneath. She likes waking up in the morning and in the semi-gloom watching Grampa prepare for the day.

It isn't Grampa's rising that wakes her, it's the unaccustomed noise. What you hear depends on which side of the milkhouse you sleep on. On the Little House side, the only early-morning disturbance is the chitter-chatter of a hundred sparrows in the thick ivy that covers the chimney from ground to roof. But on the Big House side, she can hear the clang of the milk cans coming up from the barn to the milkhouse, and the crash and clatter of milk-bottle cases being loaded into the milk trucks, and the trucks themselves driving out of the yard. And then, from the woodpile side of the Big House, comes the strident crow of the rooster, soaring into the sky, over and over.

Jackie watches Grampa dress through almost closed lids, so that he won't know she's awake. If he is ever naked, it happens in the bathroom or when she's asleep, for he always has on one-piece long underwear as he moves quietly around his room. He puts on his blue cambric work shirt and buttons it almost up. He steps into his one-piece overalls and pulls the straps over his shoulders. He fastens the straps to the bib not by button holes or snaps but with metal loops that fit around the brass buttons on the two corners of the bib. Then he sits on his bed to pull on his mottled brown cotton socks with the white toes and heels, the kind she has a monkey made out of, and then his heavy work shoes that are leather and come up over his ankles. His movements are deliberate, and Jackie can hear every one of his regular breaths, labored as though he were working hard.

Sometimes she decides to get up and follow Grampa to the bathroom for the next part of the ritual. She loves to watch Grampa shave. It's more interesting than watching Daddy, who uses a safety razor.

Grampa soaks a towel till it's steaming, then wrings it and packs it around his chin. Holding the towel in place with one hand, with the other he scrubs his wet shaving brush in the china cup of soap on the windowsill till it's thick with suds. Then he sets down the towel and lathers up his whiskers. The white mask softens his beard as he strops back and forth, back and forth his single-edge razor on the brown leather strap that hangs by the window. At last he takes the razor and starts slicing off the lather in long clean swatches. After each swipe he rinses off the piled foam under the hot faucet. He twinkles at Jackie from the mirror but doesn't speak. When all the lather has been shaved away, he uses the wet towel to wash any remaining soap off his face, dries his neck and face and ears, puts away his brush and razor in the medicine cabinet, and returns to the bedroom. There Grampa stands before his dresser and brushes his sparse hair with a brush with no handle, only a strap on the back for his hand. He buttons the top buttons of his shirt so that his damp long underwear collar no longer shows. He puts his pad of paper and a pencil in his shirt pocket. He puts on his gold rimmed glasses. "Let's go see what's for breakfast," he says to Jackie, but she already knows. She can smell the buckwheats and bacon.

15 ∝ LET THERE BE LIGHT

When Grampa and Grama come to the farm in 1906, the sources of power are hand, horse, wind; wood, coal, kerosene. Wind is harnessed by a cranky, creaky, wooden-strut windmill with wooden vanes and extending sail, snugged up close to the east side of the house, directly over the well shaft. A wood rod extends from the gear box at the top down to the pump. When wind blows, the gear box imparts vertical motion to the rod. This operates the pump, lifting water out of the well. When wind doesn't blow and reserves fall, the lifting rod is disconnected at the pump, the pump handle connected, and lifting motion provided by hand. The cows are milked by hand; the milk is bottled by hand. Milk is cooled to the 51 degree temperature of well water and is kept cold on the milkroute with ice harvested from frozen Rock River.

Water pumped by the windmill—or hand—is run into a boiler stoked with wood or coal which heats it for washing and scalding the milking utensils and milk bottles. Power for lights and lanterns comes from kerosene. But when Grampa builds the round barn in 1911, he wires it and makes it ready for electricity.

Beloit has been a pioneer in electric power. A.P. Warner (who at twelve declared he was going to be an inventor, and was told by his educated grandfather there was nothing left to invent) built his first commercial dynamo sometime after 1884, when he was 16 or so, and at 18 built, for Beloit's Gaston Scale Company, one that operated 75 lights. By 21 he had built dynamos for the Iron Works and the Beloit Strawboard Company; the latter dynamo ran 200 lights. He joined forces with another enterprising young man, and before 1895 the two formed the Wiley-Warner Electric Company, using water power from the dammed-up Rock River in downtown Beloit, and supplying electricity to businesses and some homes. They were the first with central service.

So electricity is an established part of the Beloit picture when W.J. is looking for a farm, and certainly plays a part in his decision. At the start he can't afford to hook up with city power. Fairbanks, upriver a mile, has begun to make generators for individual farm use. Their Model Z is a popular make-and-break engine with a belt coupled to a dynamo for generating electricity. Around 1910 Grampa dismantles the low-horsepower windmill and buys a Fairbanks pump jack and gasoline-powered Z engine. He installs it at the pump head. The engine pumps water to a pressure tank. Then he can turn off the engine and release water from the pressure tank as needed. He now has a reliable home water system.

When he builds the round barn he cannot yet afford a home electrical system. But by March of 1914 he's ready to remedy that. He replaces the old pump jack with a new motor-driven jack down in the pit. This is electrically powered by a new generator at the well head, which gets its power from the old Z engine just outside the wall. There is now power for pumping water, washing bottles, capping milk bottles, and furnishing light not only in the house, but in a line down to the barn. Grampa runs a line shaft, belt driven, off the well head pump motor to supply mechanical power for household items: the sewing machine, washing machine, power vacuum cleaner, dishwasher all have belt drives. In the barn a gasoline engine is used for running the shredder and husker, filling silo, and grinding feed. At 2 horsepower, it isn't strong enough to power a mechanical milking system too, now available through Hoard's, DeLaval, and elsewhere, but while Grampa would like one, he doesn't yet really need one. He has plenty of help, all of whom do their share of the milking, including Ronald and Trever. There are five or six men in the barn, morning and evening.

Though the new barn had previously been prepared for electricity, the Big House had not. Grampa's electrician drills, saws, threads wires behind woodwork and through walls, installs outlets, puts in light sockets. The chandeliers Grama has selected are hung in the living room and over the dining room table. At last the job is finished. The electrician sweeps up his mess and departs; Grama and her hired girl clean up after the electrician.

Now it is suppertime. It's dusk. The Z engine is running, the dynamo is running. Grampa waits by the kitchen doorway till everyone is seated at the dining-room table in the semi-gloom. Then he reaches around into the kitchen and throws the switch.

"Let there be light!" cries W.J. Dougan.

Brightness floods the room and shines on the grinning faces of all the family and help. They clap and cheer. Grampa stands, his hand still on the switch, laughing silently. Later in the spring Ronald, who gets a box camera for his twelfth birthday, takes pictures of the brand new machinery and fixtures.

Near the end of May, Grampa has an alfalfa field day. The whole area attends in order to view the farm's alfalfa fields in progress and learn from university agronomists what must be done to succeed in growing this new and valuable forage crop. When the newspaper writes up the event, it stresses electricity as much as alfalfa. The many men have been hearing lectures in the loft of the round barn, then tramping the fields with the professors, while the ladies have been "shown the conveniences in the house, intending to lighten the burden of caring for the large family necessary to do the work on this farm. The house is equipped with power washing machine, water system, power vacuum cleaner, and electric lighting. This latter extends to all the barns and other buildings. The place as a whole is fast rounding into a perfect plant for efficient farm work and milk production."

During the same week the paper describes a church party at the farm: "Games were played on the beautiful lawn which was illuminated with electricity, and later the 'round barn' was made the scene of much merriment." This electrical emphasis is due to the sparsity of individual home electric lighting, even in progressive Beloit, but especially on a farm. It also reflects Grama and Grampa's and the whole farm's pride and delight in the modern system.

Over the years, Wiley-Warner Electric has gone through several management changes, as well as developing in electrical sophistication and growing in scope. In 1911, Beloit's power is supplied by Beloit Water, Gas & Electric Company. A large generating plant is located on Rock River just north of the college. By 1916 a high line has been run out Colley Road as far as the crossing tracks of the Chicago, Milwaukee, St. Paul, and Pacific Railroad, to service the Perrigo sand pit operation in full swing there. Perrigo has been digging both clay and sand and mixing these in proper proportions for foundry casting at Fairbanks and the Iron Works.

At the farm, with the milkhouse in progress that same year, electrical demands are heavy. It's obvious that the farm already needs more power than its various systems can generate, about 1,500 watts. The milkhouse, with its larger automated equipment, will soon need even more. For three years Grampa has been running his Z engine hard, and maintaining the various separate systems is a nuisance. He is frustrated by the limitations of the Z. He also is beginning to have trouble getting help; he loses a number of his best workers. Many men are going into the Army, and the factories are funneling off those who don't. Why should a young man put in a grueling farm workday when he can spend considerably less hours at a factory for more pay? The ads for milking systems reflect this: their big pitch is how much labor is saved with milking machines, and how few men it now takes to manage a modern barn.

With the high line so near, and the electric company aggressively going after customers, Grampa pays $600 to have the high line extended three fourths of a mile farther out Colley Road, supplying a three-phase current direct from the city power plant to the farm. Voltage goes from 32 DC of the home generator to 220 AC. Motors and the additional wiring needed bring the cost to over $900. But as of January 1917, the farm is fully electrified, with all the power it needs.

At this juncture, remembering the alfalfa field day, Grampa, Grama, and the power company combine forces to make the farm a teaching example, to demonstrate to the rural community the advantages of electricity. Grama already has in use an electric iron, a vacuum cleaner, and an electric dishwasher. The company installs a stove, a sewing machine, and other conveniences for the event. It also adds demonstration equipment to the barns and milkhouse. It's an all-day affair. People swarm to the farm, some two hundred of them, and many not country folk, either. They watch the milking, the bottling and capping, and go through the Big House to see the wonders there. Grampa lectures from the loft floor of the round barn and the audience clusters inside or on the ramp. After the lecture a supper is served on long trestles laid on sawhorses inside the loft. Electric lights shine down as dusk gathers.

Grampa doesn't say, "Let there be light," to this gathering. But his Scots soul must be gratified that after the party the electric company presents him with some of the equipment loaned. They are glad for all the publicity and advertising, and want him to keep the stove and sewing machine.

A year or so later Grampa buys a milking system and puts an electric motor in the barn's loft over the cow vestibule, to supply the power needed to produce a vacuum in the milking machines. The barnhands learn to use the two Empire milking machines that stand back on the sidewalk behind the cows. The first day everyone stops by to watch and marvel as the tits are sucked into the tit cups, and the rhythmic expression of liquid begins. But the era of hand milking isn't over. When the machine is through each cow still has to be stripped by hand, to be sure the udder is completely emptied.

Shortly after the building of the milkhouse Grampa finds another way to expand power in the interest of economy. He buys a Freeport gas machine from the Stover company and sinks it, and a condensing tank, in a pit across the drive from the Big House in front of the milkhouse. He fills the tank with high test auto gasoline. A sleeve of circulating water keeps the tank cold. It is a kind of still. Grampa funnels off the vapor in a vaporizing tank, pipes it to the Big House, and uses it to run the boiler and the stoves. He pipes it to the milk-house to make clean fuel in that building, and also down to the barn. Then he utilizes the residual heavy gas for the Z engine and for the tractor he purchases shortly thereafter. Thus the high test gas is broken down to serve two needs.

By 1921 ice has become a problem. The farm has always cut ice from Rock River during the winter, above the dam, and stored it in the icehouse for warm weather use. Recently, Fairbanks Morse factory has begun to empty sludge into the river. Oil freezing into the ice makes the ice unfit for use, and threatens (and eventually destroys) the commercial icehouses down river. The farm tries for a while to cut ice upriver, but that proves unfeasible. The town's largest dairy, Sturtevant, Wright & Wagner, installs a large ice-making plant. Grampa knows he cannot rely on Turtle Creek for the dairy's needs; he, too, buys an ice making machine, though not as large. A Lipman, its engine in the well head, utilizes the floor of the old ice room for the ordered row of lined cavities that freeze water into cakes of ice. He continues, however, to stock the icehouse with naturally frozen ice when he has the opportunity.

A dozen years after the arrival of the high line, rural electricity is still enough of a rarity in many parts of the Midwest that in March, 1929, Clifford Gregory, editor of Chicago's *Prairie Farmer* magazine, writes to all of *Prairie Farmer's* Master Farmers, of whom Grampa is one, asking them to give their views of electricity on the farm. He says he will value Grampa's thoughts for an article the magazine is planning to run.

Grampa responds, and sends a copy of his letter to his friend Mr. Meecham of Wisconsin Power & Light, which Madison company had added Beloit Water, Gas & Electric to its constellation of area power companies in 1927. Grampa says it may be of interest to the company to know how he feels regarding his electric service and its advantages for farmers. He adds, "I just returned from a trip to Texas. Had a fine time, saw lots of things, and am glad to be a resident of Wisconsin." His letter to *Prairie Farmer* starts with the statement that he is pleased to be of help. He continues:

> I have had experience with electrical power on the farm since 1914. For the first three years I used the individual plant; then in 1917 I put in the High Line current from the Wisconsin Power & Light Company. My conclusions from this experience are that no progressive farmer can afford to be without electric current. If it is impractical to get current from a central plant, he should use one of the many forms of home generators.

My farm and business has grown to be more than just a farm; therefore my use of electricity cannot be spoken of just as farm use, and of course my farm bill is much higher than any ordinary farm. There is also another factor in my large use of electricity. I have not figured its use on mere economy in dollars and cents, but in economy of human energy, therefore adding to the pleasure of living.

In my farm work, distinctively, I use electricity in this way. First, of course, for ample light everywhere. Then the electricity lifts these burdens: it furnishes a complete automatic running water system; in the house it washes the clothes, the dishes, sweeps the floor, irons the clothes, warms cool nooks in the house, helps with the cooking, and does the sewing; in the barn it milks the cows, grinds the feed, fills the silos, elevates the grain, and elevates the hay; and in my milk plant electricity does all the work it does in any well organized city plant.

Much of this work is of such a nature that it could not be accomplished by any less vital force; and much of it is so heavy and so constant no human power could do it. It is my experience in using electricity in this manifold way that convinces me that it is one of the greatest benefits to progressive agriculture.

I have a few concrete examples showing the economy and desirability of electric power on the farm. I am enclosing a copy of my study of silo filling

Grama enjoys her electric sewing machine while granddaughter Joan, 3, looks on.

last fall. You will note there is not a very large difference per ton in the actual power cost between the electric current and the gas power. However, we have not taken into consideration the overhead expense of the two. I have run the 15 HP motor to do this filling since 1917. There has been no repair expense, and its first cost is less than one third that of the tractor. By this you can see that the overhead of the electrical power is almost negligible, while we all know that the overhead of gas power is exceedingly high.

There is but a trifling difference in the quality of power produced by the two. Of course the electric power is more convenient in starting, and this fact is largely in favor of electricity when power has to be used through the cold months. One other concrete example is the convenience of electricity in haying. I have my hay rope attached to a hoist run by an electric motor. When the load of hay comes up it is but an instant's job to throw the switch and get a start. Also there is a return drum that quickly draws the fork back to the load. We frequently unload large loads of hay in 10 to 15 minutes, and it requires in man labor only the man of the load to operate the fork, and from there he controls the drums. I could multiply almost indefinitely these incidents showing the convenience of electricity.

You ask my opinion relative to disadvantages. Of course a farm is safer from fires with no matches, no kerosene or gasolene, no combustibles, using only the natural light for conveniences; but this is impossible in civilization. Then the question comes, "Can electricity be used as safely as other forms of light and power?" In my opinion, if one realizes the tremendous energy he is working with, and takes scientific precautions to harness it aright, it can be used much more safely than any of the other forms of light or power.

One of the big dangers is from unskilled, careless wiring. My place was wired for a 32 volt current which the sellers claimed could not cause fire. I have recently gone to the expense of overhauling much of my wiring, and putting in the barns, in the exposed places, the conduits. One other danger is to allow any man to tamper with the wires. They should be handled only by those who understand the job.

You ask what might be done to improve electrical service for farmers. I can answer this in a single sentence: Farmers, use more electricity! The electric companies cannot economically install their plants, extend their lines, and give the supervision that is necessary for efficient service unless the farmers use the current to the full extent. When farmers do their share I feel the economical forces will adjust to the prices so that electricity can lift the great burdens of the farm to the advantage of our whole society.

Grampa's thoughts make up the bulk of Master Farmer commentary—some six paragraphs straight from his letter—in the lead article of the August 10, 1929 *Prairie Farmer*, "Clean, Quick and Convenient Light and Power," with a subhead, "That is What Central Station Electrical Service Gives on the Farm."

The Roosevelt administration in 1932 passes the Rural Electric Authority Act, and the Rural Electrification Administration comes into existence to carry it out. The Act is dedicated to bringing electricity to rural areas: as Grampa's last paragraph indicates, private utilities find it too expensive to run electricity to the country, and farmers find it too expensive to buy. The REA is formed to run the lines out; this subsidizes both the utilities and the farmer. But many farmers who have been using home generators are reluctant to give up their reliable source of power. If they accept the wire, they want to keep generators as backup, in case of outages. The government, however, needs full farmer cooperation to succeed—the more home plants in use, the less power bought from utility companies. Only by selling enough power will it be profitable for the government eventually to privatize the operation, which is its aim. Rock County in general supports REA, but REA's projected sweep of the nation is never completed. World War II disrupts, and private utilities do pick up on providing rural electricity where the government has not yet succeeded. REA forms cooperatives, establishes local boards, and buys power from such utilities as Wisconsin Power and Light. Daddy becomes one of the charter members of the Board, for while the dairy has Wisconsin Power & Light, Chez Nous, a mile and a half farther from town, is part of REA.

Jackie isn't aware, when her parents buy the Snide place in 1937, how recently that farm was operating on a home generator. When one is eight—unless of A.P. Warner's stripe—it isn't the sort of subject one contemplates. She knows of Thomas Edison from school, but to her, unlimited electricity is a given that has always been available at the touch of a switch—except living at Chez Nous, later, when the lights go out. She does realize electricity costs money. Daddy is forever harping about turning off lights.

And she has an experience at the Wisconsin Power & Light plant that she never forgets. She is perhaps nine years old. She's dressed in a costume Mother once made for a dance recital. It resembles Peter Pan garb, though not green but a soft pearly gray. It has britches to the knees, and a jerkin shirt, and a tunic. She wears finely ribbed gray knee socks and ballet slippers. She has a soft gray cap that comes forward to a point, has a peak that folds over near the tip, and a blue-green feather on the side. A black half-mask covers her eyes. She's in the car with Daddy. He's dropping her off at a Hallowe'en party.

But first he pulls into the huge generating plant on the river that is Wisconsin Power & Light. He needs to see someone. It's dark. Jackie follows him through a door that seems small in contrast to the immensity of the towering, windowless walls. Inside, a few lights are on, bare bulbs, but such is the vastness of space that they light up only a local area, like a candle. Jackie stands a little apart from the two men while they talk. Above her, the room dissolves into darkness; she can't see where it ends. Around her are gigantic pineapple-shaped machines, with dark metal vertical ribs. There seem to be four or five of these; they, too, shade off into the gloom. She can't really see how many, or where they end. But she feels their massive presence as almost living things. They are humming; they are quietly, pulsingly alive.

The whole space is peaceful. Nothing menaces. But being here, Lilliputian in this strange place, and in costume, makes her feel not-quite-herself. And then something odd happens. It's as if there are two of her. The Jackie that she knows herself to be is up high, in the dark on a horizontal steel rafter that the light only hints at. That Jackie is gazing down on a strange small Peter Pan figure in pearly gray with a mask and feathered cap. The Jackie on the rafter observes the Jackie on the floor, standing in a pool of light beside the conversing men, the humming behemoths. The floor Jackie is aware that there's a rafter Jackie, but does not look up. It's trancelike. It lasts till Daddy takes her hand, and they leave.

This is the first time she realizes that she can see herself objectively, as another person. It happens throughout the rest of her life: the watcher-self and the being-self. Usually it's all right; sometimes she even does it deliberately. It comes to have a name: she calls it, in her mind, Jackie-on-the-lintel, for the top sill of a door is where most often she feels her viewer to be. The vantage point is seldom so far away as the dim Power & Light rafter.

But the experience gives a sort of power, a sort of light. Isn't it a writer's habit to be watcher, observer, while also participating? It's only a nuisance when she'd prefer to be so totally immersed in an experience—just plain living—that she's not aware of herself so immersed. The watching can take the edge off the being. At those times she tries to banish the watcher. Sometimes she succeeds.

16 ⚔ SPARROW POT PIE

Trever is nine. He has a BB gun that he uses to shoot at various targets: pigeons, sparrows, his brother Ronald. The BBs only sting Ronald and annoy the pigeons, but they kill the sparrows.

Practice makes Trever a crack shot. One day he carries two dozen sparrows to the kitchen and asks his mother to make him a sparrow pie. Grama is not pleased with the idea. Trever begs and teases. Finally Grama relents and patiently cleans all the sparrows. It's a hard job, and when all the feathers are removed with boiling water, there is not much left of a sparrow. Grama decides not to behead or gut or take legs off, as she would a chicken. She merely slices the breast meat off the tiny bodies. Trever watches until he's bored, then wanders off with his gun to cut down the sparrow population still further.

"Don't you bring in a single one more!" warns his mother.

Grama bakes the slivers of sparrow breast in a pot pie with a gravy of onions, carrots, peas, and potatoes. At supper that night, she carries the little casserole steaming to the table. Trever and his pie are the focus of interest. There is much quoting of four-and-twenty blackbirds.

Everyone watches as Trever cuts the crust and takes his first bite. There is a tide of snickering at the dubious expression on his face.

"It's sort of different," he comments when he's asked what it tastes like. He slowly works away at the pie while the others eat cold roast pork and applesauce. He offers everyone a chance to sample, but everyone declines, even Grampa.

All except Ronald. He hazards a small bite.

"Ugh, that's no dainty dish!" is his verdict, and he goes to the kitchen to spit it out.

"I didn't think it could be," Grama says, "but Trever would have it!"

Trever leaves most of his pie uneaten. When he thinks no one is looking, he eases some roast pork onto his plate from the nearby platter.

17 ⋇ GRAMPA'S BLUE MEMO

It is November of 1923, and Grampa is in a crisis of faith. This is the background: Grampa had misgivings about allowing Ronald to attend a North Shore private university instead of the Ag School at Wisconsin, where he'd been first enrolled, and his misgivings seem justified. The fraternity is Ronald's main interest. Grampa writes him, in his sophomore year, "I am sorry you are not able to retrench in the harmful and wasteful expenses. If you realized that it meant quitting school if you cannot get on without these flowers and parties you would think twice before following the crowd." And later that sophomore year, Ronald and forty other Northwestern boys are carted off to jail in a raid on a "Bohemian" speakeasy, "The Wind Blew Inn." Grampa has to appear in court with all the other fathers and sons, and pay a stiff fine. The papers, even out-of-state ones, make hay of the story, with puns on how the police blew in and blew out again with the college boys in their paddy wagons. Ronald's name, usually misspelled, is in all the Chicago papers, but kind providence omits it from the front-page in the *Beloit Daily News*. Grama, heartbroken, writes her son, "When we saw this in the paper our hearts stood still till we had read it through, fearing your name would be in it."

Then, worse, he is caught smoking. Grama writes another agonized letter:

> I asked Papa if you had smoked any and he had to tell me the truth. I cannot see how you can do it. Your father has done so much for you and loves you so and you know how he feels men are so much smaller who do it. I should think you would want to tower in his eyes and do nothing that would keep him from admiring you in every way. The dear unselfish dad. He is carrying such a heavy burden and practically all alone. He cannot keep that beautiful optimistic spirit up against everything. He tells me so long as he can keep his grit he can make it but if he loses that, it is all up with him. Ronald you must be his support. He is the best friend you have, you must keep his love and respect. Oh my precious boy if you would stand firm against the cigarette I

would be the happiest woman on earth. Papa and I would rather have that assurance than the grandest home money could buy.

So thus far, Ronald's college career has not made his father happy, especially when he thinks back to how hard he himself struggled to get a solid education.

But there are other factors. There's a mini-depression in the early twenties, and Grampa is sick with financial worries. He's upset about his help — they are not of the caliber he's used to. Then there's Grama. She's suffering from nervousness, insomnia, dizziness, and spends weeks at Aunt Ida's or in Chicago at the home of friends. Even when she's at the Big House much of her time is spent on the couch. Grampa is in charge, with the help of Hilda, extra hired help, and Esther, now fourteen. He's glum about the state of the house. He finds it hard to manage everything.

By Ronald's junior year he is earning much of his own money, but at what cost? His grades are undistinguished. He has no idea of what he wants to do with his life. He shows little interest in attending church. He thinks about dropping out of school and working for a while. His father writes immediately, offering him a job as assistant herdsman, with side benefits of study and checking farm records, later crop and field work, and possibly some management. Within a year or two he would return to school with a definite aim. His letter continues:

> At my Institute talk yesterday a businessman asked, "Do you plan to continue in your present work as a life work, or to stick for a time then give up like so many do just as they are getting where they can accomplish something?" A year ago I could have answered with all assurance that I should continue to the end of life, ever improving and progressing. Yesterday I candidly answered, "I don't know."
>
> At present, the big problem is bettering the life in the home. Relieving the congestion and confusion, and making it possible to keep the family spirit. I can manage the work so as to secure leisure and life for both the help and ourselves but the constant presence of so many at the table is distracting. There is only one thing we can do about it, with our finances as they are at present. That is to refine the home under the present plan. Change service at table somewhat. Have one of the helpers wait on table, possibly serve plates from kitchen and lay emphasis upon neatness of all to come to table — quiet and time for eating, wholesome inspiring conversation etc. All of these can

be gradually brought about and make our meal hour a delight instead of a horrible nightmare.

We have help enough both inside and out to make the work run smooth. Mother and myself can and do get much time free from our duties. I, more than the average businessman and mother more than the average city house-wife who cares for her own household. Our work is so organized that this is possible. Probably we could make and save more money if we stuck closer to our job, but that is not the question. The big problem is, can we manage the work and business so as to find life and stick to the job as a satisfying life work.

Such a work should fascinate one so that he would regret any circumstance that would necessitate his leaving it. I often ask this question: Would we leave the job with regret, or with anticipation and pleasure? I feel that mother's only regret would be the cut in income and I rather think she would even welcome poverty if she could have her family to herself.

In my case there is a delight in the work itself. I like the responsibility of keeping things going. I enjoy especially the problems of the crops and the herds. Up to last spring I always entered into the cropping season with a peculiar joy of anticipation. A sense of confidence in the assurance that there will be a seed time and a harvest. Last spring I seemed to have none of this joy of the true husbandman. It worried me not to realize it. Of late the old sense of assurance and joy in my job has gradually returned.

I do not know but the cause of this is some real fellowship with Trever, also the part I am taking in the Junior Club work of the county. Trever helps me in writing down the discussions and he is really interested in this work. He says he has the best time with me. It is not the idea that I expect to make him a farmer by these means but that we can talk together and that I can get through to his thoughts and feelings that gives me real pleasure.

How about your job possibility in France? If you decide to come home I will give you the best chance possible to fulfill your desires. You will be able to earn $40 or $45 per mo. after the first two weeks. Remember, whatever you choose I will help you to the utmost of my ability.

Ronald's decision is to stay in school for the second term. Then the offer to do social work in a war-ravaged French town does come through, and he departs before the semester is over. He leaves his low grades to show up at the farm after he's gone. That summer Grampa doesn't have his elder son's help on the farm, nor his younger's, either, for Trever, instead of working shoulder to shoulder with his father, as Wesson had happily anticipated, takes a job selling fly spray.

Ronald's letters from France are filled with youthful exuberance. His eyes, dazzled, are suddenly wide open to the world. Trever goes off to the University of Wisconsin, joins its chapter of Ronald's fraternity, and acquires a jalopy. Grampa writes, "Regarding your car, cut it out. You are better off without it. Even if it cost nothing. What you need is to develop quiet strength and poise of mind and character. The car tends to develop just the opposite. Walk and think and grow great. I do not want you to use a car in Madison. Sell out and walk."

Trever is happy-go-lucky, and unlike his brother, doesn't strive to earn money. Grampa's letters have a three-note monotony: study, don't spend frivolously, and lead a pure, manly life. Concerning the budget Trever sends home in the fall, Grampa writes wryly, "Your financial statement was ambiguous. Whether you need $25 for these purchases in future, or whether you have spent this and more, I cannot make out. I notice you are not planning to eat for a month."

Grampa is also discouraged about his hearing. He writes, again to Trever, how those he takes along to write for him either think the talks are not worthwhile, lose interest and cease to write ("you and Mother of late") or become so intensely interested themselves, they forget him ("Henry and Lester"). When he gives talks and speeches, he finds the communication with his audiences increasingly difficult.

So in late November, 1923, Grampa sits down at his desk and in a letter to himself, written in pencil on tablet paper, takes stock of his life:

These have been my ideals:

1. To build a successful business that would give opportunity for life, as well as a living; to build a home that would be a model for conveniences, beauty, and a desirable place to live.

2. To inspire my family and entire household with high ideals and give them a happy life.

3. To live a straight forward christian life; to continue to grow mentally and morally; to be active in work and religious work; to have our home distinctively christian.

4. To so direct and inspire my children that they would choose the good and detest the evil, and would seek to serve, would be efficient, outstanding characters wherever found.

Regarding my feeling as to my failure in realizing these ideals,

1. We have worked hard and developed a successful business and built the house but by its own burden it is destined to fail in its ultimate aim. We have no pleasure in it now. It is not a desirable place to live. We take no pleasure in the work or the life.

There are many reasons for this: failing health, unsatisfactory help, necessity of economy in order to meet obligations, and especially the lack of interest on the part of our lads.

2. In the latter part of this ideal I have failed. The very things I have provided for making my family happy have caused discontent and unhappiness. I have given leisure and opportunity for camp and recreation. This has created a restlessness and dissatisfaction with real life.

3. In all but the first clause I feel I am falling down. Our home is becoming just an ordinary nonchristian farmhome. My church and religious work is of no account, to keep the mind alert and conscience sensitive seems difficult. Even in the personal christian faith and practice I am falling far short of the example of the Master. He had courage to undertake the difficult. He had perseverance. He had hope. He was confident of ultimate victory. He knew what he believed. I don't. In these things I am not following and it seems impossible for me to rise above my present gloom. I resolve again and again that I will face difficulties, trust in the future and have courage to go forward, but I find it is only a transitory stimulus. I pray with the psalmist, "Oh God restore unto me the joy of thy salvation."

4. In respect to the fourth ideal I cannot speak all I feel. It pains me greatly to see my lads deliberately choose the evil and scoff at the good. They seem to have no moral convictions on right and wrong. Nor any high sense of service, not even a spirit of helpfulness to myself, their mother, or the home, let alone of service to humanity. With all their advantages for education they are simply attracted by the tinsel and bright lights of the show and society. Missing entirely the worthwhile associations and studies that would develop mental and moral strength. As yet they are not outstanding characters, they are one of the crowd, really in the lower strata of the crowd.

These are the things that make me blue. Some of them can be overcome but at present I see no bright outlook. To sell and change business would not help much.

This is a bitter accounting. The returning joy and assurance Grampa wrote about to Ronald almost a year ago was short-lived. His depression now is considerably deeper.

In the explication of his first point, Grampa's words about the home are shocking. He gives reasons. This is the only place where he says *we*. He means Eunice when he speaks of failing health. Things have not improved with Grama. She writes to Ronald in France, "It is so hard for Dad to have me this way. He needs me so. But I am not much good till I get stronger." And Grampa writes, "I do not know when Mother will come home. I miss her greatly. Work is my only diversion. I do work like the dickens when she is away."

And then, unsatisfactory help. He writes Trever, shortly before his blue memo:

> Henry is not coming back to the farm. He is going into city business again. I feel very blue over my influence on the boys. Four boys have come to me this year enthusiastic about farming. After a few weeks or months with me they have had enough of it (my own included). I wonder if my ideals of work and life are right. They surely are not attractive.

And, "necessity of economy in order to meet obligations." The economic depression of the early Twenties is not yet over, and repeatedly Grampa's letters worry about money: "I've had to buy a new cooler." "I've had to take out another loan to tide me over." Grama's illness costs money. Hiring help to take her place costs money. Grampa speaks longingly of taking Grama on vacations where he, too, would get rest. But these are out of the question.

The last item, "and especially the lack of interest on the part of our lads," is the real kicker, shown in Grampa's severe and specific judgment of those lads in the explication of the fourth point. In the second point he speaks of family restlessness and dissatisfaction with real life. In the third, he is despairing of his own spiritual life. But in the fourth! "It pains me greatly to see my lads deliberately choose the evil and scoff at the good. They are one of the crowd, really in the lower strata of the crowd."

Is this fair? Certainly not to Ronald, who by now is sending home increasingly mature letters from abroad. His college sins are old, and he has been serving humanity for the past six months. If bright lights are still attracting him, they are now the lights of the opera houses, theaters, and art museums of Paris.

But Trever! Trever is only fifty miles from home, and has tobacco on his breath. His mother writes:

I was so crushed in heart and spirit after you had gone. I thought I never could write but you are my baby boy in spite of what you have done and I love you but I want to be proud of you. I was so weighed down it seemed I could not get off my bed, to think you could make light of the things that mean so much to me and that you could deceive me and do the things you knew would break my heart and hurt a kind loving father as you have. Can you trade a mother's love and a father's respect for things that are going to undermine your own character? I knew you were smoking for a long time, for you would not let me kiss you. Along in middle of the summer I kissed you and smelled stale tobacco and I knew then. I waited for you to tell but you deceived me and when I asked, you told me an untruth. You are naturally a fine boy with high ideals and good principles but one sin leads to another and it does not take long to slide down hill. I want to look in your eye and know it is true as it was two years ago. We used to be so near; don't let a nasty devil of a cigarette separate you from your best love.

Both parents write Ronald about Trever's smoking and lying, but with the transatlantic time lag, it is after Grampa's memo to himself that he and Grama receive Ronald's reply:

Your letter about Trever came this morning. Of course your worrying makes me feel rotten because I know how bad you feel. Trever's case so parallels mine that I can see both sides. My thought won't be a great deal of comfort to you, but I think it is pretty level. Here it is for what it is worth.

Smoking in itself isn't a crime for which a fellow will be eternally damned. It is the thinking that makes it so. I admit that it is injurious to health, but I don't think any more than a dozen other indulgences that are not so heartedly condemned. None of these things need to become habits, neither does a little smoking need to lead to a harmful excess. I think you both are stressing the evil of smoking so much that you are making it the chief fault a man can have. It isn't, and it doesn't need to lead to other faults. Even if Trever should continue, the matter will settle itself, for he worships his body, and when smoking interferes with his chances in athletics, smoking will go. It is hard to make a kid think it wrong morally, when he sees good and great men all around him indulging though, isn't it?

His deceiving you is more or less natural, although it hurts. He is too weak to hurt you outright, and when he slips up while he doesn't think he is committing a crime, he knows you will think so, and attempts to hide it.

Smoking isn't the great crime. A man can think straight, love and be true to his friends, and lead a life without violating friendship and honor and still smoke. Oh gee — I so want to express myself — make you feel better about it — and my words don't come well.

This is my point. Because smoking is a tangible thing that can be nailed down, don't you think you are making too much of it? It is much more to the point that he realize he should deal seriously with his friends — develop a high code of honor — that he should get enough sleep to keep him alert, than that he should take any definite stand about the other question. Perhaps by making him think he is headed for a bad life by smoking as he has, you really do make him think so. That is bad!

As to other things — Trever has the right stuff, and the right background. Don't bother about him too much. He is off on a nineteen year old tangent, just as I was a year or two ago, with its attendant questioning of everything, its tendency to coarse language, and all. Sometimes I think nineteen is a fellow's oldest period. He knows everything! After a bit, he comes to and loses his high horse.

But I'm really worried about you both. Please don't take things so hard. Know you have three pretty decent kids who are surely profiting by your teaching even when they seem to the least.

So the trigger cause of the blue memo comes clear. Trever's smoking and deceit. This against a background of remembering Ronald's shortcomings, plus farm worries, help worries, money worries, and concern about Grama. There is plenty here to make Grampa blue, to cause him to take up his pencil and assess his life.

He doesn't know it yet, but in regard to his sons, it is the darkness before the dawn. In his next letter to Trever, he gives advice and encouragement on Trever's upcoming exams, then goes on to outline a talk on "Problems of Dairying" he is soon to give in Iowa. About the last point, "Problems of Recruiting Dairymen," he says, "I am going to hold out my ideas of the opportunities in the broader field of dairy work, i.e., not just actually milking cows, but research work, teaching, marketing, etc." He adds, "You know I am to speak at a big state meet in Illinois in February. I shall use this same thought."

At that Illinois talk, someone takes down the speech verbatim, as well as the question and answer period. Throughout the speech, Grampa counters gloom. In the last section he states that farmers, by their own gloom, are discouraging those in their sphere of influence from going into farming, including their own children. He concludes the speech by saying yes, there are problems in dairying, but there is no cause for despair.

One of the questioners asks, "I would like to hear what this gentleman has to say about keeping the boys and girls on the farm. That is more of a problem than getting a good sire." The transcript continues:

> Mr. Dougan: "I do not know." (Laughter.) "I have two boys. I have talk-ed the higher ideals and tried to give them a vision of their opportunity. I thought that they were absolutely against the farm. One boy has a position in community work in France at present. His last letter was to this effect: 'I am thinking more and more about the farm,' and 'the picture and vision of the farm.' He said, 'Some people would call it kiddish, but I call it a vision.' If he works that out he will be a farmer, he will be a progressive farmer. The other boy is telling me that he is getting to think better of the agricultural course that he is taking in Madison. I don't know whether they will be farmers. We do not care especially whether our boys and girls are farmers or not. This is the thing we hold up to them: 'First be good and strong men and women.'" (Applause.) "'Then choose the vocation in which you can serve humanity.' We figure out the education to that effect." (Applause.) "I believe the farm is going to appeal to them."

There will be future discouragements in Grampa's life, future major crises. But so far as anyone knows, he never writes another memo that so questions his own spirit, or so despairs of his sons. Jackie's personal experience, in the twenty years she knows him, is of the beautiful optimism Grama writes about. To Jackie Grampa is, in the words of a famous writer, "the apple tree, the singing, and the gold."

18 ✢ ESTHER, CONTINUED

When Esther is ten, and back at country school, the teacher, Mrs. Ernie Smith, becomes pregnant and therefore has to resign. Esther's brother Ronald is now seventeen and waiting out a year before starting college. He's appointed teacher to finish the year. His sister and Eloise are two of his pupils.

When he leaves, Mrs. Hugel comes, but she's not much interested in the job and often sends her father in her place. He leans back in his chair and poses the students mental arithmetic problems all day. Though they learn little else, they all become whizzes at adding long columns in their heads, especially one student, Robert Mackie. Then the school district is consolidated and all the students are driven to town schools. Eloise and Esther, both eleven, go to Merrill School.

Esther, about ten.

Ronald, a freshman now at Northwestern, hears frequently from his parents. While his mother's letters are full of worry about the state of his soul, the state of the laundry he sends home weekly, the state of the farm finances, and accounts of Trever's doings, she never mentions her daughter unless there is trouble. In February, she writes:

> We have been having another time about Esther. She took my watch to school, and when I went to get it, it was gone. I hunted all over and when Esther came home from school I told her to hunt. She went up and soon came down with it and said it was under a box on my dresser. I asked her if

she had taken it to school and she said no, and repeated she had never had it, so I let it go. Ida was at Smiths Sunday and asked Eloise if Esther ever wore my watch at school. She said yes, one day, and Esther said she brought it downstairs and forgot to give it to me. (See her deceit?) Well Tuesday night we were alone setting supper table and I said, "Esther did you ever wear my watch to school?" She said, "No." I repeated and she declared no. I knew of course that she did, so I asked her if she had anybody's watch and she said yes, she wore a girl's watch. I took hold of her arm and looked into her eye and told her if she told me one lie more I would punish her severely. Then I repeated, "Did you ever wear my watch to school?" and she said, "Yes." Just think of the plight we are in. What can I do with her.

I tell Papa with my help problem, these new Swiss girls can't talk or understand English, and Esther, and Trever with his school and social problems, and his athletic ambitions and his underestimate of himself which makes him blue instead of cheerful, and my anxiety about my beautiful oldest boy—all these are enough to give me nervous prostration. The only thing that helps me is that God knows it all.

At school, Esther always has money. Noontimes, she'll take Eloise, and five or six other girls who carry their lunches, to a little grocery store on the corner of Porter and Copeland, just north of the railroad tracks. They will all select penny candy—jawbreakers, licorice whips, lemon drops—and Esther will pay. She's warm and generous and popular with the girls.

Later that spring, Grama learns that money is missing. She suspects Esther, and wrings the truth from her. She once more unburdens herself to Ronald:

We are going through a bad time with Esther again. She is up to her old tricks. Ed told me he had missed a box of wafers and two dollars out of his room. I could not believe Esther had done it yet could not see any other way. Up in her room I asked her if she knew anything about it. She said no—not a thing. Never had been in Ed's room, etc. I said if you have Esther God knows and he will tell me. Go to school and tonight be prepared to tell the truth or it will go hard with you. When she came home she was full of plans to go to an entertainment and said she was in it. I said we will first straighten out that business from this morning. She began to cry and said, "Well, I did take the wafers but I had nothing to do with the money and nobody can say I did." I made her look right into my eyes and tell me again and again. Then I let it drop awhile. Finally I came from a different angle and said, "Esther, what did you do with the money from Ed's pocket?" She looked at me in amazement that I should know and said, "I paid my debts with it." So after all these terrible lies she confesses. "Debts!" I said. "What debts?" She said at the little store she had got things without paying. So the next thing was to get money somewhere. Just think of the hard boiled wickedness. I don't know what we will do with her. She acts as if she had not done a thing.

In her next letter, Grama continues the sorry story:

Last week I told you about Esther. Monday morning I searched her pockets just to be sure. I told her I hated to do it. She stood still without a change of color. I felt in one pocket of her sweater and nothing but apple and handkerchief. In the other was 16 cents. I said, "Look, Esther, where did you get this?" Not a word. Again and again I repeated it. She finally put her hand in the drawer and pulled out the "Kings Heralds" envelope and said she took half of that. Imagine my feelings. I asked her what she could do with it when I had forbidden her to go to any store and forbidden the man to sell to her. She said she was going to buy candy from the teacher. I will not write more but what to do we do not know. I made her learn a prayer and say it every morning and night and learn verses from the Bible. "Be sure your sins will find you out" and "Thou shalt not steal." "Children obey your parents," and "Honor thy father and thy mother," and "A lie is an abomination unto the Lord," and "Thou God seest me" etc. She can say any of them when I ask her. It is an awful thing.

Esther, increasingly beautiful as she grows into her teens, is also popular with the boys. So popular that Eloise, when they are in ninth grade at Roosevelt Junior High School, hears the rumor that Esther is pregnant. She tells Esther, who laughs at the ridiculousness of the idea.

At the Big House, there are usually six to eight hired men. These men are single, like Ed, whose wafers and money Esther stole, and for the most part young. They take their meals with the family, and read or play checkers or listen to the Victrola in the men's sitting room, off the dining room. They wash up at a long sink in the washroom behind the kitchen. They have shower and toilet facilities closed off at the end of the washroom. The men use the back stairs and sleep, dormitory fashion, in several rooms opening off a long corridor. Where the corridor connects to the front part of the upstairs, the family area, there's a closed door. The men's sleeping quarters are strictly off-limits to

Esther, except when on washday she helps change sheets and pillowcases on the bunk beds, or when at mealtime she's sent to fetch a jar of beans or applesauce from the canning shelves that line the wall at the top of the back stairs.

The hired men—called "boys" by Eunice and Wesson and everyone—have always been of interest to Esther, sharing so closely as they do the family space. Back when she was nine she wrote in a letter to Demice, a teen-age Dougan cousin. After telling of a ride to town with Eloise and her mother, and of Trever's broken arm:

> We have four men you don't know, I ges you know Richard or Dix for a nickname. If you don't know Dix it will make five boys you don't know. We have a new highered lady, her name is Ida and her last name is Kester and we all call her Miss Kester, and her brother works here too, his name is Gie. I don't know how to write his name but the e is silent and the i is a long i like in the word, like, the i is a long one. The new boys names are Lynn, Lenard, Harry, and Gie. Our old Harry has left for good. I mean Harry Kristofson.

Eloise is in the family bathroom one day while Esther is cleaning it. The bathroom is the last room before the closed door in the corridor and shares a wall with a dormitory room. It's early afternoon, when the barnhands, who were up before four for milking, take a few hours' rest in their rooms after dinner.

"Listen," says Esther with a mischievous glance. She taps a light tattoo on the wall. There's a pause; then, from the adjacent room, the tattoo is answered. Esther taps again, a different rhythm. The rhythm is tapped back. Esther taps a third rhythm, and again it's returned through the wall.

"You shouldn't be doing that," says Eloise. "Which boy is it?"

"Oh, I don't know," Esther laughs. "Just one of them. It's a silly game we play."

Grama is not unaware of Esther's interest in the hired men. She writes Ronald at college, "Esther is so crazy acting with the boys. They even tell her not to be so forward," and in another letter, "I am glad you visited Kohlstedts. I knew you would find Mildred a nice girl. She may be quiet. I wish Esther had more quiet reserve and modesty. I bet Mildred has character anyway."

Esther and Eloise go into high school. Eloise becomes ill and loses her fourteenth year, and almost her life, to scarlet fever and pneumonia. Every few days Eunice sends over a dish of the vanilla pudding that Eloise likes. But Esther rarely visits her friend, and then only to stand outside and call through the window, for Eunice is afraid that Esther might catch something. So Eloise doesn't see Esther start off to school in the serviceable dresses that Eunice has sewn large for her to grow into, only to emerge later from the girls' washroom in gauzy, skimpy, stylish dresses, silk stockings, and dainty shoes.

Ronald, on hiatus from college, is now working in France. He writes home frequently. In late summer, 1923, he muses about French customs:

Esther, 14, the photo sent Ron in France.

Take the matter of bringing up girls. At home boys and girls play together in theoretically perfect comradeship. Here they never get together. A girl is always shielded by an older person—girls are taught to fear boys, marriages are arranged on a purely commercial basis, and there is no social life whatsoever. The only thing is, when the protection breaks down it is liable to be a sorry affair for the girl. At home girls are given practical freedom, they get a few knocks, I expect, but when they do come through they are better off—stronger, I guess. I'd hate to have the responsibility of being a parent in either country.

He goes on about his little sister, and offers advice:

I have been thinking about Esther. She is practically grown up, even if she is only fourteen. She is probably having all sorts of dreams about glittering Sir Galahads that we can't know anything about. I can remember the wonderings I had only a few years ago. We aren't so far apart, as I developed so much slower. I don't think she is exactly inclined to be the confiding sort, do you? It must take all kinds of tact to keep her confidence. Wish I were home to talk to her about the boys and girls she knows, and give her my ideas about conduct, and what not. It would never do to lecture her. I think she rather looks up to me and if I gave her a picture of the kind of girls that likable, decent fellows like, it might give her some ideas.

She is a normal, impressionable kid, but with ideas years older than you had at her age, and much older than even I had. It won't do to blind ourselves to the fact that she is growing up, and can't be disciplined much longer with lectures and "thou shalt nots."

What I'm saying is so abstract—do you mind if I make a few definite suggestions—what I would do if I were with her.

In the first place I would recognize she must have masculine idols. I would talk to her about them, never letting my ideas take over, or never condemning them or being startled at her adoration. If she finds you are more an interested individual wanting to exchange ideas without urging too strongly, the ideas will mean more to her than a thousand lectures.

Then I would accept her ideas of her schoolmates pretty much on her say so. I would try to get to know them as much as possible, and that leads to another thing. She will never bring carloads out to the house if she feels that they will be made to feel too uncomfortable by our scruples. For instance, if dancing is totally out, she will hesitate to act as hostess because, I tell you mother, dancing is the chief amusement of the whole set. When you take that prop away from a crowd too old for sliding down the straw stack, and too young to get a kick out of prolonged conversations, you drive them away. Esther is bound to dance and play bridge. Wouldn't it be better if she did those things with a good crowd of kids that you know, in your home, than away from home where it would be impossible for you to know the crowd?

Then there is another thing—she will be asked out on dates very soon, if not already. You really must know the boys. How are you going to do it if they haven't the courage to come around?

There are all sorts of things she will say if her confidence is gained that will be surprising to you, that you can't imagine a little girl thinking or saying. Keep the startled look off your face, take it as a matter of course, and by a subtly dropped word, attempt to give her your ideas. But don't think you can fit her into the mold of little girls thirty-five years ago—superficially, perhaps, but fundamentally, never.

Then about clothes—she is always well dressed, but I don't think her taste is far wrong. She would get a kick out of planning the things she is to wear. Probably you do that with her already.

About Trever, I know that after bumping around a while, he will get things straightened out. I'm sorry you don't know more of his Beloit friends. He has lots of them, and thinks something of my judgment on them. He is striving for what is best in life—therefore his discontent when he finds out how little he really knows, or can do. I do think, though, you would have known more of his friends if the house had been open to what I deem innocent amusements, and which he has done anyway, but not at home. You say by not sanctioning it, you stand as a continual protest to the state of things. I think there is another side. By condemning dancing, for instance, which is innocent of itself, when he does it, he can't help but think he is sinning, which makes other things less of a step. Oh, I express it all so badly—but this is what I mean—open up the house to Esther's friends—let them play bridge, dance, let the boys smoke if they want. That is the only way to keep the confidence of the girl. Forget you are breaking your resolutions and giving the neighbors a chance to wag their heads at your seeming change of front—it doesn't mean much anyway, if it is going to make a greater comradeship with Esther. Forgive me if I have said too much—I do think once in a while, and maybe twenty-one is pretty close to fourteen.

Eunice uses Ronald's letter as ammunition against Trever, who has just left for the University of Wisconsin:

Ronald wrote a long letter this week, mostly about Esther. That she is older than her years and is really a young woman. He hopes she will not be frivolous and foolish, but a fine type, etc. Hopes she will pick the right kind of friends, etc. I quizzed her about her friends one day and asked if she went with Margaret Branthaver at high school. She said, "No, she is foolish and paints and is silly with the boys. I won't go with such girls for I don't want to lose my rep. I tell you, once you lose it, it is hard to get it back again." That is the truth. I asked what kind of boys she admired and she said, "Oh, I have my ideas." I said, yes, but what are they? What "kind" of boy would you like to go with when you are old enough? She said, "Well I will tell you. Ronald is the kind I admire, I bet he never does that petting stuff." I said what about Trever, you always seem to like him and be so proud of him and she said, "Yes, he is a good kid but I didn't like his ways this summer. When I saw him and cousin Helen acting so nutty he went down in my estimation."

Eunice goes on to exhort Trever, whose smoking has been giving her deep distress. "You see you are judged where you least expect it. Oh, Trever, you can't afford to make yourself less than you really are." The sound advice from her elder son about his foster sister goes largely unheeded.

19 ✠ AUNT LILLIAN

Aunt Lillian, Grampa's third sister, is a trial to Ronald and Trever when they are boys. She oversees her nephews' language, manners, and play. She objects to their stockpiling frozen horse apples, which they use for ammunition in fights. She calls the droppings "choaties" and feels they should be swept up, left on the manure pile, and ignored as a byproduct of existence.

"Even people make choaties," Trever objects, but Aunt Lillian lifts her chin sharply and looks the other way.

It's because of Aunt Lillian's nosiness and barbed tongue that Ronald suggests to his parents, before he returns from France in 1924, married, that Vera trim three years from her age so she'll appear to be only four years older than her husband. It's because of Aunt Lillian that Vera burns all her diaries before Joan is born, so that if anything happens to her — she and Ron are living with Aunt Lillian, Aunt Ida, and Hazel — her most intimate thoughts won't be revealed to Lillian's prying eyes.

Joan is small when Aunt Lillian says, "Why are you looking at me like that? Why do you keep staring at my nose?"

Joan answers, "Because Mommy says you poke it into everything!"

Joan and her sisters and brother are older when Aunt Lillian objects to the words of the comic books they are reading out loud to each other. For "gosh" and "golly" and "gee whiz" Aunt Lillian makes them substitute "blank."

"They aren't even swear words," objects Craig. "They're only slang!"

Aunt Lillian sniffs. "In this house, I will not listen to such language!" "This house" is Aunt Ida's, across the street from Strong School, on Bushnell. Lillian has long lived there with her widowed sister and pays room and board. The sisters do not get along. After Ida dies, Lillian goes on living there with Ida's adopted daughter, Hazel.

Lillian comes to a family Sunday dinner at the Little House and investigates the ice box. "Who will drink the skim milk?" she calls into the dining room where everyone is seated.

"Nobody needs to drink the skim milk," Patsy calls back. "We just use that for the dog and cats."

Aunt Lillian rejoins the table carrying a glass of blue-tinged milk. "Then I'll drink the skim milk," she says. Forever after, when anyone is being a needless martyr, someone will remark, "Then I'll drink the skim milk."

Over the years, Lillian is a thorn in the flesh of her sister-in-law, too. Whenever Eunice accompanies Wesson on a speaking trip where they are away a few days, Aunt Lillian comes out to the farm. This is so that there will be someone in charge of the Big

A young Lillian, when as a train dispatcher she saved the trains at Elba.

House, her brother says, but everyone knows it's primarily to separate her and Aunt Ida for a while, and at a time when no one else — that is, Eunice — will have to put up with her. But Eunice always returns to something Lillian has done — rearranged furniture, or altered schedules and menus, or made repairs on something that was working well enough before Eunice left. One time she proudly shows how she has "renovated" all the pillows. She'd taken the ticks off, laundered them, laundered the feathers, too, restuffed them and sewed them back up. "They are like new," she boasts, but Grama fumes. "Those pillows didn't need cleaning!" she says. "Why doesn't Ida keep her home?"

She is sometimes a nuisance to the hired men. When she's at the farm she insists on washing and salving the minor cuts and scratches they get on their hands. When it's a hot day and they come in, all sweaty, she sticks her head into the washroom off the kitchen and orders, "Now before you splash that cold water all over your face, you soak your wrists real good until you cool off." Outside she bosses the men, and her brother, too, until W.J. gets exasperated and exclaims, "Oh, go inside!" He can't hear his big sister calling him "Wessie," but the men can, and smile.

Vexing as Aunt Lillian is, she has had moments of glory. She's the only one of Grampa's sisters not to marry. Aunt Della marries a rich man much her senior. When he dies she marries again. Her husbands provide her with fashionable dresses, elegant carriages, purebred riding horses, and many acres of land.

Aunt Ida also marries an older man, James Croft, who drops dead crossing

Horace White Park when Ronald and Trever are boys. Daddy's story of Uncle Jim is complete with quotes. He was an agent for the St. Paul railroad, and every morning he'd walk downtown and stop at Murray and Frank Johnson's grocery store. "He'd go in," says Daddy, "look around, take a dried apricot, maybe fish a pickle out of the barrel, and say, 'Dammit, your store smells just like a high-holer's nest, dammit, Frank!'—meaning a flicker nest; flicker nests smell particularly bad, worse than an owl's."

Facing the park was a livery stable. "I had a friend who lived next door," Daddy goes on, "and we'd build fires in his back yard, and the smoke would blow over the fence and make the stable owner mad. He had one of his outfits tied outside that day, and when he saw a man collapse in the park, he drove across, picked him up, saw it was Jim Croft, and drove him home, but he was already dead."

Uncle Jim was a difficult man, to believe Lillian, who writes in 1895, "Mother, don't mind Jim, he treats me that way too, he don't think how it hurts. There are no hard feelings between any of us, Mother. Be good to Ida for she needs our help and council, she has her social duties to attend to but I fear she is almost a slave to them, I would free her if I could but she is happier that way." Lillian is perhaps referring obliquely to Jim's drinking; later, at Lillian's expense, he "takes the cure." The "cure" is a town one goes to, that dries out alcoholics. But with Uncle Jim the cure doesn't take.

Ida is left reasonably well provided for in the Bushnell Street house, though she sometimes takes in a roomer or two, to augment her income. Her daughter, Hazel, has a beau at one point. He smokes cigars; Aunt Ida doesn't approve of him. When he moves from Beloit, he writes Hazel letters. Her mother intercepts and destroys them. Hazel feels abandoned, and no doubt the young man thinks Hazel doesn't reciprocate his love enough to reply. The missives taper off and stop. No one ever tells Hazel of the deception, and she grows old and crabbed taking care of her mother. The one time she tries living in another city, Ida becomes so ill that Hazel has to return home.

But the third sister, Lillian, never marries. She becomes a telegraph operator. She has a job as station master and train dispatcher at the Elba station, a little office at a lonely country switching near Beaver Dam. She's the only woman in all the Chicago, Milwaukee, & St. Paul Railway system, and has the responsibility of arranging thirty-four trains every twenty-four hours. She writes her mother, in the same 1895 letter where she commiserates about Jim Croft, "Your letter received this morning and I could see how every line was filled with love and anxiety for my welfare. No, Mother, I promise you I will never, never marry anyone and especially an old man, so do not worry and in just one year I will quit office work and come home to stay. We will have a piano and some few pieces of nice furniture and you shall have your home as long as you live and I will do all in my power to make you happy and I intend to have a home of my own somewhere sometime and somehow if there is only one room in it but it will be all mine and a home. When I get it—the piano—you may give one hundred dollars toward it."

She goes on to say she's been poorly for several days, a severe time with bowel trouble, but is improving. She's taking a cinnamon medicine, also hemlock in water. Her mother isn't to worry, she lies down a lot, and doesn't lift a pound or even sweep the office. She advises her not to get the cape, for capes are cold, and her cloak looks far better. She tells her not to worry that Wesson won't let anyone help him make the move, by team, to the McFarland parsonage, but to please him by letting him get everything ready before she moves in. She finishes, "Mother dear cheer up as there are better times in store for both of us I am sure. Be very careful to keep well, for I want you to live a long time that I yet may make you happy."

Lillian's office is equipped with a stove and benches, and serves as a rest house where train crews can sit while their engines are watering. There is usually no one there but herself. For company she keeps a pet blue jay and a dog, Joe.

The blue jay is a nuisance. He jumps up and down on the open telegraph key and sends out garbled messages. Lillian stops him by throwing a handful of straight pins on the floor. The jay hops down and with his strong bill bends every one. He's also a nuisance to Joe. He waits till the dog is gently snoring, spread out on the floor with his underbelly exposed, then steps up and pecks him in a tender place.

One bitter cold night Lillian is at her post when the door opens, and men who are not railroad men start filing in. She grasps a stick of wood under her telegraph table but keeps her weapon hidden. Joe raises his head from his paws and watches. He shows no alarm. The men come and come, until there are fourteen in the small office. Each man raises his hat as he passes her and says, "Evening, ma'am." They are hobos. They sit down on the wooden benches. Lillian relaxes her grip on the kindling and returns to her work.

All night long the men sit there, not speaking among themselves or to Lillian. The first time Lillian lifts a log from the wood box to feed into the red-hot iron stove, one of the men takes it from her and performs the task. From then on, one or another refuels the stove when it needs it. The only voice

Aunt Lillian at fifty-five, when she and Grampa ran the farm during the flu epidemic. She's with Bob and little Vic.

heard is the blue jay's. When morning comes the men stand up and file out. As each one passes her he tips his hat and says, "Thank you, ma'am."

It's often boring in the little office. Though it's against the rules, Lillian leaves her key open half the time and listens to people talking up and down the line. One day she hears an operator direct a freight down the track. She knows that just twenty minutes before, another operator from the opposite direction has sent a passenger train down the same track. She figures quickly and sees that the trains will meet right outside her station. She rushes out, flags down the freight, and makes a very angry engineer pull onto the siding. He no sooner has gotten his long train off the main track than the passenger train whips by from the other direction. The engineer is subdued. Lillian is a hero, but because of the reluctance of those who made the mistake to draw attention to it, and because Lillian was eavesdropping when she shouldn't have been (no matter how fortunately), she is not singled out for special notice.

All this is when Lillian is a young woman, before she comes to Beloit to live at Aunt Ida's after James Croft dies and to be a vexation to her young nephews.

Ronald and Trever are often at the house on Bushnell Street. It's a convenient place to stay when in town, or to be sent when guests overflow the Big House, or to be nursed when one is sick—for their mother, with all the work at the farm, has little time to spend on illness, while Aunt Ida's time is almost unlimited. The boys build castles on the tablecloth, using the sugar cubes Aunt Ida keeps in a lidded dish. Ronald, and once in a while Trever, gets to go around with a wax taper and light the gas lamps; at the farm there are only kerosene lamps in the house, and lanterns for the barn. Aunt Ida's is their second home.

They sometimes attend Strong School across the street, and when he's in high school, Ronald rides his bike to Aunt Ida's for lunch. He plays marbles with the boys in the schoolyard and is late to his classes in the afternoon. He and Trever know all the children in the neighborhood. They spend many a soft summer evening playing Capture the Flag or Kick the Can or Duck on the Rock. Sometimes they are knights jousting with long poles underneath the moth-circled streetlamp, with bicycles for horses. One of the boys Ronald jousts with is Lowell Putney. He lives right around the corner on Harrison Avenue.

In 1918, near the end of the Great War, an epidemic of flu sweeps the world. The strain is a killer. It's estimated, before the end, that twenty million people die; twice as many as soldiers and civilians killed in the war. Populations are decimated; whole families perish. In Beloit, one of these families is Lowell Putney's. He, his parents, and all his brothers and sisters die of the flu. Lura Marston, at the next farm to the dairy, sobs, "Oh, it's a bitter, bitter pill!" and because there is no family to mourn them, she and other friends gather in the Marston living room to pray and to recall together all they can of the Putney family.

Out on the farm, nobody is able to attend, for almost everybody is sick. Esther isn't; she's been shipped down to Aunt Ida's. But Ronald and Trever are sick. Grama is sick. Most of the hired men are sick. Every day a nurse comes out from town for a few hours, to tend everyone.

In the kitchen of the Big House, Hilda stays well. There is nobody in the milkhouse, nobody in the barn. One route man, Charlie Kellor, doesn't get sick; he works a double shift. In the morning he peddles the east side. When he's done, he telephones Grampa, who meets him with a fresh team and loaded wagon where Colley Road ends at the edge of Beloit. Grampa takes Charlie's team and empty wagon back to the farm, and Charlie delivers the west side. The next day he reverses it. When he gets his second wagon back to the farm, Grampa has the bottles washed from the first load. Then Charlie washes the bottles from the second load.

Grampa doesn't get the flu. Neither does Aunt Lillian. She moves out to the farm and dons overalls, apron, and rubber boots. Day after day, side by side, she and her brother do all the barn work. Lillian washes udders. She milks. She pitches hay and grinds feed. She shovels manure into the manure trolley and hoses gutters. She carries buckets of warm milk to the calves. She tends the horses. And when there's a pause in the barn work, before it all starts over again, she and W.J. rush to the milkhouse, washing bottles and cans, separating cream, bottling the milk. "We'll fetch it!" Grampa keeps repeating. It is his battle cry.

It's a grueling, exhausting time. Aside from a few hours, there is no sleep. There's scarcely time to eat. And the work is accompanied with knowledge of death all over Beloit, all over the world, and especially anxiety for those of the household who are struggling to survive, and those up and down Colley Road. Before the crisis is over and people begin trickling back to work, Grampa and Lillian are stumbling zombies, haggard shells.

But no one connected with the farm dies. None of the neighbors die. Every day the essential farm work has gotten done and milk processed and delivered to all Dougan customers. It's a triumph. The credit goes to the wills and stamina of Grampa, now fifty, and Aunt Lillian, fifty-five, and those few others who stayed well enough to work around the clock. Throughout the ordeal they've been upheld by Grampa's ringing, "We'll fetch it!" and the glint in his eye. But there's no energy left for celebration.

Grampa does give a special blessing of thanksgiving when all the household is finally reassembled at the dinner table. By then, Lillian is back in town.

The Dougan children grow up unaware of Aunt Lillian's past except in casual mention. To them she's a fussy, forgetful, difficult old lady. Jackie doesn't hear about the blue jay and the telegraph office, the hobos and the flu, until years after Aunt Lillian is dead.

20 ⚜ QUENTIN BOWEN

Grampa hires Quentin Bowen and his brother Alfred in 1923. Farming is not their choice. They are musicians and want jobs in a band. Quentin, years later, writes Ron about his farm experience.

Our father died, and we weren't doing well on the farm, we had to sell. So with our mother and sister we came from Minnesota to southern Wisconsin, where an older sister lived. I was seventeen, Al eighteen. But the area, and the musicians' unions, didn't welcome us. We studied the want ads, and applied for jobs at the Dougan farm.

Your father's roll top desk stood in the front room of the Big House. It was there that interviews were held, men hired, men reprimanded, and big decisions of management made. I stood before that desk with some trepidation. But Daddy Dougan hired us both.

We lived in the bunkhouse over the milkhouse, but took our meals at the Big House. That large dining room table could hold ten comfortably. We ate family style. You were in France, and Trever at the university. Only Esther was home. She was a young teenager and helped keep the spirits of a group of men in good condition.

On Wednesdays we stayed sitting after supper as Daddy Dougan read from the Bible, and explained his interpretation. The Tscharners were a couple from Switzerland. Elsie helped with the house work. They told us about dairy business in the Alps, and that they had soup to start every meal. I liked that!

Another man, from the Guernsey Islands, was on the farm as part of his education. Some men were agricultural students from the university, their stay was similar to practice teaching for future teachers. My brother and I had both attended the University of Minnesota at Morris for a short while, so we considered ourselves university men, too.

Your mother, we called her Mother Dougan, was a mother hen to the whole group. She always had time to listen to our thoughts and needs.

The herdsman lived at the Big House. He went down to the barn every night before retiring to check on the cows' comfort. I sometimes joined him. A barn full of contented cows is beautiful!

My brother worked in the fields, but I was assigned to the milkhouse. My work day began at 4 a.m. Of all Daddy Dougan's Aims painted on the inside silo, the one that impressed me most was "Life as well as a living." I sometimes questioned this one, when I had to get up so early. My first chore was to start the wood fire in the milkhouse boiler, developing steam to sterilize the milk handling equipment. Daddy Dougan watched all the operations of the dairy like a hawk. Cleanliness was everything, but he wasn't often checking on me at that hour!

At 5:00, I went to the Big House to turn on the electric oatmeal cooker, and call the maids, sleeping on the second floor. (I never got further than the staircase!) Breakfast always included that hot oatmeal. It was the only meal we didn't eat together, but in the kitchen, as each man needed it.

Until 6:15 my entire time was spent preparing for the delivery of milk from the barn to the milkhouse. I loaded a two-wheeled cart with the sterilized milk pails and containers. These were picked up by a runner who took them to the barn and returned them when filled. The milking pails were large but their tops were partially closed, and the open part covered with gauze that strained the milk when the men were hand stripping after the milking machines. Also, the first six squirts from each tit were milked into a special pail and fed to the calves. Another way of controlling bacteria.

Our milk was Guernsey, and the best in the area. You know that raw milk from Guernsey cows is rich in butterfat, though not so rich as Jersey. It is much richer than Holstein. My father said that if you dropped a silver dollar into a bucket of Holstein milk you could still read "In God We Trust."

I took the full pails of warm milk up a little outside stairs at the milkhouse, the door there opened on the top of a grid. I poured the milk into a large container, and it spread the milk out into a pipe with little holes spaced the length of it, so that all the milk cooled evenly running down the grid and into another large container at the bottom. The grid was filled with cold water so that the milk cooled quickly. Then it was ready for bottling.

One morning I was in real trouble. The bottling machine was not filling properly and it left about an inch of foam at the top of each bottle. I had a pitcher of clean milk and was pouring each bottle full before capping. Daddy

Dougan came in; he immediately saw the trouble and started blowing the foam off the tops of each bottle. I gently tapped his arm and said by my accented lips, "Bacteria." He stopped short, took the milk pitcher, and helped me the rest of the way!

One day I asked Daddy Dougan for a chance to talk. He escorted me into his office, gave me a tablet of paper and a pencil. He was seated at his roll-top desk and I at the side chair where he could

Making music in Beloit.

also read my lips. I seriously wrote that I had been there some time and my $35 per month (plus room and board) salary had not been increased. I wrote him, "I need a raise." He smiled, and told me it was not a large salary, but I should be thankful for a good life and take pleasure in knowing that the babies in our area were receiving clean healthy milk, and that I was a part of the operation. No, I didn't get the raise but I felt better for asking!

About once a month Alfred and I walked to town and spent an evening at Cosmo Hall listening to the orchestra. We really longed to play our instruments and be part of a group.

The men who milked the cows and attended the barn chores did farm work too, but those of us in the milkhouse didn't have time. My brother's work, though, was in the fields. It wasn't very different from our boyhood days in Minnesota, plowing and seeding and weeding, and he became bored. He was an entrepreneurial sort of guy, he wanted to start a business. I liked it on the farm, but after a year or so, before you came home, we left Dougans. The rest, Ron, is another story.

———·——·———

Quentin Bowen would have been surprised, and probably guffaw, at the description W.J. writes of him and his brother in a 1924 letter to Ronald in France. W.J. is beset with hiring problems, and the Bowens have recently quit for greener pastures. It shows Grampa's exasperation, even despair, and of course his lack of musical knowledge and trends:

> You ask what is the matter with labor. It is not labor but the fool age that pays for trash more than for things of value. An example. I had two boys this year. They had been raised on a Minnesota farm, also had "played in the band," often for dances. Could play (?) a dozen instruments at the same time. I paid them each $40 per mo. They weren't bad fellows, no bad habits except swearing and big mouths. Now the Oriental Cafe pays them $35 per week each for a few hours in the evening. No wonder such boys are discontent with farm work when any fool can do things like they do and the fool public thinks they are getting their money's worth!

Actually, the public does get its money's worth — the Bowens are talented, and prominent on the local music scene for many years. Quentin's band plays at the Coronado in Rockford while the movies are still silent, then he moves into the Sunstrand Corporation, though often still playing. Al stays closer to Beloit; he and his wife develop "The Ledges," homes in a unique area south of town. Elizabeth, a fine pianist, becomes Vera Dougan's helper in Mother's later job in the National Federation of Music Clubs; Elizabeth is a Wisconsin Federation president. W.J. lives long enough to appreciate the Bowens, to see them become outstanding citizens. He'd have appreciated them more, earlier, had he been able to hear their music.

21 ⨯ GRAMA'S EVENTFUL SPRING

It's a rainy Monday morning, March 29, 1921. Eunice is low in spirits. The heady weeks of evangelistic services had been concluded, and Easter was celebrated yesterday with the fullest church in her memory. Ronald had been a credit to her, though he'd had to return immediately to his second semester at Northwestern. But today the water must be heated, tubs filled, piles of overalls and shirts and sheets washed and hung all over the back room and in the cellar by the furnace, bread baked, meals made, the relentless and dreary monotony of farm work gotten on with.

Oh, the meetings had brought splendid changes. At the request of the help, Wesson had begun Bible readings and exegesis every night after supper. And everyone is behaving more soberly. But Trever … Trever … Eunice's brow wrinkles. Trever has changed for the worse, and apparently as a result of the meetings. She punches down the dough she's kneading as if she were pummeling her second son.

The meetings! Why couldn't Trever rejoice in the glory of it all? They'd begun early March, two Sunday services and one almost every night thereafter, for three solid weeks. She'd gone regularly, greedy for the singing and the Word. Most of the live-in hired men managed to attend several nights a week. Even Wesson, lacking hearing and with the exhausting work of the farm, went to a few, and encouraged everyone to attend.

Eunice, through her letters, had kept Ronald well informed. On March 8 she'd written that the evangelist had given up many alluring positions because God called him to this work. "He owes it all to his mother. All her life she had prayed for him to be a minister but never lived to hear him preach. We had them here to supper last night, chicken pie and mashed potatoes, lettuce salad, fried parsnips, parker house rolls, pickles, lemon pie, doughnuts and milk. They thought they had struck a banquet. After supper we sang—Mr. Troy, the song leader, seemed too full to sing but he managed. Mr. Cotterell tells many incidents where people have been wonderfully changed after accepting Christ."

Grama's report covers two pages. As a chaser, she throws in a talk from the annual Y banquet which she and Wesson had just attended:

> He came to YMCA work after training at Yale for a lawyer, by a little ragged boy asking him to a prayer meeting. He laughed but could not refuse the child. Instead of a church, the boy led him to a hut in a yard. He stooped and saw 4 boys in there, one seemed ill at ease. The boys had formed a club to get the neighborhood boys to become Christians. This new boy was to be prayed for. They asked Mr. Ames to help, and in doing so his own soul was awakened. From that time on he gave up the lawyer business and has been in Boys Work in YMCA, 18 years. One never knows what a small thing will turn ones life work. "A little child shall lead them," and the Bible says God uses the simple to confound the wise.

At her letter's end she'd written a long PS on familiar subjects. "Papa thinks of nothing else but how he can meet our crowding financial obligations. Of course we both are anxious for our children and want them to be the best spiritually, stand for all that is strong and right. It hurts us that Trever is so indifferent to the church. Where is our mistake. We surely have made one."

On March 11 she'd written more: "Tonight Mr. Cotterell speaks on a pure life. I think he will tell what he thinks of the dance. I am so anxious for Trever to go, but one of the girls has invited him to a private party." The letter continues with talk of the Swiss couple come to work on the farm, Elsie to help in the house, but then she returns to the evangelist:

> I told him of my other boy, that I was anxious for you to do Christian work, to let God use you. The next day after church he told me he'd got thinking of the dangers to young men, so many ways they are tempted, and what a power they can be if they take Christ as their guide, and said he could not sleep. He got up and wrote this enclosed message to you. He had a wonderful mother, it is through her life and prayers that he is a Christian. He never preaches but he speaks of his mother.

She'd concluded:

> Bring your friend home at Easter. I guess he won't smoke around here. Mr. Troy the singer said the other night how he had been to the Dougan Farm

and had never seen such a fine lot of young men. When they came in dressed for supper, you would think it was a frat but told the people, "Seven young men and not one of them smokes. Match that, you employers! You say it can't be done, but one man out in the country is doing it and has for 15 years." He said, "I plan to have that Dougan octette sing for you some night!" Well goodby again and bushels of love from your Mother. God bless you and guide you in knowledge of Him, is her prayer.

Eunice's March 17th letter expanded on the splendor of the meetings:

Every night the church is crowded. Many have come forward, Leon and Joe among them. I think Ted and Trever will come before the end. They are both convicted. There will not be so much dancing after this. Evelyn Burnette told Trever she was not going to dance any more, many others are taking the same stand. Reverend Cotterell's text last night was "What shall it profit a man if he gain the whole world and lose his own soul?" He said, What are you sell-ing out to? Some to cigarettes, some to dance, and others to money never thinking God owns it all. Some to clothes, some to society. My how true it is. He advocates clean, nice looking clothes but not paying high prices for dresses, coats, hats, etc. because you want to look better than someone else.

And she'd given Ronald a caveat:

When you come home dear be not thoughtless or light in your talk, for the boys here are all thinking. They asked Papa to have Bible study with them. My dear boy I am praying for you that God will show you the best way to be used for Him. You will find the Epworth League more serious when you come home.

PS: I wish you could be here Friday night to hear the sermon on dancing. I know he will coincide with my sentiments.

The evangelist does not disappoint. Saturday's *Beloit Daily News* considers the event front-page material:

EVANGELIST ATTACKS CARDS AND DANCING

Standing room was at a premium last evening at the Methodist Church where visiting evangelist O.L. Cotterell made "Amusements" the subject of a stirring talk. The lobby was choked with late comers. Young girls sat on the floor inside the main entrance, and the back of the church was lined with standing men and women. Members of the congregation stated this was the largest audience the church had ever housed. An augmented choir rendered anthems and J.W. Troy gave another of his popular solo numbers.

Card playing, dancing, theater-going and moving pictures have tendencies to weaken the moral fabric of the young, Cotterell charged. They are time-wasting and blur the spiritual inspirations of the church. He deplored the use of questionable posters, suggestive names of plays, and the extreme ball gown.

"Cards were first invented for the amusement of an imbecile king," he said. "They are the devil's cheap tool of the gambler. The game pours cold blood into the system of the inveterate player who would not stop at fleecing his own mother. The dance is like a cancer. It ruins one's spiritual reactions. Many plays are vulgar and degrading. The moving picture is a wonderful invention but the devil has a mortgage on it."

The meetings end the following evening. Monday's paper records the triumphant finale: "110 persons came to the altar at the conclusion of Reverend Cotterell's address on 'Eight Points to Observe in Christian Life.' During the series about 375 persons either made their religious confession or pledged renewal of faith."

What a grand total! And Trever, praise be, among them! Squirming in the pew among his friends, he must have been aware of his mother's anxious eyes on the back of his head, her ardent prayers urging him forward. To her joy, at the last minute, he had gone to the altar. Ted Selmer had gone with him. Leon Richardson and Joe Sennith had declared on an earlier evening, along with the other young men boarding at the farm.

Eunice had been ecstatic that her younger son had finally professed Jesus Christ as Savior and Lord. But her forehead creases again. This past weekend, with Ronald home for Easter, Trever had behaved abominably to his brother and his friend, to his younger sister, his mother, the hired men. He had nothing but sarcasm, sneering, and general ill humor. His face was a scowl. He teased the cat. Once in a while, for no reason, he broke into raucous laughter.

Now, on Monday morning, Eunice realizes she is depressed. The excitement is over. She's come down off her high. While the bread is baking, while the kettles are coming to a boil, she pens a note to Ronald:

I have felt bad ever since you left, the way Trever acted toward you. Not only you but me. He was worse Sat. and Sun. than I have seen him in a good while. I think he was feeling convicted since going forward, and not satisfied. He's so upset with himself he acts his worst. We will have to overlook it for a while. I have felt so bad in my head—so dizzy—I tell Trever it is because he has been acting so.

Later, after a day of hard work, after supper and dishes, after putting beans on to soak for the next day, Eunice takes off her apron and sinks down to gloat again over the newspaper's report of the evangelism crusade. Her eye is caught by an inner headline: WOMEN OF BELOIT REQUEST COURSE IN AUTOMOBILE CARE. The subhead is, Vocational School Will Offer Ten Lessons if Number Sign For Class. Eunice reads the article carefully. If enough sign up, the vocational school will secure a competent teacher to give a series of lessons on automobile care and parts, once or twice a week. Those interested should telephone 439. The article ends:

> The course as outlined will take up the following subjects:
> 1. Oiling: Kinds, types, and care of system.
> 2. Transmission: Type and upkeep.
> 3. Valves: Types, settings, and grinding in.
> 4. Clutches and Brakes: Types, adjustments, and care.
> 5. Fuel: Grades, testing, and carburetor trouble.
> 6. Steering system: Types and care.
> 7. Cooling system: Types and frost protection.
> 8. The road: Rules, and minor road repairs.
> 9. Tires: Care and Changing
> 10. General Review

Eunice reads the article again. Excitement begins to bubble at her soul. Hasn't she always wanted to learn to drive? Wesson learned years ago, Ronald and Trever both drive, even Esther, at twelve. Everyone on the place drives, be it automobile, truck, or tractor. She hates always to be driven, to her church meetings, her club meetings. There have been farm emergencies where it would have helped had she been able to take the wheel. Now here is a class, exclusively for women, that sounds like the perfect preparation! Of course she can manage to go out several nights a week, hasn't she just finished three weeks of nightly services? She'd be meeting women she'd never meet otherwise. She'd be learning something useful, challenging, different. She'd be joining the modern world. Wouldn't Daddy and Ron and Trever and the boys all

Eunice, ready for an outing, sits on the running board of the car she is learning to drive. We see Trever's back, Esther on the left.

be amazed? Furthermore, the classes are free. Eunice will call the next day. It seems almost a summons from on high.

The following week the paper announces that sufficient enrollment has allowed the Women's Automobile Repair class to begin instruction Monday April 11 at 7:30 and meet every Monday and Wednesday for five weeks.

Eunice now tells her secret at the supper table, and displays the course list. There is indeed amazement, along with good-natured ribbing. "There goes my job!" says Leon, for he sees to it that the farm's vehicles keep running. Eunice swells under the admiration.

The classes begin. His mother writes to Ronald, "I am taking 10 lessons in auto mechanism at high school. I go Mon. and Weds. nights. I drove there the other night with Dad on the seat beside me." Wesson takes along the newspaper, or *Hoard's Dairyman*, or something to figure on, while he waits. Often he dozes in the lobby. One night he goes to a movie at the nearby Rex Theater; its endorsement in the paper had intrigued him: "No more sweeping or powerful exemplification of the divine force of mother love has ever been penned." He is so pleased with the film that he sends Eunice, Esther, and some of the help to see it, notwithstanding Mr. Cotterell's distrust of the medium. Eunice writes to Ronald, "The worst characters were smoking cigarettes and dancing. 'The Woman in His House' was the name of it. Dad went while I was at my auto class, and he made me go the next night."

Every Tuesday and Thursday noon the farm is entertained by Eunice's account of what transpired the night before: how to grease bearings, or how she already knew the use of a wrench when some of the other pupils had never even held one. Her letters continue to feature the class. "Yes, I am taking night school on auto mechanism. None of you kiddies ought ever run an auto without carefully reading your manual."

The evangelism marathon has not been forgotten. Bible reading at supper is still in force; Eunice urges Ronald to read the 13th chapter of Matthew, so he'll be caught up when he visits home. And Trever is regaining his good spirits. Earlier, before the meetings ever began, Eunice had confided to her eldest how unhappy Trever was about the recently formed church basketball league. While the Methodists had two teams, neither had elected Trever to a position, though he was a sub on the True Blues. He had organized a team of leftovers, the TNTs.

Now all the church teams were invited to a party at the YWCA, where there was dancing! Eunice fumes to Ronald that Trever held back till his Methodist coach ordered him to the dance floor. "All the boys who went forward to the altar danced!" She does not connect this to Trever's improved good humor.

The vocational school class continues into mid-May. "Tonight is my last lesson," Eunice writes. "I have enjoyed it and will be much more interested in auto mechanism." And, "Papa would like to visit you at Evanston, but does not feel dressed good enough and cannot buy a new suit now. It will not make so much difference if driving an auto though — one is not expected to dress in fine broadcloth handling an auto."

The farm now expects Eunice to commence driving, and she does, some, around the driveways that circle the buildings. She hasn't learned the gears lesson well enough, for a great grinding often announces her coming. Since Wesson can't hear, he can't correct her mistakes, and he's the only one she allows to drive with her. But Wesson is frantically busy with spring planting, installing the new ice machine, tending to a myriad other matters. He does not often get time to drive with his wife.

One Sunday afternoon in late May they do go for a drive. The weather is pleasant; lilacs waft their perfume. They are on a country road near Footville when Eunice, driving slowly, rounds a bend and finds a cow standing directly in front of her. She cries out, grips the wheel, and slams on the brakes — except that she hits the accelerator instead. The car leaps forward, knocks the cow over, and stalls on top of her.

Eunice is in shock. Wesson is grim. He helps his distraught wife from the tilted car, over the awkward flank of the twitching animal, seats her on the grass beside the road, rubs her hands and shoulders, says "Now, now, dearie," in the crooning tone he uses to calm a panicked horse. It is several minutes before he can ascertain that the cow is now dead, and then he hastens in search of the farmer.

Wesson pays full value for the animal. He doesn't argue that she shouldn't have been in the road. After all, he regularly loses a cow, sometimes more than one, when they break out of the back pasture and onto the railroad tracks. A cowcatcher may catch cows, but it doesn't usually save them from their folly. Nor is there any way he can take the purchased animal home, for Eunice keeps repeating, "We mustn't tell anyone! No one must know! Wesson, don't say a word!" And surely everyone would wonder where a strange cow had come from, to be suddenly butchered, when the farm always butchers its own stock. Eunice could not stand the disgrace. Furthermore, who would be the one cooking up the roasts and ribs and hamburger and making the head-cheese and mincemeat? Eunice. She couldn't endure that, either.

He solves the problem by making an anonymous gift of the carcass to Janesville's Salvation Army, which is happy to travel to Footville to retrieve it.

Eunice never drives again. She gives excuses of busyness, both hers and Wesson's, to anyone who asks, or replies that the farm has plenty of drivers and she will finish learning in the fall, when things are calmer. By then, nobody remembers to ask.

Eunice never tells what happens, nor does Wesson, except later Wesson tells Ronald. He in turn, a number of years after Eunice has died, relates to Mother and Jackie the story of his mother's spring of 1921.

"And what about Trever's conversion?" Jackie asks.

"Oh, I think he got over it in fairly short order. After all, you couldn't leave Grama without a soul to fret about, could you? It wouldn't be kind. He probably had his fingers crossed, like I did earlier, when Grama took me to tent meetings."

22 ⚔ RONALD'S COURTSHIP

Ronald's courtship is like this: He goes off to Northwestern to college. His grades are so-so. He takes French his freshman year, gets a C first semester, a D second semester. He figures that's not so good, so his sophomore year he takes the same French again. He gets a C first semester, a D second semester. He joins a fraternity. He joins the Glee Club but never sings after the tryout, just mouths the words.

He gets into various scrapes. He telegraphs home one Sunday morning and tells Grampa not to believe everything he reads in the *Tribune*. Grampa is bewildered. He drives to town, and with some difficulty manages to find a *Tribune*. He can't find anything in it he thinks Ronald means he shouldn't believe. They call a friend in Chicago who reads them the headline of the local Chicago edition: NORTHWESTERN BOOZE DEN RAIDED. Ronald Dougan's name leads all the rest, even though, he assures his father, he had just entered the den looking for a friend.

Late in his junior year he gets a chance to go to France and work for a year doing reconstruction work. It's after the war. On a fine May day in Evanston, he gives a fraternity pin to one girl in the morning and asks her to wait for him; he gives away another fraternity pin in the afternoon and asks the girl to wait for him; he gives a third fraternity pin to a third girl in the evening and asks her to wait for him. He skips off to France the next day without taking any of his final exams.

After three months at the Methodist Memorial in Chateau Thierry he's head of a Boy Scout troop and speaks French like a native. He's sent to the train to meet a dean of women from an Illinois college. He's in short pants and rope sandals. He is not eager to meet a Dean.

Mother steps off the train. Daddy immediately changes his mind about deans. It turns out Mother isn't a dean, anyway, but had been elected president of her alumnae association. Somehow information had become garbled between Illinois and France.

Ronald and Vera's wedding, May 1924. They are in the courtyard of the Method- ist Memorial, Chateau Thierry, France.

At the Methodist Memorial Mother teaches English and piano and ballet. Daddy sets right to work courting her. They take picnics of long French bread and cheese over to the little village of Essomes; they hang over the bridge and watch the waters of the Marne flow by; they climb around the ruins of the old chateau, and from the heights of the huge hill it was built on, look down on Chateau Thierry and all the surrounding countryside.

Daddy proposes. Mother is in love, but there's a problem. He is twenty-one, she is twenty-eight. That's too much age difference, Mother thinks. And then, how will Grama and Grampa on the farm react? They will be aghast that their son, barely of age, is marrying an Older Woman. One they haven't even met.

Daddy doesn't think there's any problem at all. Every night he proposes, every night Mother refuses. She expects him to be crushed and disheartened in the morning, but Daddy shows up for breakfast as bouncy as a new pup. He's persistent and indefatigable. Finally Mother succumbs. She agrees to marry him. Daddy is jubilant. He writes dozens of pages home, telling his parents how they will love his bride, and asking their blessing. He says he now has direction in his life, he will finish school with honors, and wants to go into the family milk business with Grampa.

Mother and Daddy celebrate their engagement by going into Paris for dinner at a special restaurant. They are blissfully happy. After the *escargot* and *escalopes de veau a la creme* and *fromage*, Daddy becomes serious. He says, "Vera, I have something to confess to you."

"What is it, Ronald?" asks Mother.

Daddy says, "I've been lying to you in order to win you. I'm not twenty-one, I'm nineteen."

"Oh, Ronald!" Mother cries. "Nine years! Oh, I can't marry you! That's too much difference! I can't. I just can't."

Daddy lets Mother carry on for a little bit. Then he produces his passport. It proves he's twenty-one. Mother is so relieved that she's only a little angry. After that, the seven-year difference seems like nothing.

They are married on May 3, 1924, at noon at the Chateau Thierry City Hall, wearing their Sunday clothes. That's the civil ceremony required by French law. In the afternoon they are married again, at the Methodist Memorial, by the Reverend Doctor Joseph Harker, president of the Illinois college that Mother is not a dean at. This time Mother wears a white gown and Daddy a tuxedo, and there are many guests and cake and flowers. There's a cablegram from Grama and Grampa, giving their blessing.

After the wedding a picture is taken. The young woman in the picture is beautiful, slim, with long brown hair and classic features. She wears a look of grave serenity. The young man is dashingly handsome; his look is just a tiny bit cocky, like a rooster on top of a manure heap. They are standing on the outside staircase which has an ornamental wrought-iron rail. The staircase curves about a wall fountain down to the courtyard.

Jackie sees this picture all her life. It's enlarged and framed on Mother's dresser. When she herself visits Chateau Thierry, many years later, and walks into the courtyard of the Methodist Memorial, she stops quite still. It is a familiar place, where she has been before.

23 ⊰ THE SHOWER

Jackie attends her first wedding shower when she's seven. It's held at Aunt Ida's, and all the women of the farm go. Moo-Moo Stam is there, as are the wives of some of the other milkmen and married farmhands. Aunt Lillian and Hazel, of course; it's their house, too. And Grama and Mother and a few women Jackie doesn't know. The dining room table, where refreshments will be served, has a party cake on it, and flowers, and frilled nut-and-candy cups, each with a miniature Japanese umbrella that really opens and shuts. The adjoining living room is decorated with crepe-paper streamers. A low table is piled with the wrapped and ribboned gifts.

Jackie feels quite grown up to be considered a woman, along with Joan and Patsy. Their presents are on the table—they went shopping with Mother, and Joan bought a red mixing bowl; Patsy, a flour sifter; and Jackie, measuring spoons and cup. It's not specifically a kitchen shower, but these are appropriate gifts because the shower is for Josie, and Josie has worked for Grama in the Big House for a long time, doing lots of the cooking.

Mother's present for Josie is a soft satiny slip and a sheer white blouse with pearl buttons. "A bride needs some pretty things," Mother had said.

Till today, Jackie has never seen Josie in anything pretty. At the Big House, she wears cotton house dresses and feed-sack aprons. Her beige stockings are thick, and her flat black shoes don't lace but have narrow straps. She wears her glossy black hair pulled tight across her head and fastened in a bun behind. Her eyes are black as buttons and she has heavy eyebrows that nearly meet in the middle. She has a wide mouth. She is often perspiry, and even when her face isn't sweating, her cheeks and forehead shine bright enough to reflect the overhead lights. She's not a pretty woman. But she giggles a lot and is cheerful at the Big House table. She giggled hard enough when Al Capps told about the old woman who made a list of her many tasks, ending it with "nap" and then decided to nap first thing, to get that out of the way.

Jackie is surprised that Josie is getting married. She is so old! Old and not pretty. She doesn't fit Jackie's storybook princesses who wed the prince and live happily ever after. But then, Mr. Griffiths is hardly a prince. He is thin and has a stringy neck, and he is a lot older even than Josie. He has worked on the farm since before Jackie was born. He isn't an ordinary hired man — he's more like the head hired man, a foreman. He sometimes tells Jackie and her sisters and brother what they can or can't do, as if he's a parent or grandparent, and this annoys them. But he plows a straighter furrow than anyone on the farm, and Grampa entrusts him with all the planting. Jackie remembers when she was smaller, Mr. Griffiths sit-

Josie is second from the right. Others are Ruby Horn from the office, Daisy Shepherd who took Josie's place at the Big House, and Aunt Ria, Grama's visiting sister. Bounce keeps a lookout.

ting in the spring sunshine at the entrance to the loft of the round barn and cutting up wizened seed potatoes. He told her that in order to grow, every potato piece had to have an eye. She had to go ask Mother what a potato eye could possibly be.

Mr. Griffiths had a wife once, before Jackie was born, and two daughters. But the daughters grew up and married and moved out west, and before that, something happened to the wife. Nobody tells Jackie, but she listens in to grown-up talk when they lower their voices, and she learns that Mrs. Griffiths committed suicide. She did it because she thought she had committed the unforgivable sin. Jackie is curious as to what the unforgivable sin is, and whether Mrs. Griffiths really did commit it, but she never overhears the answer to either of these wonderings. And since she's not supposed to be listening, of course she can't ask.

She herself knows that Mr. Griffiths has committed an unforgivable sin.

A while ago Craig found him killing newborn kittens with a hammer, and when Craig went howling to Daddy, that Daddy should fire Mr. Griffiths, Daddy had said that that wouldn't save the kittens now, and he'd speak sternly to him about it. Jackie thinks Mr. Griffiths well deserves the tricks the younger men play on him — she'd heard at the supper table how he was at the gas pump with a tractor, and one of the milkmen, Howard Milner, let him put the nozzle in the tank and just as the gas started running, he pulled the switch that turned the gas off. "Mr. Griffiths would examine the nozzle," Daddy tells the tale, and illustrates it with his gestures, "he'd shake it, put it back in the tank, and Howard would let him have a little more gas before pull-

Mr. Griffiths, W.J.'s senior farm worker, ready for his wedding.

ing the switch again. He'd quick pull it out, shake it, try it again, Howard'd let him have some more gas" — by this point Daddy is laughing — "we were all watching, and after several more on and offs, Griffiths comes to the office to tell me there's something wrong with the gas pump, and he found us all so convulsed we couldn't talk. He was mad — he doesn't like to be fooled." Jackie and the family had laughed hard, too, even Mother who'd managed a "Poor Mr. Griffiths!" and "You let them get away with it, Ron!" between her laughter. Yes, Mr. Griffiths deserves pranks, and more.

As to his and Josie's getting married, Jackie manages to gathers more bits by eavesdropping. Usually, seven or eight hired men live at the Big House, and these men are single. Jackie knows and likes them all. Ernie Capps with the rotten ear, who sometimes stays with them when Mother and Daddy go out. Handsome Kenneth Liddle. Al Lasse, who is even handsomer. Shy Ockie Berg. Russel Ullius, who plays croquet with them in the evenings, and calls Joan "Punky." Mr. Griffiths doesn't live at the Big House but in his own brown stucco house, right at the head of Colley Road where it leaves Beloit. But he often takes his noon meal at the communal table.

Josie, Jackie overhears, first made eyes at Al Lasse, but Al never gave her the time of day. "In that way," Grama says significantly. And so, after a while, she started making eyes at Mr. Griffiths. The first Jackie hears about any of Josie's amorous intentions is through a near accident of Daddy's.

"Coming back from the Hill Farm just now," he reports to Mother at the Little House, "I was coming up on one side of that little thank-you-ma'am there by Blodgetts', and coming up on the other side, driving right in the middle of the road, were guess who? Griffiths and Josie, and he had his arm around her! I swerved and missed them, nearly drove into the ditch. I don't think they even saw me."

This is when Jackie begins tuning her ears to Josie-conversations and learns about Al Lasse, Mrs. Griffiths, and the enigmatic unforgivable sin. She happens to be in the Big House when Mr. Griffiths is in the kitchen helping Josie with the dishes, a remarkable occurrence in itself, and the men in the sitting room turn the radio way up when the song comes on, "Get Away, Old Man, Get Away." Veiled talk about the courtship becomes open once Josie has a ring on her finger. The teasing subsides somewhat. Now, with a wedding date set, is the shower.

Josie doesn't look like she does in the Big House kitchen. She has on a Sunday dress Jackie has never seen, with beads and a brooch. She's put a ribbon around her bun. But she is still the same Josie for laughing and giggling. She cannot stop her laughing and giggling.

They play the games Mother leads them in, matching up famous couples, and finishing proverbs about love and marriage. Hazel plays the piano while one of the women sings a medley of old-fashioned love songs: "Let Me Call You Sweetheart," and "I Love You Truly," and "A Bicycle Built for Two." They all sing along with the ones they know. Jackie knows the one she calls "Daisy, Daisy." Joan and Patsy, surprisingly, know some of the others.

And then it's time to open the presents. Josie sits on the floor beside the low table and carefully undoes the paper and ribbons. She thanks Jackie and Patsy and Joan for the cup and sifter and bowl. She gives a little gasp at Mother's slip and blouse and holds the blouse to her while everyone tells her how lovely she will look in it. She appreciates Grama's embroidered tea towels, Aunt Ida's little spoon set from the World's Fair, Moo-Moo's crochet-edged pillow cases. She thanks each giver profusely.

Near the bottom of the pile she finds a small package wrapped in tissue paper. She turns it over and over. There is no card.

"Who is this from?" asks Josie.

No one responds.

She peels off the paper. There is a brown paper bag inside, but still no card. Jackie watches as she puts her hand into the bag and is startled to see Josie startle. And then Josie begins to blush. It is a blush that rises up her neck and spreads rapidly over her face, deepening and deepening and deepening, until her shiny skin is a more livid crimson than Jackie ever dreamed skin could be.

"What is it? What is it?" the guests clamor. Someone on the edge of the circle begins to laugh, and a few others pick up the laughter. Someone tugs on Josie's arm, and someone else snatches away the bag. Josie is left clutching a pair of rubber baby pants.

Now everybody is laughing, hooting, whooping. All but Josie. She sits there a scarlet statue, her chest heaving as if she can't get her breath.

After a moment she grabs for the tissue paper and buries the rubber pants in it. Then she starts laughing, too. Her face remains red.

There are one or two more presents to open and then refreshments. Josie is still unnaturally florid when they go to the dining room.

The wedding comes, and Grampa performs the ceremony. Josie moves into the brown stucco house with Mr. Griffiths. Grama has to get someone new to help in the kitchen. She finds a woman named, interestingly enough, Daisy, and Jackie and Craig sometimes sing "Daisy, Daisy" to her. She's younger than Josie and not so plain, but though Jackie watches closely, she doesn't spot her making eyes at any of the men. They still see Josie once in a while, when she and Mr. Griffiths come out to the Big House for Sunday dinner.

The pair lives happily ever after, until Mr. Griffiths dies from cancer in 1947. Till then, he continues working on the farm. After his death, Josie goes back to the small town upstate where her family hails from.

She and Mr. Griffiths never have a use for the rubber pants. Jackie wonders sometimes if Josie threw them out or kept them still in the tissue paper in her bureau drawer. She wonders if Josie ever showed them to her bridegroom. She suspects not.

24 ❧ HALLELUJAH, I'M A BUM

The hired men's sitting room was added to the Big House before Jackie was born. Mornings the room is usually empty, unless Grama is using her sewing machine, but it's always filled with sound. The radio is there, tuned loud to Ma Perkins or Stella Dallas, so that Grama can hear the next episode while she's in the kitchen making pies. The soap operas always have organ music that quavers and swells up between scenes, and sweeps to a massive vibrato at the end, nearly drowning out the announcer asking what will happen next; you must listen tomorrow. Grama always listens.

Very early mornings, when Jackie and Craig have stayed overnight at the Big House, they get dressed in the sitting room. Jolly Joe, who advertises Cocoa Wheat, conducts dressing races between the boys and the girls.

The men—Al Lasse, Ken Liddle, Ernie Capps, Russ Ullius—gather in the sitting room before dinner and again just before supper. They listen to twangy country music over WLS, the Prairie Farmer Station, and read the paper, or just talk and kid around.

Ernie Capps is a source of fascination to Joan, Patsy, Jackie, and Craig; he has a rotten ear. Its skin looks like the skin of a spoiled apple. Ernie sometimes spends the evening at the Little House, if Mother and Daddy go out to Bridge Club or Dinner Club and Eloise is busy. Then they tease him about his ear. He's good natured about everything, even when Craig vomits all over the bed one night and Ernie has to change the sheets.

Before the Big House had a radio, the four learn, the hired men listened to a Victrola. They find this out by discovering the Victrola. It's been in plain sight all along, but obscured by the upright piano at the end of the Big House parlor, the area that was the men's sitting room before the new one was built. It's a graceful cabinet on legs, with a lid; a scarf is on the lid. A broad copper tray containing rock crystals and twisted mineral formations always sits on the scarf. The four have fingered the minerals for years; it's all you can do with them. They're a boring display. That's why it takes so long to

A musical evening, posed to accompany W.J.'s 1915 Hoard's Dairyman *article about happy hired men. Ronald is on left, Trever back, and the Victrola on right.*

notice that under the tray and the scarf there's a lid, and under the lid there's something interesting.

The Victrola is a new and fascinating toy. They all like the picture inside the lid: a little white dog sitting with one ear cocked to the fluted morning-glory shaped loudspeaker of an ancient instrument. Under the dog are the words "His Master's Voice." On the side of the cabinet is a crank they have to crank up to make the turntable go. They select a record from the many stored behind the two sets of double doors of the lower cabinet, position it carefully on the felt disk so that the metal knob comes through the center hole, push the switch to set it rotating, then carefully lower the needle arm onto the outside groove. They are enthralled with the old-fashioned records, and quickly establish their favorites. Of plain music, there's the "William Tell Overture," but with no "Hi-Ho, Silver, Away!" and a part the Lone Ranger never plays—"At Dawning," with birds twurbling, and then a storm that crackles and booms. "Stumbling" and "Four Little Blackberries" are played by bouncy, tinny orchestras. Of comic dialogues, they soon memorize a dozen routines of "Two Black Crows," and can mimic the words and intonations of the dialogues down to the "woo woo woos."

The songs, however, are their very favorites. Harry Lauder with his thick Scottish brogue sings plaintively about a wee hoose in the heather, and "I love to get up in the morning, but I'd much rather stay in bed." There's a long dirge about Willie the Weeper: "He had a job as a chimney sweeper. He had the dope habit and he had it bad. Listen while I tell ya 'bout a dream he had." The violin then weeps an interlude before the ballad relates Willie's encounter with Cleopatra while he's floating down the Nile on the back of a seagoing crocodile. The four bawl along with the singer. And they join in with the thin nasal voice of another weeping dreamer:

Last night as I lay asleeping
A wonderful dream came to me.
I saw Uncle Sammy weeping
For his children from over the sea.

They had come to him friendless and starving,
Whence from tyrants' oppression they fled,
But now they abuse and revile him,
Till at last, in just anger, he said:

If you don't like your Uncle Sammy,
Then go back to your home o'er the sea,
To the land from whence you came,
Whatever be its name,
But don't be ungrateful to me.

If you don't like the stars in Old Glory,
If you don't like the red, white, and blue,
Then go BACK! like the CUR in the story,
DON'T BITE THE HAND THAT'S FEEDING YOU!

They give all the power of their strong lungs to the last lines of that chorus. And then they find the hobo songs. Even though it's the Depression, Jackie has never seen a hobo come to the Big House or the Little House and ask for a handout. Men do come seeking work, and Grampa sometimes gives them a day or two's employment. And she sometimes sees men sitting on top of the boxcars when a train goes by in the back pasture, down by the crick. Daddy reports, at the Little House table, that he counted 110 cars on a freight train. "They were all empty, and at least one man was in every car. All going somewhere. All going nowhere, the poor devils."

She's familiar with hobos through the funny papers. They don't seem like poor devils, there. They cheerfully walk along railroad tracks with their shoe soles flapping and their possessions in a red bandana on the end of a stick. Or they sit around a camp fire cooking Mulligan stew in a tin can. But the songs on the records are sad:

> I'm ridin' the rails on a train goin' west,
> Never again will I roam.
> I'm ridin' the rails on a train goin' west,
> Goin' back to my ho-ome.
> The conductor takes the tickets,
> The engineer runs the train,
> The porter puts them all to bed,
> While I stick out in the ra-ain

And another:

> I'm a broken-down tramp without money,
> My clothes are all tattered and torn,
> And I am so weary and lonely
> That I wish I had never been born.
> All through this wide world have I wandered
> A-looking for something to do
> But whenever I ask for employment
> They say I am only a tramp

The Hallelujah song is the only jolly one:

> Hallelujah! I'm a bum.
> Hallelujah! Bum again.
> Hallelujah, give us a handout
> To revive us again!
>
> Why don't you work
> Like other men do?
> Now how I can work
> When there's no work to do?
> Hallelujah! I'm a bum ....

The four lustily shout, "Hallelujah! Bum again!" along with the record. Suddenly Grama strides into the parlor. Her face is red. She shoulders through their circle, cuts off the singer in mid-Hallelu by flipping up the Victrola arm, snatches the record in her floury hands, and smashes it over her knee. Then she stamps back toward the kitchen. The four recoil in shock. Patsy and Jackie rush after her, horrified, in time to see her lift the stove lid and thrust the shards into the flames.

They hurry back to the Victrola and hide "I'm Ridin' the Rails" and "I'm a Broken-Down Tramp" from Grama's wrath. Then they hasten to the Little House.

Mother explains. The record Grama smashed is a parody of a hymn that goes, "Hallelujah, thine the glory, Hallelujah, amen," and ends up asking the Lord to "revive us again." It's a song written during an earlier depression — as are all the hobo records they've been listening to — to protest the plight of the jobless workers. But only "Hallelujah! I'm a Bum" is written to a hymn tune. Grama cherishes the old hymn. She thinks the record is making fun of religion. That's what upset her so.

"How come she never broke it before, then?" Patsy asks.

"She's probably never heard it before. The hired men who bought the record must have known better than to play it around her."

Patsy shakes her head. "We've never sung that hymn in church."

"It's not in the Methodist hymnal," Mother says.

Jackie is relieved about the whole affair. She thought Grama had it in for tramps.

There are two tramp stories connected with the farm that Jackie doesn't hear till she's older. One is that Uncle Trever, her very own uncle, known to everyone as Pat, rode the rails for a while after college, early in the Depression. "I didn't have any job or any money," Uncle Pat tells her, "and so I'd hop a freight to get anywhere, hunting for work. There were other men on the cars, too. The trainmen knew all about us, but they'd look the other way. Little raggedy children would be standing beside the tracks with their wagons, and they'd yell and stick out their tongues at us, and throw apples. Those of us riding on the gondola, the coal car, would throw down lumps of coal and they'd scramble to pick them up. We knew that's what they wanted. And then we'd eat the apples. They knew that was what we wanted."

The other story concerns Ernie Capps. One day he goes down to the pasture to get the cows and returns without them, out of breath. He's green.

"There's a man — where our lane crosses the tracks," he manages to gasp to

Daddy. "He's dead—he's been cut in half by a train."

Daddy phones the police. The police have just gotten word from the railroad that a hobo fell off a train back down the line and could be hurt. They were trying to figure out where to look. Now they know.

"Are you sure he's dead?" the policeman on the phone asks.

"Are you sure he's dead?" Daddy asks Ernie, covering the mouthpiece.

"Look, Ron," Ernie says. "Part of him is between the tracks, everything below his waist, and the rest of him is outside the tracks, everything above his waist, and the tracks are so clean you could eat off 'em, not a speck of blood, a thousand wheels must have gone over those rails after he got hit. Now you tell me if he's dead."

"He's dead," Daddy says back into the mouthpiece.

"Oh," says the policeman. "We'll call the funeral home, then. We'll be right out. Can you supply some gunnysacks? And we'll need to know where to go."

Daddy doesn't care for the whole scene. He looks green, too. "Go get some gunnysacks," he instructs Ernie, "and they'll probably want the farm truck. We'll have to wait on getting the cows."

Ernie goes off, looking sick. In ten minutes two policemen drive into the yard. They deplore the situation. They take the gunnysacks, and do want the farm truck, rather than risk their car over the rough terrain. They want someone to come with them to drive the truck and show the way.

"Go show them, Ernie," says Daddy.

Ernie gives Daddy a baleful look and climbs in the cab.

"Do you have gloves? You'll probably need gloves," one of the policemen says to Ernie as he and his buddy climb in the other side.

While they are gone, the Rosman-Uehling-Kinzer hearse arrives, and the two attendants take out a gurney and stand it at the back doors of the vehicle. Then they wait around with Daddy. Nobody says much.

Before long the police return. Ernie does most of the work of transferring the two bulging gunnysacks to the gurney. Daddy stands by with his hands in his pockets.

The funeral home men drive away. The policemen thank Daddy and leave. Ernie has already made an abrupt departure, a spurt of gravel under his tires, to hose the blood from the truck.

After a while Daddy seeks him out in the barn and thanks him.

"I don't see why me," Ernie complains.

Daddy doesn't know if he's speaking to the universe—why was he, Ernie Capps, the unlucky one to be first on the scene?—or to Daddy person-ally—why should it be Ernie Capps and not Ron Dougan who had to scoop up the mess in the pasture? Daddy suspects he means the latter.

"I guess," he mumbles, "it's one of the advantages of being boss."

Daddy knows that had his father been on the farm at the time, instead of in town on some errand, he would have taken the gunnysacks and gone himself. Grampa takes pride in never asking a man to do anything he himself wouldn't do. Daddy follows this policy, too, and spends more time than any hired man inside the bottle washer, or at the bottom of cesspools.

Daddy tells Jackie, "It was not my finest hour."

Jackie thinks back to the record Grama broke. Uncle Pat did revive, and went on to get good jobs. But there was no reviving the poor hobo who fell off the train. She knows that none of the men on the boxcars, or in the funny papers, had anything to hallelujah about.

This photo of the Big House interior from Hoards Dairyman *was meant to illustrate the model of a well-appointed, electrified living room.*

25 ⚜ SAME OLD CAT

It's mid-August, 1918. Ronald and Trever, recently turned 16 and 14, are at Phantom Lake YMCA Camp. They get letters from their parents, two in one envelope. Their mother writes:

Dear Boys,

Papa is writing you and I will add a few lines. About the flashlights, I cannot find a one of them. I had a dark one and you had one Percy gave you, Trever, and Ronald had the one Lillian gave him, the one we had fixed before we went to Kenosha. We cannot find any of them. If I do I will send them. We have had a great concert here tonight — Hazel and the Wiswall girls were here to supper, also Aunt Ida. Ben Lentell happened to come in the afternoon and was here to supper. We had a fine one. I will send you a sample of the cake and you must not look for anything more. I am glad you are having a good time. Come home well rested and happy for the greatest help you can give is a cheerful and happy disposition.

When you get home Aunt Kate and Aunt Rose will be here. They start tomorrow from Seattle. Papa and I are going to Janesville to the fair tomorrow. I wish we had the car but we will have to go on the Interurban. I received a grand picture of Percy this week in his sailor clothes. It is just as though he were right here.

There is not much news to tell. We had a big thunderstorm Sunday morning and Walsh's barn was struck by lightning and burned. We could see it so plain. There were shocks of oats burning also. We had a grand rain then and another last night.

Vic has been a real naughty boy nights since you went away. We put both him and Bob in the barn nights now and they howl all the time. The crow is so comical. The hen that had the eleven chicks and Jet are great friends. Today I heard Jet talking and chattering so I went to the porch by the bay window to see what was the matter and there were the crow and the hen talking together. The crow was coaxing the hen to feed her. She would talk, then take the hen's bill in her mouth. She is so comical. It is ten o'clock and I must close. Lots and lots of love from Mama. We will be glad to have you home again.

Their father writes:

My dear Boys,

I miss you greatly. Not alone because of your help with the work but it is lonesome without you. We have had two fine rains which will do seeding good in Southwest field (#12) and also the new alfalfa seeding. The corn is growing great.

I am not pushing the work very hard. Am waiting for your help. Chas Kellor has been away since Sat noon to the fair at Springfield, Ill. He will be back tomorrow. He is a nice lad and learns quickly. I am sorry you lost your glasses, Ronald. I fear it will hurt your eyes to go so long without glasses. Do not read.

We are planning on going to the Janesville fair tomorrow. Just Mama and myself. We are going to take a picnic dinner. Will have fried chicken and jelly and everything good. I have had Mama preparing for it all day.

The Wiswall girls, Aunt Ida and Hazel were here to supper. They gave us lots of music.

I must close and get to bed. I hope you have a grand good time. We will be glad when you get home again. Things will be much the same when you return.

Esther with Jet, the pet crow.

Do you know that story of the lad who had been away from home for a few days and felt it was years and remarked, "Well, I see you still have the same old cat." We will have the same old cat.

Lots of love from Daddy.

Vic. The Little House is behind him.

This letter merits some comments. Grama writes about Walsh's barn burning down being no news. In 1949, the Walshes build a new barn. They certainly had one between 1918 and 1949, but this is a super-barn. The university is in on the planning and building of it. It's the newest design, special construction, air passages, fans. It's built so that a farmer can store hay straight from the field without waiting for it to dry; the barn is so constructed that the hay will dry inside the barn. Chance at last is taken out of haying, that rain will come before the hay can be dried and stored. Walshes' new, innovative barn is the talk of Turtle Township.

The barn is finished, haying time arrives, the barn is loaded with green hay bales placed just so. The fans and all equipment go into action. That night the barn burns down.*

And on Grampa's letter: His final story enters family language. When anyone returns from a brief visit where much — or nothing — has transpired, the remark often is "I see you have the same old cat."

*My father always said, "Never ruin a good story for the facts." That's the way I heard it, anyway — the fancy new barn burned down. But after writing this story, I found that the new barn worked fine, just as the university planned it, and it didn't burn. It was a new pig shed that burned down in February 1949; my brother's memory (or his diary) was faulty. Thanks to Bridget Walsh and newspaper clippings, to get the facts straight. But I'm leaving the faulty story as is; this is called poetic license.

26 ❧ THANKSGIVING AT THE BIG HOUSE

It is Thanksgiving dinner at the Big House, and the table is crowded with family and hired men. Jackie perches on a stool at one corner. Grampa has just finished the long Thanksgiving blessing. In the pause after his "Amen," as everyone is looking up from being solemn and thankful, Grampa adds a postscript.

"It gives me great satisfaction to look upon this table," he exclaims. "Do you know that everything for our Thanksgiving dinner has been grown on this farm?"

"Why, that's so, Wesson," says Grama.

Grampa beams, laughing silently, while everyone looks around and begins pointing and enumerating. Jackie looks around, too.

Dominating the table are the Thanksgiving chickens, sharing a huge platter, three of them, golden brown and crackling, with steam escaping from a tender breast where Grama's fork has pierced. Because of Grampa's words, Jackie sees the food and its source at the same time. It's more than a double exposure, however; it's a series of pictures in such quick succession that they seem to be seen all at once, with sounds and smells and feelings rolled in.

She sees the hens as chicks, adorable fluffy balls; as gawky, half-feathered younglings; as grown hens purling and prowling around the woodpile by the Big House kitchen door and racing when she comes with scraps; as laying hens sitting sharp-eyed and sharp-beaked in the box nests in the hen house, herself reaching cautiously under a puffed bosom to ease out an egg. She sees the chopping block and a headless chicken running crazily, like a balloon blown up and let go. She sees Grama plucking and singeing and pulling out all the insides, setting aside the heart and liver for giblet gravy, and with one swift stroke cutting open the gizzard to remove the gravel. She remembers the time she stood in amazement, her eyes scarcely above the marble table top, as Grama pulled shell-less, yellow yolks out of a chicken, a whole sequence of them, starting with almost usual size and then gradually smaller and smaller,

The dining room table during a normal, non-Thanksgiving meal. Hilda presides regally at the head, Grampa at her left. But where is Grama?

till there was a final itty-bitty round yolk not as big as a teardrop. And at her request, Grama gathered up those never-to-be-laid eggs, down to the tiniest, and poached them for her breakfast.

And then, all the vegetables! The golden mountain of Hubbard squash, with a peak of snowy mashed potato beside it, both with boulders of butter melting down their sides; the tureen of creamed onions; the sliced carrots swimming in cream and butter; the cucumber pickles; the cabbage slaw; the bowl of stewed tomatoes. She sees, superimposed, the garden in all its seasons: the long row of feathery carrot tops; the tangled masses of squash and cucumber and pumpkin vines, with their gaudy flowers; the rough-leaved potato plants spattered with the yellow-striped potato bugs she loathes to pick off but is sometimes ordered to.

Strawberry jam and ruby-red currant jelly share a divided dish; she sees the strawberry beds with their glimpses of red and, at the edge of the garden, the hedge of bushes laden with sour red currants, each as translucent as the jelly but with faint little stripes from top to bottom, like a beach ball, and with a little pip of something on top, left over from the flower.

The hedge and garden stop at the orchard, and there are rows of gnarled trees, all good for climbing and making separate houses, all bearing different sorts of apples, with different tastes and different consistencies: Snows and Hubbardsons and Northern Spys and Wallingfields and big, fat Northwestern

Greenings, for pies, and Daddy's favorite apple, Eastern Maiden's Blush. In the fall, after they are gathered, the potatoes and carrots and turnips and parsnips and apples and squashes and pumpkins are stored in her most private, most special place on the entire farm, in the part of the basement beneath this table: the dirt-floored pungent root cellar, where she goes during the fall and winter from time to time, just to stand in the dim light of the single bulb, amid the bins and bushel baskets, and breathe deep breaths in dizzy ecstasy.

There are the breadstuffs of the meal: the stuffing in the chickens, made with onions and celery and sage and butter, and the plump, hot rolls. Grama is explaining about the flour. Jackie knows it comes from town in sacks that Grama turns into dishtowels, after a hired man has poured the flour, in a sneezy cloud of dust, into the big square flour box beside the stove. Jackie and the others always perch on this box to be able to see what is going on yet be out from underfoot. "But we never buy a lick of bread," says Grama. "I make all those loaves every other day, enough to feed our house and Ronald's, too, so even though we buy the flour, and the yeast, we produce ourselves all the bread and cakes and pies and cookies we ever use. And the jellies — there's sugar to buy, Daddy forgot that, but that's all. And I even make my own mincemeat."

Only last week Jackie had watched Grama mince up the meat for the mincemeat, beef from a butchered cow, and helped cut up the apples and raisins, and drank in the heady fumes as she'd stood over the kettle stirring the dark mixture. And later she'd watched Grama roll out the pie dough, dough made with lard rendered from a butchered pig.

And last of all on the table, rising like the barn's central silo above the other dishes, is the tall white china pitcher of milk, and clustered below it, the other dairy products: the cream, the butter, the cottage cheese. Later, there will be whipped cream mounded on the mince and pumpkin and apple pies.

Grampa is right. It's all from the farm. You can quibble if you want about the flour and raisins and the coffee the grown-ups will drink with their pie. You can waggle your finger at the salt and pepper, as Craig is doing. But these are small matters. They have really grown all the food for their Thanksgiving meal right at home.

"The Lord, of course, gives the increase," says Grampa. "But none of this bounty would be here without the daily efforts of each of us. It is the fruit of our labor. And for this I am truly thankful."

"Amen," agrees Mother. Everyone laughs and nods, and starts passing the laden dishes.

27 ✥ GRAMA'S DEPRESSION

It's the early thirties. Grama has a mysterious malady. She's had it before, off and on for over nine or ten years, as early as when Ronald was in college. In her letters to him, she wrote about how poorly she was feeling. Sometimes she'd go down to Bushnell Street and stay at Aunt Ida's for a two-week stretch. Twice she went to Glencoe and stayed for several weeks with Mrs. Turnbull, Alan Turnbull's mother. Alan worked on the farm in 1914 while he gathered data for his Master's thesis at the University of Wisconsin. This time, like the last, Dr. Thayer can't find anything physically wrong with her. It's a kind of nervousness, a weakness. Dizziness. Depression.

Grampa has worried about Eunice's nervousness. He doesn't know what to do now, any more than he did ten years ago. He knows she works too hard; she complains often enough about how hard she works—but she does have time for her church and club activities. She always has help, and the Big House boasts every sort of labor-saving device.

Vera and Ron worry, too. The three discuss the problem over and over. They agree that some way must be found to relieve Grama of her duties until she gets stronger. She needs an extended vacation—perhaps at the Turnbulls again. Grampa is reluctant to put her in a hospital or rest home.

But someone would have to take over the Big House. It must be someone competent who understands the farm work and schedules, someone willing to work for a low wage. Grama has always been paid for her job of running the Big House, but, like Grampa's salary, her payment is more a matter of figures in a ledger than cash in a pocket. An outsider would need to be paid. And the farm's cash is at a low ebb; it's the Depression. As Grampa says ruefully while he and a route man are checking in change in the office, "It comes in dimes and it goes out dollars!"

The solution isn't a good one, but it's the obvious one: Mother. She has the competence and the managerial skills. Her salary, like Grama's, could be on the books. She lives on the place and understands its workings as well as

Grama does—perhaps better, in some instances, for she's served as a secretary for Grampa numerous times, in matters personal and business, and he often confides in her. She knows the men at the Big House, and gets along easily with everyone.

The hitch is that Vera has had four babies in five years, and Craig is hardly more than an infant. Mother already has a full-time job taking care of her children and running the Little House. How can she manage the Big House, too, with its schedule of meals and cleaning and hired men? Even with assistance?

The decision is left to Mother, and it's not an easy one. But she, like Grampa and Daddy, don't know what else to do. If it will help Grama get well, Mother wants to do it. She agrees to take over the Big House.

Grama has not been in on these discussions. Now Grampa tells her that he and Vera and Ron know she needs a vacation, and that Vera has agreed to manage her work until Grama feels stronger again.

"What?" cries Grama. "Vera run the Big House? Why, whatever are you thinking of? Vera couldn't run the Big House!"

Grampa explains how the three of them have talked and figured, and while they know that no one could run it as well as Grama can, that in order to give her some rest and relief, this seems the best plan. And Vera is willing.

Grama sputters and stews. She gets off the couch, goes to the kitchen and begins banging pots and pans around. She launches into a frenzy of cooking and cleaning. "Vera run the Big House!" she's heard to mutter from time to time.

The plan to relieve Grama dies aborning. Mother never takes over the Big House. And Grama, *mirabile dictu*, does not have any more depression—at least not for a while.

28 ⋆ PLAY HORSIE

When he was little, Daddy didn't know that boys are different from girls. He thought everybody was the same as he was. It never occurred to him that they might be different. He had no sisters. Even if he had, he wouldn't have seen them undressed. He never saw his father or mother undressed. He didn't see pictures of unclothed people, not even reproductions of the Great Masters, or photographs of Greek statues. That was the way it was, in that generation, in the Big House, when he was little.

Jackie had always heard that Daddy ran after a little girl once when he was small and pulled down her pants because he'd heard there was a difference. One day Daddy tells her that this story is apocryphal. He tells her the true story. He'd never have been brave enough to run after a little girl and do that. What happened was just the opposite. The little girl ran after him.

Ronald is six; it's 1908. He's at school, the one-room schoolhouse in the field just beyond the corner of the East Twenty. There's a curve in the road there, at the edge of the schoolyard, and a culvert under the road. It's recess time. A little girl his age asks him to play horsie. The girl will be the horse, he'll be the driver. She holds a jump rope between her teeth and hands him the ends. Ronald twitches the reins and says "Giddy-yap!" She gallops; he gallops behind her. She gallops under the culvert. They are hidden in the culvert. She says, "I'll show you what I have if you'll show me what you have." Ronald has only a broken harness buckle and three aggies in his pocket. He doesn't think these will interest her, but he's interested in what she has to show him. "All right," he says. She pulls down her drawers and shows him.

Ronald is appalled. Distraught, he stumbles out of the culvert while she cries, "Wait! You promised!" All afternoon he doesn't look at her. He goes home, he picks at his supper. He goes to bed. In bed, he starts to cry. He cries uncontrollably. He is terribly, terribly sorry for girls. The world contains a sadness he has never suspected.

Ronald, hand on hip, and Trever, in bloomers, on the last day of school—the windows are already boarded up and the older boys and girls in eighth-grade graduation finery. Miss Church is the teacher.

His mother hears him weeping. She can't make him stop. She can't find out why he's shaking with sobs. Finally she carries him to the rocking chair and holds him in her arms. She rocks and rocks and rocks and sings lullabies. She rocks him to sleep. He never tells her why he cried.

There is more to the story. It's the next day. It's recess. Ronald's little brother is four. Trever is too young to go to school but he comes anyway, almost every day. The teacher doesn't mind. Ronald watches while the same little girl, and another little girl come up to Trever. "Let's play horsie," they say. They take the jump rope in their teeth and hand Trever the reins. They gallop off across the pasture. Trever gallops gaily behind them. Ronald watches them go. They disappear into a gully. Ronald wanders off and sits behind the boys' backhouse. The infinite sorrow strikes deep within him.

29 ⚹ THE PHANTOM LAKE TURTLES

Every year Ronald and Trever go off to Phantom Lake YMCA Camp at Mukwonago. Grampa is on the board of directors. The camp is about forty-five miles from Beloit. The boys take the Chicago, Milwaukee, St. Paul, and Pacific Railroad as far as East Troy. From there they take the Interurban. Someone from the camp either meets them at Mukwonago or they walk the rest of the way, their bindles on their backs. The trip takes almost all day. Once there they live in tents, swim, hike, ride, boat, eat in the huge mess hall, sit around the campfire and hear inspiring messages followed by ghost stories. It's a week they anticipate all year long.

When Ronald is eleven and Trever nine they arrive back in Beloit mid-afternoon and phone the farm from the train station. "You gotta come get us right now!" they shrill to their mother. "We have a surprise! It can't wait! You gotta come right away!" Grama objects. All the men are in the fields. They'll have to wait.

"You come!" the boys order. "You have to come! Now!"

Grama has rarely hitched up a buggy, but such is her sons' insistence that she gives in and promises to come. She goes to the horse barn, hitches up with some difficulty, and drives down to the station. She is met by Ronald, Trever, and a sack of assorted painted turtles. The smallest are silver-dollar size, the largest, no bigger than a saucer. They roil around in the sack.

The boys are ecstatic. They can't wait to get home and fix the turtles a place to live. They impress their mother over and over with their stealth in catching them. She is not thrilled.

At home the boys drag a large, shiny, oval, copper washtub to the front lawn. Shortly before they left for camp their father brought out to the farm four young elm trees, standing up in the back of a wagon along with a new outhouse. The outhouse went behind the woodpile. Grampa planted the elms in the front yard. All four trees have taken hold; they are doing well. The boys get spades and dig a trench large enough for the washtub alongside the elm nearest the spirea bushes. The ground is still soft there, from planting the tree, and easy to excavate. The shade of the bushes and the elm will give some shelter to the turtles. They sink the washtub in the hole so that its rim is level with the ground; they fill in any unevenness around the edges. They carry buckets of water and fill the tub. They fashion a chicken-wire fence that circles the tub and the trunk of the tree, to give the turtles a little land-space, and so that they won't get away. Then they turn the turtles into their new home.

The boys are filled with pride. They bring everyone to delight in the dazzling sight of all the dark-shelled turtles with their orange and yellow and black striped necks and heads and legs, swimming in the oval tub.

Their father isn't thrilled, either. "What will you feed them?" he asks.

The boys don't know.

"You will have to go to town in the morning and find turtle food," Grampa says. He frowns at the tub sunk flush with the elm tree.

The next day a few of the turtles are missing. The boys anchor the fence better. They bike to town and manage to find turtle food. Another turtle has vanished before they get back. They fortify their fence.

As the days go by the turtles do not thrive. They either disappear or die. Trever and Ronald dig little graves. When all the turtles are dead or gone Grama demands her copper tub. The boys dig it up. Grama sends them back to fill in the hole.

BOAT TILTING·
Y·M·C·A· CAMP·PHANTOM LAKE

Hijinks and water fights on Phantom Lake.

It's not until two weeks after their return from camp that Trever remembers something. He's been raising guinea pigs. He's kept them in a large frame of a box, all sides and ends covered with chicken wire. It makes for easy pet care. He can set the box down in the middle of an alfalfa field and the guinea pigs eat the thick alfalfa right through the chicken wire floor. The alfalfa is succulent enough that they don't need water. The greenery against the sides casts a cool shade no matter where the sun is. The droppings go right through the mesh. When the guinea pigs have eaten alfalfa a day or two, the only thing that has to be done is to move the cage to a fresh spot. The little animals are scarcely any trouble at all to take care of.

They are also easy to forget. Trever now remembers that he forgot to ask anyone to take care of his pets when he went to camp. Nobody else even knows where they are. He goes down to the alfalfa field and finds the cage. The ground under it is hard and cracked. There isn't a trace of an alfalfa leaf or stem. The bare earth fringes the cage as far beyond the chicken wire as the little beasts could reach. Inside the cage are three desiccated bodies.

Trever doesn't bury the guinea pigs with the turtles. He shakes the animals out of the cage into deep alfalfa and makes sure they aren't visible. He carries the cage back to the farm and hides it behind the henhouse. He never reminds anyone he had guinea pigs, and nobody else remembers.

By the end of the summer the little elm tree is dead, too. Ronald and Trever cut too many of its roots when they sank the copper tub alongside it.

30 ⊰ SNAKES

From the very start, W.J. Dougan has held his help to lofty standards. In a 1927 article published in *Hoard's Dairyman*, "What I Am Doing on My Farm to Solve the Labor Problem" he lists the requisites of a dairy farm worker. Intelligence, because he is an independent worker and must carry a job through to completion. Clean in person and morals, for he handles "the most delicate and most easily contaminated of food." Efficient, "for there is no place on a farm for a droon or a shirk." Grampa also includes loyalty to the employer.

When a potential employee is interviewed, standing on the red rug before Grampa's desk in the Big House, the agreement is not consummated until he signs a card stating that he does not drink, smoke, or swear.

Over the years the farm has a remarkable procession of employees. Although with human frailties, they are in most instances honest, conscientious, hard working, clean living. Several, like DeWitt Griffiths and some of the milkmen, remain with the farm their entire working lives.

Uncle Pat, though, once says to his brother, when they are talking of early gallants, "There have been occasional snakes in the garden, you know."

Daddy responds, "Not to mention the slugs and cutworms!"

Jackie finds the stories of these interesting. Some were before her time, some she has been unaware of, some she has been witness to.

A man is caught smoking in the barn and dismissed. Another keeps a bottle hidden in a rumble seat; at its discovery he, too, is let go. Swearers are harder to apprehend, for Grampa can't hear them. One once takes glee in using foul language in Grampa's presence. Mr. Griffiths and others are shocked, more by the insult to Grampa than by the language itself. They tell Grama, and the man receives a tongue-lashing he'll never forget. It's remarkable that Joan and Patsy, Jackie and Craig grow up on a busy farm peopled by a spectrum of workers, yet aren't aware of the more obscene expletives of the language until they hear them at school.

Pilfering at the gas pump occurs now and then, one spate by the teenage sons of a farmhand. The boys drive across the fields and up the lane from the pasture so they won't be noticed coming onto the place. But Ralph Anderson notices, and Daddy deducts the price of the gas from the worker's paycheck. The boys also substitute new tires from the farm for their own worn ones; Daddy discovers this, too, and makes them bring the tires back.

There is some thievery of dairy products, even though Grampa and Daddy's policies are generous: milk returned from the route is free for the drinking; men who live away from the place can even take it home. The tire-switching boys, until they are apprehended, switch fresh milk for free day-old milk in the cooler and carry home the fresh.

Daddy catches and fires an employee who in his own car is plying a milk route after work with milk stolen from the dairy cooler—some fifty quarts a day. Another, who has a small farm with a few cows, puts the raw milk into Dougan bottles and peddles it on his route at a lower price to certain favored customers. He then pockets the revenue.

A rare helper at Grama's or Mother's carries off produce in a large purse. One who had previously made off with blueberries, horse blankets, and a device for bottling root beer goes too far when she tries to smuggle a watermelon under her coat.

There are certainly thieves never spotted. Willis Morecombe is one. In 1929 he left the farm, Jackie learns, and headed west. Clair Matthews, the herdsman, is glad to see his back, for Willis has been sparking Clair's wife. Several years later Morecombe writes that while employed he stole five hundred dollars. Now he's got religion and been born again. He encloses fifty dollars and will send the rest as soon as he can. He never sends another nickel, yet Grama and Grampa correspond with him over the years and on a trip to Colorado are entertained royally at his ranch in the mountains. Grampa must figure he has to collect his debt in trade.

During World War II there's a new route man who juggles his figures to his advantage and pockets the difference. He's caught, leaves the farm, makes restitution. Grampa and Daddy don't call in the law.

Of the sexual trespasses, most must be known only to the parties involved. But the advances to teenaged Esther by O.J. Miller and Walter Lake are found out, and Floyd Peters, apprehended climbing across the roof and into Esther's bedroom, is fired on the spot. Bobby Emmert, age seventeen, comes to the farm from a rural village up north and is seduced by a helper in the Big House kitchen. Frances is a woman ten years his senior. She herself is married to a hired man; they live in the upstairs apartment at the Hill Farm. She leaves her husband a note on a paper bag, saying she doesn't need him, she has a new lover. He departs but watches till Bobby arrives. There's a wild bedroom scene. Bobby, britches in hand, flees out the window, across the porch ledge, and slides down a column, splintering his behind the whole way. Frances tries to salvage the situation by urging Oscar to go after Bobby and beat him up. He replies, "Blame yourself; you shouldn't go after a kid." He disowns his wife. She turns out to be pregnant, and when the baby—perhaps Oscar's, perhaps Bobby's—is born, Frances puts her in an orphanage.

When Ronald is eleven, he tells Jackie, he wanders into the horse yard and glimpses the visiting brother of a barnhand doing something very odd to the pony. The scene makes him so uncomfortable that he backs away without being noticed. Uncle Pat adds that not the brother, but the barn worker himself, lays a carnal hand on him. At nine he's ignorant of the man's intent, but wriggles away and runs. He avoids going near that employee until the man leaves for another job.

There are miscellaneous incidents. A group of first-day detasselers flatten a large area of hybrid corn to let the breeze into the middle of the field while they play cards. A pair of farmhands steal a car in town and hide it in the calf barn. A milkhouse worker avoids registering for the draft. A farmhand beats a horse and is fired. Jackie hears, many years later, from a former farmhand of a cruelty act. Ray Skogen says, "Go ahead, use my name." He is still angry. A horse had nipped him, says Ray, "and I was hitting him with a stick and Daddy Dougan stopped me, bawled me out. So later I went to the horse barn, put a rope on that horse, and pulled his head straight up, and held it, then let it down. I did it again and again. You should have seen his eyes roll. I sure showed him."

Occasionally a Galahad falls from grace. In his old age, Jim Howard, model herdsman in the twenties, confesses to having tied two cats' tails together with a length of rope, then slung the rope over a beam in the side barn. "I don't know why I did it," he says shamefacedly. "I was instantly appalled, and managed to cut them down before they did much harm to each other." He shakes his head in bemusement at his young self.

Unregenerate, however, is Louie Kozelka. He comes from a poor family in Necedah up north and boards at the farm. Grampa and Grama have retired to the edge of town; Pat Anderson is now in charge of the Big House. Louie is an indifferent young man as to intelligence and working habits, but at the end of the war it's difficult to get help of any sort, so Daddy keeps him on. He goes home frequently, and though his stays are brief, he always carries two suitcases. He courts a Beloit girl and announces their engagement. Her family is even poorer than his. They'll be married at the Janesville courthouse. Neither family will be present. Louie hints broadly that they'd like a reception at the farm.

Pat Anderson and her husband Ralph are good-hearted. So are the other farmhands, and Grampa and Grama, Mother and Daddy. They all chip in to pay for a dress for the thin little bride. Pat bakes the wedding cake. Mother makes sandwiches and favors; Grampa and Grama buy candy and nuts. The men bring in garden flowers to decorate the dining room. There's fruit punch in a punch bowl. A lace tablecloth graces the table, and the best china and silver. Everyone contributes to the wedding present: matched sheets and pillowcases, wrapped in silver wedding-bells paper and tied with a silver bow.

Louie is expansively pleased with the reception, but his bride speaks only in monosyllables. Pat thinks perhaps she's embarrassed by the modest affair, or by what may be the skimpiness of her wedding rings, for she keeps her hands clasped tightly behind her. The couple moves into the vacant first-floor apartment of the Big House, the southwest rooms that were once the office.

Louie's wife is rarely seen. The shades are always pulled. There's no sign of housework: no sound of vacuum sweeper, no clothes flapping on the line, and only rarely smells of cooking. There are dog and cat noises, and the radio is on from early morning till late at night.

"She must never get out of bed," observes Pat, whose ears place the radio in the bedroom. "Those wedding sheets are getting good use."

But on Louie's day off they will both issue forth, dressed in their Sunday best, and with heavy suitcases head north for Necedah.

Several months go by. Daddy has called Grampa's attention to the suitcases. He's also told him that expensive seed has been disappearing from the storehouse. They both suspect Louie of stealing corn and selling it on his frequent visits home, but they're reluctant to accuse him without proof.

One day, after Daddy sees Louie enter his apartment from the outside door, carrying a laden gunnysack, he comes and knocks. When Louie finally answers, Daddy asks if he may come in and look around. Louie demands why. Daddy wants to see the gunnysack. Louie brings it to the door. It doesn't seem as heavy as it appeared going in, and contains a few potatoes and onions. Daddy apologizes and leaves, but not before glimpsing the state of the apartment. He worries whether he should force a cleanup.

Two days later Louie asks Mrs. Anderson for a plumber's helper.

"Are you having trouble with your toilet?" Pat asks. Louie says he is.

A day later Pat asks if the problem is solved. Louie is noncommittal. Pat says if something's wrong it should be fixed; he should see Erv, the farm handyman, about it.

The next day water starts backing up in the sinks and drains of the main house. Pat goes to Ron. He seeks out Louie in the barn, goes with him to his apartment, and insists on seeing the toilet. He picks his way through the darkened living room, through the darkened bedroom where Louie's wife, curled up in bed with radio blasting, and with dog and cats beside her, doesn't turn her head. He enters the kitchen. Crusted plates growing mold are piled everywhere and dirty water and dishes brim the sink. In the narrow bathroom behind the kitchen the toilet is gurgling and overflowing. There's water on the floor. Daddy seizes the plumber's helper and applies it vigorously, but it produces no results.

Louie shrugs and returns to the barn. Daddy works and works. Finally he gives up and fetches Erv. They cut off the water to the Big House. They drain the tank and stool and remove it. With all Erv's tools they can't get to any obstruction. Finally Erv inserts an auger, sets it rotating, and the trouble begins to emerge: grinding back out of the pipe come swollen corn kernels, some of them even sprouted. They dig out as much corn as they can, but the auger doesn't go far enough. The pipe seems filled solid.

They go down to the cellar. The pipe travels under the floorboards, almost horizontally, before going through the foundation on its way to the septic tank. The men break it and pull out corn from either direction. Outside, they dig up the pipe and break it again. They have to climb down into the tank and ream out the pipe from beneath. There is other affected plumbing. It takes two days of nasty work to put things to rights. Obviously someone has flushed a great deal of grain down the toilet, but because of the pitch of the pipe, along with insufficient water pressure, it didn't flush through.

Louie vehemently rejects all blame. He doesn't know how the corn got there. On a final trip through the gloom of the bedroom Daddy tartly suggests to Mrs. Kozelka that she get up and clean house. She doesn't turn her head.

Grampa is angry. "You must fire that man, Ronald," he says. But Ronald doesn't. He has no one to take his place; even bottom-of-the-barrels are hard to come by. It takes another month and another crisis before he does.

The two have departed on Louie's day off. The animals are locked in the apartment as usual. But instead of returning the next day, the pair doesn't show up. The third day comes and they aren't back. The animals are frantic, scratching at the doors. That night Pat calls Daddy.

"Ron," she says, "Louie and Ginnie have been gone three days, and there are animals in those rooms — crying. And the smell — well, the smell is seeping out into our living room, and it's pretty bad."

Daddy hurries down. He pries open a window. The stench rushing out nearly knocks him over. He climbs in to find bedlam. A dog and three cats are there, starved. Worse, they have no water. There's no cat box; messes from many more days than three are scattered over the floors. The apartment is a filthy shambles. Ralph Anderson, and Daddy muttering obscenities in French, tend to the animals, while Pat retrieves a waffle iron and dishes. She takes down her own curtains from the windows, her own sheets off the bed, and picks through piles of stinking laundry for towels, facecloths, and pillowcases belonging to the Big House.

"No wonder they never hang out the wash!" she exclaims.

When Louie and his wife finally return, Daddy tells them what he thinks of people who treat animals and property as they have. He says Louie better find employment elsewhere. The two pack up and leave, Louie in a rage. They take the dog but abandon the cats.

The farm is left with a cleanup that takes weeks. Pat uses gallons of Lysol. Layers of food and feces have to be scraped off the floors. The rugs are a total loss. The rooms must be fumigated, the walls repainted. Grampa looks in every day or so, and shakes his head. But when the job is done, the Andersons like the fresh apartment so much that they expand into it.

Two months go by. Pat goes to her seldom-opened jewelry box and discovers that her mother's wedding ring and her father's ruby ring, tied up in a chiffon handkerchief, have vanished. She suspects these are the rings that Ginnie was hiding at the reception.

Some time goes by. Ronald receives a letter, written on tablet paper, in pencil, and every other word is misspelled. It's from Louie. With some difficulty Daddy is able to read that he divorced his first wife, married a fine woman, is farming a fine farm, and wants everyone to know he's getting along just fine. The letter ends with a word that is three times misspelled and crossed out. Finally it's written in block letters, misspelled a fourth way, and followed by black exclamation points whose periods slam right through the paper. Ronald puzzles over all the misspellings until the word suddenly comes clear.

Catastrophe! The last sentence, were it legible, reads, "But you RON DOUGAN are a CATASTROPHE ! ! ! ! ! !"

Daddy whoops and pockets the letter to show everyone.

"You always look to see where a compliment is coming from," Pat Anderson observes.

31 ❧ LA MARÉCHALE

Grama — Eunice Trever Dougan — is a babe in arms when, May of 1870, she and her family sail from Liverpool on the SS England, bound for New York. Her parents are Joseph and Maria Dale Trever, on the ship's register listed as ages 40 and 39, and her siblings are Mary, Betsy, Sarah, George, Maria, Joseph, Charlotte, and Kate, ranging in ages from 19 to Eunice's six months; both she and Kate are listed as "infant." Since names apparently were required and some clerk didn't bother to ask, they are registered as John and Mary. Willie, who died when he was two, is left in a grave in Staffordshire. Two more children will be born in the United States, Rose and Albert Augustus. Joseph Trever's brother John and his large family are also on shipboard.

The reason for the emigration is a conversion. Some years before, Joseph Trever, a joiner in Newcastle-under-Lyme, had been set afire by the preaching of a revivalist. His eldest son George writes many years later:

> Father had always profoundly respected his parents' piety. Even in his gayest, most irreligious hours he was ready to defend, with tongue or muscle, the religion of the Gospel, yet was a worldly, somewhat wild young man. But in January 1855 Reverend William Booth — then a Methodist preacher, now General Booth, founder of the Salvation Army — was holding a revival in Bethesda Methodist New Connection Church, Hanley. At a store one evening a young man who waited on Father for some tools asked him to go to the meeting. He replied, "No, they will be converting me there if I do." The clerk replied, "Do go; I was converted there last night, praise the Lord, and you may be tonight."
>
> Father left in deep thought, carried home his tools, and went to the meeting. The text was, "How long shalt ye between two opinions." The earnestness of the preacher arrested his attention, the Holy Spirit fixed the truth in his soul, and soon he was under deep conviction. At the invitation he went straightway to the altar as a seeker of Christ. He remained 'mid prayer, song,

exhortation, and instruction, until the lights were put out. The workers kept telling him to believe, believe; yet somehow he could not see what to believe. At last one impatiently exclaimed, "You won't believe; you could if you would." But no light came, and Father went home in wretchedness of soul. The next night the sermon was from "My spirit shall not always strive with man." Again he went forward—again wrestled in vain, and returned home miserable in mind. The third night found him in his place at the altar once more; the sermon had been "Choose ye this day whom ye will serve." He had scarcely knelt when he saw the way of salvation through surrender to Christ and His atoning blood. Light broke upon his soul, and he arose with shouts of praise. He went home, and the moment he opened the door Mother saw with joy that he had experienced a change. As she has often said, his face reminded her of Acts 6:15, regarding Stephen, that "his face appeared as it had been the face of an angel."

His first words were, "Well, I have been converted and joined the church." She replied, "You needn't have told me, I knew it by your face." He asked her to burn his tobacco and break his pipes. When she proposed taking them back to the store, he objected, that "to do so would encourage someone else in doing wrong." Then Mother joined him, neither resting until both were rejoicing in Christ. The next morning he set up the family altar, which henceforth had the central place in his home.

The account goes on to tell of his fervor in educating himself to speak to others the Word of Christ, and also of his business acumen which led to his success as one of the leading contractors in Newcastle. He rose high in civic, social, and religious circles. But:

Owing to the growing complications in the business world, as a result of the frequent strikes and radical measures of the labor unions, my father grew tired of business life and desired a quieter occupation. This with the fact that competition, the influence of associates in trade, and the social habits of the circle in which he moved had lowered his religious tone, whilst yet he keenly felt the supreme importance of living for Christ, led him to resolve to seek a new home and means of livelihood. He therefore emigrated to the United States, sailing from Liverpool in May 1870.

Grama's sister, Ria, who was nine and never lost her clipped Midlands accent, adds details when she visits the farm. "He took the term 'convert' seriously," she tells the family, "and he turned around on his old life and made a fresh start over here." She recalls perching on a steamer trunk at the docks, surrounded by cousins and bags and boxes, waiting to board the ship, and being sent to buy another loaf of bread. She recalls her mother, Maria Dale, holding baby Eunice. Her sister-in-law looks disapprovingly at the infant.

"'Aven't you anything else for the baby but that black 'at?" she demands.

"I 'ave a little white 'ood in me bag," Maria replies.

"Prithee put it on!"

The crossing takes many days. The families travel in steerage. They bring their own provisions and take turns with other passengers cooking on the small iron stoves set in sand which the ship has provided for steerage use.

They arrive in New York June 9, and stay in a hotel. The beds crawl with bedbugs. Ria remembers her father pacing all night, smoking. In the morning he throws his tobacco away. This is the last time he smokes.

Both families are headed for Wisconsin, where a sister has already settled, but they leave New York City at different times. Eunice's family boards the train. At a stop somewhere in New York state, Joseph and Maria get off to buy supplies. The train pulls away sooner than expected, and the children are treated to the sight of their laden parents rushing, stricken, along the platform.

La Marechale, daughter of General Booth.

"That was a cryin' time, I'll tell you!" Aunt Ria comments, and Joan and Patsy, Jackie and Craig, fervently agree.

But the tear-streaked faces against the panes were soon witness to a welcome surprise: an express train on the adjacent track creeps up on them, and they spot their parents in a coach window, grinning and gesticulating as the train passes. Tears turn to screams of joy, and the family is reunited at Buffalo.

They arrive at midsummer in Brant, Wisconsin, near Chilton in Calumet County. Joseph, no farmer, walks through a field thick with clover, decides this is excellent land, and buys the farm. The next spring, when the ground is bare and frost has done its work, he discovers the soil to be filled with thousands of fist-sized stones. It becomes everyone's job to rake stones from the fields, although Joseph, to gain ready cash to support his family, goes to Chicago and helps rebuild after the Great Fire.

The other Trever family settles nearby. From Uncle George's account, "My father, as he intended when he left his English home, resumed his old-time religious zeal, and soon became the natural leader and main support of the little Methodist society that worshipped in the schoolhouse in Brant." Joseph Trever leads the way in building a church. All his toil and sacrifice are abundantly rewarded, for in this little building seven of his children come to Christ.

In England, meanwhile, another family saga is unfolding. William Booth, broken from the Methodists, has founded the Salvation Army. He is himself the father of a large brood. His eldest daughter, and the apple of his eye, is Kate. Like her father, she's an inspired and charismatic evangelist. When she's twenty-two, General Booth commissions her Captain, and sends her to unfurl the Banner of Salvation in France.

The banner is a literal one: it's the first Army flag, and her mother has embroidered it with red for the saving Blood, blue for holiness, and gold for the Star of the Spirit.

"Carry it into the slums and alleys, and preach under its shadow wherever there are perishing souls," exhorts her mother at a farewell meeting. "Charge on the hosts of hell, and see whether they will not turn and flee!"

Kate, with two nineteen-year-old lieutenants, moves unprotected into the slums of Paris, rents a hall, and begins preaching to the dregs of humanity. At first only a handful of the curious come to see the strange English girls, but they are soon joined by mobs of hecklers. These mimic Kate's halting French, tear pages from New Testaments to light their cigars, and throw mud, stones, and garbage.

A few, however, sense what Kate and her lieutenants are meaning; they catch hope from the fervor of Kate's eyes, and stay to pray. The three battle incredible odds, and the movement grows. The General raises Kate's rank to Field Marshall, "*La Maréchale*," and this is the title she bears the rest of her life.

An Irish Quaker convert and pacifist leaves fortune and family and comes to France to join the struggle. Colonel Clibborn and La Maréchale work side by side over the years, and when Kate is twenty-eight, they marry. He changes his name to include Booth, as all Booth sons-in-law must do, and becomes

Arthur Booth-Clibborn. With Kate his senior officer, he must also pledge to obey her.

Kate and Arthur eventually have ten children. They also eventually break with the General and his Army, mainly over the issue of the Boer War. The Booth-Clibborns are ardent pacifists, while the old General, with members of his flock on both sides, is a fence straddler. In addition Kate loses faith in her father's judgment to deploy his forces effectively and compassionately, particularly when it comes to his own children. His new *Army Rules and Regulations* is a document which represents such rigidity and requires such blind obedience that this contributes strongly to her regretful resignation. Through it he loses not only Kate, but two of his other children as well.

The father is enraged at his daughter's defection and vows never to set eyes on her again. He never does, though at her pleading, she's allowed in to his deathbed, but must stand behind the headboard and not make her presence known in any way.

After leaving the Army, La Maréchale continues as an evangelist. She travels the world, speaking to huge crowds in hired halls and to small groups (which sometime include royalty) in "drawing room meetings." She doesn't form a rival Army nor found her own church but sends the souls she wins to local churches or the Salvation Army.

The family comes to the United States and rents a house on Lowell Avenue in Chicago. Most of the Booth-Clibborn children are involved in the family calling. An older one is Victoria, who has inherited the charismatic gift of preaching that her mother and grandfather possess.

Vickie meets a young woman, Vera Wardner, who works at a settlement house in Chicago, the Association House, doing social work, and teaching music, ballet, and physical education to poor children. She also teaches Scottish dancing at Jane Addams' Hull House, and is an excellent pianist, having trained at the American Conservatory of Music. Vickie is much taken with the talented Vera. She urges her to help with the campaigns. The group needs a skilled pianist, one who also has deep spiritual qualities.

Vera comes. She meets La Maréchale, and is impressed with her power and presence. She meets Uncle Herbert Booth, and a number of the now-grown children. The youngest son, Theodore, plays the violin, sings, speaks, and helps in the organizing of the campaigns. Vera often accompanies him on the piano. She is held in great affection by all the Booth-Clibborns; she becomes one of the family.

Then Vera leaves Chicago to attend Illinois Women's College downstate in Jacksonville. After her graduation she teaches French, English, music, and Physical Education at Winchester High School. All during these years she remains close friends with the Booth-Clibborns, who come and go from England. Theodore cares a great deal for Vera, and she for him, but there is no engagement: one of Vera's deepest concerns is the incredible strength of the Booth-Clibborn family; every decision is made by all of them, but with La Maréchale always supreme. Vera fears that if she becomes a permanent part of such a powerful tribe she will be swallowed by the Cause. She has her own private faith, but is no evangelist like La Maréchale and Vickie. Will she lose her identity? And how can there be any family life apart from the Greater Family?

Theodore has his doubts, too, and for much the same reasons, but his solution — that in marriage he be absolute head of the household — makes Vera uneasy. She receives a job offer in France. She accepts, mostly for the splendid opportunity to do social work there for a year, but also to get a perspective on the Booth-Clibborns, and to think things over. It's agreed that Theodore will join her in France in the spring, and some decision about the future might then be made.

Vera's train is met at Chateau Thierry by a dashing young American-gone-

Vera, at right, outshines the bride at Victoria Booth-Clibborn's wedding.

native, Ronald Arthur Dougan. On his chiffonier at the Methodist Memorial he has a picture of his best girl back at Northwestern. Vera, on her night stand, places Theodore's photograph. At Christmas Vera helps Ronald select a present for Katherine, and he helps her choose for Theodore. By late winter the two are engaged, and in May they are married. Ronald doesn't care a whit who is head of the family; the issue never occurs to him.

Theodore, meanwhile, has been unable to come to France. His brother Eric, preaching the Gospel in Africa's interior, has died of fever. Eric's pregnant wife Lucille and their tiny daughter Phyllis have also been ill but have survived. Slowly and painfully, first by mule, then by riverboat, they are transported to the coast. Theodore is sent to meet them and take them back to London. From England, he sends Vera and Ronald his best wishes.

The couple returns to the States. Ronald attends Beloit College, and little Vera Joan is present at his graduation. That summer they live at the farm in the Big House, while the Little House is being remodeled.

One evening Mother receives a call. It's from La Maréchale. The family is in Chicago and are planning to come the following day to see their beloved Vera, meet her husband and baby, and the rest of the Dougan family. Mother says they are welcome. "I think she wants to see for herself that I've made a suitable marriage," she tells Daddy.

The entourage, when it arrives, consists of La Maréchale, Victoria and her husband, a sister Freida, and Theodore. They embrace Vera; they meet Ronald; they admire the baby. They are much taken with Grama and Grampa and the farm. Ronald and Grampa give them the grand tour. La Maréchale, down in the round barn, watches the sleek Guernsey cows being washed around their hind quarters in preparation for milking, each one neatly shaven. She's impressed with the spotless cows and spotless barn.

"How much is one of these cows worth?" she writes to Grampa.

"About three hundred dollars each," he replies. He can see her mental calculations on the value of the herd.

She's also impressed with Grama's gleaming kitchen, the rows of rhubarb pies, the homemade bread, the meal they are served of roasted chicken and gravy, fresh peas, and little tender lettuce. She's impressed with the family warmth and egalitarianism, with all the hired men sitting at the dining room table with the family and their guests. She's impressed with Grampa's Grace, and his Bible reading after the meal. She listens with delight to Eunice's recital of the Trever family's coming to the States when Eunice was six months, as a direct result of William Booth's preaching in Staffordshire.

In the kitchen after the meal, she says to Grama, "I should like to leave Freida here with you. Freida is not strong enough for the evangelistic work, and this farm would do wonders for her. She needs a place to be settled for a while." It is less a request than a command.

But Grama is her equal. She thanks La Maréchale for thinking so highly of the farm's healing properties, but says at this time there's simply not enough room for another person. There is a full complement of hired men, and Ronald's makes an extra family. La Maréchale shakes her head in regret.

Grama and Grampa, Ronald and Vera, do not expect the group to spend the night, but when La Maréchale asks if they would like a drawing room meeting the next afternoon, the Dougans realize she has had in mind a two-day visit. They assure her they would, and Grama rushes to see about beds. Esther is sent downtown to Aunt Ida's, and everyone doubles up. Then Grama and Vera get on the phone to invite the neighbors.

The next afternoon the living room is crowded. The hired men are all there. Aunt Ida, Aunt Lillian, Hazel, and Esther have come from town; the Marstons, Smiths, Blodgetts, Higginses, Holmeses—all up and down Colley Road and throughout Turtle Township the neighbors have gathered to hear the preaching of the daughter of General Booth. Vera plays piano as of old, and Theodore plays violin. La Maréchale leads the singing, evangelistic words set to familiar hymn tunes, but also to tunes popular at the time, and to operatic airs. The hired men suppress smiles and look at each other and at Ronald when they sing, to the tune of "A Bicycle Built for Two":

> Come, Lord Jesus,
> The spirit and bride say come;
> Come, come, quickly,
> Back to Thy earthly home ….

And these words are set to the tune of "O Sole Mio":

> Down from His glory, Everliving story,
> Our Lord and Savior came, and Jesus was His name.
> O how I love Him! How I adore Him ….

La Maréchale preaches. Ronald sits beside his father and writes the words.

"Salvation is not a theory or a dogma nor a thing of the intellect," says La Maréchale, "it is a change of heart!" Grampa nods.

La Maréchale goes on. "When I went to France I said to Jesus, 'I will suffer anything if you will give me the keys.' And if I am asked what was the secret of our power in France, I answer: first, love; second, love; third, love. And if you ask how to get it, I answer: first, by sacrifice; second, by sacrifice; third, by sacrifice!"

Grampa nods and nods. Love and sacrifice are things he much understands.

Theodore Booth-Clibborn.

Then La Maréchale's daughter Victoria preaches, and there is praying and more singing. A plate is passed to help with the work of salvation, and everyone contributes generously. La Maréchale asks the Reverend W.J. Dougan to give a benediction, and Grampa does. It's an inspiring service.

Afterwards there are tea and coffee and cookies and fresh strawberries for everyone. Eunice queries La Maréchale on the propriety of "Bicycle Built for Two." "I never heard tell of such a thing!" Grama exclaims.

"Oh, but you have," says La Maréchale with a twinkle in her eye. "Luther took the barroom songs and made them into hymns; you sing them in church every Sunday. Why should the devil have all the good tunes?"

The Booth-Clibborns stay for supper, then leave for Chicago. Before she departs, La Maréchale gives Mother a strong hug. She says she's happy for Mother's happiness, and that she will always care for her. Theodore shakes Ronald's hand warmly. The party doesn't know it then, perhaps Theodore himself doesn't yet know it, but he will return to England and marry Lucille, his brother's widow. The two couples will be friends all their lives.

La Maréchale lives to ninety-six. For her ninetieth birthday, she asks Theo to arrange one last meeting where she can meet her old comrades in the Army. Theodore asks; the Chief of Staff sends a refusal. Theodore looks at his mother weeping over the letter. He says, "Look darling, be damned to the Chief of Staff, you'll have a meeting in London, and you'll meet your old comrades." He goes down to Central Hall Westminster and tells Dr. Sangster, "La Maréchale is ninety this year and she'd dearly love to have one more meeting in London."

Dr. Sangster replies, "But of course—let her have Central Hall."

At the birthday meeting Salvationists in uniform pack the hall, and two or three thousand people unable to squeeze in wait in Parliament Square out-side. La Maréchale prays and preaches and leads the singing of evangelistic words to popular tunes. There are congratulatory telegrams from all over the world.

Perhaps this particular event is not noted in Wisconsin. But in Turtle Township, on Colley Road, for many years past and more to come, the residents sing, "Our Lord and Savior came, And Jesus was His name," to the tune of "O Sole Mio," taught to them by La Maréchale, daughter of General Booth, when she preached in the drawing room of the Big House at the Dougan farm.

32 ⁕ BEDMATES

Patsy is six. She has the flu. She's sequestered over at the Big House, on a couch at the far end of Grama and Grampa's living room.

Grampa comes into the room, carrying a bundle in his arms. His eyes are twinkling. "Would you like to have this baby in bed with you?" he asks. "Will you keep him warm?"

He peels back the blanket and reveals the snout and bright anxious eyes of a very small pig. Patsy reaches out her arms and Grampa tucks the piglet in with her. She snuggles him and strokes the top of his velvet head with her finger. She examines his quivering nose and tiny eyelashes. The pig makes high snorting noises. He roots at her. Grampa laughs silently. He leaves the room.

In a few minutes he returns with a nursing bottle full of warm milk. "This little fellow has no tit," he says. "His brothers and sisters won't make room for him, down in the barn."

He gives Patsy the bottle and she sticks the nipple in the baby's mouth. He grabs it and sucks ravenously, noisily, sloppily. Milk flows out the edges of

Patsy, without the flu, on the Little House lawn.

his mouth, but it doesn't matter. Grampa watches a few moments, laughing, and then departs.

When the pig is through, Patsy puts the bottle on the floor. She pulls the little body close to her. She runs her finger over his full little belly. She curls and uncurls his little tail. He makes sleepy, happy grunts. His grunts taper off; Patsy's stroking gets slower. Together they sleep all night.

Patsy and a calf share a quiet moment on the Big House lawn.

33 ⊰ BIG HOUSE CHRISTMAS

Christmas at the Big House is held on Christmas Eve. Earlier in the week, Grama and Grampa always give a big Christmas supper for employees and their families, and Christmas bonuses are handed out. There is cold molded chicken salad, and everybody carries home a plate of Grama's special Christmas cookies. But Christmas Eve is the party for the more immediate family—Grampa and Grama and Effie (Grama's maiden niece and helper); Mother and Daddy, Joan, Patsy, Jackie, and Craig over from the Little House; Aunt Lillian, Aunt Ida, and Hazel out from town; and all the hired men who are living at the Big House, unable by distance or work demands to be at their own homes with parents or other family members.

The parlor has the tall tree at the east end. Grama and Grampa's tree, this year as always, has its own familiar ornaments, different from the ones at the Little House, and in the darkened room its many colored lights shed a diffuse glow through the circling mists of angels' hair. Jackie loves to tiptoe into the room and stand, smelling the balsam scent, drinking in the softened colors, feeling the magic of the huge pile of presents under the tree. The quiet heap exhales that magic like perfume emanating from a hay field or warmth rising from a pasture lane. Only a few of the packages will be for her—tonight is more an evening of giving than of getting—but that doesn't lessen the anticipation.

She and the rest of the family brought their gifts over in the afternoon, in a wicker laundry basket; she recognizes the wrappings, and these have helped swell the volume of the pile under the branches. On a side table sits a crèche, and its familiar Mary and Joseph and baby Jesus, and all the kings and shepherds and angels and animals, are older, a little chipped, enough different from the crèche set up on the mantle of the Little House to merit yearly reexamination.

Out in the brightly lit dining room there is noise and laughter and much going to and fro from the kitchen. All the hired men are slicked up. Some of them are helping, others are in their sitting room, which opens out from the dining room, basking in watching all the activity. The radio is playing carols. When Jackie isn't making her trips to the sanctuary of the Christmas tree room, she's racing around with her sisters and brother, dodging into the kitchen to snatch snippets of the coming feast, and then being given jobs to keep out of mischief, such as carrying to the table the milk pitchers or bowls of cranberry-orange relish. The waiting for dinner is almost unbearable. It isn't helped any by the huge wooden chopping bowl sitting on its own little table, mounded up with popcorn balls wrapped in wax paper, a treat Grama makes only at Christmas. The smaller bowl of sugared doughnut holes is also a Christmas treat, but sometimes, when Grama is making doughnuts during the year, Jackie is allowed to drop some of the centers into the hot fat, so doughnut holes are not quite so special as popcorn balls. Popcorn balls mean Christmas.

But finally, the meal is ready, the family from town has arrived, and all are seated at the candlelit table with its snowy tablecloth barely visible underneath the best china and silverware, the bowls and plates and pitchers and platters. Grampa lowers his head and gives a long, grateful, and joyous Christmas grace. Then there is so much food that the sideboard is used as a buffet, and everyone has to stand and go past to load up his or her plate with creamed chicken on biscuits, and all the fixings. Christmas Eve is always creamed chicken on biscuits. And there are often so many guests that a few card tables have to be set up in the entryway into the living room, and these too have festive cloths and candles.

The grownups don't hasten their eating, so there's no point in the children hurrying, either, for they'll have to stay at their seats right through to the mince pie with whipped cream and the coffee for the adults. Jackie, all her life, never does learn to eat quickly—even non-holiday meals on the farm are always a ceremony, deliberate, a time to start, a time to stop, with much conversation and sharing in between. Tonight, there's plenty of time to see who can construct the best mashed-potato pie. Half the hot mashed potato is patted down into a circle, and this is covered with thick shavings of butter all over, for the filling. It is then salted, peppered, and the other half of the potato spread on top for the upper crust. The trick is to get the cold butter on quickly and evenly and then the hot top, so that the butter doesn't melt too soon and mess up the process. The edges must also be rapidly crimped so that the filling doesn't run out onto the plate. It's permissible to prick a little pattern onto the top, like Grama does; and then, of course, once you slice your pie in six and start to eat it, the filling goes all over anyway, as it does in any respectable apple or cherry or rhubarb pie. It's only the pumpkins and minces and custards that don't ooze.

But finally, the dinner is over, and then the dishes have to be cleared, and everything tidied before the next phase of the evening. But with so many hands, the cleanup doesn't take long. Jackie's favorite job — if any job at such a time can be a favorite — is to crumb the table, with the crumbing pan made of amber horn, flat with curved sides and with a handle, like a medium-sized dustpan, and then the crumber itself, also horn, shaped like the larger pan in miniature. You have to get the angle just right, to collect the crumbs and guide them into the larger pan. If you go at the job too vigorously the crumbs behave like tiddlywinks and hop all over the place, even onto the floor. And if you shepherd them all to the edge of the table, then you have to hold the large pan just so under the wide, table-clothed lip, to be sure all the crumbs fall in. It takes care and practice to be a good crumber. At the end of the job, you empty the crumbs into the bucket for the chickens, nest the small pan inside the larger one, and return them to their spot in the buffet drawer. You never wash them.

The presents are not next. The program is. This varies from year to year, but it always begins with Grampa reading aloud the Christmas story from St. Luke: "And it came to pass in those days, that there went out a decree from Caesar Augustus, that all the world should be taxed." Jackie knows it almost by heart.

Other things follow. One year Joan and Patsy sing a duet of all three verses of "Fairest Lord Jesus," while Mother accompanies them on the piano. Joan sings the melody and Patsy sings a high sweet descant that amazes Jackie: she herself will never be able to sing that high or sweet. One year she and Joan and Patsy are dressed up in crowns and bathrobes, and they each take a solo verse of "We Three Kings," with everyone joining in on the chorus. Joan and Patsy sometimes play their violins. One year Hazel, who teaches vocal music at Lincoln Junior High School, sings and plays the story of "The Selfish Giant." Grama reads a poem she's written, called "Wrapping Paper."

Another year the hired men put on a shadow pantomime behind a sheet pinned over the door of the office, on the far side of the living room from the tree. The audience sits in the dark room and the lights are bright in the office; there's even a spotlight. A shadow figure climbs on a table before the door and stretches out. A shadow doctor clamps a tit cup over the patient's nose; shadow attendants pin down his flailing limbs until he goes under and flops limp. The attendants hand the doctor his tools for the operation: a large knife, a saw, a hammer, a plumber's wrench, a horse hypodermic, a nose leader. The shadow doctor uses each tool with vigor, and there's much laughter from the audience. Finally the doctor takes a posthole digger, lowers it into his patient and hauls out a great mass of guts, which the viewers gleefully recognize as spaghetti. The doctor inspects the cavity, reaches in, and brings out and out and out what's apparently been the trouble—a manure fork. The crowd claps and cheers. The doctor replaces the spaghetti and mashes it down well with a hoe. Then using a long gunny sack needle and twine, one of the attendants elaborately sews the patient back up, the tit cup is removed, the patient sits up and makes the I'VE WON boxing sign, and all the shadows take bows amidst thunderous applause. The hired men, flushed with success, emerge from behind their sheet. And then Mother, or Hazel, plays Christmas carols while everybody sings. Grampa can't hear any of the festivities, but he's the one who enjoys them most of all.

And finally, finally, come the presents! Sometimes Grampa plays Santa Claus, sometimes the children take turns distributing. It's always hard to know what to get the grownups, especially Grama and the elderly aunts. Handkerchiefs are such dull gifts, yet everyone can use another handkerchief, Mother assures. Jackie likes the year Mother suggests little Christmas corsages to pin on coat lapels: these are bright and have bells and ribbon and pine cones, and cost only thirty-five cents each at Woolworth's. Grampa is easier. One year Joan gets him a red clay head in a dish; above the head's saucy smile and upturned nose and arched eyebrows his scalp is scored with parallel ridges; you put water in the dish and grass seed in the ridges and the man grows green hair. One year Jackie and Craig get Grampa a present they can't wrap, but have to carry in from where it's been hidden in the office—a goldfish bowl and two goldfish: a gold one with a streamy tail and a black one with bulgy eyes. Grampa laughs so hard at the bulgy-eyed fish that his own eyes disappear.

As for Jackie's presents—there are the mittens Grama knits, connected by a long crocheted string that goes through her coat sleeves, or a pair of blue knee-high knit stockings, beautiful, but which she knows from experience will fall down around her ankles when she runs. There are games and puzzles from the aunts and Hazel and Effie, or something for the whole family. Daddy gets ties and gloves and fishing lures; Mother gets candy and note paper and scarves. One Christmas when Craig is small he receives a knitted doll, its clothes part of the knitting—orange top, black pants, orange and black striped socks. It's a long slim boy doll, knit by Aunt Ria in Appleton, and named by Craig, oddly enough, "Jackie-doll." Over many years Jackie-doll is loved to shreds. One Christmas Grampa gives Grama a large set of expensive kitchen knives, and Grama is offended. The next year he knows better, and she receives a jeweled brooch. The floor is always littered with bright paper, and Grama tells at least three times every year how when she was a little girl she got only half an orange for Christmas.

The year Jackie remembers most vividly is the one when, at the end of the gift exchange, Grampa makes them get into their snowsuits and boots and mittens and follow him outside. He won't say for what; he is merry and mysterious. They form a line and Grampa leads them through the snow. Jackie follows behind Patsy. She feels cold and cross. She wants to be back in the Big House, playing with the toys she's received, claiming another popcorn ball. The moon is so bright that they don't need any flashlights. They go this way and that, out into the Big House yard, then behind, past the woodpile and henhouse, then between the barn and Big House, out toward the lane leading to the crick and then back again to the granary and the corn crib. Jackie gets colder and crosser. Where is Grampa taking them? She finds his suppressed mirth annoying. They round the milkhouse, go past the circle of lilac bushes, and are at the Little House. Grampa leads them into the back yard and stops.

There is a sudden intake of breath from all of them. Glimmering in the moonlight is a playhouse! It's large and white, with dark shutters running the length of both sides. Grampa opens the door, and they crowd through. He strikes a match and lights a candle that is waiting on a small table. The inside flickers to life, throwing their shadows against the white painted walls. Long screened windows are on either side. Two green benches flank the walls.

It's a perfectly wonderful building! Grampa is laughing silently and looking at their faces. Jackie is ashamed that she's been feeling so contrary. She rushes to him and hugs him; Grampa is smothered in a pileup of hugs.

The playhouse is a present from Grampa and Grama, Mother and Daddy. It gets constant use—as a playhouse, a clubhouse, an art gallery, a store, a summer camp, a sleep-out spot, a ticket booth, a museum, a jail. When the family moves up Colley Road to Chez Nous, it stands at the foot of the lane; and on winter days, the four huddle inside for warmth while waiting for the school cab. Then it disappears, and the four think it's stolen; after some years it surfaces on the dairy as a hutch-house for rabbits. Nobody tells them who took it or where it's been. It leads a long and useful life.

But on the night of its arrival, they can only sense its potential. Grampa blows out the candle, and they return to the Big House by the direct route. There, the grownups are waiting to hear how they like it and to tell them how the house had to be secretly delivered and put in place while the Big House party was going on. Daddy had even slipped out to be sure it was really there and to put in the candle, before Grampa started the trek.

And then Christmas Eve, like every Christmas Eve at the Big House, is finally over. Thanks and hugs are exchanged, and the family walks home on the shoveled sidewalk under the bright stars to the Little House, carrying the wicker laundry basket full of the presents they've received, and it's time to hang up stockings, put out the milk and cookies, and go to bed to wait for Santa Claus.

34 ❧ HELEN BURNETTE

Helen Burnette comes to Beloit when she's six years old. That is around 1907. Her mother is a widow with six children; her husband died three months before Helen was born. Helen first meets Grampa and Grama in church. She peers around her mother at a woman down the pew.

"What's she doing?" Helen keeps whispering. "Look, what's she doing?"

"Hush, hush," says her mother.

It turns out to be Grama, spelling out the sermon to Grampa on her fingers. After the service Mrs. Burnette apologizes to them for Helen's stares. Grampa smiles with his eyes, and shows Helen his ear trumpet.

"If you shout loud, I can hear through this," he tells her, "but we mustn't shout that loud in church."

From her youngest years, Helen is a favorite with Grama and Grampa. At one point Grama is Helen's Sunday School teacher. Grama is an earnest teacher, with well-prepared lessons. She knows that what she's teaching will affect her students' lives and mustn't be treated lightly. She won't put up with any shenanigans from her pupils, including Ronald and Trever. The class sometimes visits the farm. They walk out, have doughnuts and milk, play "Run, Sheep, Run." Then they all get a lift back in a wagon.

Sometimes Helen and her next older sister, Evelyn, come out for Sunday dinner. Grama thinks it is good for her sons to have girls around, especially such splendid girls as the Burnettes. When Esther arrives from the orphanage to live on the farm, Grama likes to have Helen visit. She tells Helen that she's Esther's older sister, and such a good influence.

Ronald sometimes escorts Helen when he is home from Northwestern. Once, on an outing, he drives the car onto glaze ice, slams on the brakes, and laughs as it spins around and around. Helen is not quite so amused.

Helen loves Grampa and Grama. For her, Grampa is the father she never had. She especially loves them both for encouraging her in her goal to go to college. She has worked several years after high school and saved her money, but she can't save much for she has to help with her family's expenses. She talks often with Grampa and Grama about how she can manage; she has only $25. This is a large sum, but not enough, for tuition is $75. In December 1923, after the Christmas program at church, Grampa hands her a small envelope. On the outside it says, "For our beloved Helen, for college." Inside is a check for $75. She's overwhelmed, especially since she knows what a sacrifice it is for Grampa and Grama to give her this. She repays some later, for she earns scholarships, but the gift makes possible her continued enrollment.

She writes to Ronald, who is now working in France:

Santa Claus was very good to me. Never was quite so happy in all my life. Listen closely and I'll tell you the glad news: HB is going to start in Beloit College January 4th! By the time you get this letter I'll be buried in books. Going to do part time work at the office and carry thirteen hours. I'll have a 7:40 every morning and be through at 10:40. I expect to work terribly hard but I know it will be worth every bit of energy I have. Seems all like a dream and everyone is helping make it so easy for me. I had a long talk with your father and mother one day and they were so determined and I wanted to go so very badly. I began to think how stupid I was. By careful planning and by working at the office I hope to be able to make it and still keep the money I have invested to use next year. Wonder if it is all I've dreamed of? I'm sure I'm going to get a lot out of it.

She doesn't mention his parents' generosity. Perhaps she is tactfully sparing his feelings, for she's been close enough to the family to know how frustrated Wesson and Eunice have been at Ronald's frittering away valuable time at Northwestern.

She also writes ordinary bits, if hair-pulling bouts between a 22- and 19-year-old can be considered ordinary:

I was out to the farm for supper tonight. Had some letters to write for your father. Trever and I made use of our spare time pulling hair. He delights in it and it bothers me not a whit for my hair is the least of my troubles now that I'm one of the "common herd" as Fran says. Esther went to a party tonight with William Duggan, a high school senior, and Trever took Bennie von Oven to a dance at Rockton. T.C. has improved a lot although I've always thought he couldn't quite be beaten. He's a dear and you'll enjoy him so much when you're together again. Tickles me to hear him say "We Delta

Upsilons." Seems to swell up all over when he says it.

Grama yearns for Ronald to marry Helen, and many times in letters to her college son she gives her candidate enthusiastic press: "We had supper at Burnettes. Helen got the supper alone and everything was so nice and tasty and dainty. She is a little queen wherever she is." "Helen was overjoyed at what you sent for her birthday. I gave her a nice cream cake and Trev gave her a record. Dad said he didn't know who was most in love with Helen — you, Trev, or me. I said I had nothing to do

Helen Burnette.

with your affairs in that line; Helen and I were always in love." And to Ronald in France:

> Helen is very busy in college and so happy her eyes sparkle. I am so glad she can go but it is sheer will power and faith that makes her go. She has a position with Dean Collie for the same pay she got at school and not so hard work nor so long hours. Everything seems to come her way and I am so glad. If any girl deserves those things it is Helen. She is an ideal girl and woman. She was out here to dinner last Sunday. She helps at home, pays rent as she did before. Anybody who works as she does deserves the best. She is so happy to be Delta Gamma and the girls are all crazy about her.

Helen also fulfills Grama's prediction that she will be a big sister to Esther. Esther writes a long letter to Ronald and Vera in France, congratulating them on their marriage, and in the way of news, besides parties, wild rides in jalopies with no windshields or floorboards, and visiting Trever at his fraternity house at Madison, she says, "After church I went home with Helen Burnette. We talked about everything from Adam to the present day, and enjoyed ourselves immensely while we lazily sat on the back steps. I then attended chapel with her in the afternoon. President Maurer gave a wonderful address to the college students."

Helen and Ronald's relationship is always brotherly-sisterly. Helen never

Helen Burnette on an outing.

indicates to Grama whether she shares Grama's dreams, although there is a faint hint of it in her letter to France where she tells Ronald of going to college: "Looks as though you're well provided for so far as your spare time is concerned. Three is a safe number, and I'm glad of it. Awfully hate to have you 'intrigued by the mystery of people' and fall in love, too. Think how stupid it would be if we all were readable—wouldn't be interesting and we couldn't have the fun of being a puzzle." She writes of Eunice being in good health and spirits, of Wesson being tired that night, and that, "with the exception of my own they're the best Mother and Dad in all the world, but I guess I don't have to tell you that. You know."

Ronald, for his part, writing from France general thoughts about love—for he has indeed fallen in love, although he hasn't revealed this to his parents yet—says to his mother, as if it is a completely new thought to him, and it probably is, "Say, you never entertained any ideas about Helen and me, did you?"

Ronald marries Vera and they honeymoon on the continent before returning to the states. Later, during the Depression, Helen marries a collegemate, Ben Wadsworth. They have a small wedding in Beloit, at the home of one of Helen's sisters, and W.J. Dougan is the minister. He embarrasses the groom by saying he'll accept for payment what his bride is worth to him. He then refuses payment, for Helen is like a daughter, but he compounds the confusion by saying, "What? Is she worth nothing to you?" Finally the joke is cleared up and everyone laughs, Grampa most of all. The couple lives in Appleton. W.J. baptizes their first child.

Many years later, Helen Burnette Wadsworth shows Ronald and Jackie the little envelope that Grampa gave her that day in church, the one saying, "For our beloved Helen."

"I've treasured it all my life," Helen says.

35 ◄ PAT AND RALPH ANDERSON

The work in the Big House becomes too much for Grama. In 1945 she and Grampa retire and move to town. Grama's niece, Effie, moves with them. Effie, aging too, has lived and worked at the Big House many years. She goes along to help at the house in town. Now who to live at the Big House and be in charge of the hired men?

The first is LaBerta Ullius, wife of Russ, the farm manager. When the Ulliuses leave, Erv and Olive Fonda take over. Erv is the farm mechanic.

In 1949, Vera at Chez Nous advertises for help, and a woman recently widowed answers the ad. Pat Gerke has three young children. She's warmhearted, likable, capable, comfortably plump. She helps with Pat Dougan's wedding, shortly after Grampa's death that spring.

Although Olive Fonda enjoys the sociability of the Big House, she doesn't like all the cooking and cleaning; she especially doesn't like the grueling schedule. She and Erv want to move. A year after Pat Gerke has been at Chez Nous Daddy says to her, "Pat, how'd you like to tend the Big House?"

Pat jumps at the offer. She's liked working with Mother, but she's a single woman raising children. She has to get up early, get them ready for school, go back and forth. Sometimes they're sick and she has to stay home. This way, they can be on the farm with her—her work will also be her home. And she knows the Dougan farm is a healthy place to raise children.

She, her daughter, and two sons move into the Big House. The kids are already familiar with the place. They can run free, help with the chores, have their own chores. Pat raises chickens for the farm, and the children feed them and gather the eggs. She tends the farm garden, and the children pick peas and strawberries. Pat is a fine cook, a cheerful and caring friend, interested in each man, especially the ones who come from foreign lands, whom she gets to tell about their families and lives. She keeps all their names in a book. The men living at the Big House are well content.

The first few nights she's there she has trouble sleeping. She can hear the milk cans clanging before dawn, the rooster crowing, other unfamiliar sounds. But after a few nights she's so tired that nothing bothers her. The place, she soon discovers, is Grand Central Station. When some of the younger men are coming in at three in the morning from Delavan's Lake Lawn, or Waverly Beach, some of the older ones are on their way out to milk.

Pat cooks three meals a day, sometimes for eight, or twelve, or fourteen people, depending on who's there—the milk tester two days a month, Doctor Knilans, the Ag School people, students from the university to study the corn yield test patches. Grampa, at noon. Sunday is her night off. Then she leaves out cold meat and sandwiches. Grama daily telephones, to see how everybody is and how the work is going. She's particularly concerned that Ron will get a hot meal, when Vera's out of town.

In 1952 Ralph Anderson hears that Ron Dougan needs help. He applies and is hired. On his first day the outside silo is being filled. He has to climb out the top and slide down the rounded slope of the cement roof till his feet hit the outside ladder. He's afraid of heights, and has never been so scared in his life. The next day he goes to work in the milkhouse, and that's much better. He stays there, his rubber boots firmly on the ground. He rooms and boards at the Big House.

"Ralph," says Daddy a number of years later, "how long did it take you to realize Pat was something special?"

"The day I went for the job!" says Ralph. "I saw her dressed up ready to go to town; she had that old Nash parked outside. I eyed her up pretty good then!"

"I wasn't thinking of remarrying," Pat says. "On account of the children. I had a funny feeling about stepfathers, a fear of them. But Ralph was living right in the house, being thoughtful and fun, and he so gradually became my friend, and so like a father to the kids, that there was never any problem."

"I impressed her once that first year," Ralph says. "They were killing chickens down at the garage, had tables set up, doing a pretty slow job of it. The next time they wanted to clean some hens I said I'd do it. I'd had some experience; my dad used to do that stuff. I got a five gallon pan of scalding water from the milkhouse, cut the throat of five chickens, took their feathers off, got those five in to Pat, got more scalding water, did five more—we had fifty done and ready for the locker in a couple of hours. She could hardly keep up with me, getting the innards out!"

The courtship spans three years, and the difficulty is with the church. Pat is Roman Catholic; Ralph has been divorced. They try to get permission from the diocese to be married in the church. Their file of appeal gets fatter and fatter, but the church can't find sufficient reason to consider Ralph's previous marriage dissolved. They finally marry in a civil service. Pat's marriage is never considered legal by the church, nor is she allowed to take the sacraments. Her brother is a priest, Father Furong, who visits frequently at the dairy. He approves. "If anyone's going to make it to heaven," he tells Ron, "Pat will!"

The marriage is a happy one. Ralph introduces rabbits. The hutches overflow, rabbit meat becomes a farm staple, and Pat's boys learn rabbit care. Ralph and Pat get a couple of ponies at the Elkhorn fair, and while the Gerke children are now too big to ride them, Ralph gives pony rides to the school children who visit spring and fall.

Ralph keeps a watchful eye on the whole place. When Jackie visits, he confides to her various farm shenanigans he fears her father either hasn't noticed, or is turning a blind eye to. "He ought to know, even if he doesn't want to know," Ralph insists. "He's too softhearted; he doesn't want to fire anybody."

"Your dad's a trusting soul," Pat agrees. "I go to the locker at Clinton where our butchering is frozen, and he tosses me a bunch of keys and says, 'These are for the locker.' I had them in the buffet drawer for six months, maybe even a year, using them for the locker, and he came in one day and said, 'Where are the keys, Pat? I have to get into my safe deposit box!' I wondered what else I'd had the keys to, all that time!"

Besides the adventures of everyday living, Pat has various unusual adventures on the farm. A recurring one is when the fire alarm goes off, often in the middle of the night. Few farms boast fire stations, but the Town of Turtle has located its station at the end of the new garage. Whenever there's a fire, the alarm clangs, the telephone tree—later, the CB radio—alerts everyone, and volunteer firemen from all over the township come streaming in, their special car-top lights flashing round and round. Then the two fire engines scream out the drive to wherever the emergency is, with the firemen clinging to the handholds, still struggling into their slicker sleeves. Some of the volunteers are farmhands who live in the Big House. If a fire comes during milking, someone not a fireman has to hurry down to continue the job.

Sometimes people show up at night. A girl stumbles in from I-90, soaking wet, her clothes in shreds. She's in shock from an accident on the throughway, but can't remember she's been in one. She's crawled through the barbed wire and followed the yard light. Pat calls an ambulance. The girl won't let anyone touch her; she lies on the cement in the back washroom and keeps calling for her boyfriend. The ambulance men come, put boards under her and carry her away. The paper next day reports the two in the wreck are in stable condition in the hospital, and Pat and Ralph are relieved.

Another night, a young girl comes crying to the door. She has no money and doesn't know which direction town is. She'd been out riding with her boyfriend. He wanted to stop and she didn't. He ordered her out of the car and drove off. Ralph takes her home, to a room on Wisconsin Avenue. "She didn't say a word all the way," says Ralph. "She was afraid even of me! But I said one thing to her—get a new boyfriend!"

"And one Saturday night," says Pat, "a tipsy woman pushed open our door; she'd come all the way from the Gun Club. We learned later she'd gone into the washroom and never come back to her party. She'd lost her high heels in a snowbank and her feet were bright red. We called the police and they said, 'Oh yes, her husband's been looking for her,' and came and got her. Her husband arrived just after she'd left."

There's one person Pat wishes had seen their yard lights. An elderly man suffering from dementia wanders away from his home on the edge of town. He's confused, and follows the road as far as the underpass of I-90 beyond the dairy before his strength gives out. He's found the next morning, dead from exposure.

And, of course, there's the adventure of the Kozelka wedding, and Pat's rings disappearing, and Louie Kozelka's flushing seed corn down the toilet in his apartment and plugging up all the plumbing in the Big House.

"When I came here to the farm," Ralph says, "I had a little sack of clothes and no money at all. Now, we're in pretty good shape. I'll be working Saturdays, Sundays, all these city slickers I know are out having a good time, they think I'm nuts. They're making quite a lot an hour. But we've been getting house and rent and food and electricity—we're making more money than they are. And it's a good life. They can't see it that way."

Pat says, "I work hard and I work well, I'm not ashamed of it. My aim has always been to get my children old enough that they can be independent, get decent jobs."

"We're chief cook and bottle washer around here," Ralph grins. "She's cook in the Big House, I wash the bottles in the milkhouse. That's the way to have a marriage."

"I sure wish I knew how many cows and pigs I've cooked, so far. Half a herd, I bet!" Pat says.

36 ❧ ESTHER, THE REST
OF THE STORY

On December 27, 1923, when Ronald is half through his year in France, he receives family photos sent for Christmas. He comments with warmth on the portraits of his parents and brother, then writes:

> But Esther! What has the girl been doing? She has always been attractive, but here she is doubly delightful. I want to get home so I can show her off. For a minute I thought Trever was sending me a picture of a beauty winner at Madison.

But soon he is responding to an agitated letter from his mother. A hired hand has made advances to Esther:

> Your letter made me wish I were proficient in profanity. I've just written to Trev airing my feelings and imagine I'll still be angry enough when I get home to give O.J. a hot half hour. I'm big enough to disfigure him. Will write to Esther. I'm all for the kid. She is as surely my sister as if she got her pug nose from Dad.

His letter to Trever is even more vehement:

> Of all the low-down hounds I've ever heard of! The longer I live the less confidence I have in the average human. That's not quite true, because I have known more of the decent sort than the rotters. Just the same, I've run across some pant-wearing sons of bitches that would turn the stomach of a worm. But about O.J. That bastard makes me want to air every profanity I've ever heard. Don't know what you have done, but if I should hear you had battered in his face I'd be all for you. I imagine I'll stay sore enough so that when I see him I'll give him a nasty half hour. Look out for the police, but there are worse things than a night in jail. Hit him for me if you can.

Whatever may be said to the contrary there is a lot of satisfaction in fists.

Trever is now starting his second semester at the university. In a letter to his parents on February 23 he writes:

> I'm beginning to agree with you, Dad, that Esther is fairly wise for her age. I was talking to Ernest and he said, "It surely is queer the way Esther can hoodwink her parents." I said she wasn't getting by with much that you and mother didn't know. Then I asked him where he got his information. He said he wasn't on the place a day before he heard that she was "fast" and that she knew how to "spoof" her folks. She seemed to be the subject of conversation around the place. He said that she let Wally "pet" her and that she wasn't at choir practice sometimes when she was supposed to be there. Mother, please don't say anything to her about the source of this information. You probably know as much as I've told you, but she will bear watching a little closer I think. As you say, if we can get her through this critical period she will grow to be an extraordinary woman. See how impressions of her are acquired, though. I've often wondered if she thinks of Ron and me as brothers. When she kissed me good bye it didn't seem at all like a little sister's peck ought to be. As I've often said, she would be better off in a good girls' school. From all the girls I've met, I think those that go away to school are the best behaved, best ap-pearing, and most reserved. I think your opinion of the boarding school type is not characteristic of the majority, judging from those I've met. At any rate she would be better off than where she is: in a high school where she has no decent companions, dirty little evil minded boys and silly, boy crazy girls, and at home where she is eyed by a bunch of evil minded no-accounts.

Wesson takes some note of Trever's warning, and when he finds a suffi-cient work-related reason, lets Wally go. He and Eunice do not alter Esther's schooling, however. W.J. writes Trever, a month or two later:

> We realize that our perplexing kids are emerging into dependable and strong manhood and will take their places in the world's work, help lift its burdens and share its joys. You have me approaching old age too fast. I am not nearly sixty. I am only fifty six and I do not expect to be any more aged in four years. Not with my boys and girl to help with the lift. Yes, the girl. Esther is a very sweet happy little girl these days. Much better since "W" left. We do hope to tide her over these critical years and save her for usefulness and her happiness.

Ronald has become engaged to an American girl in France, and then, to everyone's astonishment and some consternation, married. His and Vera's letters of their wedding precede them home. Esther rushes to relate the event to Eloise, who is slowly recovering from a winter of pneumonia and scarlet fever. "And a dog and a cat slept on Vera's wedding gown, where it was laid out on a bed the night before, and a soiled patch had to be cut out, but from a place it didn't really show; and Vera wrote, 'There'll be no dogs and cats underfoot in our house for a while!' That's what she said!"

She also dashes off a newsy letter to the newlyweds:

> Dear Brother and Sister, Well, now as all young sisters, I will give my opinion on this marriage business. I, as the rest, was very much surprised to hear about it but gradually became used to it. I know that I will just love Vera, I do already—and it will be ever so nice to have an older sister to confide in. But now, Ron, how about those little dates we were going to have when you came back? I was looking forward to them eagerly. But perhaps it will be much more pleasant to have Vera enjoy them.

She tells of visits to Madison to see Trever at the "frat" house, that she is still taking piano lessons, is anxious to take elocution and vocal lessons, and will be in a recital soon. "I am going to have a stunning dress made of orange silk and lace—maybe cream lace—Mother and I are going to plan and make the dress." She goes on to talk, cheerfully enough, about work, the early hours that had made Eloise reluctant to stay overnight with Esther: "Muddy and I did a good sized wash this morning—you see Muddy hasn't a maid now and I get up at 5:30 or 6:00 and do quite a little to help out. We get along very nicely doing the work alone." She tells of good times: "My friend and two of our boyfriends met me after choir practice and brought us home—you ought to see the little old car we had—it's an old Ford all written up with white paint, has no windshield or bottom to the front seat—rather a breezy car—every time we stop we have to pump up a tire and every time we start we have to push the car a couple of blocks—Oh! it's great fun and we enjoy it oodles. Last Tuesday night the kids came out and we made popcorn balls and had a royal good time." She ends her letter, "Well my dears, I can hardly wait for the time to come when I can see you and love Vera more—I hope we receive your wedding cake soon. Lovingly, Esther."

The newlyweds arrive in Beloit in late summer, and Vera meets the whole family. Esther shows Vera her room, and Vera notices the doll sitting on a small chair beside the dresser. "What is her name?" Vera asks, and Esther replies that it's Agnes.

During Esther's sophomore and junior years, Vera pays attention to her young sister-in-law. She assumes her piano lessons. She teaches her singing and accompanies her as Esther sings in a clear, sweet soprano. She helps with parties for her friends, a birthday celebration, a treasure hunt. They put on little entertainments in the parlor of the Big House where Esther sings and recites. Esther helps with baby Joan. Vera convinces her mother-in-law to buy Esther a white chiffon dress, on sale, just her size. Esther is thrilled. She sings in it at one of the programs and it gets smudged. When Eunice washes it, it shrinks. Vera finds Esther in her bedroom, holding the ruined frock and crying. It's the first really attractive dress she's ever had, the orange silk recital dress notwithstanding.

Esther has a number of high school boyfriends, and connections with college men. Eunice mentions to Trever, now a sophomore at the university, "Esther has just gone out with Harold Risley; he was in school with you. I don't know him, but the Burnettes say he is a nice boy. So many boys wanting to take her out—I don't know what I am to do as she grows older."

After a snowstorm several college men come to take her to a school event but can't get past the drifted railroad tracks at Marstons. They leave the car on the far side of the tracks and mush to the farm, fetch Esther, wade back on the path they've made, and thence to town. Later Eunice says to Lura Marston, in Eloise's hearing, "Well, you can certainly say one thing for Esther, she's popular with the boys. It's too bad Eloise isn't." Lura is furious. But Eloise knows that Esther has something to sell.

It's at this point that Esther's thievery finally becomes apparent. Ronald has kept a coin collection since boyhood. When the money came in from the routes, he would go through the change and trade common pennies for the rare 1909 Lincoln penny with VDB on the bottom, which had been discontinued shortly after its minting. He had fifty or sixty such pennies. He also had Liberty Head nickels, and a number of coins, both foreign and domestic, given him by people knowing his interest. At some point, when he goes to add some unusual French coins to his collection, he finds it's been stripped of everything that will pass for money. And Vera's lovely French underthings, bought in Paris from her own small salary for her trousseau, gradually vanish from her dresser drawers.

When Esther is asked about these losses she knows nothing. But Wesson moves the cashbox from his desk to the apartment of Lester and Mildred

Stam, over the milkhouse, and the route men must now go up there to check in their money.

The family isn't aware of high school whispers, but Eloise is. In Esther's sophomore year, Eloise reports again to Esther the rumors that she is pregnant. Esther laughs, tosses her head, and retorts, "I don't care what anyone says!"

By that spring, matters have so escalated that Wesson feels constrained to write to Esther's case worker, Mrs. Grube, at the Sparta orphanage:

Dear Madam,

I am writing in regard to Esther. There is no need for immediate attention, but I feel you should be kept in close knowledge of her attitude and movements. We are anxious that she develop to be the beautiful and useful woman she is capable of being, if we only can direct her aright.

The great trouble is her subtle deceitfulness, lying, and secretiveness. She tells us nothing except as we face her with facts and she must confess. Then she goes no farther than she has to. She justifies herself in this because she is afraid to tell us. This is all nonsense, as we have never punished her, and are entirely in sympathy with the young. When she is caught stealing and lying, we do not condone it or tell her it is all right, as she has an idea other parents do. We try to show the wrong of it and fix some penalty which will enforce the lesson. For example, last December Mrs. Dougan and I had to go away on a lecturing trip. We were gone three days. We placed Esther on her honor. Mrs. Dougan told her not to have any company, and not to go out, but to help in the home, study, and attend to her school work. Esther was wanting a new coat. Mrs. Dougan said if she lived right while we were away, she could have one, if not, she must wear the old one all winter. When we came home she told us she had gone to a movie with a boy from town. We withheld the coat. It is in this way we have tried to control and teach her.

It seems she is growing worse in her deceit than when she was younger. She is now justifying herself. The recent developments alarm us. Esther is bright and forward enough to carry her plans to serious consequences. She has taken to forging Mrs. Dougan's name to excuses for absences and requests for excuses from school. She has purchased at a store and had the bill charged to Mrs. Dougan. If Esther can carry this through now, what will she do when she goes into college and wants fur coats and diamonds?

This shoe dealer remarked, "The trouble is, your daughter makes a wonderful impression, and could be trusted anywhere."

Yesterday morning the school secretary telephoned to find out if we knew Esther had been out of school all the day before. It was a surprise to us. We started to investigate, both myself and Mrs. Dougan giving our entire day and evening trying to unravel the facts. After three hours of questioning of Esther, I had gathered only partial accounts of her absences and forged excuses, and where she went, and with whom. In the afternoon we went to the principal and found Esther had not told us one half of her absences. She had repeatedly lied to the secretary, putting in forged requests to be excused and explaining there was something going on at the church and her mother wanted her to help, or that her mother wanted her excused to drive the auto.

Then she has gone to shows or made dates. She asked, a little time ago, to stay overnight with one of the girls because the English teacher wanted the class to read a certain book in groups of two or three. Mrs. Dougan agreed, on Esther's promising that they would study and not go anywhere or have any boys in. Esther agreed to the conditions in a delightful sweet mode. She at once went to the Bank and conferred with a boy (one of the young clerks who is sweet on her), and they arranged a date. She never studied a minute that night and kept this from us until last night when Mrs. Dougan demanded of her to tell just how much she had been with this young man unbeknownst to us. She told of this and other times. We think she has told all in this respect. (This boy is of a good family and is all right so far as we know, but that does not lessen the danger of a young girl planning and making her own dates unbeknown to her elders.)

We have talked kindly to Esther, showed her the danger, and held up to her the possibilities of becoming a good, well educated, and accomplished woman. She seems to want to start anew and do better. We will give her another chance. This is our plan for the present:

1st. We have instructed the principal to expect her in school every minute during school hours; to mail her report card (she has signed and returned her own card once at least); and not to accept any oral or written excuses.

2nd. She is not to go to any show of any kind for at least six months, unless we take her to some we deem educational.

3rd. She is not to make any "dates."

4th. She must go and come from school in the regular bus. (Three or four boys and girls have been piling into a two passenger Ford, or one or two boys bring her home. We have never liked it. Now it must stop.)

Should you deem any of these rules too severe or unnecessary, or should you want to suggest any others, we will be glad to confer with you.

I have told Esther that if in a single incident she violates these rules, I will at once report the matter to you, and abide by your decision.

We will surely have to make some other arrangement for Esther's schooling before Fall, unless she mends decidedly. Opportunities for deceit are too great in the High School. Some boarding school might be better. We will talk this over when we see you, and after Esther has had a chance to make good.

Sincerely yours,

W.J. Dougan

The incidents and facts as reported in this letter are true and correct.

Only four days after this letter, Esther becomes ill. Eunice writes to Trever:

I must tell you about Esther. Thursday she felt kind of sick and had a sore throat. Friday she had to go to bed and have the doctor. Saturday she had a fever of 104¼ and felt terrible. I sent for the doctor again. He examined her and said it looked suspicious. Sunday he brought Dr. Field out and they both pronounced it scarlet fever. She was not very bad today but the doctor said she must go to the detention hospital. She will have to stay there four weeks. She doesn't seem to care. She has a young nurse, and if she is not bad she will soon be helping her, cooking and waiting on the other patients. We fumigated her room and sprayed lisol on all her bedding and clothing, and I guess nobody else will get it. It seems so queer that Esther is over there. Am so sorry.

Esther isn't treated at home on account of the danger of contagion to the milk. Not everyone with scarlet fever goes to the pest house. Eloise hadn't, the previous year, because she was too sick to be moved. But her father, who milked the Marston cows, had to stay out of the house for four weeks. He put his plate on the kitchen step and went away while Lura, or his mother, Mrs. Smith, put his meal on it. Then he returned and fetched it. He slept in the milkhouse and talked to his wife through an open window. Had he gone into the house, the milk couldn't have been sold.

But Esther is not too sick, and the Big House is filled with men who handle milk. It's sensible that she be the one to leave. And for Esther, living at the pest house is a reprieve. She's freed from school, freed from Big House labors, and freed from opprobrium. Her parents' rules are more oppressive than a house of detention.

She's released from the pest house the end of April. On May 25, Eddie

Pfaff, one of the men who lives in the Big House, returns late from town. He sees Floyd Peters, another boarder, crawl out of Esther's window, cross the roof, and climb into his own window. The next day he reports it to Daddy Dougan. Wesson and Eunice can scarcely believe it. They don't want to believe it.

"Wait and watch yourself," Eddie advises.

Esther's bedroom is a small one behind her father's. Its only entrance is through his room. That night, after Esther is in bed, Wesson makes his usual bedtime preparations but lies down in his clothes. Eunice's room is across the staircase, so Esther doesn't know that her mother, instead of going to bed, is outside watching her window from the bushes by the milkhouse.

The house settles down to sleep. After a bit, Eunice sees Floyd emerge from his window, cross the roof, and slide into Esther's window. She stands in the dark several moments, breathing hard and holding her arms tightly around herself; then she enters the house, goes rapidly to Wesson's room, and shakes his shoulder. The two fling open Esther's door and switch on the light. They surprise Esther and Floyd together in bed.

The pair can't deny the situation. But Esther cries, says that they have done nothing wrong, that they care for each other but they have no place to meet, no place to sit, and so Floyd has come to her bedroom. She looks straight in her father's face, with her large, tear-brimmed eyes, and swears their innocence.

Wesson, white faced, fires Floyd on the spot. "If Esther turns out to be pregnant," he roars, "she is a minor, and a ward of the state. I will see you go to the penitentiary!"

Floyd leaves but sneaks onto the farm the next day and beats up Eddie Pfaff. Wesson mails him his final paycheck.

Esther is not pregnant. Eunice reports to Lura and Mrs. Smith, "Esther just swore that they hadn't done a thing wrong, just cozied up in bed because it was chilly." Eunice believes Esther. Mrs. Smith, Lura, and Eloise do not, but they've learned long since not to say anything.

Esther spends a restricted summer and starts her junior year. She's been studying piano with Vera, but this fall she goes into town and takes lessons from Vinola Seaver. Each week she's given fifty cents to give her teacher. It's three months before Miss Seaver, a timid woman, screws up her courage and calls Eunice to ask when the Dougans are going to pay for Esther's lessons. That money and other money, Eloise knows, is going toward a Gruen watch that Esther is having held for her at a jeweler's. On the noon hour, Eloise sometimes goes with Esther while Esther pays on it. Its price is thirty-seven dollars and fifty cents, and she plans to give it to Floyd Peters for Christmas. His wages, in the six months he worked on the Dougan farm, were forty-five dollars a month; had he not had room and board he would have received sixty dollars. The watch represents more than two weeks' pay.

Later, when Wesson and Eunice learn about the watch, and W.J. asks the jeweler how he could have let a sixteen-year-old schoolgirl buy such an expensive item, he responds, "But she's a Dougan, and the Dougan name is as good as gold!"

Eloise has gone out several times with Paul Erickson, one of the young farm workers. He suggests they bring Esther along one evening. It will look like he's squiring both girls, but they'll pick up Floyd in town for a double date. Eloise is uncomfortable with the idea and makes an excuse not to go, so the plan falls through.

Christmas comes and goes. As the new year progresses, Esther, always lovely, becomes daily more radiant. Wesson puts his arm around her, pulls her to his knee and says, "Little lass, you're blossoming into a bonnie woman!" Eunice fumes. She tells Wess sharply not to say such things. "It'll go to her head, all you men fussing over her looks and praising her all the time!" she cries, and her hand jabs and jabs as she spells the reprimand out on her flashing fingers.

In March Esther is driving to town and stops at Eloise's. Out by the mailbox they chat. Eloise says, "At school they're saying again that you're pregnant." Esther doesn't laugh this time. She cries and says, "Why do they always say these terrible things about me?" She raises her large eyes to Eloise and asks point-blank, "You don't think I'm pregnant, do you?"

"No," says Eloise, and believes her.

By spring, Esther's social life has ceased. Her boyfriends, including Russ Baumann, the one she's told Eloise she is crazy about, have nothing to do with her. There are no more dates. A dentist's son, Eldon Freebach, had been trying to go out with her. She had thought him too juvenile. But now she's in need of fun and telephones him several times. Repeatedly, he refuses to come to the phone. His mother tells Eloise's mother, Lura, "I don't know what's the matter with him—he's had such a crush on Esther Dougan, and now he won't have a thing to do with her, and it's embarrassing. I know the Dougans must wonder what's wrong."

Esther turns seventeen in June. All spring and early summer, with no male diversion, Esther turns to Eloise for recreation. Eunice says to Eloise, "Esther's been more a friend to you this summer than she's been in a long time." She goes on to Lura, "She's been more of a daughter to me. She's been so pleased with everything I've sewed for her—before, she's always wanted everything so tight, and we'd fight about it. Now, she agrees with me, and thinks tight looks cheap, and she wants me to make her dresses loose."

In July Eloise goes with her parents to Camp Byron, a Methodist camp for all ages. Eloise waits on table in exchange for her meals in the big mess hall. There are dormitories, but there are also tiny cottages on the grounds, for rent or privately owned, where families can come and stay and participate in the preaching and programs, the meals, and the recreation. Eloise's grandparents have rented such a cottage, two sleeping rooms separated by a long curtain the width of the little building. Nellie Needham, Wesson's second cousin, owns a cottage. Wesson, Eunice, and Esther come up near the end of July for a brief visit. With Nellie and her sister there, too, the tiny cottage is crowded; Esther asks Eloise if she can stay with her. Eloise consents, and Esther runs back and tells her parents. She and Eloise attend that night's camp meeting in the large tabernacle but leave before the adults. Back at Eloise's cottage Esther says, "It's so lovely and moonlight out, let's not use the lamp." Eloise agrees. The girls undress and go to bed in the dark. In the morning, when Eloise awakens, Esther is already up and dressed. At one point during the day, Eloise puts her arm around her friend's waist and is puzzled to find Esther's body as rigid and hard as a marble statue. She doesn't know that Esther has wrapped herself with five yards of muslin.

Back in Beloit, in mid-August, Floyd Peters's mother comes to Lura. She tells her that Esther is pregnant and that the Dougans don't know. She knows, because Floyd told her before he left town.

"Daddy Dougan will have me in the penitentiary," he'd said. "Mom, you do the best you can." She asks Lura's advice.

"Talk to Esther," says Lura.

Mrs. Peters says she's telephoned several times to ask Esther to meet with her, but Esther pretends her caller is a salesperson. "No ... no ... no, we're not interested," Esther will say, and hang up.

Lura then advises her to go straight to Eunice.

From a friend who sells Realsilk hosiery door to door, Mrs. Peters borrows a suitcase of samples. She knocks on the Dougan door. Esther answers. "We don't want any," she states. But Eunice comes to the door and asks her in—Realsilk is a fine product. Esther stays in the room, behind her mother and outside her vision. She shakes and shakes her head and glares with her large eyes whenever Mrs. Peters pauses in her sales pitch. Quailed, Mrs. Peters takes Eunice's generous order and leaves without delivering her message.

She next goes to the Dougans' pastor, the Reverend Mr. Misdal at the Methodist Church. She tells him the story. Mr. Misdal comes out to the farm. He tells Wesson and Eunice about Mrs. Peters's visit. Esther is called in and, in the presence of her parents and minister, hears the minister repeat the story. She breaks down and cries. They call Dr. Thayer, and he comes out immediately. He takes Esther up to her room to examine her. When he comes back down, he confirms the allegation. He says Esther is over seven months pregnant.

The day after her parents learn of Esther's pregnancy, Wesson finds a letter on his desk in his bedroom, a large pencil scrawl on farm stationery:

My dearest Daddy —

I love you and know you care for me — and now I will tell you everything truthfully — since last night I have felt much better — to have you know the truth about Floyd — now in regard to anyone else — no one has ever had sexual relations with me but Floyd — all my school boyfriends have been just good pals and have always treated me very well —

I will confess though that once when I was going to kindergarten when we were living in Stoughton a larger boy followed me home and attacked me — I told my older sister and she used to have my brother wait for me at school or another sister so I wouldn't have to come home alone.

In regard to Walter Lake. He suggested to me, asking me to go for a walk in the garden etc., — but I refused — he paid little more attention to me. And O.J. — he never did suggest it with words — but he came to my room that night — he was leaning over my bed — I pushed him off — and told him to leave immediately or I would call you — he would say — but listen, I have something to tell you — I kept telling him to leave — he finally went over by the door — he said he was afraid you'd wake up — I told him — if you didn't I would awaken you anyway — and — after standing listening to whether you were asleep or not — after a while — he left my room, closed the door, and crawled out on his hands and knees through your room.

Most all boys "try" a girl to see what she is like — and when I went with Russie Baumann — he told me he respected me more than any other girl because I held myself aloof and respected myself so much. Jim Delaney said I was different from most modern girls — and he liked me on that account — I always could hold myself aloof from any boy except Floyd — somehow I couldn't resist him—I don't know why it was and I have wished thousands of times I had won in resisting him—I am glad though that seeing I didn't that I got into trouble or likely no one would have known—and I feel better about it to have my sin told to someone who understands and is considerate.

I really feel as though I am nearer to being a Christian now than I ever have been. I see things so much differently—and feel a much greater responsibility.

I feel nearer to God than ever before—for anyone in my condition never knows her outcome—and she needs God's strength as well as the love of those dear to her—

Now Daddy dear I have made my confession and feel quite assured that you will stand by me in the coming crisis altho' I don't see how you can be so forgiving—after the great sin I have been keeping back so long—

For when Floyd used to come to my room, he came several times—we had sexual relations then and when I met him after choir it happened again—But God forgive me—because I truly am repentant and see my great mistake. I know though my future life will not be ruined by it—I am going to strive for higher things and overcome my great mistake in the past—for I know I can depend on you and Mother and with the help of God I will do my best.

Another letter appears a few days later:

Dear Daddy—

I really believe that I had better try to get along without all of yours and mother's combined efforts—I really am not worthy of them all. Mother says it will be harder for you two than for me—socially, etc.—but everyone knows I am only taken into your home and it wouldn't be such a reflection on you two if I were to go away somewhere and never return—I love you and appreciate everything you've done for me, but all I've been is worry, heartache and expense—I want my baby to be with me and if I could only go somewhere where I could have my babe and then work and care for it—I ought to do something like that because I'm to blame and should be able to take the consequences. Another thing it's too much expense for you and if I could work and get money to pay for it all. The only thing I'm good for anyway is housework—because it was born in me to be a domestic I guess.

This is the way I feel—that the burden is too much upon yours and mother's shoulders and that you're doing too much for me—I am of course willing to do as you say—but God grant me find a place where I can take care of my baby—

I hope you do not misunderstand this note and my motive in writing it.

Word of Esther's condition has spread instantly. Lura says to the Marston family, "I don't believe Eloise could have gone through seven months of pregnancy without my knowing it," and she reports other churchwomen asserting the same thing. It does seem incredible. Eloise hears Eunice defend herself to Lura by telling about the menstrual cloths.

When Esther and Eloise both began to menstruate, near their thirteenth birthdays, each girl's mother gave her the standard supplies: a kit of bird's-eye pads to wear. It was Eloise's responsibility to set her soiled pads to soak in a mop pail of cold water, swish them around some, and leave them for her mother to finish in the washing machine. Esther's requirements, she knew, were more stringent. From her first period, she was to be responsible for the washing and wringing of her pads herself, getting out every trace of blood and keeping them in a place where none of the men could see them. Then she was to present them on washday to go into the machine.

Eunice tells Lura, "I noticed that I hadn't had any of Esther's pads for quite a while, and on washday I said to her, 'Where are your pads?' and she said, 'Oh, I've neglected to take care of them,' and after a bit she brought them down to me all wet and wrung out, and after that they were always on time, as punctual as clockwork." She adds, "And then she bound herself so tight … and never had a sick day."

Wesson spends sleepless nights and anguished days on the problem of Esther and her baby. Eunice is so beside herself he can't hold a reasonable conversation with her. He confides to Vera, living beyond the milkhouse in the Little House, who had typed up his letter of the previous year to Mrs. Grube. Now she types for him a letter to himself, as he thinks out loud what are the family's options in the present situation. One is that Mrs. Peters has offered to take Esther and the baby into her own home or to take just the baby and raise it, if the Dougans want to separate Esther from her child.

Thoughts on our difficult problem.

I am writing because all our nerves and tempers are wrought up and on the hair trigger. It is so easy to have a misunderstanding and say things that hurt.

This to me seems an ideal plan:

To have Esther go to the State School for confinement, give the babe to

Esther at sixteen.

Mrs. Peters, or better, to some unknown person. Then Esther come home, live a quiet life, taking some private or correspondence course of study, and music, and helping in the home. We to give her the affection, sympathy and loving direction she needs, some of us going with her wherever she goes outside of the home; not to watch her but to show her and others we care for her and stand by her. Then if she deceives us or fails again under the influences for us to follow the teachings of the Master in answer to the question, "How often shall I forgive?" "I say unto thee not seven times but seventy times seven."

Then I imagine if the Master were speaking in this age with its temptations and all thought and actions in big figures, He would multiply this to infinity.

If we were able to carry out this plan, I would be glad; but I fear it is too ideal to fit human nature. Only an unusual supply of divine grace could help us submerge the human feelings and tendencies. I can see a multitude of difficulties in it. Esther has had a good chance. Mother took her in good faith and has tried to be a real mother. She has forgiven almost up to the limit of seventy times seven, and it is not strange that she has lost confidence and hope, and cannot give the mother affection to Esther now in her trouble. It is difficult and dangerous for me and the other men of the family to stand alone in doing this.

I confess I have a tender feeling toward Motherhood. I am almost nutty on this subject. I cannot harm a mother mouse, I save the homes of mother birds, not because I want their young rascals to strip my corn and steal my berries, but because I respect the mother spirit. And, with the domestic animals, I take great delight in observing the mother pig, getting her confidence and helping her in caring for her litter. Especially does the baby heifer going through her first experience of motherhood appeal to me; and I try to heed Mr. Hoard's injunction, "The cow is a mother, treat her as such."

When it comes to the motherhood of humans, my thought and respect is only deepened and intensified. The pregnant mother is beautiful to me. This prudishness about seclusion would not be, if men and women could revere motherhood.

I mention this feeling of mine to explain my tender feeling toward our unfortunate little girl at this time, and also the danger of my manifesting this feeling as I would like to. Therefore I am convinced that under all the circumstances it is best for Esther and all concerned that she be cared for hereafter away from us. But she must be cared for!

The plan of going to Peters' is only an easy, cheap, and cowardly thing to do. There are three possible outcomes to it:

First, that F. returns and they marry.

Second, that F. returns and refuses to marry her, or she cannot bring herself to accept him.

Third, that F. never returns.

In the first: We all know he is a drinker, liar, gambler, prostitute, ignorant, suspicious, and an infernal coward devoid of every sense of moral obligation. Can we throw our little Esther into the hands of such and expect her to develop to a pure and useful woman?

In the second case: Esther would be there helpless, dependent, and under his evil sway. We can all imagine the result: a ruined life — then open profligacy or prostitution.

The third alternative is the most pleasing. Then she might become the "Hester Prynne" of *The Scarlet Letter*, truly repentant, doing deeds of charity and kindness to all, caring for her refractory child, but a pitiable figure and a blighted life.

The only plan I can see at present is to have Mrs. Grube take Esther to the hospital, then we find a suitable home for Esther and help with her support, and Mrs. Grube will give the child to Mrs. Peters. This will separate the child from Esther, will give us a chance to keep an interest in her, and will help Esther regain a normal girl's life. This plan would hold for a year or two, and the future would be determined by the circumstances as Esther makes good.

Esther is aware of the storm raging about her and the various options being considered. She knows her father has written to a Roman Catholic home for unwed mothers in Michigan, and is glad when they refuse to take her. She wants to have her baby at Peters's; she rejects the Beloit Hospital because births there are announced in the paper. She writes a letter to Eunice and leaves it on her bed:

Mother dear—

You probably do not realize that I have seen through the past years your efforts to keep me dressed and looking so up to the minute as possible,—and all your carings for me since I was about six years old. I can see how much you took upon your hands when you took me in—and I have always wished to be a real daughter and do as you wished—even if it does seem as though I have been a miserable failure—

This past summer and spring, I have really led a more sincere life than I ever have before. I have seen things through a different light. I cannot explain why and I have turned it over in my mind numberless times, why I ever let Floyd convince me, and why I yielded to temptation. It has always been farthest from my thoughts, anything of that kind—and why it happened I have tried to solve many times. Mother, I know you feel terrible for many reasons, but I want your and Daddy's help and I know I will turn out to be the right kind of woman—with your forgiveness.

In regard to my baby—I love it and have always wanted one—to say was mine. I am extremely happy to think I will have one—but the conditions of course should not be as they are—nevertheless I am willing to take what comes and know God will help me—and guide me—

I think Mrs. Peters will make it enjoyable for both me and the baby—and care for the baby especially—I think that is the best plan—but about marrying Floyd I cannot decide to do it—that will work out for itself later, possibly—

Now, Mother dear, please help me and I will do my best—

But Eunice, along with Wesson, goes up to Sparta to confer with the officials of the orphanage. There they learn about Esther's biological mother, that she ran off with another man, leaving a family of four or five young children. The father, unable to cope, put them all in the state institution.

They come back and drive into the Marston dooryard. Wesson goes into the barn with Albert while Eunice comes into the house and pours out the results of the visit to Lura and Mrs. Smith. She cries and cries. "It's in the blood," Eunice wails. "Like mother, like daughter. There's nothing we could have done, nothing."

At home she tells Wesson that blood will tell and that she will not allow Esther to have her baby at the farm. She doesn't want Esther and the baby returning to the farm, nor for Esther to return alone. She washes her hands of her. She's convinced that bad seed is irredeemable.

Although the Peters scenario is not what Wesson wants for Esther, he has no alternatives. On September 26, Esther's labor begins, and he drives her to the Peters's home in nearby Shopiere. Dr. Thayer is called. He stops by the farm and picks up Vera. At the Peters house, Wesson, his face heavy, says to Vera, "I would stay, but with Eunice feeling as she does, I cannot." He returns home.

During her labor Esther writes a letter home, remembering the things she had promised to do for Trever. She's not yet aware that Eunice has refused to have her back:

> My dearest Mother and Daddy—
>
> Since I have arrived here I have had but one pain and it's past six—I don't really know if that was a false alarm or not—
>
> Oh! I love you two so and know how you care for me and miss you both tremendously already.
>
> I am thankful to Vera and appreciate it so much to think she is here with me. She certainly is darling to do it and give me some of her baby clothes.
>
> Mother and Daddy dear—please don't feel so broken hearted—because I am out of my home, because I am coming back and let you know I can be a real daughter.—
>
> As far as marrying Floyd goes—I do not want to—I want to be single and finish my education as I planned. I know I can do it—and Mother I know I'll be a real help to you in every way—because I do not intend to have this ruin my life—and Daddy has given me such wonderful things to think about—I love you both immensely.
>
> Trev wanted his tux shirt and tie sent to him and his sweaters put in the cedar chest.
>
> Mother, could you send some handkerchiefs—my nightgown, petticoat, and teddy—If you could get me a brassiere, size 36 or 38, I really need one as soon as I am up and around—
>
> All my love and remember my promise—
> Your daughter, Esther

Mrs. Peters cooks a supper of pork chops for Vera; the doctor; her husband; Georgia, her youngest child who is near Esther's age; and Herbert, an older son who is currently living at home. Herbert has also been a boarder at the Dougan farm, his work time roughly coinciding with his brother's, though he started some months earlier, left before Floyd's nocturnal visits, and came back as a day laborer through the summer after Floyd's firing. Ronald stops by early in the evening, holds his little sister's hand for a while, and returns home.

Esther's labor picks up. Vera administers the chloroform when Dr. Thayer directs. Esther suffers pain, but her labor is not unusually long nor difficult. Before midnight, she's delivered of a healthy boy, one with Esther's same large beautiful eyes.

"His name is Russell," Esther whispers.

In the days following, Mrs. Peters acts as nurse to Esther and the baby. Georgia and Herbert frequently tiptoe in and peek at the little face. Wesson visits, and Ronald and Vera, and Floyd's other brother, Ross, and his sister, Leora. Eloise comes, too.

Esther says, "It was so funny. I just didn't show it till the last six weeks, and then it just popped."

"Well, you know," says Eloise, "I told you two times that people thought you were pregnant, and I thought maybe you were, and the third time, when you actually were, I didn't think so."

Eunice sends gifts, but she can't bring herself to come. At the Big House, on the Sunday after the birth, she serves everyone a big Sunday dinner. Besides Wesson and the hired men, Ida and Hazel and Lillian are out from town, and Ronald and Vera and little Joan over from the Little House. In the midst of the meal, the phone rings. It hangs on the wall in the dining room. Eunice answers it. Everyone falls silent so that Eunice will be able to hear. She suddenly slams the receiver onto its hook and spins around, her face flaming and contorted with shock and rage. Her mouth works; she is incoherent.

"What is it, dearie?" cries Wesson in alarm.

Eunice's hand flies, she splutters and cries, and the story comes out bit by bit. She'd put the receiver to her ear and a woman's voice had said, "Judge not lest ye be judged; forgive, and ye shall be forgiven," and abruptly hung up. It's hours before Eunice is even partially calmed down. Nobody ever knows who made the call.

The next day Esther writes a despondent letter:

> My Dearest Mother and Daddy,
>   It seems you have forgotten me entirely. Yesterday and today have been so lonesome—especially Sunday—for I thought you would be over for sure Sunday—
>   My problems are so many and I sometimes think I just can't stand it another minute.

Baby is really growing and he seems exceedingly smart. He's such a darling.

I started reading *High Fires*—read two chapters and my eyes began to hurt so decided it wasn't best, but the book is interesting.

Herbert, Ross, and Leora and her husband came yesterday—

Mother, you paid more than $5.00 for baby things, I don't see as I ought to have another $5.00. The baby layette is darling—it was so wonderful of you.

I would like some bedroom slippers if you could get them—then I will pay for them out of this money—I would like a pair with low heels and real light soles, if possible, about size seven—not so very wide. I will really need them when I begin taking care of baby nights.

My mind seems a jumble—things look so hard—and look harder every day. I just can't decide what is best or what to do—it seems as though at night I can't stand it—during the day it's not nearly as bad.

I do love you so and need your help and mostly your advice, for I want to become the kind of woman you want me to be—for I certainly have made a terrible mistake.

Ross said that Floyd went to Chicago to find work—couldn't find any, so got discouraged and started bumming west—he said until he could get some money to come back a little respectable he wouldn't come. He said he didn't intend to leave me but expected to get a job and come back after me. Maybe he means it and maybe not, I don't know.

It's getting too dark in here to write more—please come and talk to me—

All my love—Esther

Esther soon realizes she will not be coming back to the farm. When the baby is about three weeks old, she writes her father her thoughts:

My Dearest Daddy—

I have been thinking hard ever since our talk last Sunday, and I think I have decided my future—as far as I can—I am positive that this is the best place for me—for I am sure Floyd will come home before long, and I want to be here when he comes. Then if Floyd and I decide not to marry—then I have made up my mind to finish high school. There is a good opening for me—Mrs. Tomlen says they will probably be living in Rockford next year and she would like to have me live with her and finish High—she always keeps some girl that helps her, stays with the children, and goes to school—if I went down to Helen's this could not be worked out—of course everything's going to come out all right, I'm sure—and if Floyd comes back and we marry, I know he'll make a wonderful husband and I'm sure we'll be happy. But when he comes we may decide not to marry—things will have to be worked out, so I'm sure this is the best place for me—and all the Peters would like to have me stay. I know your viewpoint and you said if Floyd came back and didn't want to marry he could convince his mother that he wasn't the "only one"—Floyd knows he is or he wouldn't have run away—he knows the baby is his and mine only and so does God, so everything's coming out all right if I stay here—I'm convinced that my decision is right—and things will work out better this way—

> Love, Your daughter,
> Esther G.

Heretofore, when she has signed her notes at all, it's been simply "Esther" or "Your daughter, Esther." She signs this letter, "Love, Esther G.," then goes back and squeezes "Your daughter" between the "Love" and her signature. Her father knows that Esther has always been aware that Groose is her legal name. And Aunt Lillian has never let her forget it.

A letter from Sparta, October 16, carries on the story:

> Dear Mr. Dougan,
>
> I have been waiting a long time to hear from you in regard to Esther and her baby, understood you were to send me a copy of her letters she wrote you and Mrs. Dougan, also what her future plans were to be. Trust she has not given up her advanced education.
>
> > Best wishes for you and your family,
> > Mrs. Ada E. Grube

But a fourth scenario, one Wesson did not anticipate in his letter to himself, comes into play. Floyd's brother, Herbert, is a plodder. He has none of Floyd's sexy charm. But he has a fiancée, and they've been putting money down on furniture at Leath's: chairs, a table, a couch, a bedroom suite. As soon as they have it paid for, they'll marry.

The fiancée lives on a farm west of town, works in town, and rides back and forth with a widower living nearby. On a Thursday, she and Herbert make their final payment. They plan to be married the following week.

That Friday she doesn't return from work. Neither does the widower. They've driven to Dubuque, over the river in Iowa where there is no waiting period, and gotten married.

Herbert is shattered. It's only a few weeks after this that Esther arrives at Shopiere and has her baby. Herbert, when he was at the Big House, had always found Esther attractive—her vivacity and beauty, her laughter, her flirtatious way of joking with the boarders. He had admired how hard she worked, up at five before school to help with breakfasts for all the men; the many hours he saw her doing the dishes, dusting, vacuuming, ironing, hanging out the wash. Although Eunice always had a hired woman, there was work aplenty for three. And Esther went to school besides. Now he admires still more her courage and spunk, cast out by the Dougans, deserted by his brother, at only seventeen having a baby alone. He and Georgia sit in the bedroom evenings, and the three chat. They laugh and play games. Herbert watches Esther care tenderly for his tiny nephew. Though they never discuss it, he knows that Esther is all sympathy and indignation for the wrong that has been done to him, and she knows he feels reciprocally. It's very soon that he proposes marriage.

Again there is a letter from Ada Grube at Sparta:

> If Floyd's brother is willing to marry Esther and you say he is a good moral fellow and she likes him well enough to marry him, why wouldn't it be a good idea. The other fellow (Floyd) is a dirty skunk. Why wasn't he man enough to come back, for I feel he has been kept informed of everything all along, and give himself up and take Esther and her baby and make a home for them.

Esther accepts Herbert. He rents a small house near his parents. His share of the refund on the Leath furniture purchases a set of more modest furniture from the same establishment. The couple are married in mid-November in a parson's parlor in Shopiere. They have only Herbert's brother Ross and sister Georgia standing up with them. But afterward, there's a merry dinner at the Turtle Grange hall, put on by Eunice and Wesson. The Peters family attends, except for the baby, whom a neighbor is watching. Herbert's friends come, and from Esther's side, besides Eunice and Wesson, Ronald and Vera; Trever down from school; Aunt Ida, Aunt Lillian, and Hazel out from town; the help from the farm; and Eloise and the Marstons and Smiths. Wesson gives a little speech about wishing the couple happiness and includes a few earnest lines about the responsibilities of marriage and the importance of being loving helpmeets. Eunice says, "Well, Esther, you have a second chance, and you are lucky. Herbert is the finer man."

The only one missing is Floyd. He's not actually missing. He's sitting outside in the dark, in his car.

After the reception, the couple go to their little home. In the middle of their wedding night, the bedroom door bursts open and Floyd is standing there. He orders Herbert out of the bed. The brothers fight, Esther screams, the baby wakes and cries. Herbert manages to throw Floyd out, but has to call for help to keep him out. It's an inauspicious ending to a happy day.

Wesson, whose frequent communications to Trever at the university rarely mention family affairs but concentrate almost wholly on Trever's studies, spending, and character, in a letter dated November 21, 1926, includes a brief and weary account:

> Well, I have had a full week regarding Esther. She is married to Herbert, then the next day F. turned up. I am glad she is settled. Floyd stayed only one day. I wanted to get an appointment to see him but when I proposed this he skud again.

Helen Clarke, Director of Child Placing Department at the State Public School for Dependent and Neglected Children, is not aware of the latest developments when she writes from Sparta on November 24:

> Dear Mr. Dougan:
> You were indeed patient and kind and your attitude showed toward me and Esther was more than a little appreciated. I realize the strain you were under and, therefore, doubly value your cooperation.
> I very much hope that Esther and Herbert are going to be happy and that their future will be rosy. I shall always value the contact I had with you because of your fine Christian attitude toward your problem.

But Sparta learns the situation, and the Superintendent of the Orphanage writes Wesson in January, after Wesson writes Mrs. Grube about Floyd's return and subsequent behavior:

> I greatly fear that we have made somewhat of a difficult problem of Esther's case and I don't know what to advise. While the state released the guardianship at the time of the marriage of Esther, we are still interested. I am inclined to believe that we would take steps to prosecute the boy, Floyd, unless he leaves the vicinity and ceases his attentions to Esther, regardless of her feelings

in the matter. Should you see this young man it might be well to inform him on the former charge of his intimacy with Esther. It would be especially hard for him as she was a ward of the state at the time and he will have the State of Wisconsin to deal with and not the ordinary parents of a child.

Regretting that you are having so much trouble with this case, I am

Very truly yours,
C.D. Lehman
Superintendent

This letter is followed almost immediately by another, offering advice and Mrs. Grube's help but in effect washing Sparta's hands of the whole matter:

Dear Mr. Dougan,

It has seemed to us that probably the best thing to do is to get Esther out of your community for a while—to find her a home elsewhere where she will have supervision and time to obtain an objective attitude toward herself, the two men and the baby. We doubt if the state has any legal right now to prosecute Floyd and if we had, it would probably not do any good. The problem must be handled through Esther rather than either of the two men. Even though you were to personally prosecute Floyd we doubt if anything would be accomplished; rather antagonism on the part of Floyd and Esther would result.

By all means it seems that you should stop furnishing Esther with money after a position has been found for her. It may be difficult to find the right situation but with the combined efforts of yourself and Mrs. Grube who I know will be glad to help, some suitable place should be found.

The whole thing is a tragedy and can only be solved in our opinion after Esther develops character. If later on she wants to marry Floyd she will probably let nothing interfere. At present we would counsel no action about a divorce or legal separation provided Esther can be removed temporarily at least from the community.

But Esther is not removed. She remains with Herbert for a year while Floyd continues to heckle, harass, and court. Then she divorces Herbert and marries Floyd. Herbert is shattered again.

Floyd has a job on a road gang, repairing roads and bridges all over the county. Esther hires on as cook. Mrs. Peters tends little Russell while Esther travels with the gang. She becomes pregnant again. She and Floyd are low

Esther, mature, and always beautiful.

on money; the Great Depression has begun, and Esther's earnings are desperately needed. She tries to abort the fetus and succeeds, but so injures herself that she develops septicemia and nearly dies. She will not be able to have another child. Word of Esther's illness and hospitalization never reaches Wesson and Eunice, and in subsequent years she never tells them, though she does tell Eloise.

Ronald and Vera's second daughter, Patsy, is born shortly after Russell, followed by Jackie and Craig. Eloise, who is attending Beloit College, occasionally spends the evening with them when their parents go out. When Jackie is six, Eloise marries an engineer; Jackie is flower girl at their wedding. The couple lives now and again in Beloit but mostly all over the globe. Their two children are born in faraway places.

The four Dougan children grow up playing occasionally with Russell, when he and Esther visit the farm. Jackie knows there is something odd about her cousin besides his large, strange eyes, that he is not-quite-a-cousin, nor Esther quite their aunt, but she's hazy as to what causes the difference. In church, when she and her sisters sit in the pew beside Grama and draw during the sermon, a standard picture is of a hill with a rock part way up, and a girl tripping on the rock. She and Patsy snicker over "Esther Falling on Fool's Hill" though they don't know what they are snickering at.

Esther divorces Floyd after ten years. Grama, on a trip west with Grampa visiting Trever and his family, writes back to Ronald and Vera in May 1939:

> Then we got a long letter from Esther. She has her divorce and is happy. She is to have Russell and I am sure she would be better off without him. He will be but a big expense and maybe trouble. They are on their way to Chicago.

Esther marries again. She has a home in Shopiere with white ruffled curtains, polished floors, and snowy throw rugs. Jackie goes along when Grama visits and is given the grand tour. And in summer of 1942 Grama writes Jackie who's away at camp, "We had a fine dinner at Art and Esther's, and Trever thought she has a lovely home."

Over the years Esther works at various jobs. At one time, she's the beautiful and gracious hostess at the area's finest restaurant, The Wagon Wheel. At another, she works in the Fairbanks Morse factory. For years she manages the general store in Shopiere. When she sells candy in a Fannie May store in Beloit she assures her friends, as she presses gifts of candy on them, that employees have an allowance. Eloise is reminded of noon hours at Merrill School.

Russell Peters, high school graduation.

When Russell is grown he's drafted into the army. He marries, fathers a son, and is killed in Korea. Esther's third marriage ends; the reasons are unclear. There's a brief fourth marriage, in which she is perhaps mistreated. Her last husband, Clifford Cox, outlives her. They have had a number of happy years.

She has also been happy in her grandson, whom she raises, and who grows up loving and attentive and a pro football player. Esther and her husband take Esther's brother Trever and his wife to a football game when the Washington Redskins play in Chicago. It's a proud day for Esther.

Esther dies, unexpectedly, at sixty-seven. Her memorial service is at the Shopiere Methodist Church, and it is packed to overflowing. Afterward, there is a community potluck in the church basement. Affectionate words are said about Esther. One person said, "She lit up a room whenever she entered." It is obvious she was loved.

Later, Eloise says to Ronald and Vera, "I never knew anyone like her. She could look you straight in the eye and tell you black was white, and you'd believe her, because you wanted to believe her."

Eloise also says, "All her sins were warmhearted ones. Somehow, when someone steals something in order to give it to someone else, it doesn't seem as bad."

Esther leaves her body to science. Eloise says, "She was generous to the end."

37 ❧ GRAMPA BANDAGES

Jackie is four or five when she nearly severs the tip of her left thumb with a hatchet. The accident happens at the woodpile, out beyond the back door of Grama's kitchen at the Big House. It's entirely Jackie's own fault. Someone has left a hatchet embedded in the chopping block. This tool, unlike the ax beside the block, is Jackie's size; she can wield it, and has done so before. This time she tries to chop in half a narrow ribbon of metal she's found on the ground, perhaps a strip peeled from a coffee can by its key. With her thumb she holds it firmly against the block and hacks at it. The metal resists; she hits at it again, misses, and strikes her thumb. The thumb is saved but heals a bit misshapen, and with a scar. It serves her forever in telling her lefts and rights.

Years later, when she's grown, she can't remember who tended to the injury. She remembers vividly when she smashed the same thumb a year earlier in the Little House window seat: the excruciating pain, and Mother sitting her on the kitchen counter and bathing the thumb in an enamel basin of cold water. But the accident with the hatchet happened behind the Big House, so it could well have been Grampa who took care of her then, who applied the bandage.

She has abiding memories of Grampa putting on bandages, in the years before Band-Aids. The recipient can be a sister, a brother, herself. It can even be Grampa himself, for he's adept at putting on his own bandages. First he has to get hurt. Jackie likes to be nearby when Grampa hurts himself, for he always cries, "Ouchy! Ouchy! Ouchy!" before he heads for the men's washroom behind the Big House kitchen.

If it is a grandchild injured, she or he cries "Ouchy! Ouchy!" too, then trails behind, dripping tears and blood, and stands while Grampa rummages on the shelf above the long sink. He lines up all his supplies—cotton, a roll of gauze, a roll of adhesive tape, scissors, and the big red-and-yellow tin of Watkins' Petro-Carbo Salve, its colors arching out alternately, like sun's rays, from the lid's center. Petro-Carbo is used on people and animals alike. It smells powerfully medicinal and cures everything. Grampa rips a long stretch of tape from the adhesive roll and with the scissors carefully splays one end an inch or two deep. He sticks the adhesive to the edge of the sink.

Now he is ready for his patient's wound. While the injured one winces and tries to be brave, he washes the dirt and blood off the gashed finger slowly and thoroughly with cold running water, until it bleeds freely again. He then swabs it with cotton, applying pressure to stop the flow. He takes the end of the gauze roll and swipes it into the strong-smelling brown salve, lays the salve against the wound, and begins to wind. Round and round the finger he goes, layering the gauze up and down and over, changing hands so that the ribbon doesn't twist. He does not stint on gauze. When the bandage has achieved rotund proportions, he snips it off and takes the adhesive strip. With this he binds the finger, making sure that the two tails are spread diagonally so that they hold the layers of gauze fast to each other. Then he cuts a final strip of adhesive and uses this to anchor the bandage to the uninjured skin at its base. All the while he gives the work his unwavering attention, breathing heavily, not speaking, but sometimes accompanying the job with his familiar throat-drone of concentration. The one being bandaged, and those watching, give the work their equal undivided attention. When the bandage is finished, it's a work of art. Everyone knows there can be no better bandage; no germ would dare break through one of Grampa's bandages to start an infection.

"There you are, cubby," Grampa says.

The one bandaged sports a baton of impressive proportions and workman-ship and walks off carefully, holding it with respect.

Grampa, like all good workmen, puts his materials back in their contain-ers, replaces lids, and sets everything neatly back on the shelf, before return-ing to whatever job he had been doing when the crisis occurred.

38 ❖ RONALD PART 1 ❖
FRANCE IS SET TO RECEIVE ME!

It's an aggravation to Ronald, growing up, that he can't do things other kids do, such as playing cards, dancing. Grampa and Grama have strict rules against these evils. Not all card games are forbidden, though. From the innocuous "Authors," he and Trever learn the titles of works by famous writers, as well as noting their odd hair styles and flowing beards—Tennyson, Kipling, Shakespeare. And their parents give them "Rook" one Christmas. Rook has no face cards, otherwise it's exactly like the pernicious deck. The boys realize this quickly, and on the living room rug, beneath the benign gazes of Grama and Grampa, they play poker using matches for poker chips.

Ronald has another cross to bear. He's the smallest boy in his high school class. He can't swashbuckle in front of the girls like Chas Ingersoll or Cam Murkland; he has to pull hair and run in the halls. At a class mock wedding, the tallest, heftiest girl, Frances Timm, is drafted as the bride, and the shrimpiest—himself—as the groom. It doesn't occur to him that Frances may feel as humiliated as he does, or that she acquiesces for the same reason: to be included.

He badgers his parents to let him go to dancing school. His friends are all going to Cain's Dancing School, held at the Cosmo Hall. The leader comes down from Madison every Friday on the train, and wears a silk hat and Inverness cape. Miraculously Grama and Grampa are persuaded, but Ronald must pay the weekly fee. He also has to ride a horse to town, blanket the animal, and arrive at the class smelling horsey. It's too much; he quits after three sessions.

Still, he wants to go to Junior Prom. He takes Elizabeth Macklem. The two spend the evening stumbling on each other's feet, apologizing. After that misery, Ronald gets a hired man to teach him behind the barn. There on the concrete, with the horses in the horse barn looking out over their shoulders, he learns the step-step-glide of the waltz.

Ronald does fine with girls when he's part of a crowd—a hayride, a sleighride, "Poor Pussy" at Sunday night Epworth League. He distinguishes himself there when he responds to the leader's question, "Why do you come to Epworth League?" with, "To see the girls!" But his experiences with girls one-at-a-time are another matter.

When he's a freshman, alphabetical order in one class puts him at the head of a row of desks and a girl he greatly admires, Mary Foster, at the foot. He keeps leaning out and looking back, to drink in her image, until she sticks her tongue out at him. He doesn't look again.

As a junior, he sits behind

Ron worked summers on the farm, and a year between high school and college.

Theodora Dinsmore in geometry, her name falls alphabetically next to his. Her father teaches at the college. He invites her to attend "Shepherd of the Hills" with him at the Wilson Opera House. Once home, he discovers in his pocket the five dollar bill he brought for emergencies shredded into tiny bits.

Then at a party at Waverly Beach he stands with a different girl on a little bridge. He gathers courage in the moonglow, and takes her hand. As their clasped palms grow sweaty, Ronald becomes desperate, for he hasn't any idea how to let go. Finally Emily gently extricates her hand and he cringes with mortification.

Even a sleighride isn't immune. The couples around him are spooning. Ronald is encouraged for his date, though silent, has leaned against his shoulder. He again gathers courage—this time he ventures a kiss on the cheek. There is no response. He retreats into himself, and it's several minutes before he realizes that the young lady is asleep.

Not all Ronald's high school is social ineptitude. He does well at his studies, especially English; he's also good in math. He's valued on the debate team. He attends an assembly where the speaker is the Honorable Henry Morgenthau, former U.S. ambassador to Turkey. The *Beloit Daily News* offers a prize of five dollars in Thrift Stamps to the student who submits the best report of the address. Morgenthau reads all the entries. Through the paper, Ronald receives a letter from the famous man, telling him he's the winner; the *Daily News* also publishes the report "exactly as it was submitted to Mr. Morgenthau." He gets an impressive headline:

RONALD DOUGAN IS MORGENTHAU PRIZE WINNER

Ronald stays out a year before college for he's young, seventeen. He delivers milk; does farm work; when the current teacher becomes pregnant, he fills out her year at the District school that he attended years before, across the East Twenty. Eloise and his young sister Esther are two of his pupils. Apart from church activities he has little social life. So it's a heady experience when at the last minute he cancels his enrollment at Wisconsin's Ag School, and his reserved room, and goes with the local Methodist minister's son, Cranston Spray, down to sophisticated Northwestern University. This is the result of the Sprays having dined at the farm at a crucial moment: their enthusiasm about Cran's freshman year persuades Grampa and Grama. Cran further paves Ronald's way by championing his admittance to Delta Upsilon fraternity.

Shortly into the fall Ronald writes a letter to his parents, full of homecoming floats, house decorating, and other freshman shenanigans:

> Did I tell you about our "kid" party? The freshmen came dressed as "kids."
> I wore my pants turned under so they looked short, wore a big green sash,
> turnover collar, and socks. This left my knees bare. When the sophs came to
> break up our party they got an awful beating. I got a scissor hold on some
> chap's neck when he was trying to get away, it quieted him in a hurry. Two
> sophs were hurt pretty bad, but they were all right the next day.

At this point it occurs to Ronald that his parents might need certain reassurances:

> I am going to study all afternoon and evening. I have a theme to write, a
> report to make on my sand dunes trip, some math to do, and two chapters of
> Latin to catch up in. I don't write much about my classes because they would
> be uninteresting to you. The same things happen in the same order. From

this letter you might think study is the last thing I think of. I wish it could be, but it is on my mind most of the time.

He then finishes his letter with an abrupt change of subject which, with no introduction or explanation of "them," indicates that this is a conversation he's had before with his father:

Dad. I am still afraid of them. I am doing my best to overcome my fear. The way I see it, getting to know people, this includes girls, is part of a college education. If I were to go through school and still know nothing about the average girl, I would figure I had lost a lot. Am I right?

One family of girls, however, Ronald has always felt comfortable with. Mrs. Burnette, a widow with six children, attends the Methodist Church. The youngest becomes a favorite with Grama and Grampa. Grama yearns for romance between Ronald and Helen, and in letters to her college son gives her candidate enthusiastic press. But she's too successful in making Helen family. To Ronald, she's like a sister. She's not considered "them."

In another letter Ronald brings up the touchy subject of dancing. For after the brief high school breach, the prohibition has been renewed. His father responds:

My Dear Boy Ronald: I realize you are laboring to solve one of the problems of life. I trust to your strength of character and manhood to guard against the temptations of the social life you are entering. I will leave it to you when you see immorality and immoral influences coming through the dance to cut it out. Or when you see the dance is taking your time and strength from useful work and clear thinking, restrict it or cut it out entirely.

I feel you could be a happier, stronger lad if you did not allow this temptation to draw you. I shall expect you to be careful in the amount of money you spend in this and also the time it takes from school and other work.

Two courses are open to us in this matter. Either to absolutely forbid you to go and enforce the order, or to allow you to go and assist you to guard against the evil influences and help you come to a strong Christian life. The latter is the course Mama and I have decided to follow.

You are a noble boy. We love you and are anxious for you to be a good and strong man.

Your loving Father

It's not long, though, before W.J. spells out his fears:

I see that my letter has not impressed you in the right way. You are starting just the course that is most objectionable. I have seen many freshmen go to the racks in just your way. You have an ambition to excel in scholarship and athletics. The social pace you are starting is sure to beat you in this. It will do this in three ways, any one of them will turn the trick. First, you are getting your thought and interest in shows and dances. You cannot do good mental work under these conditions. Besides you are crowding out your study hours and exhausting your energies. At the end of the semester you will be conned out. Or at least pinch through with unsatisfactory grades and get but slight good from your studies.

Or second, you will strive desperately to keep up grades and near examinations study day and night, and either ruin your eyes or break down in some way physically from "over study."

Or third, you are going to spend so much that you cannot return second semester.

At your present program and pace you are beaten at the outset. Regarding that freshman party. You freshies are the poor fish that these Northshore sharks are after. I did not object seriously to your college parties and dances among college boys & girls. But these hotel dances are the worst of public dances. Any harlot or reprobate with money can go and mingle with you sweet little boys & girls. If the frat continues to hold this ideal, you will have to cut out the frat and its ideals, or cut out college. I will not have to enforce this edict. You will do it yourself in one of the three ways above mentioned.

In the envelope is a second letter that Grampa writes the following day:

You know my practice of not mailing a letter until I am sure it is the right thing. I have reread your letter and there is one part I may be a little wrong in. That is that at those hotel dances you join in the public dance. Do you have your hop in your private dining room? If so the moral influence is not so bad. However the influence upon your schoolwork is just as fatal.

I wish you were absorbed in your great opportunities. Think of the great institution you have there. The equipment for the increasing of knowledge and disciplining the mind. Then the grand men and women who are longing to know you and help you. Also the athletic field ready to help you excel in strength of body and fortitude of mind, and to think of you missing it all for just a mess of pottage. You will be better known to the gilded hotel keeper and bellboys than to the great men and women of the faculty.

I appreciate your writing us so fully and am only anxious to help you to see and get the worthwhile things of life.

There are stories of Ronald's freshman year he tells only to his brother, and later to his children. It's dubious his parents know of fraternity hazing: Ronald perching on a branch and commanded to sing like a bird; Ronald with a mouthful of lake water, climbing the fraternity fire escape on hands and knees, entering the building at the third floor, crawling down the stairs, and finally spitting his mouthful onto a fire in the fireplace. He must collect exactly two pounds of horse apples—this means weighing them in a drugstore, taking the sack outside and adding or subtracting apples, and weighing them again. At the frat his sack is checked and he sets it on the hearth. A few days later an upperclassman says, "What's in that sack, Dougan?" "Horse shit, sir," responds Ronald, and he's paddled for foul language.

Something occurs during Ronald's freshman year that surely makes a difference in his social life

Ronald, off to college.

as well as in his feelings about himself. He grows. From being the high school squirt, by the start of his sophomore year he's six feet. This affects his father's pocket book—the letters are full of discussion about new clothes, old clothes altered at the tailor's, which items are indispensable, which merely fashionable. And surely his mother spent the previous summer taking down cuffs until there was nothing more to be lowered.

On October 2, a Sunday, his father writes his sophomore son:

I have spent the day in reading. I am interested in your letters. I cannot believe they are pure diplomacy—nor can I believe you are so free of the thought of the girls as your letters seem to indicate. I think your work has a different grip upon you than it had last year. You have a fine course and one in which you ought to grow both in mental grasp, vision, and knowledge of facts.

Trever and Mama are making great plans to go to Evanston the 14th to see you and the ballgame. I cannot go. I would need a new suit and overcoat. I must get Trever a new suit next week. He is pretty shabby.

You spoke of that "soliciting ads" job. I did it in Madison. It is not pleasant and takes lots of time. Instead dig hard at your studies. Take good regular gym work. Get outside all possible. Don't be a hothouse plant.

On October 10 his father writes again:

I guess you are still yourself and still playing square with me. I am much encouraged both on the money question and girl question. You are beginning to realize how hard and slow honest dollars come (and honest dollars are the only ones worth possessing) and how easily they vanish.

You have been in school all of three weeks today. You have spent $24.76 besides your regular meals, room, barber, laundry, books, tuition, and traveling expenses. The $24.76 is purely social expense. $8.25, ⅓ per week, for stepping out is too much. You seem to realize this. Situated as you are, I will not say that all this expense is unnecessary but I am sure you cannot afford to spend this much as a rule, or even half of it. I am not as good at analyzing the girl question so I will pass that.

Whatever the question is, Ronald seems no longer afraid of "them," but in his letters mentions this girl and that he has squired, or at whose home he has enjoyed Sunday dinner. One frequent name is Eleanore Aubere, who lives with her mother and brother. The family is Roman Catholic. After Eunice and Trever's trip to Evanston, Eunice writes a letter filled with alarm:

I am sorry you are not more connected with the church. Eleanore may be cute and pretty and have many good qualities but I am sure she is not the one for you to be so intimate with. I do wish you would go with girls brought up as you have been. You are on dangerous ground. I had no idea it was Eleanore's house you went to. I thought another home and she went there with you. I never knew till this morning. I thought "O'Bear" was another girl you liked.

And Grampa writes, at about the same time, "Regarding your girl plan. I do not know as I care to have you settle to any one girl as a regular. When you do this you want to be mightily sure she is near your same plan of life in thought, taste, religion, and that her habits of expenditures are also on your level."

As a student, Ronald doesn't distinguish himself. He does enjoy a busy non-scholastic life, what with dating, fraternity, and work. For after a short while he takes jobs passed on to him by his frat brothers, including the one his father advised against. It's soliciting ads for desk blotters, having the blotters printed, then distributing them free to students. There is a nice profit. He also becomes a puzzle editor: a firm runs a cluttered drawing in a newspaper, and the contestants are to name everything in the picture beginning with, for instance, "B." Book, baby, burglar, bugle. He doesn't have a master list, but selects several of the longest entries and composes his key by cross-referencing these. It's then a simple matter to select a handful of fairly complete entries for the judges to choose from. He's paid $150 for each puzzle.

Ronald becomes so good at making money that he's able to relieve his father of some expense. This is appreciated, but it presents W.J. with a new worry—he points out to his son that he's in school for an education; he can earn a living at home.

And in spite of Ronald's earnings, things continue tight at the farm. "I do enjoy your letters and your open heart. I see you are weighing some problems and I believe I can trust you to find the truth and to have manhood and courage enough to follow it." He regrets Ronald's wasteful expenses. "Mr. Morgan once told me that he could always excuse a mistake the first time but when the same thing was repeated he had no patience. It seems to me you have had experience enough to spot the needless." And with finances as they are—W.J. says he will be $1,500 behind this month on running expenses and bills—excessive spending could mean quitting school. This seems to give him an idea:

PS: What would you think of staying at home after this semester and taking the place of Wallace? I will pay for that job this year $45 or $50 per mo. What effect would it have on your course? So far as the job is concerned you cannot find a better one for physical development, gain in useful knowledge, or net cash saved.

But Ronald stays in school. In February he breaks his father's trust by being one of some forty Northwestern students hauled to jail in a raid on an establishment suspected of selling liquor. Its colorful name is, "The Wind Blew Inn." His parents are in shock. Grama writes:

> You have two pretty sad and sorrowful parents tonight, dear boy. To think that such an experience could come to you. I knew you were not living as you should. That is why I am so anxious & nearly heartbroken every time you come home. You cannot serve God and Mammon. Just as sure as you play with the devil you will get bit. When God's people are putting up such a fight to rout out evil and put down the filthy booze, my boy, who ought to be one of the fighters, has to be routed out. It is an awful blow. You may try to make light of it but no explanation can take away the fact that you had no more self respect than to go to such a place. That is the result of the miserable dance and that is why I lay awake with my heart heavy the night you told me you must learn to dance. I knew you could not tamper with it without losing your religion and your conscience would be hardened to that and gradually to other things. Cannot you realize, Ronald, what a big sacrifice we are making so that you can have an education? Does it mean anything to you that we have planned and looked forward to your college days and that thus far we are so disappointed we can hardly bear it.

Ron during fraternity hazing.

Grampa writes:

> Mama has written you a good letter. I cannot add to it. We have been unable to get a hold of the press notices. Please send clippings of everything the papers published.
>
> I am under the impression you should change your plan of Easter vacation.

Come home. I will not try to write more tonight. I will withhold my judgment until I get all the facts from you.

When the Northwestern boys are brought to court, W.J. and other fathers are there to pay the fines and fetch their sons. Grampa feels the shame is punishment enough.

By the following fall Ronald, now a junior, seems very much at ease with the opposite sex. He writes his mother that after a "Y" dinner for foreign students he hastened to the House and the season's first formal party; he took Mary Day, a Theta and a senior, and lists all the girls he danced with that his mother knows. To his brother he writes:

> Went to lunch with Katherine Redfern and had a peach of a time. She talked about you and resolved you should come down here to school and be put in charge of the Gamma Phis — nice girls, and every one a lady as far as I know. I offered Katherine every form of graft I ever heard about or read about, or that I could imagine on the spur of the moment, but she turned it all down flat and is resolved to turn my scheming brain into the paths of righteousness.
>
> For the first time since school started I've been seeing a bunch of good new girls. I'm all set to tear but haven't any time. Have been cultivating a Tri Delt freshman a trifle but my ardor is cooling — met a cool eyes, slow drawling, beautiful Kappa today. Guess I'll give her a thrill. Eleanore is still holding a strong place in my affections. Don't draw the conclusion that girls have my goat again. Such is not the case.

It's at this time that Ronald commits the near-unpardonable sin. He's caught smoking. His frantic mother exacts a promise from him to stop; perhaps he does. But Ronald is restless. There is again talk of his dropping out at the end of the first semester and working at home. There's also talk of an overseas job he's applied for, but it seems a long shot. Grampa writes, mid-January, 1923:

> Regarding your decision to quit school. I do not want to influence you one way or the other. I know, however, that I can give you good training, physically and mentally, good food and a good time. I need you to take responsibility.
>
> I am planning if you decide to do this to start you in the barn as assistant

herdsman. You help do the work in the morning then study and check records in the PM. After about two weeks you will be familiar with the herd and hardened to physical work so I can put the other assistant to other work.

In April I will want to take you out of the barn and onto the farm. Helping to prepare the fields and put in the crop. If you do not go to France, by next winter you will be able to assume management and let mother and myself spend some time in California.

I do not want you to think of stopping your schooling at this period, but to plan to return after a year or so to your studies with a definite aim, then take the highest training in your chosen line. If you finally decide to come home I will give you the best chance possible to fulfill your desires. You will be able to earn $40 or $45 per mo. after the first two weeks.

How about your work in France? I fear it is like my Tennessee speaking trip. Mine will not materialize this year at least. $280 is more than they can handle, Mr. Hutton writes, and he cannot get other states interested at present. I can go any time by paying my own expenses.

I am planning to spend a few days in Madison with Trever next week. We will not try to take in all of the Farmers Course but will see the UW at work, especially the agriculture classes. I discovered by a remark of his that he has no idea what the course is, nor a clear idea of college instruction and methods. I feel it will be a profitable week for him.

I must close. Remember, whatever you decide I will stand by you and help you to the utmost of my ability. You have my keenest interest and sympathy.

Again, Ronald stays in school. In late spring the France job is offered. He's to come at once. Simultaneously, he is profoundly shaken by the death of Eleanore's brother. The young man, riding on a car's running board, was hit by another vehicle:

The papers called it a feud but in reality it was just the two classes cutting up. I went to Auberes immediately and have been down every day since. Eleanore and Mrs. Aubere are holding up as well as can be expected. They look on me as one of the family and I feel I have helped them a great deal.

We buried Louis at Crystal Lake today. Mother, I have been closer to God this week than ever in my life. I have been to church to pray a couple times a day, went to Mass Sunday and to the service today. I enjoy the Catholic ceremony and can see how the creed has a lot of good points, although I was at variance with the priest even during the funeral service on some points. It is all symbolic of course, and I don't understand that, but I should think a good Catholic would get as much out of his religion as a good anything else. The priests have been a great comfort.

I never realized till this week how many good true people I know. Let me tell you, Mother, if at the end of three years Trever has as many acquaintances together with a few life long friends of the quality I have, you have nothing to fear. This talk of the younger generation going to the bow-wows is all bunk. At least as far as my generation is concerned.

I'm not going to argue schools but this is straight. Northwestern has the finest moral tone of any school in the middle west with no exceptions. I only wish I could be as sure of Trev's surroundings at Madison, where things are so much looser, as I would be if he were down here under the tutelage of such boys as Don Calhoun and George Kershaw, and such real girls as Eleanore, Marian Case, Katherine Redfern—the people he would mix with of necessity and choice. Knowing Eleanore has meant worlds to me. When I think how good and sincere she is, I wonder if I can ever do anything that would shake her faith in me. It is the same with the others—I couldn't play fast and loose with any girl—this crew of girls have taught me what is real and lasting, just when the average fellow is thinking it is smart to tear the limit.

Ronald continues about money—he's spent a lot with the sad activities of the weekend, but if he can drop on his father's neck pretty heavily for a short while he'll soon be financially independent, and wealthy in francs. "PS: Tell Trever, Katherine Redfern is all O.K. She is really a princess—I know you would all approve. S. S. & G., which translated is Sweet, Simple and Good."

Thus Ronald leaves Northwestern near the end of his junior year and is off to the Continent, flinging back a second PS at the end of his letter: "France is set to receive me!"

39 ⚜ TREVER GROWS UP

Trever, like Ronald, attends the one-room District School across the field by the crick. Sometimes he goes to Strong School for a spell, downtown across from Aunt Ida's. At home he has his chores, his cows to milk, but he finds farm tasks irksome. He prefers puttering around the shop, the cellar, putting things together. Figuring things out. Making inventions. Summers, he likes the sessions at Phantom Lake YMCA Camp. All year round he goes with Ronald to the church young people's group, Epworth League. He attends Beloit High. He has various escapades with his friends, which his father rarely hears about. He participates in debate, is a Hi-Y member, and joins the ROTC.

When he's a junior, and his brother a freshman at Northwestern, his mother's letters to Ronald often include accounts of Trever's activities. She describes the intensive three week evangelistic campaign during Lent. She herself attends every night; most of the farm help do. Trever drags his feet. Grama prays that he'll catch fire, answer the altar call, and dedicate his life to Christ. On the last night he finally succumbs to the unrelenting pressure, and his mother is ecstatic. But being converted does not make Trever happy. On Easter weekend he's surly to everyone, including his brother, visiting from school. Eunice writes Ronald afterward, "I think he was feeling conflicted since going forward and lets himself act his worst."

She also frets over Trever's lack of confidence, and the basketball situation:

> The Federated Church has inter-Sunday School games every Tuesday night. Poor Trev. He wants to play so bad but the Methodist teams seem to be organized without him. The True Blue class is one, and the Live Wires another. Trev is a "True Blue" sub but never gets to play. Dad let him fix up a nice place in the barn and bought him a $12 basketball to practice with. He says he is organizing an independent team, he is calling it the TNTs, and they will practice in the gym.

But she laments an unfortunate outcome of Trever's being a True Blue:

> The YWCA girls entertained the Blues at their rooms last week. In the course of the evening Miss Eddy asked the coach if he objected to them dancing. Boardman said no so they went to it, all the boys who had gone forward! Trever hung back till Boardman came up to him and told him to get on the floor. I could tell him what I think of him!

Trever's spirits rise as the repression of the evangelism recedes, but they fall again later in the spring. The ROTC officials decide to make a parade ground behind the high school. This involves removing a hill. The laborers to accomplish this task, with shovels and wheelbarrows, are the ROTC boys. Camp is set up; the boys wear uniforms daily, sleep in tents, and cook their own meals. The officials rub their hands in congratulation. This is providing a real taste of army life. Trever is initially enthusiastic. But the heavy work is monotonous, the weather often unpleasant, and the hill big. He must take his turn standing night watch, and drag to his classes in the morning. When he goes home on weekends he spends his time sleeping. Once, because he's in bed, he misses an event he'd been anticipating—going across the back fields to the Morgan farm, to see the Curtiss airplane due to land there. He's glad when school lets out.

As a senior, he travels down to visit his brother at Northwestern. "Meet him in Chicago," his father writes Ronald. "Go to the Art Institute and one or two places of interest, then take him out to dinner and the game. Plan to have

Trever studying at the University of Wisconsin.

him see Rev. Kohlstead, and also call on Turnbulls. Give him a good inspiring time. He will arrive at 10:05 a.m. via C&NW. Ry."

Trever may travel sedately by coach the first time, but he soon learns to save his fare home:

> Dear Ron—Everything went along smooth after I left you. I went to the depot and noticed how the ground lay. I couldn't find Gharrity so decided to go alone. At first I couldn't get through the gate. There were a dozen men there and no possible hole to dodge through. I spied a funny little door way over to the opposite side and found it to open. I hiked down the yards as fast as my pins would carry me. Two or three of the men followed. I ran around a bunch of cars, dodged in and out, then hid in one for ten minutes or so. Then nosed around and smelt about a bit. Of course there were lots of men, baggage men, cops, brakemen, etc. I headed for one who seemed least like an authority to get the right train. He said, "You bumming? This is no place for bums, in fact, the worst place in the U.S." I said I was a passenger, lost my whereabouts, etc. He pointed out the right train and just then I saw the same men who had chased me. I put two or three trains between me and them. I next went across several trains to my train. This was the best way because no one could very well see me as there were only small alleys between trains. I rode the blinds and nearly froze my nuts off. However, at the first stop I went into the cab and warmed up. The engineer told me to come back at the next stop. From then on I wasn't cold. Gee, Ron, you know where I would have been for the next 30 days or so, if I was caught in the Chicago yards. Nothing short of the piss house, I take it. I was pretty lucky. When I arrived at 5 I saw Gharrity getting off a coach. He paid his way.

Trever is not above boasting about such exploits at home. Grampa writes to Ronald, "By the way, your baby brother has broken hobo records. He has marched right through the Chicago gates, boarded a palace car, and rode to his destination. Well, I hope he has had his craving for being a tramp satisfied—I shall have him insured for financial security before he has a chance to risk his neck again."

By spring of 1923 the decision has been made that Trever will go to Wisconsin in the fall and study agriculture. Trever urges Northwestern, but his father has been having serious misgivings about Ronald at a frivolous north-shore college; Ronald's indiscretions include smoking and a night in jail with forty of his classmates after a police raid on an Evanston speakeasy. Trever writes his brother that he is playing lots of poker—"fun when you're win-ning"—and surmises that Ron must have improved his game, since he sel-dom hits the parents for money anymore:

> Gee, you sure pulled some bright ones in those letters to the folks, Ron. Be-lieve me, when I get to school I'm going to keep darn still about my pranks. No wonder I am queered as far as Northwestern is concerned. But I believe a fellow that is half awake can get into just as much deviltry at Madison. I will know more about it after I get there. But wherever I go, I have your mistakes to profit by.

On May 20, Trever writes his brother a birthday letter: "How does it feel to be of age, Ron? Just think, now you can wave aside all parental authority and use your own wings, blaa!!" And, "Did anyone tell you that I smashed up the Dodge? Had an accident that knocked off the fenders and bent up the frame. Now Dad won't fix it till I get away. I also got pinched for speeding a while ago. I sure have hard luck."

At the end of the month, Ronald cuts short his junior year and with his fa-ther's blessing heads for France to spend a year doing youth work at the Meth-odist Memorial in Chateau Thierry. Trever disappoints Wesson that summer by not working on the farm as anticipated, but taking a job as a flyspray sales-man. His father repairs the Dodge, and Trever uses it to ply his trade. His first cousin Helen Trever visits for a month: the two have a mad romantic time, to the disgust of his young sister, Esther. His social life enlarges to being rushed by the fraternity boys at Beloit College, and to visiting, on his own, the Delta Upsilon house in Evanston, where he dates the girls Ronald left behind. He is harum-scarum, handsome, quick tongued, and full of Irish charm.

Late in the summer he uses his earnings to buy a used Ford. His father, searching the flivver for some tools, finds tobacco and pipes under the front seat. Trever endures several days of grim silence while he waits for the ax to fall. Then W.J. lectures him, and says he will not pay for his schooling unless Trever quits smoking. Trever agrees. His mother is not told of the incident. Trever writes Ronald about it, though, and takes gloomy stock of himself:

> Are you getting a lot out of your experience in France? You ought to come back a man, to have lost all your kiddish ways, to have forgotten all about the fairer sex and to have stopped smoking. I believe you are very moodish and tempermental. Your letters show me you are trying to cultivate your

Trever at college.

imagination and sense of beauty. I wish I could. I feel I'm getting worse and worse in being able to carry on an intelligent conversation and in being able to see the finer things in life. I don't read enough and bullshit too much. I wish I knew if I had the will power to stay away from smoking to please the folks, if I had enough will power to tend to my business at school. I sort of doubt it, with the state of mind I'm in now. I wish I knew how I could revolutionize my thinking.

Trever, about to cast himself on the world, misses his brother, though he veils it. In the same letter he goes on, "I think of you a lot, Ron. When you write those touching letters of our boyhood days it almost makes me shed a tear." But then he too reminisces: "Remember way back when I shot you in the leg with our Daisy BB gun? You had me locked up in that old shed but I had the gun and I shot through the paper on the roof and made you hop around up there." And, "By the way, Ron, I did something the other day that made me kind of lonesome for my worthless brother. I got that old cider press of Luty's and pressed out a bunch of apples. It sure reminded me of last summer when we used to guzzle it down." He wishes he could join Ron in France, making high jump standards for his Boy Scouts:

> How we would fight without anyone to interfere, or hear you swear. I have to take all my vengeance out on George now. It was his birthday yesterday. We fought for a half hour and broke both our beds before I could get 18 swats on him. (Mother and Dad were away.) Remember that egg fight we had last summer? When I got you behind the ear?

He closes the letter by saying he has to go to Janesville and write for Dad, and signs it "Horseshittingly, T.C. Dougan." Ronald's reply chides him on his language. Trever's response drips with sarcasm:

> So you think I am blasé! I'm sure there was nothing in my last letter to give anyone that impression. I'm sorry I shocked you by some rather "rough and

useless" words. I forgot that you were working in the kind of place where one cannot give vent to all his thoughts. I cannot tell you how bad I feel that I forgot myself so entirely that I said such things to my noviette (French!) brother. But it is all in a lifetime, I suppose; if you hadn't heard that kind of embellished language before, you would later.

At Madison, Trever takes beginning agriculture courses. He has little enthusiasm for them. He pledges Delta Upsilon, Ronald's fraternity, and thanks his brother for running interference. He goes out for track and discovers he's a swift runner. He becomes known as "Pat Dugan." His father writes him regularly, exhorting him to study, spend only what he must, avoid frivolity, and live clean and pure. In November he tells him to sell his car, to "walk and think and grow great." And about Trever's financial statement, "I notice you are not planning to eat for a month."

At the same time Trever is writing his brother:

> We just had our midterm exams. They were terrible, I know I flunked one. Guess I have started out wrong, got into too many things. I'm a swimming instructor at the "Y", that takes 6 hours a week. I'm on the Frosh Track Squad, and due to my selling experience I have a job on the Octopus staff, I suppose they took me partly because I have a car. When fraternity politics came along, I was head over heels in that, got a job out of it as chairman of a committee. Belonging to Skull and Crescent means one party after another—I have to pay for them anyway so why not go. We had a formal party just last night, and Saturday we have our formal fall party. I have the best looking girl in school dated up for it. Oh yes, and I'm on the house bowling team.

Trever recognizes the problem but does little to alleviate it. His work first term is only fair. He writes Ronald that he'd drop out for a while, if it weren't for his wanting the fraternity pin. He does start to appreciate his father: "Ron, we have the best dad in the world. I'm beginning to see his true values more and more—his judgment is just right on any subject under the sun and he will do everything for us that it is possible for a father to do." But in the same letter he says, "I have been smoking too much, been a regular furnace since exams began. Ron, between you and me, are you still smoking? Dad thinks you have the habit and can't quit. I'm going to quit as soon as exams are over."

And Wesson writes to Trever, in mid-March:

Your letter of the 14th is at hand. It is a good one and shows the inner life of a real man. I know the thoughts that are teeming through your mind, and the problems you have to solve. Mother and I never had the auto to speed us or the dance to allure us. If it was present it cut no great figure in our lives. I realize you are living in a faster age but realizing this I know that all the more you will need to strive to be master of yourself and of your destiny. I see you growing this year in "wisdom and in stature and in favor with God and man." You were a trial to me last year in many ways but I look forward to a better time this year. I do hope you can work with me this summer. I am looking for your application.

Your conclusion that good parents have all bad sons and bad parents all good ones is certainly too sweeping. First, you are not in a position to judge the good and bad parents. God and the child seeth the heart. I explain the phenomenon in this way. Many times when the son of an apparently good dad goes wrong that dad is not what he appears to be and the boy knows it as well as God does, or the dad, if he is really good, has not lived close enough to his lad to let him know his real worth. Or has just lacked tact. In the case of the bad dad and good son, there is inert goodness in the dad that God and the boy have seen and it makes the boy. He is doing what the dad might have done. Well, anyhow, as good as I am and as bad as I know I am, I am gaining confidence that my lads are going to improve on the old stock. I can see in both you and Ronald that you are thinking manfully. You are looking to a large, useful life, you will not draw to the low and sordid but look up and strive to attain the best.

Trever sticks in school and is initiated. Of that he writes, "Dear Brother: This now has two meanings, Ron, for this day of March twenty-third in the year of our Lord nineteen-hundred-and-twenty-four I have been formally initiated into the Wisconsin chapter of Delta Upsilon." He continues with a description of the solemn event, then tells of the earlier, hellish mock-initiation: "We had to undress as fast as we could, lie down on the floor and have chickens peck cracked corn off our bellies. It was painful! One little fellow had his penis pecked—guess the chicken thought it was an angle worm."

During spring semester Trever's work does not much improve. His father writes, "You can be assured if you should fail to get the necessary marks to pass but have done good honest hard work you will not be in disgrace in the eyes of your instructors or of me. But if you get lazy or dissipate your energy you surely will stand in bad."

He sits on his father's application until he hears the flydope job is not available again, and then returns it. He also sends a Mother's Day letter

Mother dear,

I've been thinking of you a lot today. I look back on all the years of attention and anxiety you have bestowed in "bringing me up" and wonder if I will ever show myself worthy of it. Think of all the hours you have spent in reading to me, counseling with me, and teaching me. I think I am beginning to appreciate it, Mother, but I realize I will have to do more than just that to make your labors fruitful. It's a responsibility that I have, to make my time and energy count, seeing you have given me such a good start. I remember all the little incidents that have gone to make up our home life. Things that in themselves seem petty but have really accumulated to form character. And I can see your influence and guiding hand thru it all. Of course you and Dad are of the same mind and Dad has molded the lives of us kids to a very great extent. However we have been with you more, as all kids are. Mothers get the advantage of a greater influence on this account. I can't say, though, that you have had more to do in teaching us because you both have absolutely the same principles and try to pass them on to us with the same degree of earnestness. I see that now it is up to me to carry on and if I fail, the blame is mine. But I think that in all probability I will pull through all right.

I'm so sorry I couldn't get down this weekend. I certainly wanted to. This weekend was not half as full as last week. I had a date Friday night and studied some Saturday night. I'm rested and ready for the work of the week which will be getting more and more strenuous. I'll do my best, Mother, and hope you can be proud of me when I'm through the year.

All my love, Trev

PS: I'm wearing a big red carnation in honor of my mother on Mothers Day.

His mother promptly reports to Ronald:

After reading your letter I still held a fat one from Trever in my hand — a Mother's Day letter. It touched my heart and made us both rejoice. I am enclosing it to let you see how dear he is. Save it, for it is one of my treasures. I think God has answered my prayers.

Trever is going to work at home this summer. Your father sent him a questionnaire. He kept it a couple of months and it came filled out Monday. He only answered 2 questions, we knew all the rest. One, do you smoke or

Trever, back at his old job in his old work clothes.

use tobacco? He said no. The other was, When can you commence work? He said, June 16. We went to Madison two weeks ago and ate dinner with him at the Delta U. house. The boys are nice and they gave us a good time but they smoked at the table. It does not suit me to have Trever under that influence all the time.

And Wesson writes to Trever:

Your letter to me and your application came today. I think today's mail brought the most precious messages to Mother and myself of any one day mail in our lives. Mother got splendid, soulful letters from France. I rather feel that your dear letter to Mother is the best of all.

Your application is accepted with sincere pride and confidence. I so anticipate our work and play together this summer. The place is looking grand. When I get things picked up a bit better and the fields all growing, you will be proud of it. Before long I will send you a case of milk and cream. Enough to give the boys a treat.

Trever works amicably on the farm that summer. But on his first day, as he drives the loaded manure spreader out of the barnyard, a hired man yells after him, "Trev, I see you've got your old job back!" Trever is not amused.

40 ⁂ INCOME TAX

It is 1913, spring. W.J. Dougan has not been working outside at the planting, nor at manure spreading, nor even in the barn. All afternoon he's been laboring at his desk against the north wall in the back section of the parlor. It's a large roll-top desk. Once in a while, Ronald and Trever are allowed to roll up the top, so that it's magically swallowed inside the desk, and then they get to pull it down again. The desk has many cubbyholes along its back, which the boys are not allowed to explore. Each cubbyhole has different papers and receipts in it. The drawers at the side hold large clothbound ledgers held together with fat steel pins. All afternoon no one has disturbed their father at his desk.

Suppertime comes. Grama and Ronald and Trever and the hired men are waiting. Grampa is a few minutes late. Grama goes and calls him again.

Grampa comes into the dining room holding a legal size envelope. His face is severe. He puts the envelope beside his plate and sits down in his seat at the side of the table. Ronald feels uneasy. The hired men stir. All eyes are on the envelope.

Grampa bows his head. The others bow their heads, too, except for Ronald. He cranes his neck to see the address on the envelope, but Grampa has placed it face down.

Everyone waits for one of Grampa's usual weekday blessings, the one that starts, "Bless the Lord, O my soul," or the one that starts, "Praise the Lord, all ye nations, praise Him, all ye peoples." But Grampa pauses a long time, then clears his throat and says something new.

"Render unto Caesar that which is Caesar's, and unto God that which is God's. Amen."

Everyone looks up, startled.

Grampa picks up the envelope. No one moves to pass the platters of food.

"Our government has just instituted an income tax," Grampa says gravely.

Everyone nods. The income tax has been a topic of discussion before, at the table, and Ronald and Trever have talked about it in school.

"I have spent the day computing my income tax," Grampa continues. "I completed it just before supper, and I have written the check and placed it in this envelope." He holds up the envelope and studies it, then reads aloud the address.

He raises the flap and plucks out a large tan farm check. He surveys the check even longer than the envelope. Ronald can't see what's written on the check. Nobody can see it.

"For mercy's sake, Wesson!" cries Grama impatiently. "Get on with what you're going to say!"

Grampa, taking a much deserved moment of ease.

Grampa can't hear her. He examines the check another serious moment, then casts a sudden mischievous glance at the assemblage.

"My income tax for this year is thirteen cents," says Grampa.

The table dissolves in laughter, with Grampa laughing the hardest of all.

When order is restored and the dishes begin to move, Grampa looks around merrily.

"I am happy to do my share," he says.

BOOK FIVE
AROUND
THE FARM

The Dougan herd heads to the barn at milking time.

1 ❧ TWO FINGERS

I t's early spring in the midforties. An out-of-state friend mails Daddy a prayer from their church bulletin. Daddy shows it to the family and Grampa. It's called "Prayer for Precipitation."

> O Lord, send us and our dusty neighbors around the world a good soaking rain of about $1^1/_2$ inches over a fifteen hour period, at the rate of no more than a tenth of an inch per hour, preferably at night, and repeat once a week until May 15 with the exception of three weeks appropriate for spring planting; and thereafter once every two weeks until the soil moisture deficit has been eliminated, or until the farmers wish it would stop, whichever comes first. Amen.

Everybody laughs, Grampa the hardest. "Somebody's read my mind," he exclaims. "I regularly instruct the Almighty!"

"But how to get Him to obey?" says Daddy. "Do you suppose He prefers rain dances?"

He tacks the prayer to the bulletin board at the office.

The spring goes on. After the initial rains, there is nothing. The seed is in but hasn't come up. The pastures are parching. The hayfields are browning. If there isn't rain quickly all the farmers will suffer heavy losses.

Daddy doesn't pray the prayer for precipitation. Instead he shakes his fist at the sky. "What's the matter up there?" he yells. "Let's have some rain down here! Don't you know how to run your own business?"

The skies blacken and four inches pour down in the space of a few hours. The deluge washes out a lot of seed and topsoil.

Daddy is inclined to blame the catastrophe on his neighbor Lang, who, he says, must have been plowing on Sunday. But another neighbor, Howard Lentell, thinks differently.

"Next time, Ron," he says, "shake only two fingers."

2 ⋊ THE COLT

Jackie is five. She's sitting on the back step of the Big House, by the boot scraper. She's eating one of Grama's fat sugar cookies, the kind that's always in the cookie jar except for special times. Then you might find oatmeal-raisin or date nut bars or even peanut butter cookies crisscrossed with fork marks. But the day-in, day-out cookie that usually fills the cookie jar is the fat yellow sugar cookie. Jackie is slowly eating and watching Grampa.

Grampa is in the large graveled area bounded by the Big House, the round barn, and the milkhouse. He's breaking Beauty's colt to halter. Jackie knows Little Beauty. He's had the run of the place ever since he was foaled and is everybody's pet. He regularly gets out of the horse yard and wanders the farm. He has to be chased from the grain bins in the upper barn. He eats the pig swill. He begs apples and sugar cubes. He has become a butterball. Now Grampa has decided enough is enough, that Little Beauty is old enough to go to work. But first he has to be broken.

Little Beauty is skittery for he's never had anything on his head before. The halter straps around his muzzle and over his forehead and behind his ears are frightening to him. He also has a blindfold over his eyes, Grampa's large blue bandana hankerchief. Jackie thinks she'd be skittery, too.

Grampa fastens a long rope to the halter. Little Beauty wants to break free but he can't, for Grampa holds fast to the end of the rope. Tossing his head, the colt starts to run in a large circle around Grampa.

Grampa's rope is taut. He turns as Little Beauty runs. He turns faster as the colt gallops harder and harder. On every rotation the colt sweeps close to Jackie, but not too close. Other people go by on their own businesses, giving the action wide berth. Nobody else stays to watch. Jackie knows that Grampa sees her, but is far too busy to chat. He shouts encouragement to Little Beauty. "That's a good laddie! On, boy, on!"

Finally the colt begins to tire. He slows down, falters, finally stops. Grampa comes up to him, pats his lathered neck, speaks soothingly. Little Beauty stands there trembling, nostrils flared, breathing hard.

Jackie takes another bite of sugar cookie. She watches Grampa bend and peer closely at Little Beauty's fat belly. Then he jerks something from under it.

Little Beauty lets out a screaming whinny and leaps straight in the air. He lands bucking and pitching. He rears up on his hind legs, flings forward on his front ones. He flails and kicks and lunges off at a gallop. Grampa hangs onto the rope. The colt is jerked short and Grampa is jerked too, nearly off his feet. He staggers and recovers. He's dragged hither and thither. He bellows, "Whoa! Whoa, lad, whoa!" He steps nimbly, skips this way and that to avoid flying hooves. Jackie's bite of cookie lies unchewed in her gaping mouth.

At last Little Beauty slows his frenzy and comes to a nervous standstill, snorting and stamping and switching his tail. Again Grampa pats his neck and speaks to him gently. When he's finally calmed, Grampa takes the blindfold hanky off and swipes it all over his own face.

Jackie realizes she has something in her mouth, chews up her bite and swallows it. Grampa turns, sees her on the step. His face crinkles up. He begins to laugh silently.

"Did you see us dancing?" he shouts.

Jackie laughs and nods her head.

"Did you see the foolish thing I did that upset him so? A hair! He had a long hair hanging down from the middle of his belly—oh, at least a foot long!—and without even thinking I pulled it out—to tidy him up. Oh, didn't he just go crazy!"

Jackie laughs harder.

"Poor little laddie," croons Grampa, stroking the glistening colt. "I'd have done the same! You'll get a good rubdown at the barn." He looks all around and back at Jackie. He whispers loudly, "Did anyone see us?"

Jackie shakes her head no.

Grampa looks sheepish. "We'll not tell anybody."

Jackie nods agreement.

Then Grampa reconsiders. A twinkle comes into his eyes. "No," he says firmly, "I'll tell Ronald. I'll tell the men. It's good for everyone to know that no matter how old you get, you can still be a fool. Even the boss can be a fool."

He leads the trembling colt back toward the horse barn. Jackie skips into Grama's kitchen to be the first to tell her what happened when Grampa jerked the long hair out of Little Beauty's belly.

When Grama hears she says, "Well, what a fool thing to do!"

Jackie helps herself to another cookie. "That's what Grampa thinks, too."

3 ✥ CORNSHOCK TEPEES

It's a sunny fall day, and Jackie, Craig, Patsy, and Joan are playing house in the cornshock tepees in the field across Colley Road. Jackie is seven; she's played house in cornshocks every fall since she can remember.

A cornshock is made of bundles of cornstalks stacked upright against each other, and the way to turn one into a house is this: You select a tepee that has a likely gap between the bottoms of two bundles. You pull and push to make the gap bigger, and then, down on your knees and stomach, shove and hunch and worm your way into the shock. In the middle there is a little space where the original two or three bundles were propped together, tripod fashion, to start the shock. Inside the tripod you can almost sit up, and by more shoving, with arms and shoulders and back and feet, you can either move or compact the stalks till you have a small parlor, with space to entertain one or two cramped visitors. You burrow out to make a back door, too.

Once the house is finished you visit back and forth across the corn row stubble to other houses. You bring your dolls and stuffed animals. For your larder, there's chocolate milk and orange, and you raid the orchard for apples, and the garden for anything still in the ground, such as a stray carrot.

This fall Patsy is being very mysterious about her house. She won't let anyone in. But after a bit she has to fare forth for more materials, and then they see what she's up to. She is paving her floor! She's husked the dry corn ears from all the exposed stalks inside and outside her dwelling and hammered them into the ground like bricks. Now she goes around to the other cornshocks and gathers more ears. She plans to pave her house all the way from its front entrance through to the little center room and out the back door.

Jackie marvels. A yellow floor! It's hard like a floor, and each brick is slightly humped. The whole pavement has a pebbled effect, on account of the kernels. Craig and Joan also admire the improvement. Their own dirt floors now look shabby. Patsy explains how she had her happy inspiration while the rest rush to husk ears and pave their houses, too. In a short while, all four entrances are aglitter in the autumn sunshine. Joan arranges her ears in a criss-cross fashion, to make a parquet pattern. Patsy finishes, and adds a vestibule. They all save the dry brown cornsilk to make little pillows, for the gleaming floors are not too comfortable to sit on.

They see Grampa heading toward the orchard. They hail him. They want him to come into the field and look astonished at their houses. They want him to burrow on his hands and knees over their elegant yellow pavements.

Grampa sees their beckoning. He veers and comes across the stubble. His face is

We kids burrowed inside these cornshocks to fashion cramped houses.

filled with mirth. Patsy rushes to show her house first, because she had the idea and besides, hers is finished.

Grampa beams until he gets to Patsy's door. Suddenly his face changes. It becomes stern. He bends and looks into Patsy's house. He stands up again and looks at the other three houses. All the while he shakes and shakes his head. Patsy and Joan, Craig and Jackie, are dashed.

"Cubbies," says Grampa finally, "don't you know why the corn is shocked this way?"

The four shake no.

"It's to keep the corn dry during the winter, so that as it's needed, the men can load it and bring it into the barn for the animals. The corn you've husked will freeze into the ground. The kernels will rot. And the mice will find it easy to get at, and the pheasants. You'll have to dig it all up and bring it in to the corn crib."

Grampa squats and pries up an ear from Joan's patterned hallway. He turns it over. Earth is caked between the kernels. He shakes his head again. "You'll have to take a stout brush and get out all the dirt, too."

The four stand dispirited as Grampa leaves. Then they begin to dismantle their pavements.

"Well," says Craig, "I'm glad I only got mine half done."

"You can go get the wagon," Joan says curtly.

Craig fetches the silver wagon. He brings a stiff brush from the barn. It takes several hours and many trips to get all the corn to the corncrib. They can't pile the wagon very high or the ears fall out. Even level, they bounce out as the wagon bumps over the ridges in the field. It's an unhappy job. They are snapping and snarling at each other long before it's over.

As they are hauling in the last load, Grampa comes out of the tool house. They indicate to him they're finished. They offer an ear for his inspection. They pant and stagger and roll their eyes, to show him what an awful job it's been.

Grampa nods approval. His silent laughter is sympathetic. He says, "You've heard of Heaven, where all good cubbies go?"

The four nod.

"And that the streets there are paved with gold?"

The four nod again.

"Well," says Grampa, "when Saint John had his vision, and wrote it all down, he forgot to tell us an important detail. But I've had my own vision, this afternoon, and now I believe I can fill in the Scriptures."

His eyes twinkle. "Do you think the Lord would use anything but the very finest gold?"

The four shake their heads.

"And what's the finest sort there is?"

The four begin to smile.

Grampa bobs his head vigorously. "Yes, I agree. When you and I get up to Heaven, we're going to find that golden paving made of—" he pauses, holds up both hands, looks merrily enquiring.

"CORN!" cry all four in chorus.

"Corn," repeats Grampa firmly, dropping his hands onto his overalled knees.

4 ⋇ ALAN TURNBULL'S MASTER'S THESIS

In 1914 Alan James Turnbull, a Master of Science candidate, comes from the University of Wisconsin to work on the farm and use it as the basis for his Master's thesis. The thesis is titled, "A Study of Efficiency in the Management of an Accredited Farm."

The Introduction starts with location, size (176.5 acres), description, and climate—the average temperature is 46.7 degrees, precipitation, 32.68 inches, and the average growing season, 150 days. The last killing frost is May 6; the first in the fall, October 3. Topography and character of the soil follows: black, underlaid by a fine yellow clay below which is a layer of sand and gravel. Drainage is via Spring Brook (here called by an earlier name, Sunnyside) into Turtle Creek and thence into Rock River.

The introduction continues with the buildings: a large round barn; a barn for young stock, dry cows and calves; a horse barn; icehouse; and milk room. There is storage space above each stable, and the second floor of the round barn has the general granary and corn crib. There are the usual tools plus a husker and shredder. The barn boasts a litter carrier, and hand tools for herd care. For dairy work there are milk pails, a milk cooler, bottles and cases, a power capper, a steam boiler for heating water and running the turbine bottle washer, and two delivery wagons.

Six to eight men are employed the year round, and nine horses. Engine power consists of a kerosene engine used for pumping water, washing and capping bottles, and furnishing light. In the barn a gasoline engine is used for running the shredder and husker, filling silo, and grinding feed.

The herd for the past year has consisted of thirty-seven milking cows, seventeen heifers, eight yearlings, and five calves; all but two are grade Guernseys. Two purebred bulls are kept for breeding purposes.

The farm dwelling is two story with an addition in the rear of one story;

the latter contains sitting room, dining room, kitchen, and milk room. The family occupies the front rooms on the lower floor while the help occupy the upper rooms. One woman is employed to help with the household work. The help are a part of the family.

The body of the thesis has six parts: "The Soil and its Management," "Crop Management," "Herd Management," "Marketing Products," "Labor Management," and "Personal Equation in the Management." Most of the sections are furnished with copious graphs and charts, and the appendices at the end are generous.

The "Soil" section goes into glacial deposits and concludes, "The soil on the Dougan farm is mainly made up of material that was carried from farther north and deposited to great depths over the farm. This soil, known as prairie soil, occupies areas known as outwash plains." The soil resembles Waukesha loam and Marshall silt loam, both soils underlaid by fine clay and then sand and gravel. In one field the soil is over twelve feet deep; atop a knoll in another, the gravel comes to the surface. On the whole the Dougan soil possesses good properties: firmness, good tilth [tillability], ability to hold water, the power of absorbing and retaining heat, and a porous, open condition that permits the circulation of air. In addition, the texture and structure of the soil—terms taking several pages of explanation—are also favorable.

The methods for the control of soil moisture are tillage, mulching, drainage, and adding organic matter. An inch of mulch is left on the tilled surface to prevent rapid evaporation. Two fields where pockets have collected water have had vertical drains installed; there are also a few lines of under-drains.

Chemical soil analysis shows the land to have sufficient nitrogen, calcium and most other needed nutrients, but to be acid and deficient in phosphorus. Turnbull recommends adding manures and commercial fertilizers. If rock sulphate were used in the barn gutters in addition to slacked lime, then the manure that is spread on the fields every day would carry the needed phosphorus.

Soil is plowed six or seven inches in depth, then double disked, harrowed, and when possible, spring toothed and finely rolled before seeding. Tilled crops are cultivated throughout the season, starting with a drag. Alfalfa is treated somewhat differently. The cost per acre of raising different crops varies. Corn, on account of its constant cultivation, is the highest, alfalfa the lowest. The cost of man labor is figured at slightly over 10 cents an hour; for horse labor, about $6^1/_2$ cents.

The "Crop Management" section notes that the principal crops on the farm are corn, clover, and alfalfa, with small grains such as barley and oats grown only for seeding down land. The grain is then used for feeding the stock on the farm. Sufficient potatoes and garden stuff are raised for household use. Considerable experimental work has been done with alfalfa. Turnbull analyzes each field of the farm and then works out a rotation plan, covering the next five years. He also analyzes the gain or loss of the previous year on each crop, taking into account labor, seed, interest, taxes, threshing expenses, and interest on and depreciation of tools. His conclusions are that oats are an unprofitable crop and probably should not be grown; barley, though yielding a fair prof-

Alan Turnbull in front of the entrance to the lower barn.

it, should be limited; crib corn should be grown after all silage corn demand is satisfied; and alfalfa should be increased, as it is the most profitable crop.

"Herd Management" states, "It is around the herd that all the other lines of the farm activities centralize as it is from it that the income of the farm must come. When trying to increase the yields of crops one is only making it possible to keep more cows hence to increase the product. The herd is necessary also to build up and retain the fertility of the soil, and to breed and rear calves." The housing of the Dougan cows is described, and the summer and winter schedules that are generally adhered to:

> Winter Period
> A.M.
>   4:00-4:30 Cows fed grain and groomed
>   4:30-6:00 Cows milked
>   6:00-6:10 Feeding silage
>   6:10-7:00 Feeding hay or stover [corn stalks and leaves minus the grain]
>   7:00-9:00 Cleaning stable

9:00-11:00 Cows let out for water and exercise

11:00-12:00 Cows put back in stable and fed grain

P.M.

2:00-2:10 Cows fed grain

2:10-3:30 Cows groomed

3:30-5:00 Cows milked

5:00-5:10 Feeding silage

5:10-5:30 Feeding hay

5:30-6:00 Cows put to bed

Summer Period

A.M.

4:00-4:30 Feeding grain

4:30-6:00 Cows milked

6:00-6:10 Feeding silage

7:30 Cows let out to pasture

7:30-12:00 Cleaning and working around barn

P.M.

1:00-2:00 Work in barn

2:00-2:30 Putting cows in barn and feeding grain

2:30-3:30 Grooming cows

3:30-5:00 Milking

5:00-6:00 Letting cows out to pasture and cleaning in barn

During dry, hot periods in summer the cows are kept in the barn during the day, and fed some soiling crop, that is, a crop cut green and fed to livestock immediately such as green alfalfa, clover, or corn. At night they are turned out on pasture, which is mainly clover and blue grass. The cows' feed is mostly home grown, ground barley or corn, mixed with purchased bran and oil meal. They receive all the silage they can clean up. During the winter each cow receives about 6 lbs. alfalfa daily. Clover and mixed hay are fed more abundantly, and stover is fed during the winter months. Water comes from the creek, and from a 65 foot well, pumped every day as the cows need it. In winter the chill is taken off before the cows are allowed to drink.

A herdsman is employed by the year, and at milking is assisted by three milkers. He does the ordinary veterinary work, except in cases of severe sickness, when a veterinarian is called. The milking is done in a covered pail with a head consisting of two rings. A layer of absorbent cotton is put between two pieces of medicated gauze. The gauze and cotton is placed over the top of the smaller ring and the larger drawn down tightly over it. The head is then placed on the pail. After each cow is milked the milk is taken to the milk room in the barn, weighed and put into cans. These are taken to the milk room at the house. The milker washes his hands after every other cow and if through accident his pail head becomes soiled, he takes a new one.

With milk at 10 cents a quart it is very expensive to feed calves. This is helped by buying pasteurized skim milk and a quality calf meal for them.

The herd bull has become worthless as a breeder because of insufficient exercise. It is planned to give the new sire more exercise by training him to work and making a sweep to which he may be tied for a part of the day.

During 1914 the herd produced 273,332 lbs. of milk with an average production per month of 22,778 lbs. The average amount per month per cow was 617 lbs. and the average per day, 20.28 lbs. The greatest amount produced per cow was in June and the least in October. Turnbull gives many charts that calculate the costs of producing milk, including a chart of the ten best and ten worst cows. The best, Peggy, earned the farm $108.02 over the course of the year, with her runner up, Violet, only bringing in $73.53. The other eight, Minerva, Nellie, Lucy, Star, Hazel, Marie, Brownie, and Dot, ranged from $68 down to $43. On the other side of the ledger, Mary lost the farm $10.69, while Margaret, Ivy, Daisy, Portia, Jersey, Lydia, Jennie, and Bonnie lost from $11.34 to $68.85, with Wilma at the very bottom losing a whopping $71.66.

"Marketing the Product" tells how the milk is cooled immediately on receipt from the barn, bottled, and placed in crates. During summer the cases are filled with ice before loading. All utensils are washed immediately after use and steamed once a day. The milk is delivered directly to consumers at 10 cents a quart, and 50 cents for cream. "There is a feeling of trust and confidence grown up between the customers and Mr. Dougan. The business is continually growing and most new customers come through the recommendation of old ones. People are glad to get the milk even though it is two or three cents more a quart than the ordinary milk." Milk tickets are sold for $1.00. Cash is expected for them, but credit is given if it is understood that it shall not exceed more than two dollars. In cases where it's not convenient for a party to pay for each dollar's worth of milk they are allowed to have a $25 milk book. The payments in this case are made every two weeks or monthly. As a result, there is very little money lost through bad debts—in the previous year, less than one-half percent.

Alan Turnbull in World War I uniform.

The monthly cost of delivery ranges from $110.09 in January when the roads are bad, to July, at $83.80. The hot weather then causes it to rise and it continues upward for the rest of the year. The amount of the product sold is the chief factor which influences the cost of delivery. One wagon cannot handle all the milk and there is not full work for two. With business growing, however, it will be only a very little while before there will be sufficient business to keep both wagons busy.

Data in an appendix compare the income if the milk were sold to a creamery instead of the market already established, and Turnbull concludes that with its present equipment and methods the farm would lose money selling to a creamery.

The section, "Labor on the Farm," describes how every man's daily work record is kept, and transferred to a monthly summary sheet. Wages are $15 to $20 a month for inexperienced labor; more experienced labor ranges from $25 to $50. Board and room have to be figured in. The cost of horse labor as well as man labor is figured higher in the winter, when there is not as much work. During the winter months it is as high as 13 cents for man labor and 10 cents for horse labor, in the spring falling as low as 11 cents and 5.5 cents respectively. The average length of day for a man is 11.5 hours, and for horse labor 4.2 hours. "The labor of the farm is low per hour and also efficient; the returns from crops bring this out clearly. The efficiency of the labor is also due to the spirit with which the work is done. Every man on the farm is there to get all he can out of the work so as to fit himself to manage a farm of his own or make himself a more efficient hired man. The spirit of the farm is to get the work done and done right."

The final section, "Personal Equation," analyzes the manager:

> In looking back over the different fields of management, the soil, herd, etc., upon the Dougan farm, one is impressed with their quality and how efficiently they are managed. They are not ideal but they are far above the average.

What is the cause of this efficiency? It is the manager himself. It is he who does the planning to produce these results. In order to be a successful manager like Mr. W.J. Dougan there are certain qualities that the farmer must have. The foremost is that of knowing what to do, then how to perform it, then getting it done. He has to be the leader and it is to him that the hired men look for an example to follow. A more difficult task for a manager is that of handling the hired help. Very little is done toward efficient management if the manager is without the respect and admiration of the men he employs. It gives the men a personal interest in doing their work and seeing it is done right. Great tact and skill is called for. A thorough knowledge of the farm work helps to win their respect, and also firmness in all dealings with the men.

To manage a farm rightly calls for scientific and practical knowledge, and alertness. Mr. Dougan can often find out more about the condition of the herd by merely walking through the barn, than the man who has been with the cows all day. From a question here and there and from close observations the manager often has to make important decisions that have at the back of them some fundamental principle.

The foregoing qualities of a manager have all been more or less related to the money side of farming. There are others. The manager must be willing to cooperate and help his neighbors in every way possible. He must be content to be a farmer. He should make farming his life work. There is one other factor in the success of a farm and of a manager. That is the home, the farmer's wife and family. The happiness of the home, its wholesomeness and spiritual influence, contribute greatly toward the success of the farm.

Alan Turnbull's thesis is approved by Professor D.H. Otis on June 9, 1915. It is bound in black leather, and joins all the other Masters theses in the university library. But Alan gives a copy to W.J. Dougan, who spends many a thoughtful evening at his desk, studying and annotating it.

5 ⚹ K P I P

When Ronald is twelve an elderly man comes as a day laborer for a week in August. He's a grizzled, glum looking fellow, slow of movement. He leans on his pitchfork and says, "You want some good advice, Sonny?"

"Sure," says Ronald. He's always willing at least to listen to advice.

"KPIP," says the man.

"KPIP?" asks Ronald, puzzled.

"Keep Pecker In Pants," says the man.

6 ❖ RONALD PART 2 ❖ I AM MARKED WITH A LUCKY STAR

In 1923, before the end of his junior year at Northwestern, Ronald is off to France: the Methodist Memorial in Chateau Thierry. His letters home are full of detail, and a dramatic change from his college letters of fraternity, parties, and girls.

His first evening in Paris was spent with dinner (50 cents), the opera (Rigoletto), and an open garden market. "Dad, you would go wild over it!"

The peasants come in great two-wheeled carts packed in the most precise manner with washed vegetables, and pile them in little stacks on the walks. I saw blocks of stacked carrots, cabbages, radishes — everything. Acres of strawberries big as walnuts! Then the meat markets — shelves on shelves of pigs feet, veal heads, rows of halves of beef. I bought a basket of strawberries and went to see the flowers. Roses, lilies, bachelor buttons — masses of color. I watched till dawn. Had coffee in a place called "Restaurant au Chien qui fume." The farmers were there in some numbers, a very comely proprietress, and several chippies — gee, but the town is full of them, and the evil is so evident that anyone can recognize it and easily avoid contact.

Ronald in the courtyard at Chateau Thierry.

I bought a few cents worth of flowers and continued my explorations. As soon as a peasant finished arranging his produce he or she would climb aboard the cart, curl up in a corner, and let the horse find his way home. The place was lousy with cats, or maybe it was the same cat walking back and forth, for all I saw were black. Peasants slept on the walk—all were pleasant to us and laughed and talked.

I love the dignity, the harum-scarumness of Paris. The funny little shops and winding streets, and crazy roofs and chimneys. I went to Notre Dame and then to St. Chapelle—possibly the most awing experience I've ever had. When one thinks of the history and traditions of these buildings it makes me gasp. I sure am raving—find I can talk a little French. I'll pick it up rapidly.

The next letter is from Chateau Thierry:

Jimminy, it is wonderful! My job will be biking, swimming, and generally working with twenty to twenty-five boys. The town is surely old—odd little shops and narrow hilly streets. The Chateau is of Roman origin, rebuilt by Charles Martell in the eighth century. The church is about four hundred years old, now being repaired of damage by the Germans.

The Wadsworths are kindly, Christian people with whom it will be easy to work. I will do my best to measure up. My room is at the top of the house. My salary is $75 a month minus 300 francs for board and room. I am a little lonely when I think of all I left behind. I won't have any girls over here—how they do guard them!

16. - CHATEAU-THIERRY. - Vue panoramique

Chateau Thierry, from the hill of the old chateau.

A few days later, July 1:

> Emotions — I guess I am too romantic — at any rate things I see and do get under my skin. Today I have been in a highly exalted state.
>
> A young couple called last night. They are so happy and are getting such a kick out of life that I was able to put myself in their shoes and get a secondary kick. Wish I knew when I would be settled in such a satisfying way.
>
> This job is giving me a chance to think. Already I am wondering about my future schoolwork, how I will use it, and where I will find a big enough life work to fill my demands.
>
> Speaking of emotions, though, after the couple left I climbed to my little room under the eaves and almost sang — I can look down into the court and see everything going on, or I lock the door and shut out the world. I feel like shouting and jumping around with the Count of Monte Christo, "The World is Mine!"
>
> Am in love with the town, the life, everything. We are having a village fete Sunday, celebrating the life of John Fontaine. This was his village. There will be torch light processions!

In a July 3 letter, Ron says his work is all play and planning good times. He takes boys on an all day hike, and at their return, a general songfest. What he doesn't say is the purpose of his being there, and the Memorial's — that Chateau Thierry was one of the most devastated towns in the Great War, leaving most of the children fatherless. The Memorial, funded by the Methodist Church's Missions Fund, is serving the community on many levels. Ronald's job is to lead a boys' program, to be a worthy role model. No wonder he must measure up.

He takes stock of his inadequacies, says "every once in a while I find myself marveling at the fineness and squareness of my mother and dad." He will make them proud of his schoolwork on his return. They needn't worry about the girl question, with the town so thoroughly chaperoned. Why, Mrs. Wadsworth walked down to the station with him and Miss Sedgwick — "forty-five and shows it" — to avoid talk!

Letters continue with the work of rebuilding the country; the miles of underground tunnels filled with champagne; the pattern of farm fields and farmers' lives, with farmers living in the villages and going daily out to the land.

On July 10 Ronald accompanies to Belleau Woods a former soldier who had been wounded there. Ronald encounters for the first time the trenches, now overgrown with brambles, and filled with corn willie cans, old rifle shells, grenades, rotten tents, barbed wire. The soldier finds where his best friend perhaps was buried. It's a sobering trip.

A letter describes a meal with a Paris family: "Little bits of helpings coming on one at a time—you think you'll starve—the courses are so numerous, though, that one nearly always overeats." He visits the Cluny Museum and Luxembourg Gardens. "I've come to love some of the fountains and especially two or three of the statues there—fills some longing I've always had, I guess."

He doesn't forget the farm. "Dad, don't think for a minute I don't want to hear how the work is going, what fields are what, how heavy the men are sleeping, and what the cows are doing—there is nothing that interests me more. Sure do think about home a lot."

On Ronald's day off he visits Rheims cathedral, and says that every French king since Clovis had been crowned there. It was there that Joan d'Arc was blessed and anointed. He discusses politics—the attitudes of the French toward President Wilson and the Armistice. Midway he says, "As it is, the Germans claim they were never beaten, they are preparing for the next war by building ammunition and guns in subsidized factories in Russia." He finishes, "The children in Berlin schools are now repeating every day, 'Who took Alsace Lorraine from us? France! Who is going to get it back? We children!' Unless the rest of the world acts together, it looks as though another war is almost upon us."

An addition, "It seems as if Nationalism is a curse, but what is going to supplant it, and how?"

In August Ronald, again in Paris, marvels anew at the age of the Old World: "the same crooked streets and battered cobblestones that Napoleon, and those before Napoleon, rolled over." He rhapsodizes over a concert: "By closing my eyes I visualized so many tranquil times I have had—oh, tending cows for instance, or helping Dad plant the garden, or talking with you, Mother. Never have been in love, but I have some wonderful friends. Funny how music will bring them back to you at their best."

President Harding dies; on August 10 a ceremony is held at the Memorial. "A French girl played 'Nearer My God to Thee' very softly the whole time. That piece always makes me feel rotten—perhaps because when I was a little kid I was made to visualize the band on the Titanic bravely playing it as they held their horns at a ninety degree angle to keep them out of the water as the boat sank beneath their feet."

Of his job, "My life is made up of study, reading, camping, and talk. I'll analyze each. I am putting in an hour a day with a French grammar. I am fast coming to understand the stuff. For instance, yesterday a farmer and I compared relative prices for milk in France and America, the size of cows, relative cooking, the exchange, and whatnot. They get about 7 cents a quart here."

Of studies, "The older woman, Miss Sedgwick, is directing my reading—French literature. I am learning history, cathedral architecture, politics, education."

Haven't missed home social life much, though I would like a farm meal, Mother, and an argument with you on evolution, directed from my flour-box throne. Do you still think Bryan the scientist without peer? All here including beaucoup ministers think he is sincere but off his head in his latest dabbling. The evil in education he is fighting is real enough. But instead of suppressing study for greater knowledge, and a reconciliation of the principles of the Bible to science by deeper understanding, he should work for a more thoroughgoing faith, based on everything we know to be true. Our

Ron can outswim his Boy Scouts.

system should be able to show youngsters a way to thinking things out, or to leave the mass of people in superstitious ignorance but with an abiding faith. The trouble with the latter is it leaves the mob to follow a few leaders who may or may not be scrupulous.

He gives his parents wise advice about his young sister, and describes the differences between the French and American raising of daughters. He reassures his parents about Trever; he himself has so recently been his brother's age and in his shoes. He recalls school, and while not deploring fraternity life, labels it kiddish and mainly a time waster. When he returns he' ll hit the books and earn top grades.

In at least one of his son's lengthy missives, W.J. numbers the paragraphs and writes at the end, "Just right letter."

There's a touch of homesickness to Trever:

> When I get back we will go out in the barn and jump on each other till neither of us can wiggle. The trouble with our fights is that someone always breaks them up. As long as we don't get angry we are a close enough match that neither gets hurt. When we do go off our nuts, don't the eggs fly though! These French kids don't know how to roughhouse. They take it out in talk and nobody gets a nose rubbed in the dirt.

He adds, "By the way, that is one hold I do have on these boys. Although they do many things better, I can take any two and pile them into a neat bundle. I can also dive better and swim faster. My body is getting hard as nails, my knees brown and scarred, and the muscles in my chest and arms, heavy."

Mainly letters to Trever are filled with advice about organizing his brother's upcoming studies and university life—Ronald lists priorities: "1. School: Make good grades your first two years and the last two will come easy. 2. Fraternity: Only include regular athletic work and freshman duties. 3. Social life: Girls are the same all over, and oh the money and time they take. A date occasionally is necessary, though." He advises Trever to write home often. "The folks feel pretty rotten about us both. Try to make them happier in your school than they were in mine." He confesses he's not one to preach, since he didn't follow his own advice.

And he has a telling line about play. He's nostalgic about school starting without him, but:

> For three years the moss has been rubbed off one side of me. It's high time I shifted my bed and allowed another side to get smooth. My school has been no end worthwhile, but unsuccessful in a way, too. I'm no end lazy and pleasure loving. Never having played in high school, college took me off my feet. Possibly the social side will not hit you so hard.

Throughout these summer letters one sees a young man whose eyes are truly wide open. Ronald has realized this from the start. To his parents, "It seems that I am marked with a lucky star. Every boy wants to get to Europe, but how many, hardly turning a finger, find such a wonderful opportunity? Of course I must work my head off for success, possibly already the little gods are chuckling and rubbing their round stomachs as they lay snares for me, but

A postcard that Vera sent home in 1923: "A close-up of our building. Beautiful grilled doorways. Over the doors float the American and French flags with, to the right, a sculptured American soldier, to the left a French one."

they have blessed me so far with a wonderful family, the best of friends, and a widening horizon that is astounding."

And later:

> A foreign country surely broadens ones thinking and sympathies. Can't say how lucky I feel to have an American heredity and customs back of me. Guess English, Irish, and Scottish ancestry is the best possible in this world! It is remarkable how much time I have to think, and how much greater influence abstract ideas have than they did three months ago. I am mixing with older people, have more leisure, and am getting so many different viewpoints from the French people I know and from the Americans who work with them.

He starts looking toward the future. "My life plans are still in the kettle but I can see a year or two ahead." He lists many options. At the close of a page of such musings he writes, "Dreams! I've got lots of them! The beauty of it is that they cost nothing, are no end enjoyable, and there is always the chance that one of them may be 'the dream' that will materialize."

He assures his parents that love and marriage are distant. "Personally, I like this sisterly stuff. So far I'd much rather love a girl abstractly before a fire, with her picture on the mantle, than be confronted with the actuality." And, "The art of living with people is surely to be cultivated. It is so easy to hurt another person and all so useless, that a chap is a perfect fool if he doesn't learn by experience. Hope I am getting a deeper understanding of human nature. Someday I want to be a decent enough chap to make some girl happy, and have kids of my own to worry over. That's ages away though." And again, mid September, "As to my school affairs, I'm rather glad not to be back this fall. I feel a perfect infant as far as falling in love. I'm too unsettled to know myself. It will be years before the desire to marry overtakes me, and years after that before I'll be in a position for any consummation."

But between this letter and the next, dated September 22, something occurs that will profoundly affect the rest of Ronald's life:

> Tonight has been no end worthwhile. People—jimminy how I like them. Dear Mr. and Mrs. Wadsworth. They managed such a homey, comfortable evening for us—the clever little American girl just arrived from the middle-west, the preciously delightful, accomplished American-born continental-bred Englishwoman, the little French girl, and me. We had a cosy grate fire, casting shadows on the walls and throwing rosy, flickering light on our faces, some candy, and a light, humanly analytical short story.
>
> And then the conversation, starting with a discussion of the story, and leading rapidly to the commonplace associations of our lives—plays, the atmosphere created by the new books, the worthwhile things that are so enjoyable and mentally refreshing. Oh it makes a fellow want to grow in knowledge and appreciation of what life has to offer. It makes him want to deepen his appreciation of human nature and to become more worthy of real friendship. And then it makes him wonder if life can keep increasing in interest, becoming more worthwhile. It really must, for what does a boy of twenty-one know about life? Love, marriage, life work, accomplishment, all veiled in a problematic future. Yes, for the short space of a life, the unraveling of the thread must gain in absorbing interest. And that's as it should be, isn't it?

Ronald's head has not yet realized the significance to him of the American girl's presence at the Memorial, but his heart is already speaking with eloquence. And in the nearly four months he has been in France, he has grown enough that both heart and head are ready.

7 ⚔ MANURE SPREADER

I t isn't just the barn and milkhouse that Grampa insists be clean. He wants the whole place tidy and sparkling. Buildings are regularly painted a gleaming white, lawns mowed, sidewalks swept or shoveled, driveways neatly graveled, fences repaired. If a horse drops horse apples in the drive, before long somebody comes along and removes the offending heap. Trash isn't allowed to accumulate in corners, nor old machinery to sit around rusting beside a roll of discarded bob wire. Weeds are cut. When there's a slack hour, or when a neighbor or church member prevails on Grampa to give a young teenager some Saturday labor, he sets the hired hands, or the lad, to policing the outdoors.

He's particularly persnickety about the manure spreader. This is a steel wagon with its end side a revolving spiked drum. It's drawn by horse or trac-

Joan beside horses and manure spreader on the drive between the Big House and milkhouse.

tor, and in it manure is transported to the fields from the pile behind the barn. The bed of the wagon has a track made of chain, and when the driver throws a lever, gears that drive the chain engage with the wheels. When the wheels are turning, the chain moves slowly along the bottom of the wagon, pulling the load of manure backward against the spiked drum. The drum is on a different chain belt connected directly to the wheels, so it spins all the time that the spreader is moving. Its spikes catch the advancing manure and fling it in a wide, fanned arc up into the air and onto the ground. When the wagon is going from the barn to the fields, a wooden tailgate is slipped down between the load and the drum, so that no stray manure will jostle back to the spinning spikes and be scattered in transit. Grampa is emphatic that the tailgate must always be in place. He wants manure only where it's intended.

The only way from the barn to certain of the fields is along the driveway beside the Big House. If a driver is careless about the board, and any manure and straw litters the driveway or sidewalks, Grampa meets the offender on his return and hands him a broom. If Grampa isn't around at the time, he seeks out the culprit later.

It's 1940. Cleo Reinfeldt is spreading manure on a field across Colley Road. Molly is pulling the wagon. Molly is a wily little mare, and a notorious runaway. If she's in the fields and the driver isn't alert, she's suddenly half way to the barn. If she's in the horse yard and someone leaves a gate ajar, she's off and away. For Molly, the grass is always greener somewhere else, and with a quick and calculating eye she restlessly watches every opportunity.

Cleo has finished spreading his load. He turns from Colley Road into the driveway, past the Big House and back to the barnyard. Since there's no more manure in the wagon, he hasn't pulled the lever to stop the moving chain. He hasn't put in the tailgate. He pulls Molly up beside the manure pile. The wheels of the spreader stop, the wagonbed chain stops, the spinning drum stops. Molly stamps impatiently while Cleo forks a new load of manure into the wagon. It's just about full, and Cleo is thinking he'd better put in the tailgate, when Milton the herdsman shouts from inside the round barn.

"Cleo! Come quick, quick! Gimme a hand with this cow!"

Cleo sticks his fork in the manure pile and hurries to oblige. He's scarcely inside the barn when he hears the clatter of metal wheels on cement. Heedless of Milton's plight he rushes back outside, but Molly has already made it to the open gate and is tearing out onto the driveway. The spreader is bouncing behind her, and manure is spewing out in a thick whirl of black hail. He races after her, his arms only half protecting his face from the shower. He doesn't manage to catch her until she's heading into the orchard across the road. Manure drenched, flinging furious remarks as much at himself as at Molly, he throws the lever, slams in the tailgate and wrathfully drives back along the filthy and aromatic aisle that the drive from barn to road has just become. Fortunately Daddy Dougan is nowhere in sight but everyone else is, out from the barn, the milkhouse, and Big House, to hoot and grin.

Cleo can see that the cleanup job is almost hopeless. It will take him hours, maybe even days.

Ronald comes out of the office and shakes a sympathetic head. "You know what Hercules did when he had to clean out the Augean stables—do you want to try diverting the crick?"

Cleo isn't amused. He decides the field job had better wait until he at least tidies up the area in front of the main door of the Big House, and tells Mother Dougan—through the screen—to let Daddy know that he will finish the job on his own time. He closes Molly in the horse yard, scrubs his face and arms in the horse trough, sighs deeply, and goes to find a broom.

The farm's manure spreader poses for a formal portrait.

8 ⚔ BACK-FENCE WALK

It's a Saturday afternoon in early autumn. Jackie is eight. She and Joan and Patsy and Craig are playing school in the old schoolhouse beside the corncrib. Joan is the teacher. She punishes infractions severely; all her pupils sit facing corners except Jip, who has scratched to be let out for recess.

Grampa flings open the door. "Come along, cubbies!" he shouts. "It's too fine a day to be at lessons indoors. I'll show you some outdoor lessons! Come with me for a back-fence walk."

The four are willing enough to go. They're tired of playing school. So is Jip. He runs ahead when Grampa turns down the lane toward the crick.

"Most people follow roads," Grampa says. "You can see a lot of things on roads, if you keep your eyes open, but there are so many things you miss by not following back fences."

They cross the crick, balancing on the stepping stones, except for Jip who splashes through, pausing midway for a noisy drink. They go through the pasture toward the gravel pit. Jip finds a gopher hole, and Grampa looks around till he finds the gopher's back door. He tells them that little animals that live underground always have a back door for escape if something, like Jip's nose, comes poking in their front door. They know this already. Jackie wonders how Grampa can tell which door is the back one.

The gravel pit is always a good place to play. There's a weathered wooden bridge in it, with a hole as big as a cistern cover in the middle. There's no water under the bridge, just a place to stand a farm cart. The hired men shovel gravel through the hole into the cart below. It's easier to shovel gravel down than up. But when they play, the four of them don't use the hole for its purpose. They jump down through it, in Follow the Leader, or slide down through it with a gunny sack full of stones and sticks over their shoulders, being Santa Claus, or pop up through it as the troll, trying to catch the three Billy Goats Gruff who, one by one, trip-trap over the bridge. This last is the most satisfactory of the games, for there are roles for each of them: Joan as the fierce troll and the other three in ascending order as the billy goat brothers.

On the floor of the gravel pit, Grampa bends and picks up a smooth, round stone. "Do you know how this stone got here?" he asks. "There were great glaciers that covered Wisconsin with ice, and when they melted they left behind these gravel deposits. Their immense weight grinding over the bedrock crushed it to gravel, and then the ice rolled and carried the gravel under and before it, and the streams that flowed out from under the melting glaciers tumbled the stones some more. That's why so many of these stones are smooth and rounded."

They climb the hill on the far side of the gravel pit. At the fence they turn east. Grampa checks the fence posts and bob wire as they go. He says, "Just as I thought. Some of these posts are rotting out. They'll need replacing. And the wire needs tightening up. We don't want our cows getting into our neighbor's alfalfa." He walks on a bit and adds, "But a three-wire fence never holds a cow if there isn't something in her own field to eat."

There's a kind of broad-bladed grass growing along the fence. Daddy has shown them all how to pluck a blade, place it length-wise between their thumbs, and blow through the small slit their pressed thumbs leave between them. The blade vibrates and makes a rude noise, rather like a razzberry. They show Grampa their whistles and demonstrate, though he can't hear them.

"You've made whistles," approves Grampa. "I taught your father and uncle

Cows with Spring Brook, fences, gravel pit, and distant Mackie farm.

to blow on grass blades when they were small. Do you know that all this bromegrass belongs to me?"

They nod.

"The grass knows it too," says Grampa. "Every blade has my initial on it." He shows them one. In a different shade of green, at about the middle of the blade, an unmistakable W stretches from side to side.

"For 'Wesson,'" twinkles Grampa. "Like a cow brand out west. But my brand doesn't hurt them. They grow my initial willingly."

The four pounce on other blades of bromegrass to see whether they all have Ws. They all do. Joan reaches through the bob wire and plucks a blade. "This one is on Mackies' land!" she writes to Grampa. "Why does it have a W, too?"

"Oh my," says Grampa. "It's just wanting to see if it will grow greener on the other side of the fence!"

They all laugh. They know Grampa is fooling.

Patsy takes a blade, turns it upside down, and points to the marking. She makes a letter M in hand language, then spells, M F-O-R M-A-C-K-I-E.

"Well, well," says Grampa. "The grass on that side must know they belong to Mr. Mackie."

They reach the end of the field by the Mackie farm. Grampa examines the corner post, which has to be in especially good condition since it's so important, supporting fencing from two directions.

"Look at this bob wire," says Grampa. "Notice how it's made, by twisting two wires and regularly inserting the barbs. See how they circle the twist. This wire of mine has only one barb." He walks to the adjoining fence. "This one of Mr. Mackie's has double barbs. And there are other varieties, too. The farm stores have great rolls of different sorts. Bob wire was invented, I think, only fifty miles from here, down at DeKalb. My, you should see the mansions of the families who've made their fortunes on that invention! But have you noticed how some farms have pastures with wooden fences? Those are for horses. Cows won't get tangled up in a bob wire fence, but horses will. They can rip themselves badly."

C-O-W-S S-M-A-R-T-E-R? spells Joan.

"About fences, certainly," Grampa says.

They follow the fence down to the crick. It's where the stream almost meets the curve in Colley Road. They cross the stream again.

"The school you were just playing in stood right here," Grampa says. "Your daddy went to school here, and so did Trever and Esther and Eloise.

Your daddy even taught here for a short while before college. They called it the Dougan School because it was on the corner of my land. Then, when it became cheaper to send you District 12 children to town than pay for a teacher and supplies and building upkeep, I bought the school for twenty-five dollars and moved it across the field to the farm."

The four nod. Jackie has studied the picture in Grama's album of kids wading in the crick, in front of the schoolhouse. There's a picture, too, of Daddy and all the other boys standing on the roof. And Daddy has told how he and his pupils skated on the crick. At Todd School, there's no wading or skating or climbing on roofs. It would have been a lot more fun if District 12 had decided to keep the old school right here.

Grampa pulls up the bottom strand of bob wire, and one by one, the four lie down on the grass, their arms tight against their sides, and roll under. Then Joan does the same so that Grampa can roll under. Grampa always rolls under bob wire fences, although the hired men usually step on the bottom strand with their heavy shoes and pull up on the next strand, making a gap to crawl through. Jip always gets through on his own.

Now they are on the Mackies' land. They follow the crick as it winds past the Mackie gravel pit and through a long pasture. A clump of trees is at the far end of it. This is all new territory for Jackie. She hasn't explored beyond the boundaries of the farm. The others haven't, either. Grampa tells them how Spring Brook originates in marshy land beyond Clinton. It flows into Turtle Creek shortly after it goes under Colley Road, close to town. Jackie knows where that is: Spring Brook's spindly red iron bridge, and Turtle Creek's flat black bridge are almost double bridges. The two streams meet just beyond the double bridges and just before the railroad bridge, in the flood plain beyond the two bridges.

"Then Turtle Crick joins Rock River in South Beloit, and Rock River joins the Mississippi at Rock Island, and the Mississippi flows into the Gulf of Mexico. We are connected to the sea by our little Spring Brook watershed."

"Where does Turtle Crick start?" Jackie writes.

"Up near Mukwonago, where Phantom Lake Y camp is. From a shallow lake near it called Mud Lake."

They've reached the end of the pasture; the clump of trees is on the other side of the stream.

"It's a woods!" exclaims Craig. He pulls Grampa's arm and points.

"We'll go over there in a moment," says Grampa. "I want to see something here, first."

Jackie looks down the bank as they walk. Below them the crick has broadened and the water runs still and deep. There are huge ancient willow trees with shaggy bark and slender young shoots springing up beside their thick trunks. The trees lean untidily over the water, dropping their thin yellow leaves. Some leaves are carried sedately downstream by the even current; some, like small curled barques, twirl slowly in dark eddies. Jackie feels delight. Who would have thought there was such an enchanted place so close to home?

Suddenly, their way is blocked by an immense chasm. It's too wide by far to jump across. Its sides drop like cliffs. Its mouth opens into the crick like a waterless river, and the dry riverbed winds back into the land east of them as far as Jackie can see.

Grampa shakes his head. "This is what else I came to check."

They retrace their steps till they find a place they can climb down the bank. They return along the narrow gravelly stream verge to the gully and stand at the bottom of the great gulch. They walk into it a little way.

Grampa says, "This is a terrible thing. Bad farming practices in the fields above here have caused this erosion. At every storm, rain runs off the land and uses this pathway to get to the crick. The rain carries the topsoil with it, and the force of the water digs this gully wider and deeper. The world depends on its farms for food, you know, and we're letting our precious soil run down into the sea. Have you noticed that after a storm, the crick in our back pasture runs thick brown?"

The four nod vigorously.

"Most of that mud is coming from here." Grampa shakes his head some more. "I should hate to see this spot in a freshet."

Patsy points out the black color of the soil at the top of the gully, and its change to mustard yellow at the bottom.

"Yes," Grampa says. "It's cut through the loam right down to clay and gravel. We have some of the richest and deepest topsoil in the world, right here in Rock County, but every year we're losing inches of it. When we get to clay and gravel, there'll be no more crops."

"Can't it be stopped?" pantomimes Craig.

"Oh, yes. If the hills were left in grass, and not plowed, there'd be scant runoff. The roots would hold the soil. Or if the plowing went around the slopes instead of up and down. Then every furrow would be a little dam. Of course it's not just water that causes erosion. Wind does, too. We're only beginning to recover from the worst erosion this country has ever known, where the Great Plains were plowed, and then came drought, and then wind—and all the topsoil, that's taken tens of thousands of years to build up, has been blown away in dust storms. There's been terrible loss and terrible suffering. You've seen pictures of the dust bowl."

Soberly, the four nod.

"Your father and I are trying to farm so that we increase the soil rather than lose it," Grampa says.

Jackie plucks a snail shell from a band of soil at the level of her hand. She shows Grampa.

"Yes," says Grampa. "That shell's been there a long time. When you're older you'll study geology and learn the workings of

Patsy, Joan, Jackie, and Craig at the back fence. Notice the barbed-wire and fence post.

the powerful forces that form and fold the rocks"—he flings his arms above his head—"and lift them from the ocean bed to glitter above the clouds!"

N-O M-O-U-N-T-A-I-N-S H-E-R-E, spells Patsy, shaking her head.

"No, but there was once an ocean. This was all a warm shallow sea and that's where the limestone that we have so much of has come from. When sea creatures died, their shells rained down to the bottom; and after eons, the shells built up to such great and heavy thickness that they were pressed into rock. If you study the rocks, you'll find in them the fossils of creatures that once lived."

Jackie tries to imagine such age, such vast numbers of sea creatures. It makes her almost too dizzy to think.

D-I-N-O-S-A-U-R-S, Craig spells.

"Yes, dinosaurs," Grampa agrees. "Dinosaur bones were recognized for what they are shortly before I was born, and dinosaurs burst into fame when I was a little lad. My, how interested I was in learning everything I could about them! Everyone was filled with wonder that such behemoth creatures once roamed our world."

Grampa hands back the shell and Jackie carefully pockets it. He crumbles a bit of soil from the gully wall and shakes his head some more.

"All this land isn't Grampa's," Joan says, and then spells to her grandfather, W-H-A-T C-A-N Y-O-U D-O? She stabs a finger at him to emphasize the question mark.

"Education," Grampa says. "The university, and the county agents, and the Grange—the federal government, too—are all working to improve farming methods and to let the farmer know about them. I can help there, learning myself and informing my neighbors. What we—your father and I—have been doing, is renting the Snide farm, where this ditch starts, and now your parents are buying it; it's the new farm." He points up the gully, but nobody is tall enough to see over the top. "Now we can fill in the gully up there and then farm so that the erosion slows down and stops. It will be a challenge; that farm is almost as hilly as the Hill Farm."

They walk back down the gully to where it reaches the crick and follow the verge to a shallow place where the water runs quickly over gravel. It makes a cheerful gurgle. Here, the falling willow leaves are swirled and whisked downstream rapidly.

They ford the crick; Jip stops in the middle again for a sloppy drink. On this side, the bank slopes up gently, and behind the willows the woods begin.

Joan is behaving oddly. She looks at the trees, walks a few feet, and looks again. Then, still looking, she walks backward. She tugs Grampa's sleeve. R-O-W-S, she spells, and explains to her sisters and brother, "Look how the trees are all planted in rows, and they're all the same kind of tree. This is a planted woods!"

Jackie walks backward and forward, too. So do Patsy and Craig. It's true. The big trees are in orderly rows. It's strange.

"There's a story to this grove," Grampa says. "Back at the time of the Civil War, men were drafted to serve in the Union Army. But if you had money enough, three hundred dollars I think it was, and could find someone else who was willing to go, you could pay him to go in your place. The man who then owned the Blodgett farm paid a man to go in his stead. That man was killed. Mr. Houston felt terribly guilty. Well, some years later, there came a man along the road with a horse and wagon. He was a Union Army veteran and had lost a leg and was blind in one eye. He was going from farm to farm selling catalpa saplings—catalpa wood makes excellent fence posts. And Mr. Houston felt so guilty that he bought the whole wagon load, to salve his conscience."

"And planted them here," Joan exclaims triumphantly.

"He planted them here," repeats Grampa, not knowing he's repeating. "But he didn't feel so guilty that he used his own strength and sweat to plant them. He had his son-in-law do it. It was a hard, hot job and the son-in-law thought he'd never get to the end of planting catalpa trees. I know all this because it was the son-in-law—Mr. Hill, who used to live on the Obeck place, who told me the story."

"They must not have used many trees for fence posts," Patsy observes. "There are still a lot here."

"I don't think he ever used these trees for fence posts," Grampa says.

Joan spells to Grampa, Y-O-U N-E-E-D F-E-N-C-E P-O-S-T-S.

"Yes." Grampa laughs. "And we will cut them out of our own woods at the Hill Farm."

The four walk back and forth some more to see the rows shift. Grampa points out the large size of catalpa leaves, and the long seed pods hanging from the branches and littering the ground. They peel back the brown husks and see the hard, fat, shiny seeds lying in a row inside, like beans.

"Some people call catalpas 'bean trees,'" Grampa says. "Locusts are bean trees, too, and some others. Catalpas are late budding out—every other woods will be green before this one. My first spring here, I thought this entire woods was dead."

Jackie adds a bean to the shell in her pocket. She will call this special place "the Catalpa Forest."

They leave the woods and head back to the dairy. As they go through the farm gravel pit again, Jackie picks up a small stone rounded by the glacier and adds it to her treasures. Grampa notices her do it. She spells to him, Y-O-U C-A-N L-E-A-R-N A L-O-T F-R-O-M S-T-O-N-E-S.

"Yes," says Grampa. "God's hand has written history as definitely on the pages of rock beneath our feet as on the pages of Scripture. We just have to learn to read them."

Back at the farm, they thank Grampa for the back-fence walk. He goes off to check on the milking. Jackie sets out the shell, the bean, and the stone on the well lid. She contemplates them. There are many more kinds of reading, she decides, than what Todd School teaches.

9 ❧ CHUCK KELLOR

Ron Dougan and Chuck Kellor are high school classmates. They also both go to the Methodist Church, and are in Epworth League together. In their later years, they tell Jackie about it.

"Sunday nights," Ron says, "I'd saddle up a horse and ride into town. I'd smell all horsey."

"I'd walk up from South Beloit on those wooden sidewalks," says Chuck.

Epworth League, held in the church basement, starts with a bit of prayer and Bible, followed by a business meeting. It is more social than church, a good place to meet girls. And there are good times with girls. They play guessing games. They play circle games where hands are held. They play hide-and-seek type games through the dim stairways and Sunday School cubicles and darkened sanctuary of the echoing church. Ron wishes he had the courage to sneak the kisses he suspects Chuck and the other boys sneak.

Every evening includes refreshments. Sometimes these constitute the program and entertainment: once they decorate a number of areas as different countries, tell about the country, and offer samples of that country's cuisine. Occasionally there's a box supper, where Ron and Chuck have to do quick detective work to find out which boxes have been prepared by the girls they want to sit with and possibly be allowed to walk home. At the bidding, a popular girl's box may go for seventy-five cents or even a dollar. Ron is forced to keep his bidding modest, for a man's wages, on the farm, are room and board and a dollar a day. Proceeds from such box socials and other money-raising events swell Epworth League's treasury, to help pay its missionary pledge or send chosen members to state conferences. Chuck has to bid low, too, but both boys usually win the girl they want. As Ron quotes a well known saying, many years later, "But if you're not with the girl you love, you love the girl you're with!"

There is, of course, no dancing or cards, although the minister stuns them one night by stopping in and saying, "I have something to report. They've

Gathering alfalfa haycocks, 1917.

started a dance class in a Methodist church in Milwaukee. What do you think of that?"

Sometimes W.J. drives a hay-covered wagon on runners to the church, and all the young people have a sleigh ride out to the farm. Grama feeds them oyster stew, they sing and play games, and then are driven back. Ron, in a friendly scuffle with Ethel Hopper on one such trip, knocks her into the snow and a runner goes over her arm. He's stricken, but the snow is deep and soft and she isn't hurt.

Chuck is one of the sons of Mark Kellor, the carpenter hired by Grampa to build the round barn. Mark Kellor's full name is Mark Twain Kellor but he doesn't broadcast this. He's also the builder of the milkhouse, the Big House additions, the Little House, and the Mackie barn on the adjacent farm; later he'll turn the sheds at Chez Nous into the first corn dryer in the area, and work on the remodeling of Chez Nous itself. He was the builder of the large Methodist Church on the corner of Pleasant and Public streets, where Ron and Chuck go to Epworth League.

For the summer before his senior year, and then weekends, Chuck works on the farm. He's planning to go to college, and needs to save money. His first task is pulling weeds in the garden across the road. One section is so weedy he assumes nothing else is growing there, and pulls up all the young vegetables too. "How could I tell?" he says later. "Wasn't I a town boy?" He has no dif-

Alfalfa haycocks, protected by canvas caps, the bane of Ron and Chuck.

ficulty identifying pea pods. The crop is heavy, the rows endless. He then has to shell them; Mother Dougan and Hilda are canning peas in the kitchen.

W.J. approves of him. In mid-August he writes to Ron, who with Trever is at Phantom Lake Y Camp, "Chas. Kellor has been away since Sat. noon to the fair at Springfield, Ill. He is a nice lad and learns quickly."

All summer the garden interests Chuck. He makes a plat of it, noting where everything is planted. The next spring he directs the planting, making sure that nothing is in the same spot again. He has learned that different plants take different tolls on the soil.

Both summers, with Ron, he has the chore of tending the caps on the alfalfa haycocks. When alfalfa is new and not many are growing it, it's considered a precious crop that must be cured carefully, to keep the sun from bleaching out the nutrients in the leaves, to keep the stems from becoming woody. The alfalfa is cut in the field and gathered into mounds to cure. The haycocks are protected by four-foot squares of white canvas, whose corners are weighted down with half horseshoes.

Once the alfalfa is mounded, Chuck and Ron drive a horse and wagon through the field. The wagon bed has been removed, leaving only the long reach, over which the canvases are draped. They go from cock to cock, taking a canvas off the reach, slinging it over a cock, and adjusting the horseshoes to anchor the cap's four corners smoothly. When the hay has been cured they return with the wagon, remove the caps one by one, and sling them back over the reach.

This is a job Ron has hated since he was old enough to be employed at it. In lifting a canvas off the reach there is almost no way to avoid having a horseshoe swing around and catch a bare shin. The same is true of pulling a canvas off a cock and replacing it on the reach. There have been summers when Ron has been bloody from ankles to knees. Now he and Chuck, both in long pants, develop a system as synchronized as a dance, each on one side of a canvas and side-stepping to or from the cock. This alleviates the problem somewhat. After the hay is cured and the canvases gathered, they both help load the cocks: a whole mound at a time on the wagon.

Once Chuck graduates, he moves out to the farm full time. He lives in the bunkhouse above the milkhouse, with Ted Selmer, George Meredith, and Dan Kelley. Ron moves over there, too.

Away from the supervision of the Big House, the young men engage in various hijinks. "One night," says Chuck, "I had a date, and found the buggy that Daddy Dougan made available to the help had had its wheels switched — the big wheels in front, the small in back. I took the buggy as if I didn't even notice, and drove with my girl through town with both of us leaning back so far we were almost lying down. She was a good sport. We'd all worked out a rotating schedule for the buggy, and the next guy — Ted — said, 'Hey Chuck, get out there and change the wheels!' 'I rode through town that way,' I told him. 'It's great for seeing the stars!'"

The group prepares another trick on Chuck. The entrance to the second

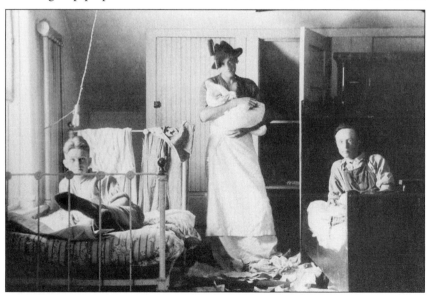

In the bunkhouse over the milkhouse, Ron has the left bed, Chuck Kellor the right. Howard Brant graces the center.

floor is by way of a folding staircase pulled down from the milkhouse ceiling by a chain. They gather all the tinware, all the pails and pans they can find around the place. They balance these on the folded stairs. "When I came in from my date," Chuck says, "I pulled the chain to get up to my bed, the staircase swung down, and everything spilled on top of me. They all laughed like crazy! I laughed, too, but left everything there and they had to put the stuff back, or Daddy Dougan would have got after them in the morning!"

In late summer W.J. puts Chuck on one of the milk routes. His team is afraid of storms. Rain doesn't bother them, but thunder and lightning make them crazy. At their first skitter, during the first ominous rumble, Chuck learns to head for Strong's Livery Stable on Broad Street. The stablemen know him and his horses. They have the gates open waiting as he gallops in. He sits out the storms there with his nervous team.

The horses are also afraid of the Interurban train. Chuck says, "They'd stand quietly while a regular train went by, but when they'd spot the Interurban on Fourth Street, they'd start to run. One time I was away from the truck, delivering, when an Interurban came in view. The horses took off without me. I telephoned the farm, and Daddy Dougan met them at the edge of town, just as they were heading off Milwaukee Road onto Colley Road. They hadn't turned the wagon over; they were simply going home."

When some streets are so deep in mud that he can't get his wagon through, Chuck dons knee-high rubber boots and delivers on foot. And when the Spanish flu strikes the other routeman during the terrible epidemic of 1919, for almost ten days he runs both routes, afterwards returning to the dairy to wash up a truckload of bottles with Daddy Dougan, for the milkhouse workers have the flu, too.

"I stayed two years on the farm, doing something of everything," Chuck says. "Then I was ready to leave. I'd saved my money, had a room reserved at the University of Illinois, and had my suitcase packed. But shortly before my departure something strange happened. I fell asleep early one evening and later my folks couldn't wake me. The next day, when they still couldn't wake me, they called the doctor. He couldn't rouse me, either. I finally did wake up—I never felt sick—but those peculiar sleeping spells continued on and off. Because of them, I felt I couldn't go away to school. Instead, I took an accounting course locally and got a business job. The spells weren't ever diagnosed but eventually they went away. I sometimes wonder how my life might have been different if I'd gone on to school."

Chuck marries and has a family, as does Ron. Over the years the two

Farmhands by the side barn, with alfalfa, wheelbarrow rider, and bull. Herdsman Art Kassilke is on the left, Lonnie Richardson in the wheelbarrow, then Charles Marlow and Ted Selmer.

friends greet each other on Sunday mornings at the Methodist Church that Chuck's father built. Sometimes they tell their kids about the things they used to do in Epworth League. Sometimes they even tell them about their pranks when they were high schoolers, both working on the farm.

"One thing I haven't told them," Chuck says to Ron and Jackie. "Before I ever worked there regular, still a kid, maybe thirteen, fourteen, I helped Dad put a roof on the Big House extension. He told me I could drink all the return milk I wanted, it was in a box in the cooler—I spent so much time drinking those little bottles of chocolate milk he had to haul me back to the shingling. From on high I could look down into the barnyard, and they brought the big bull, it was long before artificial insemination, and they kept bringing cows to him, cow after cow after cow, and he mounted them all. I was amazed at his endurance! Maybe it was just a job to him. But it was sure hard for me to keep my mind on *my* job!"

10 ❧ ANGLE OF REPOSE

If you've ever played with dry sand, in a sand pile or at the beach, you know you can make a pyramid only so steep. You can make it higher and higher, but no matter how much sand you pour on top it will slip down the sides and stop on the same slant. The slant will never get slantier. This angle is about the same for all dry measure: sand, gravel, corn, oats, soybeans. It's the angle where dry things cease slipping over each other and come to rest. Since ancient times it's been called "Angle of Repose." The dictionary puts it, "The angle of maximum slope at which a heap of any loose solid material (as earth) will stand without sliding." Daddy's knowledge of the angle of repose—when he remembers it—saves him time, trouble, and money when he's building the pit silo.

Since 1917, the farm has gotten along with two concrete silos. But in recent years, green ears and husks, mixed with some corn, have been available to area farmers from the Libby Canning Plant at Janesville, for only the cost of transportation. When Daddy first took advantage of this cheap fodder there was a near disaster, for the wet silage was too heavy and cracked the central silo. Now that silo is useless. Daddy wants to use Libby's, and so needs more storage space. He decides to build a pit silo. He decides rather late, and has a deadline for when the Libby's silage will arrive.

Pit silos, sometimes called trench silos, are a new idea. Research has shown that silage, corn or grass, will keep satisfactorily lying in a bin on the ground, or dug into the ground. If packed properly, there will be very little spoilage. Such construction is much cheaper than building a tall circular silo. Daddy had earlier tried blowing the silage onto the ground, like a hay stack, and then tramping it down, but this didn't work—the spoilage went too far in on the sides and top.

Daddy hires an engineer to design a pit silo. It will be a concrete box built into a hill, open at the top and one end. The cost is estimated at two to three thousand dollars. The site is down the lane toward the crick, where the lane

Ron directs a race of schoolkids in the empty pit silo. The concrete sides rest at the angle of repose.

ends at the pasture gate. At that spot the land slopes down, and the underlying gravel is close to the surface. Bulldozers dig out the area for the box. But it won't stay dug out, as it would if it had solid earth sides. The gravel from the hill slides down and rests at the angle of repose. The workmen have to clear a much larger area in order to make a space broad enough for the concrete floor.

Once the floor is laid and hardened, they spread heavy paper on part of it, and use the floor as the base on which to construct a reinforced 6 x 12 concrete slab. This will be set vertically, as a portion of one of the sides. When it's ready to position, a hired hoist lifts it. But something skips on the hoist, and the slab falls from a height of ten or fifteen feet and smashes.

The workmen construct another slab. It takes several days to cure. They then clear the edge where it's to go; the hoist lifts it and sets it in place at the inner end of the pit. Everyone stands back to admire. But before it can be secured, gravel from behind slides down against the slab and throws it on its face. It smashes.

The engineer and contractor stand perplexed, rubbing their chins. What to do? They decide to construct a row of deadheads—a kind of deep-sunk posts—fifteen feet back in the field around the silo. An iron chain will go on each deadhead, and fasten to a slab. The chains will keep the slabs perpendicular. The cost of the pit silo is now estimated at seven to eight thousand dollars.

To Daddy, time and money are fast going out of sight. He also can't see what will keep the gravel from slipping under the chained slabs, forcing them up and destroying them again. The cost will continue to rise, and the silo will be finished too late for this year's Libby's corn. He looks at the gravel resting at the angle of repose.

"Why do the walls have to be vertical?" he asks. "Why not let the gravel slip till it comes to rest naturally, and then cement over that?"

The contractor and engineer look at each other. They're astonished at the simple idea. They figure and confer. They decide it can be done.

After that, the silo is constructed in about three days. The concrete is merely laid on the stationary slope. There's no need for hoists and chains and deadheads; the pit silo eases into the hillside like an old lady into her rocking chair. It waits for Libby's to fill its lap.

When the trucks come they drive over the ground to the upper end of the pit and dump their cargos on a concrete platform. Then a Dougan tractor, equipped with a front-end loader, pushes the green material over into the pit. The same tractor is also equipped with double rear wheels and carries a large concrete block. The heavy tractor travels back and forth over the silage, packing it tightly, getting out the air that men tramping in boots could never accomplish. Once the pit is filled to overflowing, a heavy vinyl cover is stretched across the top and weighted down with old automobile tires. The tires are moved and the vinyl peeled back as the silage is used. It's scooped up by an endloader and taken to fill bunks in the barnyard, out of which the cattle feast.

Before long Daddy finds an additional reason why the pit silo is better built this way. When the silage is put up against the slope, on the angle of repose, it packs itself. As it ferments and shrinks down some, it merely packs tighter. With the vertical walls of other silos, he notices, as the silage shrinks it draws away from the walls and lets air in. And air, of course, causes spoilage.

Except for a little fermented drainage into the creek at the start of each season, and the aesthetics (for black vinyl strewn with tires like gigantic ripe olives is hardly handsome) the pit silo is entirely satisfactory. It costs considerably less than the initial estimate.

Daddy is pleased with himself. He brags, "There's more than one way to kill a cat besides choking it with cream!"

11 ⚹ FOOLS' NAMES

I t is 1909. Ronald is seven. For his birthday, he has a new jack knife from Aunt Ida. Trever is jealous.

"I want a jack knife too," he declares.

Aunt Ida assures him, "When you're as old as Ronald, I'll get you a jack knife. Five is too little for one."

Trever has heard that story before. When he is seven, Ronald will be nine. Aunt Ida will have forgotten about the knife. She'll be buying Ronald an air rifle, telling Trever that seven is too young for an air rifle; she'll get him one when he's as old as Ronald. Trever knows he never will be as old as Ronald.

"Let me use your jack knife," he wheedles.

"No," says Ronald. "Five is too young to play with a knife. You'll cut yourself."

Ronald uses his new knife at every opportunity. He sharpens sticks, he tries to make willow whistles, he fashions parts for his red coaster wagon.

One morning at school he raises his hand. Miss Church excuses him and he goes to the boys' backhouse. While he's sitting there, his jack knife falls out of his pocket onto the floor. He picks it up, opens it, and begins carving an R on the inside of the door. He stays a few minutes longer than his business necessitates, to get a good start on it. At recess he finishes the R and starts on an O. O's are harder, because they are entirely curved.

Whenever he has to raise his hand during the day, and at lunch and recess, he works slowly and meticulously on the backhouse door. Sometimes he raises his hand when he doesn't really have to go. He's careful not to stay in the backhouse too long.

The other boys are much interested. They envy him his jack knife. They make bets on how long it will take him to finish his name.

At last it's complete. The backhouse door is chiseled out in large, deep block letters. RONALD DOUGAN. Ronald is satisfied with his workmanship. The boys are respectful.

That night after supper Trever shouts into Grampa's ear trumpet, "Ronald carved his name on the backhouse door!"

"Shut up! Shut up!" Ronald shrills.

"What?" says his father.

Trever shouts as loud as he can. "RONALD CARVED HIS NAME ON THE BACKHOUSE DOOR! WITH HIS NEW JACK KNIFE!"

Understanding breaks over Grampa's face. He looks sternly and sorrowfully at his elder son. "Ronald, is what Trever tells me true?"

Ronald hangs his head.

"I am disappointed in you," says Grampa. "You'll have to remove it. Come along." He takes Ronald's hand. They go to the tool shed. "Select a plane," says his father.

Ronald looks at the three planes on the worktable. They are all large. They are all heavy. He takes the smallest one.

Grampa keeps ahold of his hand. Together they walk across the plowed furrows of the East Twenty toward the schoolhouse. Grampa takes long strides. Ronald has to trot fast. The plane in his other hand gets heavier and heavier. He cries. Behind him at a safe distance Trever capers and flings taunts.

At the boys' backhouse Grampa opens the door. There is the name: RON-ALD DOUGAN.

They survey it together. To Ronald the once splendid letters now seem to move and dance, to be red with the licking flames of hellfire, like the printing of the devil's whispers in one of his storybooks.

Grampa shakes his head. He says, "'Fools' names and fools' faces always appear in public places.'" He lets go of Ronald's hand and stands holding the open door steady.

Sobbing louder, Ronald begins to plane the letters. On the farm, he has always liked to use the plane, to run it along a board and have the sweet smelling curl form behind and fall off. But he's never planed on a vertical surface before. It's terribly hard. He tries going from bottom to top. He tries going from top to bottom. He tries going from side to side. That's the worst, for the plane is heavy and keeps slipping.

His father gives no advice.

Ronald settles on bottom to top, crouching before the door in order to get more shove pressure. The wood curls fall down around his knees. Slowly, very slowly because he carved them so deep, the letters are erased. He has to come at some parts of them from all different directions. The plane grows so heavy he can hardly move it. Often it nicks and chips and is balky. He can scarcely see through his tears. Grampa stands silent. Ronald knows he will not be finished till nothing more can be seen. The swatch he planes gets larger and deeper.

Finally his father says, "There."

Ronald gets up, stands back, wipes his eyes and nose with his sleeve. The spot is now smooth and light-colored against the seasoned surface. No trace of RONALD DOUGAN can be seen.

Grampa closes the door. He points to the mound of shavings left on the ground. Ronald scrapes them up and hides them between the bushes by the fence. Then he and Grampa start across the field again. His father still holds his hand, but now he walks more slowly, matching his stride to Ronald's, and he carries the plane. Trever is nowhere in sight.

In the middle of the field Grampa stops. "Look. There's an oat, just starting to come up." He kneels.

Ronald kneels, too. A little green shoot is pushing its way out of the furrow. The hull is still clinging to the blade.

"It's such an ordinary thing, springtime, and crops coming up," his father says, "yet every time a seed sprouts, it's a tiny miracle. Look down the furrows—all the seeds are pushing up. It was the rain yesterday."

Ronald looks, and in the slant evening sun sees the faint green flush of oat seedlings all over the field.

"Grow, little fellow," croons Grampa to the oat, touching it gently with his finger. "Grow strong and sturdy in the sun and the rain! Grow to make feed for the cattle and bedding for their stalls! Grow to do your little bit in the universe!"

Ronald thinks how little a bit it is, one oat plant! But multiplied by a field of oats, by fields and fields of oats, the granaries overflow, the strawstack is a golden mountain. He does not know why, but his spirits lift.

They stand up, return to the farm, replace the plane in the toolshed. Nothing more is ever said about fools' names.

12 • RONALD PART 3 • WHY NOT FARMING?

It's September of 1923 when Vera Wardner joins the staff at the Methodist Memorial in Chateau Thierry. She will be working with girls, teaching English, piano, ballet. Ron Dougan has been there nearly four months, his Boy Scout troop thriving. He continues writing home. Depending on boat schedules, a letter often takes two weeks to arrive at the farm, two weeks more for its reply. Almost all his letters now contain warm references to Miss Wardner. October 12:

> I had a royal two-day vacation with Miss Sedgwick and Miss Wardner. Miss Wardner is a charming girl from Chicago who has just arrived—really awfully nice. We did everything—walked the length of the Champs Elysees, sat in the Tuillerie Gardens, wandered through the Louvre and saw originals of all the copies we've known all our lives, we went to the opera, saw Notre Dame and St. Chapelle again, and climbed to the top of the former. Counting hotel, carfare, taxis, meals, and all, the two days cost me six dollars.

Ronald writes he's feeling rotten about the cost of Northwestern. When his job is over he'll tear home and earn money. He hates traveling alone, anyway. Still, it seems wrong, once here, not to learn all he can of other countries. About college, he's no nearer knowing what he wants to do. He likes science, government, business—in fact everything, now he's taken a fancy to French. Maybe an Econ major?

"Perhaps I think too much about work I'll find satisfying. Why not farming? It is fairly sure, healthy, and a man's head doesn't go to sleep as is proved by you, Dad. You know me so well—is it just plain dislike for any work that makes me hesitate about farming?"

He confesses his current ideas are as elusive "as the famous Irishman's flea of Dougan mythology."

November 6 brings, "I do think studying and reading and letting my mind run is a good sign." His field of enjoyment is broadening: "To my surprise, classical music isn't distasteful. The girl from Chicago plays the piano well, and in Paris at the opera I get a big kick."

> Then books! How long since I have spent an evening curled up reading? Now it is most nights from ten till after eleven. And walks and bicycle rides! The river winds through a broad valley. The rolling hills on the horizon have a cover of bluish haze, while the nearer ones show more vivid coloring. We do not have the isolated farm houses as at home, here from almost any point in the valley one can see from three to ten limestone walled red-tiled villages.

Ron and his Boy Scouts on a camping trip in the French countryside.

He finishes, "How is the farm going? I wonder if I am a farmer?"

On November 24, "My life has settled into such quiet lines that when I say I am enjoying myself immensely, studying every day, getting to Paris now and again, enjoying my congenial family here, I have said it all." Of the American girl: "We have a lot in common, and our trips to Paris are no end fun. Then, in doing the same things together every day we are able to twinkle at each other on lots of little things. Don't worry—it is the quiet sort of companionship that is so much worthwhile—none of the tumultuousness of college dates. I am well, and thinking about home—haven't had codfish gravy since I've been here."

He writes on December 19:

> The three girls and I have formed a Porridge Club. Every afternoon at four we brew something to eat, and are planning to get fat. I weigh over 150 lbs. stripped. We have more crazy fun.
>
> This sort of thing gives us a kick. Our washer woman came in last night, all cut up. They wash their clothes, even in winter, in little houses right over the Marne, in the cold running water. She let a suit of underwear of Vera's (the American girl) slip out of her hands and it had been washed down the river. Or last night—I was in my room typing songs for my scouts when I heard singing in the garden—Monsieur Dougan, Monsieur Dougan! I opened the window and in the half light saw Vera and Marcelle—the French girl. They were serenading me. I don't know why I did it, but a cup of water was on the sill. Over it went and caught them head on. They claim they might as well have been cats, and are thankful I didn't throw my alarm clock.
>
> About school, I am keen to finish. I am ready to cut out everything that doesn't lead directly to getting my degree.

For Christmas Ronald receives portraits of his parents, Trever, and Esther. He raves about them. "I want to hurry up and get to be your age, Dad, so I can have that nice twinkle around my eyes." He describes Christmas festivities at the Memorial, and that he and his scouts, bare-kneed, rode bicycles to Belleau Woods and helped place wreaths on the graves of unknown soldiers. He has spent two days in Paris: the Louvre, Notre Dame, a Middle Ages mystery play. And, "I went with Vera Wardner and Margaret Gaston. Margaret is a young English girl teaching in a girls' school here. I like her, and find Vera very wonderful indeed."

Ronald's mid-January letter is a paean to his parents, which for

Women washing clothes in the Marne sometimes lose a garment.

all its hyperbole, must have been gratifying and reassuring to them. He starts, "Dearest Mother and Dad, so you want to hear something of my daily program! I'll start on that. No telling how soon I'll shoot off on a tangent, though, and start expounding my limited understanding of love, war, or dramatics. Just take the subject of love, for example." The tangent has already begun.

Ron speaks of his parents' marriage, how they seem to have worked it out, all fifty-seven varieties. That if youngsters realized how much their parents knew of life, that they'd had similar ques-

Portrait of W.J. sent to his son in France, 1923.

tionings and wonderings, the parent-child relation would be perfect. "You for instance Dad—I've always known of your strength of character. Just the same, I'm only lately beginning to appreciate the fineness of your life, your marvelous courage—and then your quiet tact, your sympathetic understanding of people that shows itself in your eyes and sensitiveness of your mouth." He assures that this isn't a love letter; love letters exaggerate and look through rose-colored glasses.

"A blundering fool could make life such an emptiness for a wife. I had a funny thought a while ago. Of the men I know, I tried to picture one I could marry if I were a girl. Hardly a one could I put up with—mainly because they are so tactless—so lacking the traits you have."

He turns to his mother, the portrait by his bed:

> Yours is surely the head and carriage of an idealist. I can see generations of straight living and clear thinking back of you. You sometimes think I don't accept fully enough your ideas and ideals—what idealist does see actualities measure up to the goal in view? It bothers you when I bring out foolish arguments, when I see all ideas subject to a friendly debate. Of course it does—but do you think for a moment your good life, my home training, the breeding of generations of Christian men and women, doesn't profound-

The clear-eyed portrait of Eunice,
sent Ron in 1923.

ly affect my life, my impulses, my thinking?

Why do you suppose I'm not a moral weakling? Why do you suppose my tastes run to the beautiful, rather than the base, if it isn't my home and breeding that has made me? An English boy told me that he couldn't be alone in Paris for two hours without allowing some girl to pick him up. Why do you suppose that sort of thing interests me not at all and I'm as safe in Paris as I am on the farm, if it isn't you and Dad, and generations back of men and women like you that have made me? Why do I get more kick out of Browning than silly jingles, like a sunset better than artificial light and noise, like bonfire smoke better than a roomful of cigar smoke, like Chopin better than ragstuff?

And to both parents: "I may lack a number of necessary qualities in my makeup. Just the same I do have something in me that makes me want to play the game of life according to the rules—to live and love like a man. I don't lay this to any deep thought on my own account, but to what you have given me. The backing to think straight, to tell the true from the false. Let's see, I started out on the subject of my daily programme, didn't I?"

The letter following discusses his parents' worries about Trever. He ends it, "As to myself, I'm turning more and more towards the farm. It is a great life—will write more on that subject next time." And it is "next time"—January 30, 1924—that he drops on his parents the first of a series of thunderbolts.

13 ⨯ THRASHING

Whenever Jackie reads stories about farms, the yearly thrashing is given prominence. That's as it should be. On a farm, thrashing is a major event.

It was an event when Daddy was a little boy. He remembers the harbinger of the thrashing machine, the lumber wagon full of soft coal that rumbled into the farm a day or two ahead of time. It was the responsibility of each farmer to provide the coal for his own thrashing. The coal was used to stoke the thrashing machine's steam engine. He remembers better yet that day the thrashing machine arrived for the first time in his life. He was in the upstairs bathroom when he heard the commotion coming up the road from Marstons. Iron wheels were loud on the gravel; there was the shivering and shaking of metal, the pounding and chuffing and huffing of the steam engine. He ran to the window in his room, and the sight was as awesome as the sound: a metal behemoth lumbering along, filling the whole road. Tubes lying against its sides were like elephant trunks. The men were ants beside it. Ronald rushed downstairs and out to meet it, pitched over a croquet wicket in the front yard, and broke a toe.

He also remembers how it was when the thrashers quit for the day. There'd still be a little steam in the engine. He and Trever would go out and blow the whistle.

Thrashing is always an event for Jackie, too, and her brother and sisters. For days ahead, over in the Big House kitchen, one or another of them sits cross-legged on the flour box, out of traffic, watching Grama and Josie singe and clean chickens, roll out twice as many pies as usual, snip and shape and oil twice as many loaves of bread. Sometimes Jackie helps, snapping beans or stirring a pot. Over in the tiny kitchen of the Little House, Mother, too, and her helper, Geneva, are cooking ahead for the thrashers, long baking pans full of scalloped potatoes and cakes with coconut and brown sugar frostings. Nearby neighbors, whose farms are part of the thrashing circle, are also pre-

Pleas   Pleas   Pleas
Pleas
Pleas Dear Grandpa,
Please   Do you mind
if we slide down the straw stack?,
If we climb up on one side and
slide down on the same side?
Please let us gramps, we
haven't slid down it for ages,
it seems, and well try not
to knock it down ~~any~~ more
than it is. ~~Daddy would~~
~~sign~~ Daddy said he
would us if you'd sign, your
name on this paper. Please
let us *Please*

Jo, Pat, Jack, & Craig

Your Signature _ _ _ _ _ _ _ _ _ _

PATSY DODSON

Did Grampa give his consent to this plea?

paring. Hattie Blodgett always makes more pies. Mrs. Mackie chops cabbage and celery into pale jellied salad rings that nobody really likes. Lura Marston is responsible for platters of tomatoes and cucumbers. Then the thrashing machine comes, scarcely different from when Daddy was a little boy, except now it's pulled by a tractor and is powered not by steam but by a long belt that stretches from it to a tractor standing nearby. The machine is owned by a group of farmers on Colley Road, and they thrash in turn. Jackie doesn't know where it stays from August to August; it's never wintered on any of the Dougan farms. By not seeing it standing idle through the year, it's always a fresh surprise to her, its size and strength and the mystery of its voluminous innards. She can't see inside it to see how it does what it does, and there's no opportunity during the year to explore.

The thrashing begins. First the thrashing machine pulls in beside the stacked sheaves of oats that have already been cut by the binder and brought in behind the barns. These conical stacks are not easy to construct; the bundles have to be placed in such a way that they will drain and still not slide out of the stacks. Daddy says his always bulge or slide. But Albert Marston is the area's master stacker. He starts with the sheaves sloping down a little toward the center. When he gets near the top he gradually raises the center until he has a watershed.

Now the spike man, or spike pitcher—another skilled worker—stands on the edge of the stack and organizes the bundles as they're tossed to him from various parts of the stack. He straightens them out and pitches them into the traveling feeder trough, the throat of the thrashing machine, always grain heads first. The tractor roars; the belt tautens and spins. The machine gulps the bundles up, shivers, shakes, rattles. The longest tube, now an elephant trunk stretched out, spews the first golden straw onto the green ground, and the straw stack begins building. On the side of the thrashing machine the oats first trickle, then pour out into a wagon box.

Children aren't allowed in the field behind the horse barn where the thrashing is taking place. It's too dangerous. But there's a fine view from the horse yard fence or from the lane down to the crick. Jackie and Craig sit on fence posts in the sunshine. Behind them on the dusty lane, the heat rises in shimmering waves.

The elephant trunk rises slowly as the stack grows and grows. The men who are working in the straw are naked to their waists, their chests and faces and hair thick with straw dust. Heaped wagons roll in from the fields, bringing bundles that have been stacked there. The work and the noise and the flying straw against the blue sky go on and on. Then everything shivers to a stop. In the sudden stillness, a bird sings. Something has happened to the machine. Usually, it's that someone has lost a pitchfork into it, and the machine breaks down. Then all the men climb off the wagons and stack, drink water from five-gallon milk cans or bottles of orange drink and chocolate, and throw themselves down in the shade while the farm mechanics repair the damage. There is always ribbing that the pitchfork went in on purpose, for thrashing

The early steam threshing outfit. The engine drove a long, long leather belt …

is heavy, dirty, grueling, relentless work.

At noon comes the dinner. Mother is over, to help Grama and Josie, and so is Geneva. Fannie Veihman has come from the Hill Farm. The thrashers wash up and troop into the Big House dining room. They fill the entire extended table. Some years the dinner is set up on trestles in the front yard of the Big House, and then Jackie and Patsy, Craig and Joan run back and forth replenishing the pitchers of milk, the bowls of meat and gravy and vegetables, the plates of butter. After all the thrashers have eaten, the kitchen crew eats. Then Jackie and the others are employed as dish wipers for the mountains of dirty dishes.

This routine goes on for as many days as it takes to thrash the Dougan grain. As soon as a day's work is over, the four rush to play on the unfinished straw stack. Once the thrashing is finished, they know this will be forbidden.

"Those stacks are carefully built to shed water," Daddy always says when they beg. "Every time you stick a foot in the straw, that makes a pocket to collect water and rot the straw underneath. Sure, it's fun to climb up and slide down. I used to do it, too. But we just can't let you."

And then the machine crawls away, a great prehistoric monster, its rackety din fading down Colley Road. It goes to a neighboring farm where the process is repeated. It leaves behind bin after bin of gleaming grain and two huge and shining stacks of straw.

One summer, 1941, the pattern changes. Grama has been ailing; she's not up to feeding all the thrashers at the Big House. But Grampa and Daddy

... to power the dusty theshing machine.

have an idea. During the past year Geneva Bown has bought the Subway Cafe down on Third Street near the Beloit Iron Works. Earl Bown still drives a Dougan milk truck, but now if Jackie and the rest want to taste Geneva's chocolate pudding or Lazy Daisy cake, Daddy takes them downtown to sit up at the counter of the Subway.

This year, Grampa and Daddy ask Geneva if she'd be willing to have them bring all the thrashers downtown. Geneva is delighted. She plans to serve the men after the workers from the nearby shops have their noon hour. There is the plate-lunch special for twenty-five cents or the full dinner for thirty-five cents, she says. The full dinner is this: all the bread and crackers the men can eat, along with free coffee and milk. The first course is soup du jour, either bean or vegetable. The entree is roast beef or T-bone steak or two breaded pork chops or fried chicken, with two scoops of mashed potatoes and gravy and side dishes of vegetables. Dessert is chocolate or lemon pudding. A slice of pie is ten cents extra. Daddy and Grampa agree on the thirty-five cent dinner for each thrasher and pie for whoever wants it.

The first day of thrashing, all the thrashers but David Collins wash up, pull on their shirts, and pile into the back of the farm truck. David sits by himself in the shade of a bush, wolfing down the hefty sandwiches his mother has packed for him. He's fifteen years old, a town boy, and is working on the farm for the summer. Every day he pedals out on his bicycle with his sack lunch in his basket and does whatever Grampa tells him to do. Today he's been working in the thrashing. He's a greenhorn. He doesn't realize that thrashing is an event. He only knows that he's much tireder, much dirtier, much pricklier, and much hungrier than he's ever been before.

As the truck leaves the drive, Grampa spots David under the bush. "Stop!" roars Grampa, and the truck stops. "Come along, laddie, get in, get in!" Grampa shouts.

David wipes the crumbs from his mouth and protests. He points to his empty sack, tries to explain he has already eaten, but Grampa is in a hurry and pays no attention.

"Get in, get in!" he insists. "Come along, come get your dinner!"

David shrugs. His job is to do what Daddy Dougan tells him to do. If Daddy Dougan tells him to come eat dinner, then he will eat dinner. He runs to the truck, and the men in the back give him an arm up. The truck rumbles off down Colley Road to the Subway Cafe, where Geneva serves David a second meal.

World War II brings an end to Turtle Township's neighborly exchange in farm work. As the years go by, there are simply not enough men. No one farm has enough help to be able to take off and spend days thrashing the fields of nearby farms. Mrs. Wehler, when she's ready to thrash, can find in the way of a field hand only one black man. When two of her neighbors arrive with their teams and wagons to head up the work and see the man, they turn around and go home. "We're not going to work with any nigger," they sneer. The anger and animosity this breeds is lasting.

But even with most of the labor force gone, the work must be done. In addition to the country's own needs, Europe, with its food production seriously crippled, places new demands on United States agriculture. Innovations make it possible to produce more food with less labor. The first needs are for silo filling and thrashing. Thus come the forage harvester, the successor to silo filling, and the combine. While the latter is known before the forties, it hasn't been widely used in the Midwest. It goes through a field cutting the standing grain, separates the kernels and funnels them into an accompanying wagon, and spews out the straw, either spreading it on the ground to return to the soil, or windrowing it. If windrowed, the straw is baled and carried to the barns in another operation.

In Turtle, in 1944, Ralph Meech and Vern Moore go in together and buy a Gehl Forage Harvester. Phil Holmes, with his own and his father's farm to harvest, looks longingly across the fence at their machine. The next year, he buys one, too. He hires out, and that year, also using his 1943 combine, he fills silo and thrashes for seventeen farms.

By the end of the war, combines have made communal thrashing a thing of the past. The huge thrashing machine disappears; when it occurs to Jackie to wonder what happened to it, nobody seems to know. Perhaps it ends in Dick Post's barn, dozing to rust with other obsolete machinery. Or perhaps it gets hauled up to Janesville and rattles and chuffs at the yearly Labor Day Thresheree, for the amazement and amusement of droves of city folk. It must also be a wonder to the younger farmers, those who have never lost a pitchfork, accidentally or on purpose, into its insatiable maw.

14 ⚔ ROADS

It's 1912; Ronald is ten. He wanders out to Colley Road, in front of the house. Down the road a bit, towards town, is a very slight dip, and a culvert. There is activity there. Ronald heads down to see what is going on.

He recognizes Mr. Popanz, the County Road Commissioner. Mr. Popanz is working with a helper, a team of horses, and a drag. There's been a recent rain; water is still in a few puddles. The men are leveling the rutted dirt road with the drag. Ronald watches.

An automobile comes from town. The men move the horses and drag aside and stand back while the automobile speeds past, spitting out little stones and dirt from its tires. Automobiles are still not common, and especially not on Colley Road. Ronald doesn't know the driver, nor do Mr. Popanz and his helper seem to, for they don't touch the brims of their hats.

Mr. Popanz watches the automobile until it turns the corner above the dairy and is out of sight. Then he turns to Ronald.

"The automobile is going to be the death of good roads," he says. "Do you know why?"

Ronald shakes his head.

Mr. Popanz squats down and rolls a ball of mud from the edge of a puddle. He lays it in a wagon rut. "There," he says. "Now when a wagon wheel goes over that mud, what does it do?"

Ronald looks at the mudball. "It presses it down," he says.

"Right," says Mr. Popanz. He squashes the mudball firmly down with his thumb. He takes some more mud from the puddle and lays it in the wagon rut.

"Now, when an automobile goes by, what happens to the mud?"

Ronald knows the answer to this one, too. He's jumped back from the edge of a road more than once, especially in wet weather, when an automobile has roared past.

"It splatters it right off the road," says Ronald.

Cars parked along Colley Road for a farm event appear to be doing no damage.

"Right," says Mr. Popanz, and with a fast scoop of his hand flings the mud into the ditch. "Well, that'll be the end of good roads." He stands and glumly motions his helper to get the horses and drag moving again.

Ronald continues to watch the Road Commissioner at work. He agrees with him totally. The logic is irrefutable.

15 ⚔ STUART PETERSON

Stuart Peterson is a slow-witted man who has for years been working for Ruby Obeck on the Obeck place across the road from Chez Nous. With instruction, Stuart can do most things. He's strong and burly and good-natured. On Saturday nights he goes to the Shopiere tavern. As the beer flows, some of the locals turn to Stuart for sport. He's always good for a laugh, for he takes their teasing literally.

"Tell us about that lady we seen you with, Stu," one starts.

Another builds on it. "That gussied-up blond, cheek-to-cheek with you, down at Waverly Beach last night!"

"I never was at Waverly Beach!" Stuart protests. "I never was dancing with no lady!"

"Oho," cries the first. "You admit it, she wasn't no lady!"

"I never been to Waverly Beach!" Stuart insists.

One winter day he's working in a snowy cornfield east of the Obeck farm buildings, across from the Dougan fields. The cornstalks have long since been cut, tied into bundles, and the bundles set into large shocks, fifteen or sixteen to a shock. They make the field look like a village of Indian tepees. Every few days Stuart loads all the bundles from one shock onto a wagon and takes them to the animals in the barn. He's whittled away at the field; it's now half empty. He pulls up alongside a shock near the road and pitches the first bundle onto the wagon bed. As he turns back for the second, he sees something and recoils. He looks again, carefully. Feet are sticking out from underneath the bundles. Feet in worn brown work boots, and a bit of leg, covered with a ragged cuff. It slowly becomes clear to Stuart that there must be more of that leg, and another leg, and that the body attached to those legs is certainly dead and frozen. He makes a gargling noise, wheels, and scrambles over the fence, through the ditch and out onto the road, where he flails his arms at an approaching tractor.

Gilbert Gjestvang, Grampa's farm manager, stops. Stuart gibbers and points. "A dead man! A dead man under the corn shock!"

It takes Gilbert a few moments to digest the unlikely words. Then he says, "You're kidding!"

Stuart insists.

"Come show me," says Gilbert.

But Stuart won't return. He points out the shock and then paces agitatedly while Gilbert scales the fence and starts through the shallow snow into the field. Near the wagon Gilbert looks back over his shoulder. Stuart urges him on.

Gilbert approaches. He, too, sees the feet. He feels a distinct jolt. He looks again at Stuart and nods affirmation, and Stuart nods vigorously back. Gilbert walks slowly around the shock. The snow is undisturbed. Nothing else is showing. A man, lying full length on his stomach as this one seems to be, since the feet are turned down, would have to have a head … right about ….

Gilbert abruptly lifts a bundle and tosses it to one side. Nothing there. He lifts and throws another one, and a third. This last reveals the head, turned sideways so that he sees an ear, a cheek, the nose. He involuntarily turns away, bile rising in his throat. Then he forces himself to look again.

The body has been here for a long time, long enough for the rats and mice to find it. The ear is almost gone, the lower lip eaten away, exposing teeth and gum. It seems to be an older man, thin, with sparse, graying hair. Gilbert doesn't think he's ever seen him before. The mottled cheek and brow look dreadful, with the eyelid half open, but there doesn't seem to be much decomposition of the flesh. The body must have been put here after the freezing weather began.

Put here—that means murder. Someone had to put him here. Or could he have been drunk, might he have crawled in here to get out of

Stuart found the dead man under a cornshock.

STUART PETERSON

the weather and died? But his position isn't huddled up, a man trying to keep warm. Well, he could have died by some natural means, and a companion stashed him here, not wanting any problem with authorities. But that's not likely, either.

Gilbert doesn't remove any more bundles. He strides back to the road. "Is Ruby home?" he asks Stuart.

"She's gone to town."

"We'll call Ron, then," he says, "and he can call the police."

Stuart hurries after Gilbert to the Obeck farmhouse, whimpering all the way.

"You've found WHAT?" Daddy bellows over the office phone. "A dead man?"

Gilbert and Stuart scarcely make it back to the road before Ron races up in the Buick. Gilbert leads him to the spot, and he circles from head to foot and back to head, swearing under his breath in French and shaking his head. "The poor bastard," he finally says. Then he goes to the Obeck farmhouse to telephone.

By the time he returns cars are streaming up Colley Road from both directions and half the employees of the Dougan Farm are clambering over the ditch.

"Go back to work, you ghouls," says Daddy, but nobody pays any attention. It's only a few moments more before the neighbors begin to show up, and a stranger from Walworth County who's just happening by and stops to see what's going on. Each new arrival looks at the face, makes an exclamation of revulsion, and says that as far as he can tell, he doesn't know the man.

Once it's established that the corpse is a stranger, the mood of the crowd becomes almost festive. Comments such as, "Sorta chewed up, ain't he?" give way to crude jokes. Those on the edge of the group, where Stuart has come closer and is circling, start to rib him. "Hey Stu, how'd you kill him?"

"I didn't! I didn't! It wasn't me!" Stuart protests.

Two police cars and an ambulance roar up Colley Road, lights flashing and sirens wailing, and the crowd cheers. Daddy again orders all his people back to work, and the farmhands reluctantly disperse. The neighbors and the man from Walworth stay.

Everyone falls back to let the officers through. They survey the scene, confer, pull out tape measures, a photographer snaps picture after picture. Out on the road the ambulance attendants lean against the ambulance, waiting. The policeman in charge questions first Daddy, then Gilbert, then the cowering Stuart. They then begin stripping back the corn bundles, taking pictures as they go.

"Are we needed to stay and watch this?" Daddy asks the policeman in charge. He says no, and Ron, Gilbert, and Stuart walk back to the road.

"I didn't do it, Mr. Dougan!" Stuart protests. "I didn't do it!"

"Nobody thinks you did," says Daddy. "Take the rest of the day off if you want to. Go to a movie. Tell Ruby I said so. Here's a dollar."

"But the stock's gotta be fed," Stuart wails. "And that shock—that shock—nothin' should eat that shock—"

"Gilbert'll get somebody to load one from the far end of the field and haul it to the barn," Daddy says. "In a couple of days, when the police are finished, you or somebody can make a bonfire." He then heads for the Hill Farm to tell Grampa, glad that his father has been working on fences there and missed the commotion.

For a week the sensation of the stranger under the corn shock dominates township conversations—who he could be, where he came from, how he'd gotten under there, how long he'd been there. The *Beloit Daily News* publishes an initial story, then a follow-up, but these are of little help. The man, though clothed, had no identification or money on him, nor anything traceable in his pockets. He fits the description of no missing person on file. Forensic experts find no evidence of foul play: no bullet or stab wound, no strangling, no head bashed in. There's not a liquor bottle anywhere around. The autopsy tells nothing except that he hadn't eaten recently. He was probably under the shock two or three months. The verdict is: a person unknown, perhaps an itinerant worker, dying of causes unknown, on a date unknown, and either crawling under, or being placed under, a corn shock in a field adjacent to Colley Road, Turtle Township, Rock County. If placed, it was by a person or persons unknown, and the death would have occurred in a place unknown, but probably near the field where the body was found. The police don't pursue the puzzle any further.

Nobody ever learns anything more about the man. Before long he's forgotten, except by Stuart and a small group of tormenters.

"Tell us about the dead man, Stu," someone says at the tavern. Others take up the game. "Why'd you do him in? Huh, Stu? Tell us! Why'd you kill him?"

"I never! I only found 'im!" Stuart insists frantically.

"Oh come on, Stu, confess! We know you done it. Nobody's gonna catch you now. You can tell us! Did he steal your girl?"

"I never done it!" Stuart sobs, and tears roll down his cheeks.

16 ❧ CHUCK HOAG'S
MASTER'S THESIS

Charles Dodge Hoag's Master's thesis on the Dougan farm is titled, "An Economic Analysis of an Accredited Farm." An "accredited farm" is one which has been accorded "the distinction of being placed on the accredited list of the University of Wisconsin, which thereby recognizes not an ideal, but a suitable subject for advanced study toward a Master's Degree." The thesis is submitted in 1917, and in the credits Hoag states that he has used the 1915 thesis of Alan Turnbull, which covered the operations of the farm for the year 1914, for comparative data. He is particularly indebted to W.J. Dougan; D.H. Otis, Professor of Farm Management and Chairman of the Accredited Farm Committee; and Mr. O.A. Juve, Scientific Assistant of the U.S. Department of Agriculture, together with his assistants in the Department of Agricultural Accounting. Hoag's final credit goes "to each employee of Mr. Dougan, whose hearty cooperation has made this work possible."

Hoag is on the farm for sixteen months, from September 1915 to January 1917. During this time he takes "an active part in every operation on the farm, including dairyman, deliveryman, herdsman, horseman, fieldman, and manager, and operating every machine in use on the place." His economic analysis covers the year 1916.

His thesis is ambitious. From Part I, the Introduction:

> When a study is made of any particular farm, the investigator is apt to neglect one or more operations of the entire enterprise, placing special emphasis on some particular feature, and attributing success or failure to that alone. Thus, we may find a farm specializing apparently in purebred cattle, yet the bulk of the profits may come as the result of exceptionally good crop management, which has resulted in low feed costs and greater apparent profits in the cattle operation.
>
> By setting forth this thesis the writer has endeavored to make a complete

Howard Brant and Chuck Hoag clown before the milkhouse-in-progress, 1916.

analysis of every operation on a particular farm, for one complete year, from the technical standpoint as well as the accounting standpoint, putting credit where credit is due.

Detailed labor and financial records, individual feed records of all stock, individual production records of all cows, detailed data pertaining to all milk room and delivery operations and miscellaneous crop data were kept during the entire year. Sufficient freedom from farm work was allowed the writer to keep these records. Each regular workman was requested to fill out a daily time sheet stating time and nature of each work performed while all extra labor was recorded by the writer. Feed records were secured from data furnished each month by the herdsman. Production records for all cows were posted at time of milking by the milkers. The dairy and bottling department and the delivery department each kept daily records of their transactions. All time books and supplies used during the year were furnished by the Office of Farm Management of the U.S. Department of Agriculture. Time sheets and monthly milk production records were summarized by that department, in cooperation with the University of Wisconsin under the direction of Mr. Juve.

Part II, "The Farm as a Unit," is mainly statistical and echoes the Turnbull thesis as to the farm's location, topography, soil composition, growing

Charles Dodge Hoag, in World War I service uniform.

season, number of hired men and their place in the family. Horses now number ten, with four used almost exclusively for milk delivery, the other six for general farm work. The herd now numbers fifty milch cows, with thirty to forty head of young stock. An addition to the Turnbull thesis is a chart of distribution of capital: The farm, worth $40,747, is divided into fixed capital, with the land worth $19,415 and the buildings $11,965; and operating capital: stock, $5,590; horses, $1,190, and machinery, $2,587. "The intensified nature of the business accounts for the higher percentage of capital in buildings and machinery than is found on most farms." This section also states, "The farm is devoted to one major enterprise, the production of a high grade market milk, which is bottled at the farm and sold in Beloit at ten cents per quart, the highest price paid in that city for milk. The equipment of the farm is all planned with this object in view."

Part III, "General Management," forms the bulk of the thesis. It starts with "The Farm Plan" and has beautifully drawn maps of the farm and detailed charts and tables of crop rotation. The text discusses how the two rotations, clover and alfalfa, worked out by Turnbull and W.J. Dougan, are progressing and how they have been adapted. Rotation is projected through 1925. "The Farmstead" shows the arrangement of buildings and yards and outlines projected improvements. The description of buildings goes beyond Turnbull; we learn that "the dwelling" is heated by a hot air furnace and that at the present time running water is piped to the kitchen only.

Hoag lavishes loving care on his floor plans of the round barn, and gives statistics on all the buildings:

> The dairy barn consists of one large round barn, 65 feet in diameter and an annex barn, 40 x 30 feet. The silo, located in the center of the barn, is 14 feet in diameter, 47 feet in height plus 9 foot pit and is built of concrete.

Capacity, when full, is about 210 tons. A third barn, 65 x 24 with one lean-to, 32 x 14, on its south side, and another 24 x 14, on the west end, houses horses and young stock. A substantial shed, 17 x 65, adjoining the horse barn is used for storing machinery and housing young stock. There is a good poultry house, 12 x 34, capable of housing about 100 hens, but this department is only run to supply products for the table. The icehouse, 16 x 12 x 14, has a capacity of 55 tons of ice. Two sheds, one on each side of the icehouse, 8 x 16 each, are used for storing the two delivery wagons. The one story shop, 24 x 16, contains a work bench, the usual storage rooms for miscellaneous small tools, and bins for grain storage. A small engine room adjoins the house and contains a 2 H.P. gasoline engine, pump, and electric light plant. The engine runs both of these and furnishes power for the milk room machinery and washing machine for the house. The milk or dairy room is 18 x 12, being a part of the one story wing of the dwelling. The essential improvements on the farm during 1916 have been made to relieve the congestion in this department.

1916 has indeed been a year of major change. "A large new milkhouse was constructed during the year. This is a two story building, fireproof through-out, foundation being of concrete and superstructure of hollow vitrified tile. This building was not ready for occupancy until January 1917, but was prac-tically completed during 1916."

The milkhouse is not all. During July, a complete sewage system is laid, and the entire cow yard graded to allow thorough drainage, then 490 square yards of it paved, which, Hoag notes, substantially reduces the fly popula-tion. A concrete floor is laid "in the cellar of the dwelling," and new maple floors laid over the entire first floor of the main portion of the house. And full electricity comes:

> In building the new milkhouse it was found that the additional power and light required could not be supplied by the plant then in operation. Ar-rangements were therefore made to run an electric power line from the city of Beloit, supplying a three phase current direct from the city power plant. This was completed during December and the farm is now (in 1917) being lighted and furnished power by this means. The line which was extended for a distance of about three quarters of a mile from the nearest connection, cost the farm approximately $600. The cost of motors and necessary additional wiring brought the total to $900. This power is, of course, highly desirable,

especially in cold weather, when the gasoline engine starts with difficulty. The exact comparative expense cannot be determined at this early time, but the first two months of service indicate a reduction in cost of more than 50 percent.

Hoag notes that "considerable improvements have been undertaken during this one year. This was felt a great deal, when time spent on improvements should have been put on crops and other farm enterprises. Practically all the improvements were necessary, however, since the increased size of the milk business made the old milk room inadequate." He does not add something he probably doesn't know: that W.J.'s policy is to match every improvement in the business with a comparable improvement in the home—hence the maple floors and cellar paving. Of course adequate electricity and a sewage system improve the operation of both home and farm.

Hoag then lists projected improvements: better housing for the young stock and horses, another silo (which was built in 1917), a new machine shed, and the paving of the remainder of the cow yard. "The extent and rapidity of these improvements will depend largely on the profitableness of the cattle breeding industry on this farm." He doesn't mention another improvement soon to come: the raising of the roof over the one-story section of the Big House, giving it an additional story. This provides a number of dormitory rooms for the hired men and frees the upstairs of the main part of the house for family and guests. Perhaps he doesn't recognize that need, for the second story of the new milkhouse, reached by a pull-down stairs, is in service as a bunkhouse well before he leaves the farm.

The section on "Farm Labor" starts with "Man Labor" and describes the men and the work day:

> The majority of those employed are agricultural college men, of both the Long and Short Courses, all of whom are interested in the most advanced methods of agriculture. A spirit of friendly cooperation exists between the owner and the men, and among the men themselves. Each man is placed on his own responsibility as far as is possible. The daily routine work is apportioned among the individuals, thereby eliminating friction, uncertainty, and loss of time. These operations are not so complex, however, as to prevent one man taking another's place in his absence.
>
> The working day is from 4 a.m. to 6 p.m. with about half an hour out for breakfast and an hour at noon, the daily calendar varying with the season.

At 4 a.m. one man goes direct to the bottling room and puts up all the milk ready for delivery before he goes to breakfast. In the forenoon he washes his utensils and cleans up the milk room. In the afternoon he washes bottles, milks, separates the cream and cools the remainder of the night's milk preparatory to bottling in the morning. The other six men go direct to the barns, feed the cows and horses, curry and wash the cows and do the milking. This is completed about 6 o'clock. The two deliverymen then get their break-

fast while the other men are hitching up and loading the milk wagons. The deliverymen return to the farm about noon. One or two men are kept busy with the cows and young stock the entire day. Milking starts again at 3:30, with generally five men to milk. After milking the barn is cleaned, the cows fed, and the work of the entire farm finished by six o'clock.

Each man is given a full half day off duty from noon on, without any evening chores or other duties for that day. This is given with the idea of making up for the time which must be spent at

Fun on the Big House lawn, 1916. Chuck Hoag and Ron are supported by Jesse Hunt and Howard Brant.

Sunday work, as on any dairy farm, and is based on the theory that the man is entitled to one-seventh of his time off. Each man is given a regular membership in the Beloit YMCA with all its mental, moral, social, and physical advantages and privileges. With the necessity of having five men to milk every afternoon from 3:30 on, and with one man off duty each afternoon, managerial skill is required to make the outside field work progress rapidly enough.

In an ingenious passage Hoag figures the cost of room and board for the farm help. He calculates the cost of running the entire household first, separating it from the cost of running the farm, and includes, for room: interest on the value of land, house and equipment; taxes; insurance; heat; light. He estimates that 70 percent is attributable to the hired help, and comes up with a cost per man per month of $4.09. For board, he includes groceries; meat; dairy products; poultry; garden; farm labor for the house; and household help. This comes out to $14.56 per man per month, or a total cost per month of $18.65. He explains his reasoning for each item, e.g., "Household labor was charged at the amount actually paid the various women employed, while all farm labor expended on household work was charged at the average rate for the year. This includes labor such as mowing the lawn, running the washing machine, attending the household fires, and assisting Mrs. Dougan with housework when other help was not available." It also included the cost of horse labor for the household, such as plowing the garden. The chart that goes with this section shows, among other data, that during 1916 the Big House consumed 114 quarts of milk at 7 cents, 1931 quarts of milk at 6 cents, 3061 quarts of skim at 2 cents, 113³/₄ quarts of cream at 40 cents, and 233¹/₄ pounds of butter at 25-45 cents. Hoag continues, "Of the $18.65 for board and room per man per month, $10.47, or 54 percent was paid to sources outside the farm, while 46 percent was actually carried by the farm. This is in support of the theory that has been advanced by other agricultural accountants, that about half the board cost is carried by the farm." He then adds up the total cost (for a year) of board, wages, and YMCA memberships, divides by the number of hours worked (exclusive of manager) and comes out with the average cost per man hour of 15.55 cents. "It was found that the average labor rate for each month, figured independently, varied only slightly from month to month. This indicates that the work is so managed that practically the same length of working day is secured at all seasons of the year, the total number of hours worked in any given month being practically the same as any other, except where additional help was hired."

The section on "Horse Labor" shows that of the ten horses normally kept on the farm, in 1916 two were mules; these and two horses were used regularly on the two milk delivery wagons. The horses were fed three times a day: at 4 a.m. and at noon they received grain and a light feed of hay, while at 5:30 p.m. the hay feed was heavy. Hoag goes into detail on the grain feed for horses under light or heavy work, the proportion of ground corn and oats, the addition of bran, and the problems of straight ground barley. During the late fall bundle corn was fed the horses, one bundle per meal, and in such cases replaced the ground grain for one or two meals each day, and lessened the amount of hay consumed. Hay is also detailed: largely a good grade of clover and timothy, with alfalfa fed in the early summer. "During October, November, and December, barley hay was used with very satisfactory results in connection with the bundle corn. This hay was dead ripe when cut, having been ruined for threshing purposes by heavy hail just at harvest time."

All horses were groomed thoroughly every morning, whether worked or not. "Harnesses are not generally removed at noon except in special cases of harness galls, etc., that require special care." And Hoag notes that the usual precautions of not watering a horse when extremely hot, and of cutting down grain ration when not doing work, are closely observed.

In a number of tables Hoag gives the items of expense involved in the keeping of the horses. The first details the yearly cost of horse labor, and includes total cost of stabling, from interest on land and barn through taxes, insurance, depreciation, light and water, and repairs. There are interest, taxes, insurance and depreciation on the horses themselves. Wagons and bobsleds that haul feed are figured; the cost of harness and its upkeep; hayforks; feed grinder; and the use of the big engine. The cost per month comes out to $3.07 per horse. The next table gives the cost of feed by month, and adds in the cost of labor involved in the feeding.

Further tables break down the cost of work horses compared to delivery horses. Hoag comments:

> The feed, labor, and shoeing costs were divided between the farm horses and delivery horses according to actual consumption or use by each class. Manure was credited at $1 per horse per month. It will be noted that the figures from month to month on the delivery horses are much more regular and present less variations than do those on the work horses. This is because the delivery horses have the same task every day, winter or summer, rain or shine. They are on full feed ration at all times, while the farm horses have their ration cut down when not working, or working only lightly. This explains the fact that it costs an average of $18.19 a month to keep one of the delivery horses as against $16.68 for the work horses. The figure of $201 for keeping a horse one year is about double the usual figure considered but it is the belief of the writer, after a careful study to verify the figures here presented, that they are correct.
>
> It is customary to use the delivery horses for farm work only when all

the others are already in use. During the entire year the delivery horses only spent 545³/4 horse-hours on work other than the delivery of milk. Although the hours worked by the farm horses during the spring and summer months were far in excess of any one month by the delivery horses, still, the latter showed an average per horse for the year of 2190 hours as against 1583 hours by each farm horse. Of the delivery horses, each one works an average of 5.96 hours per day for the entire year. The farm horses average only 4.33 hours per day. This, however, is an excellent average figure, since Warren shows an average of several Minnesota and New York farms as 3.5 hours a day.

Hoag sees the irregular distribution of horse labor as a problem on practically every farm in the northern states. But to a certain degree the problem on the Dougan farm devolves itself upon the amount of available man labor. With the large amount of help required with the herd, especially after 3:30 p.m., and with one man off duty each afternoon, it frequently happens that the horses are idle simply because there are no men to drive them. As to 1916, the highest number of hours was attained in May, when plowing, disking, and dragging was being done with one man handling three- and four-horse teams. The fall season was a very late one, plowing being continued as late as December 6th. "During October and November it was possible to keep two sulky plow rigs going a good deal of the time, but owing to the large amount of chore work to be done, the teams were late in getting to the fields every morning and had to quit at night." Haying was the large item of horse time in July. In addition to this, because of all the concrete work being done on the milkhouse and cow yard, the horses were employed extra hours in hauling gravel from the farm pit.

Hoag goes on to chart how many horses and men are needed for each farm task, and comes to the conclusion that the farm could save by eliminating one horse, and hiring a regular farmhand from June through November. The horse would save $200, the man cost $30 a month, plus $10 for board, equaling $240. The extra man, however, would cut out the need for hiring seasonal day labor, which would be the equivalent of two months' salary saved. Also, he would be available from 4 a.m. on, three more hours per day than a day man, "and would thus help to start the whole day's work of the farm a little earlier. The difficulty in getting day help at rush seasons would be prevented. Lastly, there would be one extra man for Sunday work which would make that phase of the work more agreeable."

Building alfalfa haystacks.

The section ends with a discussion of the distribution of man labor, with a chart showing that dairy work takes 68 percent of the total work hours. Light, water, and power is then briefly noted, before the thesis moves on to a full discussion of crop production and management.

A table of farm machinery leads this section, for the purpose of assigning charges, and lets us know much of what was in use on the farm in 1916: Three plows, disk, spring tooth harrow and drags, grain drill, corn planter, potato planter, three cultivators, mower, three rakes, tedder (a machine for stirring and spreading hay to hasten drying and curing), hay loader, grain binder, corn binder, manure spreader, roller, wagons and sleighs, haycaps, and miscellaneous hay equipment. The silo filler is calculated elsewhere in the document. And not here, nor anywhere, is there a whisper about a current tractor, or the desirability of any tractor to come.

Individual crops and fields are described, as well as a great deal about the weather, for that summer could be considered close to disastrous. "Field 6 was sown to barley, 90 pounds to the acre, with clover and timothy seeding, about April 20. The ground was twice disked with a tandem disk-harrow, and dragged once with a spiketooth harrow prior to drilling in the grain. The grass was seeded with a hand, rotary seeder and the entire field dragged."

Hoag continues field by field, noting seed crops, cover crops, planting dates, soil conditions, weather. May and June are wet, then comes drought:

While the character of soil on this farm is such that the moisture remained in it fairly well, still, the intense heat caused all three fields to ripen about the same time, even though planted at one week intervals. The final "turning" came very suddenly, so that the grain was a little overripe and very dry at the time of harvest. Field 6 and all of field 10, except two acres, were cut July 24th and 25th. At noon of the latter day, a heavy hail hit the small area in which the farm lies, knocking down all grain left standing and threshing off the overripe grain. The remainder of field 10 was cut with the binder, but the bundles were very light and contained little grain.

After alfalfa, hay, corn and silage ("In filling the silo, a stream of water was kept running inside most of the time while filling, and frequently at night, to insure enough moisture and packing for the dry corn.") comes the final crop listing: "Potatoes were a total failure, entailing a loss of $90 in labor, seed, and land rent."

Hoag finishes this section with a review of the farm's crop year. "It was characterized by general poorness of crops. The whole chain of events, from the fall of 1915 on, prevented giving the proper amount of attention to the crops at the proper times. The spring season opened with general lateness of work. Not enough fall plowing had been done the previous year and the corn, especially, was late in planting."

In the next paragraph the mote of irritation that has crept into the thesis in the lines quoted above, now becomes a beam, evident with the word "apparent," for in earlier sections Hoag had deemed the improvements to the farm "necessary." He writes, "On account of the apparent congestion of the dairy department, extensive improvements were undertaken, notably at the wrong time of year—the rush time of July and August. This made haying late; prevented giving enough time to corn cultivation; and caused the grain to get too ripe before cutting could be done. If grain harvest had been started one or two days earlier, 200 to 300 bushels of barley might have been saved that was otherwise wasted by hail." He finishes with a glum account of hay. "The hay crops grew very slowly after the middle of July, and a general shortage resulted. As a result it has been necessary to buy alfalfa hay all during the spring of 1917 at $24 to $25 per ton."

But what would Hoag have called the "right" time of year? The building of the milkhouse—necessary by any calculation—was a massive undertaking, and involved extensive use of concrete. Concrete must not be poured in cold weather; strength and composition are affected. Hoag lists the last kill-

A farm hand plows.

ing frost for the area as early May, the first in the fall, early October. These were Grampa's parameters. Yet had the bulk of the work been done in May and June, planting and then first-haying would have been more profoundly affected. We are not given any reason for the lack of fall plowing the previous year, but are told the 1916 spring planting is late on account of wetness. Then comes the drought that causes the hay to grow slowly and all the barley to ripen simultaneously; it doesn't take much reading between the lines to see W.J. hastening to get the grain in as fast as he can. But how could he have predicted hail? It strikes midway, which ruins the rest of the barley harvest, and does vast damage to the shredded, albeit insufficiently cultivated, corn. It seems the weather is more responsible for the poor crops than the time expended on improvements. Could Grampa have begun the milkhouse in September? That, too, a harvest month, allows scant time for the concrete work to be completed, and throws the rest of the construction into autumn and winter.

What about the summer of the round barn, five years previous? That building enterprise was far vaster than the milkhouse and attendant improvements. How did Grampa manage the daily and seasonal work then? No one was writing a thesis to tell us, and if Grampa kept a diary, or records (and he almost certainly did the latter), nothing for 1911 has been found.

The "General Management" section now turns to "The Herd." Hoag first describes the buildings and equipment, and the advantages of a round barn as compared to the traditional rectangular barn. He is especially impressed with the ventilation system, the amount of light, and the convenience.

"Care and Management" is divided into calves and cows. Cows are usually dried off four to eight weeks prior to calving; lengthening the period between milkings is the only drying-up method used. Grain ration is cut down unless the cow is in poor flesh. At calving time she is put into a clean, light, freshly bedded box stall. Water is carried to her if the weather is severe. After calving she is put on full feed, care being exercised to guard against milk fever. If she fails to clean properly in 48 hours, a veterinarian is called. The calf is allowed to suck for two or three days. After that it is fed whole milk by pail, about six pounds per day, three times a day for about four weeks, or longer if the other demands for the milk are not too great. During the first two weeks care is taken to feed the calf from its mother's milk only. After four weeks the whole milk is gradually changed to skim and the amount increased; the calf continues on milk for about six months.

Clean clover and timothy hay is fed as soon as the calves will touch it; a grain mixture of corn, oats, bran and a little oil meal is fed after each milk feed, also as soon as they will take it. After six months the ration is hay and silage and a little grain.

Heifers are first bred at 18 to 20 months of age. All bull calves are sold for veal; all the healthy heifer calves are retained.

As to cows, they daily receive 25 to 30 pounds of silage, ten to fifteen pounds alfalfa and mixed hay, five to ten pounds corn fodder, cut or in bundles, and up to 12 pounds of grain, varying with milk production. In summer their feeding is largely good pasture, with small silage and grain supplements. Later the pasturage is supplemented by hay, green corn and green alfalfa. Salting is done every two days in the manger. Cows are watered twice a day.

The routine for caring for the cows is much as Turnbull gives it in 1914. Hoag is a bit more detailed: in the winter, after the afternoon milking, "the cows are turned out, the barn cleaned, silage and hay fed, and the cows put in for the night. At about eight o'clock each night, the herdsman inspects the herd, rearranges the bedding and sometimes feeds a little more hay."

There follows discussion of breeding:

> Most cows require only one service, but a few have required as many as three or four, and one has proved sterile. Only one cow was seriously out of condition; she was disposed of. One broke her hip and was sold for beef. Eight or

ten failed to clean properly at calving time. There were ten cases of abortion, premature birth or weak calves that had to be killed. While every precaution was taken by way of isolation and disinfectant where contagious abortion was suspected, it is believed that none of the cases were of contagious origin. On June 2nd Dr. F. B. Hadley of the College of Agriculture was called to perform the complement fixation test for contagious abortion. Fifteen animals showed a positive test, but only three of these have ever given any trouble with abortion.

Two purebred sires are kept, each in a separate box stall. They have a small yard for exercise, or are tied to a long sweep. In summer they are staked out on pasture; this is their summer ration. In winter they get hay or corn fodder. A very little silage is given occasionally and a grain ration when the bulls are in particularly hard service. Both bulls are given regular service, though rarely oftener than once a day. The danger of spreading infection by bulls is lessened by frequent syringing of the sheath with a mild disinfectant. Inbreeding and line breeding are never resorted to as bulls unrelated to the cows are always purchased.

Poor milkers are culled out, as well as those showing any tendency toward getting "off feed" or having udder trouble. "During the year twelve cows were disposed of for these reasons and two went because of their reaction to the tuberculin test." New cows, always tuberculin tested, are added to the herd. The average length of the milking period is 314 days for each cow, and the average yearly production is 6342 pounds. Hoag gives many tables and charts examining and comparing every aspect of cows and costs. He supplies, as does Turnbull, a table giving the individual records of the ten best and ten worst cows, but he identifies these cows by number rather than name. The best cow gives 11,641 pounds of milk, at a profit per quart of 3.92 cents. The worst gives 3024 pounds, and loses the business 1.87 cents on every quart of milk she produces.

The foregoing chart shows only one cow that is actually producing milk at a loss, but doubtless the high prices received for the milk, under these particular conditions, cause a number of these animals to come in the profit class rather than the loss. Should any of these conditions be materially changed, the profit from any individual cow will change. As more and more of these "marginal" cows are thrown into the loss class, by the rise in feed and labor costs, the demand becomes more evident for higher prices for the producer and for the more highly efficient cows. Just as it seems necessary to maintain a breeding herd, apparently at a loss, likewise it seems necessary to keep the cows which show only a very narrow margin of profit, but under conditions on the Dougan farm, where it is necessary to purchase considerable feed, those showing a loss under any set of existing conditions should not be kept.

The "General Management" section goes on with discussions of bottling and the milk room, milk delivery, and a summary of the cost of the entire business. The final table is the profit and loss statement for the entire farm for the year. The dairy turned in a profit of $3,378; the breeding herd lost $312. Field crops made a small profit; feed, a loss. Labor, a profit; exchange labor, a loss. Hogs made a modest profit. In all, receipts came to $35,028 and expenses to $31,615. The profit was $4,561, losses, $948. The net profit of the farm for the year was $3,412.44.

Hoag finishes with a summary of the entire thesis:

> In the foregoing pages we have attempted to analyze and in a measure chronicle the operation on the Dougan farm for the past year of 1916. Although we have been intimately connected with the farm during the whole period, and while we feel reasonably sure of the accuracy of the data shown, still, we do not feel qualified to make any recommendations in addition to the suggestions that have been noted.
>
> It must be remembered that this farm is distinctly individual in every way, from the history of its rapid growth and its present position, to the character and personality of the owner and manager. Upon the latter rests the success of the enterprise. Mr. Dougan's farm and well defined business policy in dealing with his customers has placed his product on the Beloit retail market where it has no competition. He has always endeavored to deliver the very highest quality of milk that eternal vigilance and modern methods can produce. The trade and price have taken care of themselves and come as a natural, but sure result. More than that, Mr. Dougan has the power of instilling his spirit into all his employees and the personal relationship is felt at all times.
>
> On the farm everything has a definite plan, although the plans may be changed, perhaps frequently, as necessity demands. Experimental evidence is always carefully noted and considered. Money is freely spent for enterprises which are really productive, and carefully withheld from those which are not. The rapid growth of the business since its institution about ten years ago has made necessary the constant enlargement of the entire plant. The enlargement process has about reached its climax, and the time for the development of greater internal efficiency has come—larger crop returns and better cows.

All in all, the Hoag thesis is a fine and informative job, enhanced with its handsome charts and many detailed tables. It represents an astonishing amount of work, entirely apart from the farm labor that Hoag fully participated in. And it surely did take the cooperation of everyone on the place, and many at the university. It's no wonder that young Ronald looked up to Charles Hoag as a hero, and wanted to be like him.

If one were to analyze this thesis in light of future practices and the present day (at the time of this volume, nearly one hundred years later) obvious differences would leap off the page. In 1916, for instance, Hoag makes no mention of tractors and little of mechanization, nor can we find 2-4 D, the universal weed killer of later years, or any insecticide. This analysis, beyond the scope of this book, is left to the reader.

There were other university men placed on the farm after Hoag—George Hotton (whom Grampa later cites as a disappointment), Laurens Fish and Elmer Carncross among them. But farm and university records indicate that only Turnbull and Hoag wrote Dougan theses. It's too bad that a master's candidate didn't show up every five years or so throughout the life of the farm, to chronicle, assess, and analyze its growth, changes, and demise. These would have given a detailed picture of Wisconsin farming development and agricultural pressures on a family farm and business for three quarters of a century. What a treasure that would be!

17 ❧ SAUSAGE AND PETUNIA

Jackie is a senior in high school, Craig a sophomore. Fido is a friend in Craig's class. Her real name is Lois Van Woert, but she's gained her doggie nickname because her bangs are so long they nearly cover her eyes. Early in September Jackie says to Fido, "Why don't you skip school tomorrow and come to our big annual pig auction? Craig and I are skipping; we always skip for educational things. And you love pigs."

Jackie knows this because of the Youth Fellowship Penny Carnival at church last spring. Jackie's contribution was going to be a small pig in a big cardboard box. The carnival goers could view the pig for a penny, and for an additional penny stroke its silky baby head. But she hadn't taken into account the pig. She'd gone to the barn shortly before the carnival, separated a piglet from its littermates and was scaling the planks of the pen, the little beast awkwardly under one arm, when it had twisted out of her grasp. She'd lunged for it and missed. The squealing pig had streaked off across the barnyard, under a fence and into a plowed field. Jackie was slowed by the fence but then followed in hot pursuit. For a moment she thought it would be an easy matter to overtake a very small pig, but she was wrong. It ran, screeching, faster than any animal she'd ever tried to catch. And she had to catch it — for the pig's sake, the farm's sake, and her own skin. The carnival was unimportant.

It took two fields and a flying tackle to down the runaway, and she lay there in the furrows gasping, clutching the small beast against her chest. Her own heart was dinning in her ears. But she could feel the little pig's heart pounding like a trip hammer. She was afraid it would have a heart attack. She was filled with fear and contrition.

Walking back across the fields holding the exhausted pig she decided she'd still better take the animal with her — keep an eye on it at the carnival. It shouldn't be returned to the rough and tumble of the pig pen in this condition. And at the carnival it was Fido who sat off in a corner all evening, tenderly cradling the little beast, crooning tunes to it and spooning in sips of water as it slowly, slowly recovered.

Now Fido considers the pig auction. "I've never skipped school before," she says, "but I'd like to come. I'll ride my bike out. I do love pigs."

When Fido joins Jackie and Craig at the dairy the next day, the place is abustle. Cars and trucks are parked all over, and more are arriving from both directions on Colley Road. Farmers are wending their way to the auction site, the large new garage east of the round barn. Inside many are talking in small clusters, or looking at the pigs, or are already seated around the auction ring on bleachers or folding chairs or hay bales. Henry Wieland is busy ruffling papers at the auctioneer's table and consulting with Mr. Beadle, the Dougan pig man who is in charge of the sale. Daddy and Grampa and auction helpers are much in evidence.

The three admire the Durocs ready to be auctioned. They've been scrubbed and oiled so that they gleam. Some are crowded in a pen at the far end of the garage. They snuff and grunt. More are fenced outside. The smell of clean, sunny pig is a pleasant one.

"What will happen to the pigs?" Fido asks guardedly. "Will they … will they … "

"Be butchered?" Jackie finishes for her. "Not Mr. Beadle's pigs. Everybody knows he's the best pig man in the state. People want these for breeding stock. To improve their own herds."

Grampa loves his pigs.

Dinner is always welcome.

"I love pigs," repeats Fido. She caresses them with her eyes.

The auction begins. The pigs are lined up in a passageway from the far pen to the ring, snout to tail in the chute, except that hired men hold slatted gates to separate them. They allow the pigs into the ring one at a time. Inside, Mr. Beadle guides the pig around with a long stick, showing it off from every angle, while Henry Wieland announces its pedigree and its number in the catalogue. The farmers on the bleachers and hay bales study the pig. Then the auctioning and bidding start. The bidding is done with nods and signals, and it's a good thing, for often the animal on display gets agitated and with flapping ears rushes wildly about. Its snorts and squeals almost drown out the auctioneer. Mr. Beadle rushes about, too, trying to control his charges. It's entertaining.

Fido and Jackie and Craig watch pigs come and go for much of the morning, the boars and then the gilts, and near noon meander off to the refreshment stand for hot dogs and chocolate milk.

"Aren't there any babies?" Fido asks.

"Not to be auctioned," Craig says.

They go into the barn beyond the horse barn to look at the two sows that have recently farrowed. The older set of babies is robust and active, squealing and pushing and rooting in the straw. They pay little attention to their sleeping dam, nor does she seem to want them to, for she's lying on her tits. The other set is new-born. Their red-gold mother lies with eyes shut, her massive side slowly rising and falling with her deep-sleep breaths. A roiling heap of piglets work at her double row of tits.

"Aren't they darling!" cries Fido. Then she notices something. "But what about those two tiny ones, off there in the corner? They aren't nursing!"

"Those are the runts," Craig says ruefully. "There's always a runt or two. They can't compete. The bigger pigs crowd them off the end of the cafeteria line."

"Can't someone pull some of the bigger ones off and let the little ones get a turn? Can't we?"

Jackie shakes her head. "The sow might have a fit. Sows are very dangerous. Grampa nearly got killed by one when he was a little boy."

Craig recounts the story of a Chez Nous neighbor, Bub Weller, who recently went to check on his pigs in the middle of the night, pulling his trousers over his pajamas and holding them up with his hand. When he stepped over the fence a sow attacked him; in trying to defend himself he dropped his pants around his ankles and then couldn't move, and the sow knocked him down and went for his throat. "He got his arm up and she chewed it," Craig relates, "and he thought, 'This is the end of me.' But all of a sudden the pig just quit and walked off. He was really lucky."

Fido surveys the placid sow dubiously. "Will the runts die, then?"

"Probably," Jackie says. "Unless they get bottle fed. Grama always used to have a runt pig or two in a box behind the stove, in the Big House kitchen. We helped feed them. But she and Grampa live in town now. I don't know if anybody feeds them."

"Mostly farmers figure runts aren't worth the trouble," Craig adds.

"I'd take the trouble!" Fido declares.

"Why don't we all?" Jackie suggests. "Want to raise a runt, Fido? We'll take one and you take one, till they're big enough to go back in with the others."

Fido's eyes gleam out from behind her bangs. "Oh! Could we?"

The three go in search of Grampa. They detach him from the auction and bring him to the new litter. Jackie writes that she and Craig and Fido want the runts. Fido writes how careful a parent she'll be. Grampa reads and nods. "With a name like Fido, you will be faithful," he says. "The little fellows do need homes."

Grampa leads them to nursing bottles and nipples in a cabinet in the tool shed. They take skim milk from the cooler. They wash the bottles in the office kitchen and warm the milk in a saucepan on the office stove. They fill the bottles. Then they return to the pens.

"We must be careful not to alarm the mother," Grampa says. "Sows can be vicious." He speaks to the sow soothingly, then enters the pen, plucks out the runts and lays one in Craig's arms, one

Sausage and Petunia's competition.

in Fido's. Fido cuddles hers gently. Following Grampa's instructions she works the nipple into the runt's mouth. For a moment it doesn't respond, until the pool of milk in its throat forces it to swallow. Then it gives a choke, a feeble suck, then another, and suddenly it is sucking ravenously, making frantic little grunts at the same time. Craig's pig follows suit. Everybody laughs.

"They'll be all right now," Grampa says. "Keep them warm and clean. Pigs are naturally cleanly and affectionate."

"I'll take good care of mine," promises Fido.

She names her boar pig "Sausage." Jackie and Craig decide on "Petunia" for their little gilt. They help Fido pad her bicycle basket with a gunny sack. They pack Sausage, the bottle, and a quart of milk into the basket and lace the basket across the top with a web of binder twine so that nothing can bounce out. Fido rides carefully off toward town.

At school, Jackie and Craig get daily reports on Sausage. Yes, Fido's mother was surprised but she's used to Fido bringing things home. The toy bulldog, Tiny, only sniffs. Sausage seems happy in his cardboard box. He has a hearty appetite. He likes to have his neck scratched.

At Chez Nous, they tell Fido, it's much the same with Petunia. She drinks lots of milk and is soon running around the garage. She too likes to be scratched.

The Van Woerts are not Dougan customers, but every delivery day the Dougan routeman, Dobby, leaves several quarts of skim milk on their doorstep. Sometimes he's invited in to see how Sausage is doing. Then he tells Daddy in the office how the piglet is fattening up, how he's paper-trained, and how he has won the dog over so that the two are now buddies. Fido says her mother is fond of the pig, who keeps her company in the yard while she hangs out the clothes. Sausage is now eating table scraps along with his skim milk, and is especially partial to oatmeal with raisins and bananas.

But his life as a town pig ends the day he learns to jimmy open the gate of the fenced back yard. Out on the sidewalk he and Tiny follow a woman down the street. The woman starts to run and the two animals run after her. The woman's yelps bring Mrs. Van Woert to the scene. She scoops up dog and pig; they're the same size. "They only want to have their necks scratched," Fido's mother calls, but the woman doesn't stop for explanation or apology.

The next day Sausage rides back to the farm with Dobby in the milk truck. He joins his sister at Chez Nous, where the two trot all over the farm, and when tired sleep side by side on the lawn in the October sunshine. They are the size, shape, and color of burnished footballs.

"A pair of pigskins," comments Daddy.

When Fido brings Tiny out to visit Sausage she learns her pig's abilities have transferred to his new home.

"He can open the screen door with his nose," Jackie says. "He works it open and Petunia squeezes in under his chin, and then he pushes in after her. They go all over the house, exploring."

"Pigs are practically the smartest animals there are," Craig says.

On an Indian summer afternoon Mother is entertaining Federation of Music Clubs people at Chez Nous. It's an important board meeting and important people are there, such as the National President of the Federation, and national head of the musician's union, Caesar Petrillo. He is known in the United States as "The Music Czar." The house is gleaming, and Mother, beautifully dressed and coiffed, is serving an elegant tea. At a lull in the conversation the patter of little hooves on a polished floor is heard, and a murmur of enquiring grunts. Then Sausage and Petunia appear at the entrance to the living room, side by side, looking all around. Mother takes it in stride. She calls Craig, and he comes and escorts the animals out.

Even with Sausage returned to the farm, Dobby goes on delivering skim milk to the Van Woerts. They tell him to stop, but the bottles keep appearing. They try to pay and their money is returned. They finally give in, become Dougan customers, and are charged for their homogenized milk and cream and cottage cheese. The skim milk still comes free. So as not to waste it, Fido drinks it, and develops a lifelong preference.

By mid-November Sausage and Petunia are as big as their siblings. They are a friendly nuisance, and their space in the garage will soon be needed by the car. They are taken back to their littermates at the dairy. All winter long they demand extra attention, which the swineherd gives them.

When the pig auction comes the next year, Mr. Beadle doesn't have any trouble keeping two of his charges in line. His main problem is trying to stay on his feet as they bunt against his legs, for even in the auction ring Sausage and Petunia demand to have their necks scratched.

Craig and Jackie and Fido—who is skipping school for the second time—don't warn the purchasers. *Caveat emptor.* Let the buyer beware!

18 ⚔ YOU AND HEREDITY

Jackie can't remember a time she hasn't known about Darwin. She often hears Daddy tell about sitting cross-legged on the flour box in the Big House kitchen, at fourteen, arguing evolution with his mother till she is wild eyed and punching down bread as if she's doing personal battle with the author of *On the Origin of Species*.

"Monkeys!" she splutters. "We are made in God's image! We are but a little lower than the angels! We are not descended from monkeys!"

"How do you know God isn't a monkey?" Ronald says. "How do we know the angels aren't monkeys? Why should people be the supreme creation?"

Grama finally refuses to talk, working in red-faced, grim silence. She knows there's no point in appealing to Wesson. She and her husband have never agreed on evolution. In fact, after Ronald was born but not yet christened, Aunt Lillian referred to him as "Little Darwin," scoffing playfully at her brother's views.

Nor do Grama's brothers, Uncle George Trever and Uncle Bert Trever, agree on evolution. Uncle George died before Jackie ever knew him; he was the oldest of the twelve Trever children, while Grama was the tenth. The baby, Uncle Bert, Jackie knows and loves. He's the head of the History Department at Lawrence College in Appleton, and author of a highly regarded two-volume text on ancient history, a text that Jackie will use in college. (He is also the alleged author of "A little boy fell in the Anheuser Busch and Schlitz his pants. Was he Sadler Budweiser? Pabst yes, Pabst no.")

Uncle Bert has a PhD. Uncle George had one too, and a ministerial degree as well. He was a strict biblical literalist. Daddy says that some of his most entertaining times, when he was a boy, transpired in a buggy with Uncle George and Uncle Bert, the two of them arguing theology tooth and claw. It was probably from listening to Uncle Bert that Ronald got the evolutionary fuel to use on his mother.

It's hard to see how Grama can argue against natural selection, for it's the foundation of farming. Animals and plants have been developed into different breeds and strains over thousands of years, with pre-farmers and farmers aiding nature as selectors. Jackie and her sibs listen in to talk, usually around the table, between Daddy, Mother, Grampa, visiting agronomists, geneticists, artificial inseminators, and others involved in the study and improvement of cows and corn. Corn and cows. Sometimes a lima bean figures prominently. It's always interesting, but, until she's older, often beyond Jackie's capacity.

There is a little tan-covered magazine that comes into the house every month, called *The Journal of Heredity*. Jackie always studies it. The text is usually so technical that she doesn't get much from the words. She gets a lot from the pictures, though. There are enjoyable photos of the Dionne quintuplets, though the article's title is "Diagnosis of the Dionne Quintuplets as a Monozygotic Set." There are photos of generations of people who have an inherited white blaze of hair on their foreheads, called piebald spotting. More repugnant but more titillating are revealing pictures of the naked lower torsos of males, in a family where the men inherit rough and scaly penises. Here the text makes it clear that the line is dying out after a few generations because the afflicted men can't find women willing to marry them. And pictured is a whole family that for generations has been born with split hands—usually just a thumb and little finger, looking like claws or pincers. Balancing this article, in another issue, is "Four Generations of Extra Fingers." This particularly interests Jackie because she heard once that Grampa was born with an extra thumb which was removed when he was a baby, though she's never asked him about it.

But she doesn't really start to understand what scientific breeding is all about and how it works, either in cows, corn, or people, until Daddy brings home a book when she's in fifth grade called *You and Heredity*. It's for adults but written so clearly and interestingly, and has such fascinating diagrams, that she reads it all, and so do Craig, Patsy, and Joan. Actually, Jackie doesn't read quite all of it. Mother fastens one chapter shut with paperclips, and tells the children that it's an adult chapter, and not to read it. Jackie obediently doesn't, but both Joan and Patsy take the paper clips off. They later report to Jackie that the chapter is about hermaphrodites, who are both men and women at the same time, and homosexuality. Jackie finds the former intriguing in that it's even possible; she finds the latter incomprehensible.

Probably the most interesting of the allowed chapters is about the inheriting of mental capacity, and tells about two families who have spawned great numbers of dim-witted children who in turn have produced progeny definitely under par. From then on, when the four fight, they can hurl new insults at each other. "You Juke, you!" "You Kallikak!"

An early chapter tells how an individual, whether pea, pig, or person, inherits traits from its parents through chromosomes. Every cell in a body contains a certain number of pairs of chromosomes—under a microscope looking like little worms side by side—one of each pair coming from the father, the other from the mother. The exception to this are germ cells—the sperm cells of the father and the egg cells of the mother. In these the chromosomes have divided in a process called meosis—reduction division—so that each germ cell has only one chromosome of each pair. When a sperm cell unites with an egg cell to form a new individual, then the single chromosomes find their partners, which results in a return to the somatic chromosome number of the progeny. If this didn't happen, the number of chromosomes in a somatic cell would double with each generation. Nature might have tried this, eons ago, and found it didn't work, and so devised this method.

The chromosomes are made up of genes, rather like beads on a string (this was the metaphor then), the genes on one chromosome matching up with the genes on its mate—except, in most animals—vertebrates—the sex-determining pair. In mammals, this pair of chromosomes are named X and Y, the X being the long female, the Y, the shorter male-determining chromosome. The X chromosome has a length of genes that are missing on the Y chromosome: there's an X stretch with no Y genes to pair up with. If a pig or person inherits two X chromosomes, it becomes a female. XY produces a male.

Genes determine all phynotypic traits of an offspring. Take, as the book does, eye color. Suppose you inherit a blue gene from your father, a brown from your mother. What color will your eyes be? You won't end up a blend, for certain genes dominate their mates. Since brown dominates blue, you'll be brown eyed. You can only be blue eyed if each of your parents gives you a recessive blue gene. But you'll be brown eyed if only one parent gives you a dominant brown.

Applied to their own parents, since Mother and Daddy are both brown eyed and yet have produced blue-eyed Patsy, they must each carry a recessive blue gene (or blue "allele"—a more accurate term; an allele is used to describe different forms or "states" of a gene). Mother and Daddy have to be mixed—heterozygous—in regard to eye color; they are brown-blues. They can't be brown-browns, which would produce all brown-eyed children, or blue-blues, which would make themselves have to be blue eyed, producing only blue-eyed children.

But what genotype combination, then, are the three brown-eyed Dougan children? Brown-browns? Or brown-blues? You can't tell by looks, but there are probabilities. Here is where Mendel comes in.

Mendel is a new name to Jackie. He was a monk in the Austrian Empire, who in 1857 began doing breeding experiments in his monastery's garden patch. He developed purebred strains of peas by eliminating those that did not breed true—that is, did not replicate their parent exactly, generation after generation. He did this by breeding the plants back on themselves—in-breeding—and discarding any plant that didn't have the parental trait he was breeding for, until he had, say, a strain that would always produce a smooth pea, another that would always produce a wrinkled pea. Then he crossed the pure wrinkled strain to the pure smooth strain, and observed what happened to the offspring. He took the offspring, bred them to each other, and observed the results in the next generation. He did this with a number of different traits and through many generations. His conclusions have come to be known as Mendelian Laws of Genetics, and these laws are the cornerstone of modern-day plant and animal breeding.

These are his conclusions, put in modern terms, for he wasn't aware of chromosomes and there was no way yet of observing the details of cell division. Nor did he give his elements the name "genes"—they only later came to be called that.

1. The inheritance of traits is determined by genes.

2. The genes that control a particular trait occur in pairs; genes of a pair may be alike or different alleles.

3. When the genes are different, the effect of one gene will be observed (is dominant) and the other will remain hidden (is recessive).

4. The genes controlling a particular phenotype separate during germ-cell formation, so each germ cell carries only one allele of that trait. (Phenotype: The visible properties of an organism that are produced by the interaction of the genotype and the environment. Genotype: The genetic constitution of an individual or group.)

5. At fertilization there is a random uniting of germ cells, which results in a predictable ratio of the alternate alleles among the offspring.

6. When two pairs of traits are studied in the same cross the traits can match up independent of each other.

Back to eye color: referring to Number 5, if the law of averages carries in so small a sample (which of course it doesn't), Mother and Daddy would have, at each birth, given a child either a brown (B) or a blue (b) allele. Those children who turned out to be brown-eyed could have been Brown-Browns (BB) or Brown-blues (Bb). The normal odds are, one BB, two Bbs, and one bb, which everyone already knows is Patsy. So it's probable that one of the three others is a Brown-Brown, the other two, Brown-blues. But there's no way of knowing for sure, until those three have children, which will shed some light on the situation, if any of them have a blue-eyed child. (Also, it's a long time before Jackie begins to understand how an occasional kitten, through somatic mutation, or chimeras, can be born with one blue eye and one brown eye.)

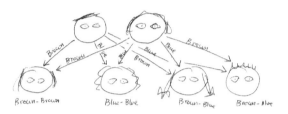

An understanding of genes and inheritance makes it possible to breed for certain traits in a much more exact way, and much more swiftly, than in previous ages. Before Mendel (and for a long time after, for his work wasn't recognized till close to the end of the nineteenth century, and after that the implications were still being slowly worked out), if one wanted a cow that gave lots of milk, it was common sense to keep the calves of a mother who was an excellent milker. In corn, the farmer saved out for seed the ears that by their looks best exemplified the traits desired in the next generation, or crossed two desirable strains and selected the best of the progeny to form a new strain. Breeds and pedigrees developed this way in both animals and plants. But in selective breeding there was never any guarantee a trait would be repeated in the progeny, and certain elusive traits simply couldn't be bred for.

The *You and Heredity* book, of course, knows nothing of DNA, RNA, or any genetic science beyond 1939; it later proves to be wrong about some very basic things—it says there are twenty-four chromosomes in the human cell, for instance—and is vastly over-simple about others. These are corrected in later editions, though no books can keep up with the pace of the science, which now, in the twenty-first century, is into genetic engineering, cloning, and has mapped genomes from fruit flies to humans. But this first edition is Jackie's written introduction to Mendel, to Darwin, to natural selection, and to scientific breeding.

Later on, she even reads the paper-clipped chapters.

19 ⨯ RONALD PART 4 ⨯ I MUST FALL IN LOVE WITH MY COWS

On January 30, 1924 Ronald sends a thunderbolt from France: "Dear Mother and Dad, this letter is bound to be almost entirely about a girl. For the first time in my life I am seriously considering settling down, finding my work, and preparing to be responsible for a home."

He warns his parents:

> Don't get excited because I am thinking along this line—it is common enough among chaps my age. I know how far I am from being the staid sort, and how long it must be before I will be in any position to marry. Just the same it is in the back of my head, and that will lead me to more serious work, and help kill my wanderlust. Actually, it consists mostly of thinking about tearing, rather than pulling out of quiet moorings and going.
>
> I suppose you are anxious to hear about the girl. I won't hold forth at great length, for I couldn't make you see her as she is. Suffice to say she is everything either of you could ask. Religion, ideas of life, home background, education, capability—Dad, you would take a pardonable pride in her, and Mother, you would fall in love with her the minute you saw her, and continue to love her more as you came to know her better.
>
> Jimminy, I haven't led you to believe she is French have I? Nope, American for generations, resident of Chicago, and of Nordic and English extraction. I have forgotten to mention the little matter of her name—Vera Wardner.

He says that living and working at the same place they have come to know each other under many conditions, nothing like school dating. His head keeps level around her, in fact, it was his head that first directed his heart. He reminds his folks of the letter about the Wadsworth evening. "Guess that was the first time I fell greatly to admiring her."

Continuing, "Of course I am thinking what to do next. First, finish my school. After that I don't know." He muses over various career avenues, then,

"You are anxious to hear about the girl."

"Farming, though, appeals to me more and more. The confinement is a disadvantage, but any business entails that, especially during the first years. Working into cattle breeding is attractive. The outdoors life, coupled with my taste for reading and enjoyment of music, ought to go well together. After I get my degree, why couldn't I work with you, and take the middle course at Madison for a couple of years?"

He compares the farm life he knows with the city life he imagines:

Like most boys I have seen the rough side of my father's profession, as well as the rosy. I have seen the leisure of middle aged men in city life, but not the hours of drudgery and application that has given them their place. The idea of any kind of work is just beginning to lose its distaste. I am seeing now there is no rosy path to accomplishment, and the more I think about our type of farming, the fuller the life seems as compared with the harrowed existence of most city men. There is enough change and head work to keep it absorbing, while at the same time, the future is fairly sure. Later on, I could make politics or community work a sideline without losing touch with my vocation. I could even write if my talents develop at all.

Ronald admits he's painting a kiddish picture of farm life, "but judging from what you have made of it, I am sure it can be shaped to fit my temperament." He knows his parents will be shaking their heads over this letter, and adds a PS: "Wish I knew how a chap could work out the problem of help. We haven't hit the solution exactly yet, have we. The idea of having men constantly underfoot doesn't appeal to me. Wish we had a class in America that is born, lives, and dies contentedly under the same employer—in this country when a man finds congenial work, he is set for life!"

W.J. does not respond with shock. On February 15 he relates some details of home life and family health, then continues:

> Your "girl letter" is sensible and straight-forward for one in your state of mind. There is no senseless raving and you show a clear conception of the meaning of life and the significance of a choice of this nature.
>
> Your description of "the girl" is fine—while we cannot draw a mental picture it is entirely satisfying. It shows poise and good sense on your part. I can believe it is the real life of the girl you are attracted to and not merely the looks or the eyes or the physical form.
>
> However we may be taking your statements to mean more than you intend. Is Miss Wardner of the same mind toward you and are you engaged?

Eunice assumes so. "Your letter made me feel sad and glad. I can hardly think of you as being engaged but from your other letters I knew you admired this girl from Chicago. Is she tall or short, small or large, fair or dark? I am anxious to see her picture. Oh yes, can she cook? I am glad she is not a French Catholic."

Most of Wesson's letter concentrates on Ronald's future plans: "You have

"The first thing is to fall completely in love with my cows."

a broad foundation now in your N.W. classes; and with your touch with city life and business in Chicago; and in your travel and work abroad; to fit you to take the best advantage of the next two years in the School of Agriculture. Not confining yourself to technical lines but to the larger principles of agriculture, fitting yourself for a world farmer and in sympathy with the whole life of all the people."

Whether Ronald continues in actual farming or goes on into diplomatic work or other fields, two years at Madison would be the best possible preparation. He could earn his bachelor's degree; in the choice of profession he still has time.

He does not find Ronald's letter kiddish: "Some farmers would consider your picture of actual farming with its intellectual and aesthetic side as foolishness. I do not. You are grasping something of what I mean by the farm yielding life as well as a living. I lecture at a state meeting next week, in which I bring out some of these points. I am also giving a talk this winter on opportunities in agriculture in which I suggest its broad field of activity and larger life."

He encourages Ronald to travel before coming home and describes different modes:

> Some see only a hasty impression of shops, bell hops and taxis. Nor is it sufficient merely to view the art and beauty, and the outstanding points of historical interest. These are the vital points to note. How do the people live, where and how earn their support. What standard of living, what moral standards. How does the prevailing political system affect the daily life of the citizenry. If there are great monuments and magnificent architecture is it the expression of a grateful happy people or is it the ground down enslaved and crushed souls and lives of millions of human beings?

His father makes, then retracts a wistful suggestion.

> You spoke of wanting someone to travel with. I am tempted to volunteer. No! I am not prepared. It is the companionship of the place you visit that you want. Get acquainted with some common people. Find a humble home in Switzerland and work for your board for a week. Then go to Denmark, study cooperation among farmers. Of course you will visit your English cousins and possibly touch the Emerald Isle. You should take weekend trips to points in France or take a week off so as to have France pretty well explored before

your time is up. It would be fine to take a trip to Guernsey Island. We have a lad here now from Guernsey. His people would welcome you. Knock around alone! You will have the better time.

Ronald has not received this letter before he writes his next one, February 6, which deals entirely with the vocation of farming: "If I decide to be a dairyman, it will be because I think it will give me the fullest possible life, and not because it means a relatively quick way to get established in business." He outlines again the disadvantages of various careers. If he were to rise to an executive position in some firm the routine of catching the same train each morning, buying the same paper, dictating the same letter to the same stenographer, the killing noise and rush of a big city would make him unhappy.

On the other hand, even knowing the disadvantages of farm life, I know its possibilities. You have proved what can be done—my ideas are still hazy. I do know, though, that I could start out with congenial work, and it would continually increase in interest. I wouldn't be away from my home for weeks at a time. Breeding and testing cows is no end interesting. Big success is possible by careful breeding. As the work develops, it would mean a profession about which I could write and talk, later, perhaps, some travel. As far as avocations go, there are absorbing side lines to farming. Farmers mostly lack leaders, I think. After establishing a reputation, there could be work in the Farm Bureau. If it interested me sufficiently, I could lay plans along political lines, and backed by the farm vote become something of a power in middle west politics. That section is going to be run more and more by the farmer vote, and the man that can swing that will have an immense field of usefulness in bettering economic conditions in the country.

But all that, says Ronald, is problematical. "The first thing is to fall completely in love with my cows." The rest will fall into place. "It is your primary interest in your work, Dad, that makes men listen to you. I am becoming more and more convinced that I can do that. I have never been discontented on the farm. The reason you had to push me at times was partly my youth, I think, and that my reading and school loomed important."

Ronald realizes he's taking much for granted. He doesn't know how his father would like him as farmer and potential partner. Once he's served his apprenticeship, he could take over some managerial duties to give his parents a little leisure. He'd like to do that for them. Eventually, "we could work out

W.J. with hired help and visitors, 1914, the only photo where Grampa has his ear trumpet. He ceased using it early.

a plan whereby I could gradually take over the place and furnish you and Mother with capital to do with what you please."

He worries the question of hired help some more. What about a couple in the Big House, and his parents building where they've always wanted?

> During the last fifteen years, your plan of giving your men a home has worked in a number of cases. All the same, I don't think your sacrifices have been fully appreciated. Wouldn't the present crowd be as well off under some other arrangement? Your influence over Chuck, Percy, Alan, and a lot of others is worth plenty, but couldn't that influence now be exerted in working with the boys, and in having them in to meals once in a while, if they were comfortably housed away from the family? It is the occasional conversations that count with the men I think. Surely having Ron and Trev under their feet continually didn't sweeten their dispositions.

Wesson's response to this letter is dated February 24. He spends all Sunday afternoon on it:

> Your letter regarding farming was read with considerable interest. I think I have something of the feeling my mother did when I told her I was going into the ministry. I thought she would be elated. However she seemed to

hesitate and questioned my decision. She either felt I was not smart enough or I was not good enough.

I want you to choose a lifework where you can live the largest life and do the biggest service. Your letter has a fine tone and shows a clear analytic mind. You surely do see the drawbacks to other lines of activity. You are not so clear on the advantages of farming. However your second paragraph, the one on possibilities of farming, could have well replaced a paragraph in my lecture last week at Dixon.

You are also right in judging my influence. That is why I declare that when I fail in farming I shall not try to tell the other fellow how to do it.

Wesson hits the managerial question head on, and in doing so, lumps his sons together:

The picture you paint is ideal. Should it work out from the motives and with the ideals you portray it would suit me to the dot. I note you realize how much you have to learn to be competent as manager. However I fear, knowing you and Trever as I do, that you may find it irksome to take a subordinate position until you gradually and naturally step up. It has always been difficult for you boys to take training. You have a native genius that enables you to do most anything fairly good the first time. Therefore you do not take well to training in gymnasium or athletic work. Both of you want to jump right into the match games. You must learn the truth: "It is only by the slow toilsome process of self culture that one can achieve great success."

W.J. takes up the help question:

We, especially I, had an idea about help that was different. Several factors determined our plan:

1. The thought of a home for the boys.

2. Economic considerations: a) we could care for help much cheaper in this way and b) lack of money for a suitable boarding house.

3. Better management by closer touch with the men.

When young Greene took over the management of the Brookhill Farm at Genesee he would not live in the mansion with his people. He had his room and board with the men in the boarding hall. He said he had better control that way.

Let me suggest a possible solution: Mother and I build a comfortable cottage on the edge of the farm. Mr. and Mrs. Stam occupy this present house and board any single men. You live in "the birds nest in the orchard" for a time. If this plan works and we make money enough, we could hire another married man to live in the Little House and you could build a better home. This main house is well situated and properly remodeled to take care of several men.

I am changing my idea toward the quality of men to hire. Inexperienced labor takes too much close supervision to get the work done right or nearly right. I am now adopting a policy of better men and better pay. Lester Stam and Clair Mathews each get the equivalent of $100 per mo. Clair rents his own house in town and goes home to supper. Stam has the little house and boards himself. He gets $65, house, garden, light, water, milk, etc., equal to $35. Both will get still more. They are good men. I want to get another good man to head the farm work, at an equal salary. I am going to Madison tomorrow for this purpose.

NO! There is no great bug-a-boo regarding the farm labor problem. It resolves itself to the question of making the farm pay enough to do the work in the right way at the right time. If you become the right sort of man, get the right sort of wife, and have the right sort of habits and a high ambition, I guess we can work out the details all right.

His father now pushes his agenda on Ronald's schooling:

If you decide on the program now appealing to you I have no question in my mind. With your cultural courses in Evanston, and your year abroad you now can afford to confine yourself to your future work. Two years is all too short for training in animal husbandry, etc. Another reason you should graduate at Madison: its reputation in putting out men accomplished and expert in agriculture is nationally known. Also the associations will help in any public effort. I can name many men who have been called to positions at Washington because the heads of departments there knew these capable men at Madison.

Wesson finishes with an account of his personal activities: "I have had a full week but have scarcely seen my own job!"

Tuesday we went to Dixon to a big State Agricultural meeting. All the aristocracy of Illinois gathers here. College presidents, teachers, governors, deans, farmers, and their wives. The program includes such as Loredo Taft, artist; Howard of Farm Bureau; and speakers of national note. I told Mother I could not see why they were so eager to have me on their program. The Sec. wrote me last July to reserve these dates. To let him know if I had any call for dates during this week so he could adjust his program so as to get me on it. I could not understand at the time and was still more amazed when I got there and met the aristocracy. I felt a great responsibility to fulfill their expectations. I made a good talk. It was logical and a needed truth.

Ron doesn't neglect his France job while considering his future. Here he's camping with his scouts, under a tree reputed to have shaded a campsite of Napoleon.

I got home Thursday night. Canvassed for funds for the University Church Fri. and Sat. and spoke this morning at the Methodist Church on this subject. Our subscription is small to what it ought to be but we did our best. Raised about $800. Mother and I gave $200. That will pinch us but it is needed.

Grampa probably does not realize that these final paragraphs are a template of what his son is proposing for his own life. But surely Ronald realizes it, when he studies this thoughtful letter. However, due to the slowness of the mails, he doesn't receive it for several weeks. He plies his parents with more startling revelations, waits, chafes, and writes home some more.

20 ⨯ FARMER'S DIARY, 1947

R on Dougan is not a diary keeper, but in 1947 he comes on an old leather bound empty diary. In it he keeps a sporadic record, mostly of the work of the farm. At this time Russel Ullius is farm manager. His wife LaBerta runs the Big House, where some eight hired men room and board. Ron lives farther up Colley Road at Chez Nous. Grampa and Grama live at the edge of town. Grampa (called "Daddy" by everyone) still comes out to the farm every day. He finds it impossible to give up the reins.

> January 7: Rock Co. Breeders meeting in Janesville. Much talk about firing Glassco as County Agent. I have never entered into his condemnation as heatedly as others, my remarks implying, "If he is so poor why don't you fellows do something about it?" Well, they have. Petitions, pressure on the new County Board Ag. Committee. I feel bad for Glassco but I'm sure county work would be better served with a new man. However, my neutral stand, which may be based on lack of community interest and inertia as well as dislike of taking an open stand led Eddy to laugh at me as "Chicken Hearted Dougan." Maybe he is right.

> January 8: LaBerta Ullius called much upset while I was in Janesville last night. Then she called before I was up today to say everything was settled. It seems Russel told George [a middle-aged milkhouse worker] that if he were sick they would cut out the radio, but it was such a part of their life they intended to continue to play it. George has times when he gets quite upset, when he can't sleep he gets down pretty badly. I think it will be O.K. for a while or until the work roughens up. Had a long talk with Russel. He asked how I felt about his handling of men. I said I thought he was a trifle rough on them and I, as he thought, might be too soft. I think time will patch most things up, though I didn't say this.

January 9: Russel told me he'd have to quit come fall if things didn't straighten out. He said Daddy made the statement that Russel "didn't know enough to know if Kirkpatrick was lying." It doesn't matter what Daddy said, that is the way it was construed. Some of the barn men overheard. The Ulliuses think Lyall has been gunning for them. They think he is lying down on the job and isn't loyal. Russel doesn't want me to hire Nyall as he thinks brothers will lead to trouble. He thinks there are too many bosses and that is the "gripe" of every man that leaves here. Daddy tells him to investigate farm machinery and then when he finds a problem, Daddy turns it down without discussion. Every day he has to "battle for his rights." It is giving him ulcers. One night the milkmen ran the farm truck out of the garage and left it — he wants order in the garage. LaBerta thinks we consider her only a glorified farm hand.

I don't know what to think about "too many bosses." I can see some justification. On the other hand both Daddy's and my interest in the place is so intense we can't sit back and do no work, and to work we need men. Maybe the answer is planning farther ahead, and conferences —

To Madison with Vera, Beadle and Mrs. Bjerk. Saw Griffiths in the hospital, who looks bad. Spent three hours at the University with Andy Wright interpreting the corn yield test. Brink wants us to put in an alfalfa test. Meals are high. At the Lorraine Hotel the "Chef's Special Lunch" consisting of dried up turkey left over from previous meals, served in a tomato sauce and a few mushrooms plus potatoes, spinach, etc but no dessert cost 75 cents. While we were gone, Daddy shelled corn. Hope he didn't get too tired.

On Friday, January 10, Ronald does office work. His father starts by shelling corn, but the sheller breaks. They switch to dusting corn. The next day Russel and Nyall fix the sheller; W.J. and several day-men shell a thousand bushels by 4:30. Other day-men dust with Ronald. "Everybody seemed happy."

January 27 Ron, understandably, doesn't write, but W.J. details the day to Trever:

Ronald has had a hard day. We were going to go over our plans for crops and seeds and fertilizers. I got nicely settled in the back office and I missed him. Miss Glenn said the state milk inspector and the city health officer came to go over our operations. He spent many hours with them. They inspected and tested everything — every can and pail and bottle, took sediment tests of the

"Have been feeding stock up here and enjoying it. 12 below doesn't seem to bother them."

producers' milk as it comes in, inspected can washing and storing bottles, washing, refrigeration, ventilation, etc., etc., etc. — they made corrections and gave suggestions. A friendly but thorough job. They were easier than I would be. On top of that Ron had to take four cans of milk back to producers because it was condemned by the inspector. Also when the inspectors got through he had to work an hour with Wright & Wagner in lowering the price of milk and during it all one of our men in the plant demanded a $30 per month raise which Ron cannot comply to. He will let him go. I suppose R. is still at the office or grading corn. I am going to bed.

January 29 [Ronald continuing]: Blizzard following several days of warm weather — lightning, thunder — 13 inches of snow during evening and night — a family froze to death at Johnson's Creek trying to drive home from the village to their farm —

January 30: Drivers got off with great difficulty. All roads blocked. Got milk through from east with horses. Reimer, Weeda, Toft, and Holmbeck met our horses at Brewers at five o'clock. I was able to meet Palmer by taking the truck onto 51 until where the road was closed — then walked and met them and was able to break through on the next road east —

January 31: Roads a trifle better — Have put two men on a milk truck — Milner had two trucks go to pieces. Garagemen worked till midnight getting equipment in and fixed. The hauling truck is standing up wonderfully. I've been walking to work. Completely closed in.

February 1 and 2: One of these days it thawed enough to settle snow so that the high winds didn't drift so badly. However after our road was plowed, it blew in again and wasn't plowed till late in the week. In fact, at this writing, Feb. 6, many roads including our own are still blocked.

February 3: Have been feeding stock up here and enjoying it. 12 below doesn't seem to bother them. Jackie's goat doesn't like the close proximity with the cattle. I've turned her loose with them and she spends her time in a corner bleating plaintively.

February 4: Between dragging in frozen trucks I have been studying cow records. Our proven bull program is paying off in a fine bunch of heifers. [The journal lists pedigrees.]

February 5: Worked on plans for seed corn fields for '47. Won't plant as much this year —

During this incredible snow, Jackie has finals for her first semester at Beloit College. It never occurs to her that weather is an excuse to miss a final. She skis from Chez Nous to the dairy and rides into town on a milk truck; two tire-tracks width have been cleared. She finds most students who live in town, even some living on campus, are missing their exams. Later, with Craig, she pulls groceries on a sled from the dairy to Chez Nous, a mile and a half. Daddy writes on February 6, "Am enjoying Patsy and Jackie at home. Jackie took her last exams at the college today — she has fun with Richardson and other teachers — Children downtown tonight at Gramp's. Craig to go on milkroute with Lester tomorrow."

There are blank pages from then until April 5. But on March 12 Ron writes a letter to Nellie Needham, his father's second cousin, to whom he sends a newsy note twice a year when he pays the interest on the money she lent W.J. to build the round barn, so long ago:

I have been busy all day getting out my income tax returns. We are in the midst of our corn selling period. Today we sent two loads of seed corn over to Hebron, Illinois, where they will be dumped into a freight car and shipped to New Orleans. There they will be joined by seed from all over the midwest and shipped to Europe. I think this shipload goes to Albania. Most of it will be doled out in small amounts and planted with a hoe.

There is an anachronistic entry on March 19, the date amended to 1971:

Snowed in with heavy wet snow. Dozen juncos, one cardinal, one song sparrow, hairy woodpecker. Yesterday a downy came regularly. Threw down hay for 18 little beef heifers. Ready to sell? Skunk in garage Tuesday night. We both retreated. Chess club Wednesday here. Decided to play another year with matches as organized by the Whitewater club. Missed Art Luebke—he was held late to hear a jury's verdict. Won against Manning after he graciously returned my Queen, lost in an oversight. Wrong to take back a move.

[Back to 1947] **April 5:** Vera, Effie, Daddy, and I drove to Appleton to Aunt Ria's funeral. Stopped at Watertown and had coffee and cake with Nellie Needham. She thinks the Lord has forgotten her, He is letting her live so long. She and several other old ladies are going to charter a bus pretty soon if He continues to overlook them.

April 6: Craig and I cleaned office. Went to Easter service. Worked in office in p.m., introduced Craig to intricacies of the adding machine. Saw Bette Davis and Claude Raines in Perception. Raines reminded me of Uncle Bert with his cute little mannerisms.

April 7: Cold rainy spring—no one in the fields yet anywhere— Finished grading and cleaning the first generation oats purchased from Tower and Bumstead. We now have enough oats for our own planting and our commitments. Jacqueline and Craig helped load oats. Their sinus trouble showed up immediately—the slightest dust—what to do with Craig? Too bad all the things I'm interested in like corn, oats and probably barn's dust bother his nose—
Went to S. E. Farm Management meeting in Janesville in evening. Took Ed Huebbe —there's a fine fellow—also his son-in-law Fritz. I don't see how the S.E.F.M. group can get very valuable information from the records we farmers keep—

April 16: Couldn't begin to plough or disk because of snowy and cold weather.

April 19: Rain. No field work yet except about 20 acres of disking and a little plowing—no grain in—Mixed 6# of brome grass to 2 bu of Vicland oats per acre for seeding permanent pasture—will add grass mixture later— Vera to Detroit. We are all alone—Craig, Patsy, Jackie, Haaken the dog, and I— Went to 35th Waukesha Guernsey sale. Told Miss Glenn as I took a blank check that if I bought anything I should be restrained and examined. Came home with three. Gramp is afraid to go to sales. I should be, didn't examine until they were in ring. I should be stung but am optimistic I won't be. Am pricing grades from $175 to $275. Sold four cows to Reuben for $250. I'll tell him we can spare a few more—

April 21: Started seeding brome grass and oats on fields 2 and 3—Abbott called at 2 a.m., his wife had a baby boy. Lyall and I are to go on his route—

On April 22, after Abbott's route, Ron helps seed and reseed parts of fields 2 and 3. Three acres next to the Clinton oats have no fertilizer; "Lyall and I will fix fertilizer attachment tonight —I broke it by letting a wrench get in." Porter Brothers of South Beloit will put 100 tons of limestone on the field across the tracks that's to go into spring wheat.

The diary is blank till May 10 when Ron reports the last of the grain in. "The latest spring I have seen. Terrifically harried by inadequate labor." Lyall, the garageman, has left to form his own business. He comes out every day for emergency work and upkeep on milk trucks. "However, general upkeep of machinery and older trucks is bound to suffer." Corn sales are slow. "We are good growers but we must do better as salesmen. The direct selling methods of competition are cutting the ground out from under our dealers. We must develop new outlets." The next entry, May 16, reports the planting of the university test plot, and the start to planting the strip test, with details of types and bushels. It rains heavily that night and all the next day. "We are behind. Most people have some corn in. Emil Punzel has a lot." On Sunday he accompanies Vera to Madison on music work. He sees Ed Blaney, another seed corn grower, who says Blaneys are just starting planting. He gets home at 9 o'clock and dusts seed corn into the night.

May 19: Albert Marston helped with planting. He says brome grass needs lots of nitrogen. Planted through the noon hour—Daddy brought us out lunch. Got rained in at 3 o'clock. Lots of breakdowns but nothing serious—manure loader, bottle washer—last minute, big tire on Farmall tractor was punctured by a boy ramming manure loader spike into it. Plowed from 6 to 9 p.m. and was relieved by Earl Brunke who will plow till midnight on field south of main house.

May 20: Got up at 4 o'clock—plowed for a while. Loaded out corn to East Troy with Beadle. Selling good. Finished strip trial in P.M. with Albert Marston. The field is planted in following order, starting at South:

There follow two pages of dense listing; the strip trials are sample plantings of Dougan's and other growers' varieties of seed corn, grown under the same conditions on the same field. In the fall people will be able to study the various varieties in close proximity, including the university's test plot. The growers are DeKalb, Nichols, Pfister, Funk, Jacques, Pioneer, Crow, King Krontky.

May 21 is all day planting into the night. May 22 Albert Marston starts at two a.m. and plants for several hours. Ron diagrams the layout of the field. Albert lays off, returns to planting in the afternoon. Rain halts it at 5 o'clock. "Big tractor (Case) broke right rear wheel hub."

Friday, May 23, it's too wet to work in the morning. "Marston planted south of house from 3 p.m. to six. Russel changed horses and planted till dark. Crave also plowed on Albert's farm from 3 o'clock on. Sent to Racine for hub—got no rivets—now what—"

Albert, on Saturday, again plants all day. On his farm "we had one man plowing with his outfit most of day and in P.M. two plows on his East field. Gramp, Craig, Jack, and I went to Madison to see Joan graduate. In evening to Janesville to Vera's state music convention. Haven't managed to work out repairs on Case yet." Sunday, Ron attends music events in Janesville. "Vera presiding—very impressive—well worked out as to details. Craig worked with Ed on tractor wheel all afternoon, five hours."

May 26: Started field work after lunch—too wet before. Albert on 464 south of house. Our plows and other equipment on his 20 acre east field. His tractor, plow and harrow with our man on his west field. Russel worked after supper taking Albert's place as corn planter.

"Marston planted south of house from 3 p.m. to six. Russel changed horses and planted till dark."

May 27: Used 116 sacks of 8-8-8 and 3 sacks of 3-18-9 on Albert's east field. Started at 3:30 in the morning planting south of house, Field 11. Albert came at seven and we finished field just at eleven. Got started at his place on 606, east field before noon and worked till six—Albert on planter most of the time. Started planting 464 with Bradley planter, west field, considerable trouble adjusting it. Brunke worked late—till dark—planting. Had 5 acres plowed in field east of house at Hill Farm. Probably a mistake, as hind sight is so good. It had a good stand of wheat and clover seeding. It is too near other corn and is wet. However we wanted a place for 595, and at the time it seemed best. Beadle shakes his head.

May 28: Had Marston's horses fed and harnessed, fertilizer in field and ready to start planting before five o'clock and it started to rain—rained all day. At six p.m. still cloudy and cold. Temperature just at freezing. Snow reported in West. In office most of day. Rotten break on weather. Lots of corn to plant yet.

The above entry has an addendum in Joan's handwriting: "Jo started working at the Rock County Breeder's Cooperative—7:00 every A.M.!" This is followed by a joyous little smiling face. Thursday, May 29, Ron takes his farm manager up to the university: "Allen says grass silage has a place. Cows don't eat it as well as corn silage. It is just as palatable if grain is put on it when fed as if it was put in at filling time. Use silo to put in grass during bad hay weather. If you save leaves on good hay the protein is as high as silage. Cows need hay. Use silage in August, etc."

Ron sees Professor Hull of soils, about shavings, and Professor Duffy on machinery.

On the way home, "picked up Pete Bertelson from Missouri, hitch hiking. Student at Carnegie—nice boy. Gave him a bed for the night."

Early the next morning Ronald types out the day at the university for his father. The farm's interest in shavings is that they get them free from a Beloit factory, for use as bedding. But what happens after the shavings go to the manure pile? Later W.J. annotates the margins briefly; his more extensive comments have been lost.

I think we are sounder on mastitis and the effect of feed on udders. Allen also said there could be no relation between the feed a cow gets—corn in her grass silage, or the grass silage, and the way the calf behaves as to scours.

Duffy could only give us a few minutes. With the wet, the hay business is in an awful turmoil. The mow driers aren't yet successful. Unless we are crowded to get the work done, the impression he gave me was to go slow about new haying ideas.

[W.J. annotates: Good. We have good methods now. I am not anxious to try the new until it is well proven. I would suggest to bite off a little smaller amount at a time. Get a surer better hay.]

I went to Hull, in soils, the man who surveyed this farm, and asked him about shavings on the land. He was ambiguous. Had no reason to believe they were harmful. The only thing they did, he said, was to tie up nitrogen for a period. However straw and cornstalks do that too. When they eventually decompose all the nitrogen is released. Thus, suppose you do tie up nitrogen for a period of years, you are adding more in the form of commercial fertilizer, and eventually the shavings will start releasing nitrogen regularly. You will reach a place when the old shavings release as much as is tied up with the new application. If you ever stopped using them, for a period of years you would have a regular release of nitrogen into the soil as the shavings continued to break down.

Shavings can do little harm—at least considerable less, if spread on top of the ground —seedings, etc. They will fix little nitrogen that way. I wonder what happens when eventually they are turned under? It is better to spread them immediately than to pile them up. The heating drives off most of the nitrogen as you know.

So I have arrived at the conclusion that if shavings are good bedding and absorbent, it is foolish to save straw after a combine. It seems to me contrary to the general trend to save as much high priced labor as possible. However, there is another consideration. If straw is worth from twelve to eighteen dollars a ton

W.J. and Joan, plowing for the kithen garden.

baled, and if it can be baled and stored cheaply, which I don't know, why isn't it a good cash crop in these times. Also, if shavings are in demand, why wouldn't it be a good idea to install a baling outfit on them and bale each load as we get it and sell in carload lots any surplus we have. Perhaps this idea is foolish. Or we could advertise locally, sell shavings to surrounding farmers at a price which would give us our hauling costs back. [W. J.: the only way]

Saw the alfalfa man, Brink, and they expect to be down in about a week. We should work up the field again. They will let us know a day or two before.

Saw Neal and John Maloney, his right hand man. I bought seven pounds more of 595. I now have plenty of border, and enough female to plant five acres of crossing block besides. Maybe we should plow that strip a little wider. I keep thinking of all sorts of shifts to get in a better corn field for the 595. That ditch bothers me, and the fact that it can't be too well fitted. Or am I wrong. Is that an excellent field and will it raise fine corn? We could put the 595 on my farm now, but that would require 20 rows of border the whole length. Then the early corn would require 20 rows of border the whole length on both sides instead of only on one. If we bring the 595 down to my farm it means silage or hard corn on the Hill Farm, and for silage it is quite a ways away. Then I hesitate to keep changing plans — the boys would take it all right, but unless there is some real reason developed, it shows too much uncertainly on my part.

("Border" refers to the rows of male corn that must flank a hybrid field to insure that pollen from nearby cornfields without the proper pedigree will have little chance, statistically, to fertilize the corn protected by the border.)

May 30: Albert started at 7 a.m. on his East field of 606, planting until 6 and finished. Pretty wet — Big job on my hill. Three plows part of the time. Disk and drag. Too wet. Almost impossible to fit. Brunke, Albert, and I got Albert's west field mucked in — started late.

May 31: Got both planters ready to go. Albert worked all day on my hill getting 464 and 416A in. He finished the seed corn. I took W. J. and Munji and got the Hill Farm field started with 595. Russel took over at noon. I went to Geneva bull meeting with Prentice and others. Vera called me that Mr. Griffiths had died. We went to Madison in the evening and got Josie. RAINED HEAVILY ALL NIGHT.

June 1: RAIN

June 2: Plowed on sod in p.m. Too wet.

June 3: Griffiths funeral at Beloit at 10, then to Dodgeville to the grave at 2. To Milwaukee for a radio broadcast at 6:00. Russel and W.J. were at Dodgeville too as was Albert, This held up our corn planting although it would have been hard to have fitted the fields ahead.

Broke the Case tractor. It jumped out of gear and in trying to get it out it dug into ground. Either then or earlier the rod third from the front went out. Somehow water got in the gasoline too — Corn planting all over state is in terrible shape.

June 4: Broke the Deere trying to get the Case out of hole — just a case of asking a tractor to do more than it can. Fitted land ahead of Albert on my farm. The land is in terrible shape. Plowed too wet and in some cases poorly. Got Joe Lentell and his tractor. Started work at 9 and ran to 12 when we were rained in. Promised repairs by Clinton dealers on both Case and Deere tomorrow.

Big party — 5 tables bridge. The Beadles were special guests. Cooked the Lentell turkey. Everything especially nice.

June 5: Got into field at noon. Albert planting on my hill. Joe Lentell started at one and worked till six on Obeck's west field. I thought I'd seen the worst in plowing but haven't. Joe disked twice, then dragged with horses and finally got planter going at 4 o'clock and planted till dark. If we can cultivate the rows I planted it will be a wonder. I couldn't see the markers half the time.

June 6: Got started early and was planting on same field at 7 o'clock. Finished at noon. Russel came on with bigger equipment and got field in only fair shape. Used 10 bags of 3-18-9 on 7 acres and a little over a bushel of seed corn 464.

Got onto Obeck's west field of 11 acres at noon. Albert finished my field using silage blend (2 kinds) and got to Obecks after lunch. We drilled silage blend, finished at 6 o'clock. We planted on the same land, one planter following the other. Worked OK. The land was well fitted. Joe all day with tractor —

June 7: Started very early. All men in field n. of Obecks by 5 o'clock. I got team in field by seven by the time first land was fitted. Joe worked from 8 until he was rained in, at 4:30. Albert worked same length. Daddy changed horses and relieved him during noon hour.

I went to bull farm at Madison on field day with George Conway — a marvelous job. Stopped and saw fish removal near Madison — swept rough fish out of a slough — disposed of carp and suckers. Heavy rain.

Planting continues on Sunday. On Monday Ron is up at 3:30. He looks into the milkhouse to see what a new pesticide, Cyanogas, has done to the "population" — and concludes, "Plenty!" It's a continuing battle with cockroaches in that building, but Ron keeps the upper hand through constant vigilance. He then spends over an hour catching a team of horses in the pasture — they've apparently had it with the difficult plowing.

Several men continue planting until dark. A crew from the university puts in their corn borer test on fourteen acres, "no fertilizer in the plow sole." After supper Ron works with Amos Grundahl, the inseminator, on bull books.

Tuesday, June 10, they finish corn planting. Joe drags the alfalfa patch; the university comes down and puts in the alfalfa trial. W.J. plants a garden at Chez Nous; Joan is his assistant. Beadle alters and vaccinates pigs.

Wednesday: rainy. Cousins visit; Ron takes them fishing at Delavan Lake. He notes that Ray Fadner has built a 54-compartment martin house. Thurs-

The horse-drawn hay loader, a precursor to baling machines.

day, in the office: "No field work. Heavy rain—over an inch at night. Since May first we have had nine inches."

Friday: "Fields flooded. Can't get on to cultivate." Ron declares a holiday—everyone goes fishing at Delavan. He catches fifteen bullheads. The next day reports: "Rain and mist."

On June 17 Ron arranges to use a one-hundred gallon sprayer for thistles that he mounts on the International farm truck. The rest of the week men are occupied spraying thistles and weeding. The family heads north for a week's fishing; the diary is silent but for a single sentence, July 1: his pig man, Leonard Beadle, is quitting Thursday. "Shabby trick on such short notice."

Ron reports on July 4 that he's been pulled into the hay job. The farm, not yet baling, still uses the hay loader behind the wagons. "Lot of trouble with the track in round barn—we must investigate methods of making hay that are cheaper in effort than putting up long hay." He drops a wagon tongue on his toe. "I lived through it." And he worries about "handling the job"—apparently referring to the whole farm operation, for he lists "hogs—corn sales—mechanic—etc." He offers a mechanic $175 per month. "He is subject to epilepsy but has good recommends."

> July 5: Went on #2 milk route with Craig. He is a good fellow and developing nicely. He ran and I drove for most part as my toe pained badly.

Slept in p.m. Movie in evening—Sea of Grass. An improbable picture based on the truth, however, that a lot of land in the West should never have been plowed.

July 6: Last conference with Beadle. Got Ed Pfaff out to check on stuck bottle washer. Found a dry bearing. I surely need more maintenance supervision.

Ron and Vera call on Aunt Lillian and Hazel. Lillian (in her eighties) "is lively as a cricket." He lists where all his children are, this evening: "Kids all gone. Patsy with Lewie. Jo to Ohio with Karl. Jackie calling on her various college professor friends. And Craig has hitch-hiked to Chicago with Ed Grutzner, he called from Western Springs where they are staying with Jerry." (Craig's first cousin.) Ron has started reading Gunther's *Inside U.S.A.* "Big storm Saturday night. Grain stood well. Corn growing well. We will get crop." Tuesday starts dusting. "Began at dusk and finished at 1 a.m. Conditions good. Used 26 bags DDT on 28 acres = 1/6# 3% DDT to acre. Lots of egg masses and some feeding." He hires a mechanic at $160 a month plus electricity with a $10 raise Sept. 1 if OK. He hires a milkhouse worker for $200, who will live in the flat over the milkhouse for $25 a month. He hires a swine herdsman, Harlan Whitmore, to take Beadle's place. "He and Russel will go to state Duroc picnic Saturday."

The DDT dusting continues; Ron with Craig and Joe spray thistles on all the farms with 2,4-D. On Saturday a light rain ends field work. "Haying going on at great rate. Lots to do yet. It is getting pretty old." July 14, Monday, more DDT dusting and thistle spraying. "Rained twice, very heavy showers. I wonder if both the DDT and 2,4-D were washed off." July 16: "DDT has proved its worth on the earlier dustings—only one new egg mass per ten hills on the dusted portions, four in ten show feeding on the hills left undusted for a check." The farm manager says he's found another place; Ron asks what it will take to keep him. A hired man asks to borrow a thousand dollars. Ron tells him it's impossible but he'll help him distribute his pay to satisfy creditors. There's a PS on this page: "Motor on bottle washer burnt out. Joe Brocolli had it out, repaired, and reinstalled by 10 o'clock."

July 17: 5:30 a.m. DDT on triangle field of 641 A. Strip trial shows a lot of feeding. Started to dust in evening (second application) but machine broke. Dusted on Hill Farm at noon. Big pump broke at 6 p.m. Orville came out and we got the spare well going. Will fix pump tomorrow, I hope. And so to bed.

July 19 sees the second dusting of the strip test. The yield trial doesn't get a second application. The duster is removed and the tractor returned to Albert Marston. Ron talks with his farm manager about the prospect of his staying. On the 21st he checks for tassels and finds none showing except on the 416 corn south of the office. "Must plan to get in the last of week." By July 25 he's hired eight boys 16 years or older, earning 50 cents an hour with a 10 cents bonus. He works all day with the crew, detasseling. Wes Wieland comes with his plane and dusts DDT on the cornfields. Ron and his father spend the afternoon looking over the grain fields. "The Clinton oats are wonderful." The men hay till midnight, when a bad storm stops them.

The day following, Ron takes a corn trip and nets two seed salesmen — one works at the Green County Farm Bureau, the other, a former employee, at Juda Lumber and Fuel. July 30 brings combining of oats. August 1 finds Ron at show day at the Green County Fair; his swine herdsman, Harlan, shows the Dougan Durocs. They win first and second on young boars, first on aged boar, and fourth and fifth on young gilts. Ron talks all day with other seed dealers: Moew, Renk, Tracy, Walker of Wisbred. With growing conditions bad all over, they are debating prices to set on what crop they have. Seed will be in demand. They also discuss what percentage of retail the salesmen should get, and on what seed.

The diary skips to August 9, a bare listing of dairies in Michigan. Daddy has taken this trip to look at bottle cap assemblies: the usual cap, and then a cellophane hood, and the machinery to cap bottles this way. He's been getting flack from a vocal customer to cover the top of the bottle, for sanitary reasons. She's a Beloit College wife, and commands an audience. On August 14 he's cleaning Clinton oats, on the 15th, thrashing Vicland oats.

A caller from Purdue University stops by who remembers W.J. vividly from 25 years ago. He's sure Daddy Dougan shipped milk to the Versailles peace treaty. Ron strongly doubts it.

The diary entries grow fewer, mostly listing corn and oat prices. George Schreiber moves to Milwaukee to open a grocery store, presumably with no radio, so he's out of the hair of Laberta Ullius. A tractor has had $385.81 already put into it, and now the repair man says it has to have a new crank shaft, sleeves, and pistons — total cost, $576.

September 5, Ron goes to Wonewoc, "north and west of Spring Green in the unglaciated sand hills along the Baraboo and Wisconsin Rivers. Clay on hill tops, sand in valleys, they tell me." He arranges to take over the salesmen of a retiring friend, stays the night and gets in on a big wedding party. The next day he sets up advertising, a warehouse, and meets sub-dealers.

Most of September's pages are blank. On the 27th, fires to dry the corn are started in the corn bins. On October 9th, Ron notices that the 464 corn in the tin bin is spoiling in the center where it isn't getting enough air. "Not bad yet but must change method." The farm manager agrees to stay on at $300 a month, no bonus, no discount on milk.

The next week of entries are one-liners keeping track of corn drying, with October 15 saying, "This completes our seed corn harvest."

On October 23, when the university yield test is picked, Ron lists the pickers and their hours. "Included dinner @ $2.50 for five men, added wages @ 75 for all but King and divided by 75 and arrived at 72^1/$_2$ hours for which I charged the university $54.37."

October 24's entry is a list of ten "Visitors," from as near as Sharon and Footville, to as far away as Mineral Point. This is the final entry. What Ron doesn't say is that this day, and the following, are "open house" days for the yield tests, that there has been an extended writeup in the *Daily News*, explaining what the tests are and their meaning, and that crowds have visited the farm on these two days to examine the results.

Yet for all its gaps, for all that's left unsaid, it doesn't take much reading between the lines to see the life of a diversified dairy and seed farmer, his range of activities, hours, problems, worries, satisfactions, family commitments. This is Section 32 of Turtle Township in Rock County, Wisconsin, in a trying but — in the farming world — an overall typical, atypical year.

21 ⚹ BRAHMS' LULLABY

It's a May morning in 1958. The air is tender; the leaves are tender; the narrow green blades of grass are tender. A kindergarten class from Todd School is visiting the farm. This is Mrs. Wildermuth's fourth farm outing so she knows what to expect—not every detail, for each tour brings surprises, but there are certain popular features that she knows will be repeated.

The children are tender, too, but as they burst from the cars, all elbows and knees and noise, they seem hardy little plants indeed. They, too, know what to expect, for they've heard about the farm visits from classmates and siblings in upper grades. And they have a secret. They and their teacher have been preparing it. It has to do with something Mr. Dougan said to Mrs. Wildermuth when last year's kindergarten sang the chicken to sleep. "Why is it that the only lullaby kids know is 'Rockabye Baby'?" he'd asked. "Gertrude is always glad to hear the children sing, of course, but she wonders why it's always the same song."

The class whispers together. Mr. Dougan is going to be surprised, this year! And Gertrude, too!

Mr. Dougan meets them in front of the milkhouse. He greets Mrs. Wildermuth and the two mother-helpers. He repeats each child's name: Alison, Freddy, Billy, Charlene, Kenneth, and all the others. There is nudging and giggling and warning shakes of heads as they think of the surprise. Ron Dougan doesn't notice anything unusual; in his experience, all five- and six-year-olds nudge and giggle.

The first stop is the cow barn. The cows are still in the pasture, but Ronald explains about the round barn and its advantages. The children all crowd to the center section and take turns peering down the silo shaft into the depths of the near-empty cylinder and then looking up its vast height to the wooden fretwork and tiny windows at the top.

"The cows eat silage all winter long, when they can't go out to pasture," says Mr. Dougan. He picks up a handful of silage from the trolley and offers it around, himself nibbling a disk of corn. A few accept, taste tentatively, and screw up their faces.

"The sourness is from fermentation, which keeps the corn from spoiling," Mr. Dougan says. "Then the cows' bodies turn the silage, along with their hay and grain, into milk. They think silage is as good as candy."

Those who tasted the silage look disbelieving.

"Can we milk a cow? My sister milked a cow last year!" cries Raymond.

"Later," promises their host. He shows them the cows' drinking cups, positioned low between every other stanchion. "All summer we use a large tank on wheels to take water to the cows in the pasture; when they're in the barnyard they drink from the big concrete cow tank. But in the winter, or when they get thirsty here in the barn, they'll use these drinking cups. Cows have broad round noses, you'll see, and when they press their noses against this curved grill in the cup, it releases a valve that lets the water in. They have to share, two to a cup. Do you ever have to share?"

Everyone agrees they do. Ronald lets the children clean out the straw bits, then press the grills and fill the cups with water. Next he organizes races on the circular walk behind the gutter. He tells how he and his brother used to race their wagons around this same track, and so did his own children. Now his grandchildren race when they come to visit.

The class goes down the passageway into the side barn, and Ronald pokes two fingers into a calf stall. A calf with wobbly legs and rolling eyes grabs and sucks noisily. A few brave students poke their fingers in, too, and calves seize them eagerly. The children squeal and jerk their hands out again, tingling and slobber-covered.

Then all troop down the back lane, pause to swing on a metal gate wide enough for a hay wagon, and go through to a pasture. "Watch out for cow pies," warns Mr. Dougan, pointing out an impressive green-brown splat on the grass. "You wouldn't want to step in one, would you?" Each child shows respectful interest in the cow pie while giving it wide berth. They look around to mark any other spots of danger.

At the crick Mr. Dougan says, "This is Spring Brook Crick, it runs into Turtle Crick down closer to town. If your teacher tells you you should say 'creek,' you tell her that all good Turtle Township farm kids say 'crick.' Tell her that's colloquial English."

Ralphie asks, "Are there any frogs in the crick?"

"Look close; you might see tadpoles."

The group crouches on the bank and studies the shallows.

Schoolkids play with tires used to hold down the pit silo covering.

"What's that? It's moving!" cries Charlene.

"Aha, what sharp eyes you have! It's a hair snake."

Charlene blushes with pleasure as Mr. Dougan gently extricates a smooth black string coiled around a reed and holds it writhing on his palm. "It's harmless. When I was a kid I used to put hairs from horses' tails in the crick, hoping they'd turn into hair snakes, but they never did. Never could figure out why." He sits back on his heels. "Listen to the birds, singing and marking out their territories. I know where a killdeer's nest is; you can see it if you're very careful. The mother will pretend she has a broken wing; she'll try to lure us away from her eggs. You'll have to cross the crick on stepping stones."

He leads the group farther into the pasture, and, sure enough, a brown bird rises from the grass and hops and flutters ahead of them. But they aren't fooled and approach close enough to see the speckled eggs lying in a hollow on the ground. Then they back carefully away.

"She'll return as soon as we're gone," says Ron Dougan. "Look. The cows in the next field are coming to see us. Did you notice that they were in that far corner when we first arrived? Now they're almost here. Cows don't look it, but they're very curious. If you run and yell they'll bolt, but if you stand quietly by the fence, they'll come right up to you. That single strand is an electric fence — it gives the cows a small shock, enough to keep them in the pasture. Don't you try touching it!"

While the cows graze their way toward them, Ronald relates the story of when he was ten and given a dime to tend cows but let them wander into Mr. Blodgett's corn because he was so absorbed reading a book. By the end of the story, the cows are in a row before the still children. Two of the boldest cows stretch their necks over the fence and chuff their grassy breath into the children's faces. There is a long quiet pause of child-cow communication. Suddenly there's a screech. The cows rear back, the children jump back, and then there's another, wilder screech.

When the moment is untangled, the cows have high-tailed away, Billy is blubbering with his fingers in his mouth, and Charlene, bawling, is struggling up from the ground. She's smeared with manure from shoes to hair ribbons. The class is aghast, the teacher and mothers frozen.

Mr. Dougan strides to the little girl and pulls her up by one slippery arm. He pats Billy on the back. "Now we've all learned that electric fences work," he says cheerfully. "Billy's a true scientist, experiment and see. Stop crying, Charlene, any kid that can spot a hair snake can handle a little cow dung. We'll go to the Big House and you'll be right in no time."

At the crick, he and Charlene scrub their hands and Ronald wets his handkerchief to wipe the worst from her face. Then, with a sniffling Charlene holding one of his hands and a chastened Billy the other, he leads the way back up the lane. He tells them all, "It's a matter of how you're raised. A country kid can run through a pasture and never step on anything, while a town kid picks his way, and steps on everything."

Charlene manages a wan smile.

He tells them Mrs. Anderson lives at the Big House and cooks and cleans for the hired men. She's the sort of woman, he says, who is a match for any emergency.

At the back door he introduces Charlene. "We have a little job for you here, Pat." With clucks of sympathy, Mrs. Anderson is already pulling Charlene into the house.

Ronald takes the others into an empty circular metal grain bin and closes

Ron tells Gertrude that the children will sing her to sleep.

the door. "This is the hollering house," he tells them in the dark. "Let's hear you holler." The deafening reverberations that roll off the metal are highly satisfactory to all the hollerers.

They go to the milkhouse and Ronald sets first Mike and then Betsy on a huge scales. "Just as I thought," he says. "A kindergartener still weighs about half as much as a full milk can." He shows them the bottling process and passes out white milkhouse caps for everyone, with an extra to the teacher for Charlene. As they leave, they meet a child dashing out the back door of the Big House. She's dressed in shirt and blue jeans, the sleeves and cuffs rolled up and the waist well belted in. It's Charlene, dressed in the clothes of Mrs. Anderson's youngest son. She's had a shower, shampoo, and her clothes are in the washing machine.

The children troop up into the haymow of the round barn. At this time of year the hay is practically gone, and the dark rafters are far overhead. Mr. Dougan reads them "The Aims of This Farm," printed on the silo. A photographer shows up and takes their picture throwing ears of corn into the feed-grinding machine. They wince at its rattle and bang, and then poke their fingers into the stream of bran and corn meal pouring from the spout. Ronald munches, but they decline to taste it. Then they go again to the lower barn.

The cows are there, now, lined up in their stanchions. The barn hands are washing udders before milking. Ronald shows how to hold the tits. Billy is the first one on the milking stool; he manages to squeeze out a few drops. After everyone who wants a turn has had one, Ronald takes over and squirts milk into the mouths of the daring while all the rest squeal. He never misses. "I could hit a sparrow at ten feet when I was your age," he brags. "Well, maybe not five or six years old. But by the time I was eight I was milking two cows a day. I knew every freckle on Daisy's udder." The kindergarten faces show respect and envy.

Someone remembers the secret. "When do we sing Gertrude to sleep?"

"Let's get her now," says Ronald. They go to the henhouse and crowd in to see the eggs. The laying hens look at the intruders with sharp-eyed distrust.

"Where are you, Gertrude?" Ronald croons. "Ah, there you are. Here's a fine bunch of children waiting to sing to you." The children whisper and nudge as he captures a white hen and tucks her under his arm. They go to the lawn in front of the milkhouse and sit in a circle. Ronald flexes Gertrude's foot for them, showing how she and other birds can go to sleep on a perch and not fall off, since their weight settling down on their legs causes the claws to tighten, rather than relax, and grip the branch firmly.

"Now what does a bird do with her head when she's ready for sleep?"

"She puts it under her wing!" cries Alison.

Ronald tucks Gertrude's head under her wing and holds her in front of him like a neat package. "Now, if you'll sing a lullaby while I rock her, I think we can put her to sleep. But you must sing very sweetly and soothingly. Can you do that?"

All heads bob vigorously, eyes dart at one another, giggles are smothered.

"Ready, boys and girls?" says Mrs. Wildermuth, and hums a note. Then their voices ring out, "Lullaby, and good night, wi-ith roses bedi-ight …."

Ronald, swinging the chicken back and forth, opens his eyes and mouth wide. He grins all the way through the lullaby, and the children's eyes dance

Cows and kids cautiously parley.

Success as a milker!

while they sing. At the last note he sets the chicken carefully on the grass. She lies there, motionless. Everyone is quiet and breathless, watching her.

"Your singing has put her into an enchanted sleep," Ronald whispers. "It's the first time she's ever heard 'Brahms' Lullaby.' Before, it's always been 'Rockabye Baby.' Maybe she'll sleep a hundred years. How can we wake her?"

"With a kiss! My brother told me!" bursts out Ralphie.

"Do you want to be the prince who kisses her awake?"

Ralphie recoils. "I wouldn't kiss a chicken!"

But Charlene will. She creeps forward on hands and knees and kisses Gertrude's feathers. The chicken leaps up with a flap and squawk, and Charlene falls backward for a second time that day. Everyone cheers. Ronald catches Gertrude and gives her to a hired man who has just come up with a case of chocolate milk.

"Are you ready for a treat?"

"Yes!" cry the class, and whirl to look not at Ron Dougan and the milk but at one of the mothers, who is coming with a broad flat box. She sets it on the grass beside the milk case, and the class squirms into a tight knot around their host. "Open it! Open it!"

"Something will jump out and bite me," objects Ronald.

"No, no! Open it!"

As Ronald lifts the lid, Mrs. Wildermuth gives a note again, and the class bawls out, "Happy birthday to you, happy birthday to you …."

"A cake!" Ronald cries. "How did anyone know it's my birthday today?"

"It was listed in the church bulletin," Mrs. Wildermuth says.

"And we made you cards!" says Freddy. The other mother produces a sheaf of brightly colored manila folders.

Ronald cuts the cake, after admiring the frosting: chocolate, with a white chicken, white egg, white bottle of milk, and white writing saying HAPPY BIRTHDAY RON DOUGAN. Then everyone eats cake and drinks chocolate milk. Ronald exclaims over each card and identifies the artist. Charlene snuggles close as a burr until Mrs. Anderson calls from the Big House. Then she scampers off, to return in a few minutes in her own clothes. They have been washed, dried, and her hair ribbons ironed.

She holds Ronald's hand as they walk to the cars. "Can I write about your accident in a Dougan's milk ad?" he asks. "Put it in the newspaper?"

"Oh, no!" cries Charlene, mortified.

He shakes his head regretfully. He'd like to use the line about town kids and country kids. Maybe on the next visit someone will only step in a cow pie. And there's plenty else to write about from this visit. The hairsnake. The killdeer nest. Billy touching the electric fence. The birthday surprise. The different song.

"Thank you for the party," he says to the children. "And thank you for 'Brahms' Lullaby.' Will you tell your little brothers and sisters that that's the lullaby Gertrude wants when Mrs. Wildermuth comes again with next year's kindergarten?"

"Yes! Yes!" they all cry.

"It's such a long time away," says Ronald. "How about an encore right now?"

Mrs. Wildermuth gives the note and there's a final sweet chorus before the class climbs into the cars and is driven away. Ronald watches them out of sight, then turns toward the office. Time to squeeze in some of the more humdrum aspects of running a business; two more classes of schoolchildren will show up tomorrow, morning and afternoon. It's great advertising to have every kid in the city visit Dougan's. But that's not the only reason he does it. He hums the tune of Brahms' Lullaby as he goes inside.

22 ⋇ FERNWOOD SCRIMSHAW

There are so many cats on the farm that it's pointless to name them. The house cats, of course, have names from kittenhood—Mittens, Malty, Effie's cat Buff at the Big House. But the barn cats go nameless. Except that Joan and Patsy and Jackie and Craig always name them anyway, for it's fun to name. A nothing becomes a something with a name. One cat can be distinguished from another. Usually they name the cats after some characteristic: Spotty, Snowy, Boots, White Whiskers, Spitfire. And the Spotties and Snowies come and go, like the rhythm of the seasons.

One season they name the cats differently. Mother has been involved in music club work. She's an officer in the National Federation of Music Clubs. She gets letters from all over the state and country. The return names in the upper left-hand corners of the envelopes intrigue Jackie and her siblings. Letters come regularly from the same names. There are Vi Kleinpell and Maude Blackstone. There are Hinda Honigman and Jennie Schrage and Julia Fuqua Ober and Sadie Orr Dunbar. There is Quaintance Eaton, whom Mother says the blind pianist Alec Templeton calls "Shouldaulda" because of the song, "Should auld acquaintance be forgot." There's a music to the names of Mother's music club friends.

Two adorable kittens are born in the barn. The four decide to call them Sadie and Maudie. Mother laughs when she hears. Sadie is especially fun to cuddle, for there's a song to sing to her, to the tune of "The Bells of St. Mary." Mother wrote the words for everyone to sing at a national convention, when Sadie Orr Dunbar was being inaugurated as president.

Jackie rocks Sadie in her arms and sings,

> We're singing to Sadie,
> We're loving you, Sadie,
> For you are the lady
> We've come to adore.

So to you, beloved,
We pledge our devotion;
Each heart and hand at your command,
Dear SA-DIE ORR!

It sounds funny, of course, to refer to a little ball of fluff as a lady, but when Jackie sings, "For you are the kitten we've come to adore," it spoils the rhyme.

There are other kittens born in the barn, and they are named Jennie and Julia and Vi. There's one sleek black kitten with no white on her, not even a whisker, and to this one they give the name they like best of all, Fernwood Scrimshaw. They don't call this kitten by her first name only, but by her whole euphonious name. They summon her, "Here, Fernwood Scrimshaw! Here, Fernwood Scrimshaw!"

Fernwood Scrimshaw

Fernwood Scrimshaw grows up into a long, lean black cat. She gets mange on her neck. Daddy brings her into the house and doctors her. He doesn't want all the barn cats to become mangy. He rubs Petro-Carbo salve on her neck every day for weeks. He cures Fernwood Scrimshaw but in the process she loses all her hair in the affected area. It never grows back. Now she's a long, lean black cat with a long, lean black neck with no hair on it. In the process of getting over the mange she becomes a house cat, but she retains her barn habits.

One Sunday afternoon Fernwood Scrimshaw walks past Jackie with a sparrow in her mouth. The sparrow is cheeping and fluttering. Jackie grabs for the cat. The cat runs. Jackie chases her around the lilac bushes and onto the lawn of the Little House. She screeches, "Fernwood! Fernwood Scrimshaw! You drop that! Drop that right now, Fernwood Scrimshaw, you bad cat!"

The long, lean black cat with no hair on her black neck looks even longer and leaner as she streaks up the choke cherry tree and sits on a branch, looking down. The sparrow's wings are like whiskers drooping down either side of her mouth.

Jackie gives up and turns around. There's a strange car beside the Little House. A woman with a startled expression is standing on the front step with Mother.

"Jackie," says Mother, "I'd like you to meet Mrs. Fernwood Scrimshaw."

23 ✴ ROCK COUNTY BREEDERS

Artificial insemination is not new. Nature has been doing it for millennia. Certain spiders, for instance, lack copulatory organs. A male deposits semen on a small mat spun by himself, dips his feelers into the semen, and plunges them into the abdomen of his spouse. In Biblical times shepherds knew to drain a ram's ejaculate from a ewe's vagina and bathe the cervix of another ewe with it. There's evidence fourteenth century Arabs knew this technique and used it with camels.

The first scientific research was done by an Italian, recorded in a 1785 treatise, *Experiments to Serve in the History of the Generation of Animals and Plants*. He used frogs. The unfertilized eggs, ejected by the female, were fertilized by the male spraying semen over them in the water. This allowed Spallanzani to study the development of the eggs independent of the female and under controlled conditions. He learned that spermatazoa or ova, each by themselves, were incapable of development into tadpoles. Tadpoles resulted, however, when the male sperm came in contact with the fresh eggs. To demonstrate that spermatozoa, and not just the presence of the male, were essential for fertilization, he made small panties of oiled taffeta for the male frogs. Eggs did not develop when exposed to pantied males under conditions otherwise suitable for fertilization. Development did result when the eggs were exposed to males without the panties. He also found he could obtain semen from the males and spray it over the eggs, thereby fertilizing them in the total absence of the male.

In 1780, Spallanzani successfully inseminated dogs. He later observed that chilling or freezing stallion semen in snow "did not necessarily kill the 'spermatic vermiculi' but held them in a motionless state until exposed to heat, after which they continued to move for seven and a half hours." This latter, and much else, is reported by Enos Perry in his book, *The Artificial Insemination of Farm Animals*, first published in 1945, with revised editions in 1947, 1952, and 1968. Artificial insemination was begun in horse breeding in Europe in the 1890s; a Russian was the first to artificially inseminate horses on a large scale, starting in 1899. He was also the first to inseminate cattle and sheep successfully. In Denmark, a breeding co-operative for cattle was organized in 1936. In this country, some calves were born in Wisconsin and Minnesota as a result of artificial insemination.

But it isn't until June of 1938 that the concept of fertilizing a female animal by artificially injecting the male sperm is begun on a commercial scale in the United States. Professor Enos Perry of Rutgers College of Agriculture, returning from a sabbatical in Denmark, initiates and helps organize a cattle breeding co-operative in Anandale, New Jersey.

Dr. Wayne Munn is a Janesville, Wisconsin physician whose avocation is cattle. He is president of the Wisconsin Guernsey Breeders' Association. He learns of the New Jersey co-op and thinks Rock County ripe for such a program. He gets a number of prominent farmers interested: Ron Dougan, Lon Markham, Walter Craig, George Conway, and Fred Eddy. In August of 1938 the six men incorporate the Rock County Breeders Co-op. It's the second in the country. The men each ante up three hundred dollars to get the venture started, and appoint themselves and a few others as directors. Daddy is elected secretary-treasurer, a position he holds throughout the life of the co-op.

The directors volunteer their own best bulls. Daddy contributes Valentine Rubina's Lad, who has the highest bull index in Wisconsin at the time, and V. Vingt-huit de Chez Nous, a younger bull from a proved sire and a dam with 489 pounds of butterfat in 305 days of milking. Although V. Vingt-huit's name is merely a coded way of saying he's the twenty-eighth animal to come into the Dougan herd in the year V, which is 1935, he's always referred to as "that French bull." One more Guernsey, three Holsteins, and two Jerseys round out the stud. At the start, Brown Swiss breeders opt out from donating a Brown Swiss bull.

War comes, and vets are drafted. Those left aren't available as inseminators. The co-op hires a young layman, Amos Grundahl, who has studied the techniques. Amos stays on permanently as Rock County's artificial inseminator.

Amos comes to artificial insemination in this way. During the Depression he's a student at Platteville State Teachers College. Teaching is a good and honorable vocation; he should be able to make a living. Even though he has no money, he's determined to get his degree. He and fifteen other young men rent a house and make their own meals. Amos goes to butcher shops and collects the beef hearts and livers of old cows which are too tough to sell. He goes to grocery stores and they give him the scrap potatoes if he'll carry them

Amos Grundahl, inseminator, returns his equipment to his car.

away. He and his friends each spend two dollars a week on the group's food.

Amos graduates, and in 1938 goes to a small town in northeastern Wisconsin, as an agriculture teacher. Part of his job is to teach seventh and eighth graders some manual training and shop, the girls as well as boys.

To stay alive in Wausaukee after 1932, almost every farm family has a cow. Some have one or two, some five, some ten, up to herds of forty. Amos decides that part of his program is to teach his students to test their own farm's milk. The school has a Babcock tester for this purpose.

The Babcock tester, invented in 1890 by an agricultural chemist, Stephen M. Babcock, treats milk with sulphuric acid and then whirls it centrifugally in a bottle with a graduated neck. The fat is brought to the top, and its amount is read off directly by the gradations on the bottle's neck.

When Amos studies his students' results, he's appalled. The production of their cows is so low that the farmers even of the larger herds can scarcely make a living. He sees them working their hearts out, trying to wrestle subsistence with poor stock on poor land. He occasionally has supper at a farm he's visiting; three or four of the families live in log cabins with sand floors. They have oil drums for stoves, and the sowbelly and potatoes they share with him are fried on these oil barrels. This is not the boondocks of Appalachia; this is northern Wisconsin during the Depression.

Most farmers can't afford a bull, yet a cow must calve regularly if she's to continue as a milker. The need is met by jumper bulls. A jumper bull man brings a bull to a farm and leaves it for a while, until the cow or cows are pregnant. During this time the farmer feeds the bull and pays rent for him. Then the bull's owner returns to take him to another farm. It's an easy living for jumper bull men, for while some are honest, many charge more than the service is worth. They have their bulls boarded, they need maintain no barns or pastures, and when the bull is several years old and becoming dangerous, they sell him for beef. For the hapless farmer, there's no way of telling if the bull is one with a good background. He could also be spreading disease.

Amos attends a University of Wisconsin Agricultural Extension meeting in 1939 and discovers something has been going on at the university of intense interest to him. A primitive technology, artificial insemination, has been brought to the USA from Denmark! The university has imported an artificial vagina from Italy, made several of its own, and is collecting semen from bulls with breeding pedigrees. Cows inseminated with this semen should produce better calves than those fathered by the usual scrub bull. The semen can be carried to cows in many locations. The farm bull and the jumper bull can be eliminated.

Amos catches fire. If he can do anything to help get this industry started, he wants to do it. He sees artificial insemination as the way to pull his farmers out of poverty. An ag teacher at Oshkosh has managed to get the plans for the artificial vagina and has made one. Amos and Jim Wilson, another ag teacher from Wisconsin's brush country, visit Oshkosh. They get a vagina and some semen, and return home to experiment.

An artificial vagina is a hose within a hose. The outside hose is some three inches in diameter, lined with gum rubber; the inner one is soft rubber, sterilized and then lubricated with a sterile gel. The outside hose is filled with warm water the temperature of bovine blood. The inside hose has a tube at its end to catch the semen. The bull is led to a cow in heat, tied up in an alleyway. When he mounts her, his penis is deflected into the artificial vagina and the bull ejaculates into it.

Amos is worried about safety at the start, but he uses only young bulls, no more than three years old, who are not as irascible as more mature bulls. He soon gets used to handling them. Besides, the bulls aren't much concerned with the man alongside the cow. Amos's favorite bull is a single-minded lame one, who no sooner ejaculates than he is ready to hit the cow again, and who, even after his jumps, pays no attention to the men around.

Wisconsin's ag professors are upset that non-professionals are dabbling in this activity—it's a job for veterinarians. Dr. Heizer, head of Dairy Husbandry, writes Amos and advises him to stop.

But Amos keeps on. He goes from Wausaukee to a teaching job at Cadott near Chippewa Falls, and organizes a stud there. He helps organize other studs. He and Jim Wilson, also active, must do unceasing promotional work to educate farmers. At one point he enlists in the Army himself, but is turned down because of a varicose vein.

Despite the university's grudging attitude toward non-professionals, Amos keeps in touch with developments there. By 1943 the Ag School has realized that vets are washed out as artificial inseminators, and to keep the program going they will have to turn to laymen. Dr. Ernest Zehner and Dr. George Werner give Amos an intensive week's training, and he becomes a certified inseminator. He's taught to place the semen inside the uterus, but later finds that it makes little difference if it's there or left at the mouth of the uterus, the cervix.

Plastic equipment is still in the future. The long rubber gloves worn to enter the cow's rectum are expensive, don't last very long, and must be continually washed. Fragile glass rods and syringes used in the insemination process are always a hazard; an uncooperative cow's sudden move can cause them to break. The inseminator must then work the pieces out of the vagina. He must carry a number of rods, syringes, and rubber adaptors. He must also carry an icebox that will keep the liquid semen between 38 and 40 degrees Fahrenheit. In the wintertime, when outside temperatures are well below freezing, he must take care to keep the semen warm enough. The glass equipment must be washed with a recently developed detergent and placed in a sterilizer; preparing the equipment every day is time consuming. It isn't until the early fifties that plastic replaces glass, semen is packaged in separate ampules, and the job becomes easier. Somewhat later comes frozen semen and special refrigerators.

There are operator hazards in inseminating a cow as well as equipment ones. The inseminator must take care not to thread the tube into a blind pouch beneath the opening of the cow's urethra—a pocket peculiar to cows that serves no obvious functional purpose—or into the urethra, the passageway to the bladder. These are easy confusions. If this happens, the cow gets upset, as well as the purpose of the insemination being thwarted. Once the rod is positioned at the cervix, the inseminator slowly presses the syringe, which he has filled with one cubic centimeter of semen and extender. Sperm are sensitive organisms, and while a natural ejaculation shoots them cervixward at a dizzying speed, the inseminator doesn't want to put any pressure

Amos Grundahl, Wilmer Vanderkoii, and Ron Dougan admire a Dougan cow shown as "Production Queen" in a recent Herd Builder, *an American Dairy Cattle Club publication.*

on them that might ruin them before they can do their work. He counts ten seconds in releasing the semen.

At the start, success is not high. Only about 40 percent of the cows settle. Another half conceive on a second service. The rest, cows that aren't easy to breed, or who don't have management that gets the inseminator there in time, take a third service, or don't conceive at all.

After his training, Amos goes north to Ladysmith to replace a vet. He breeds one or two cows a day, and is having an enjoyable time, for he also starts to date the vet's girlfriend. But after three weeks he gets a call from Janesville. The Rock County Breeder's Co-op needs an inseminator; they are discouraged with losing vets, and unless they can find an inseminator they may have to close shop.

Amos visits Janesville. George Conway is at the YMCA to meet him. Pretty soon Ron Dougan comes in, and Lon Markham, followed by Art Harris and Walter Craig. The five interview him, and are so pleased that they offer him the job on the spot. Amos accepts.

During this period, Amos has been having pressure from his family. His father was content with his son as a teacher; in Norway teaching is an honored profession. He is vehemently against Amos being an inseminator. "Don't come home!" he rants. "You're crazy to leave a fine job teaching school! What you're doing is meddling; it's against nature! Leave breeding to God!" The

Amos Grundahl inseminates a cow.

Grundahls' god is a good Norwegian Lutheran one, and Amos can't see that He would be against improving the lot of poor farmers. Luckily, Amos is in Rock County, where he has a generous gas ration to visit farms, while his family is up north with no fuel available to visit him. They couldn't have stopped him, anyway; his zeal is too great. Amos becomes the first layman technician in the area.

Until near Amos's arrival, the vets for the Co-op have been gathering semen without the aid of an artificial vagina. Their method is more dangerous, for there's no cow to keep the bull's attention, while there are other aspects that irritate him mightily. Wearing a rubber glove the vet goes into the bull's rectum, feels through the rectal wall and gently massages an internal gland, the ductus deferens, to give the bull a mild orgasm, then lets the semen gravity-drain down the penis. A companion catches the semen as it dribbles out the end of the sheath. This is a cumbersome method, unsatisfactory not only for that and its danger, but also because it's not hygienic. They clip the hairs around the bull's sheath and keep cleansing the area, but they cannot sterilize the penis and sheath sufficiently. However, before long it becomes possible to buy quality Guernsey semen commercially. The Co-op sells off its Guernsey bulls.

It's a good thing they do, for the bulls have become a source of friction on the River Road. A neighbor strongly objects to the stud's being there. He fears the bulls, while outside fastened by their nose rings and exercising on the bull sweeps, will get loose and jump the fence. He's an influential Beloiter and manages to bring legal pressure on the co-op. Stew Barlass takes his Jersey bulls back to his farm, and so do the owners of the Holsteins. The co-op divests itself of its last live-in bull the day before Amos comes on the job. However, his arrival coincides with the police's impounding of the co-op's new Chevrolet, the last off the line on account of the war. Until the directors manage to get their car back, Amos has to drive his own. It's an inauspicious welcome to someone who will prove to have a long and faithful commitment to the Rock County Breeders Co-op.

24 ⚭ THE SEA OF GALILEE

Grampa is not a singer. That's understandable, on account of his deafness. But Daddy isn't a singer, either. Once in a while he sings "The Spanish Cavalier" or "The World Owes Me a Living," and when he has his many grandchildren visiting at the Pleasant Lake cottage, he leads them single file over the hill to the little local tavern for root beers, with all of them beating on pans and singing, "We're Marching to Zion."

Daddy says he thinks he doesn't sing for a couple of reasons. "When I was twelve I rode my bicycle down to a tent meeting—those bicycles were called 'ice wagons' because you got so cold riding them—and I was singing in the choir. And when I got home I said to my mother, 'Why does Mr. Putney do such funny things with his voice? He goes way down and way up and he doesn't follow the tune. What's the matter with him?' 'Why, he's singing bass,' my mother said. I was confused, because I was sitting in the bass section and singing just as low as I could. I figured I'd been making a fool of myself."

And then there was Grama's singing. It was always embarrassing to stand next to her in church. She sang out on the hymns in such a loud and piercing alto that he always wanted to crawl under the pew.

"I did join the Glee Club in college," Daddy says, "because everybody in our fraternity had to, but after the tryout I never sang, only looked like I was."

Daddy often has vivid dreams. He has one once about singing. He tells it to everyone at the breakfast table.

"I'd been asked to sing in a quartet," he says. "We were going to sing on the steps of the Congregational Church that overlooks the park, and the park was just full of a big crowd of people. The other members were Bill Shauffer and Hobart Weirick and Percy Herman, and it seemed a long way off so I said yes. Then, like it does in dreams, time flew, and here we were, dressed in tuxedos, standing back in the church ready to go on, and we'd never done any practicing. I was scared to death. I said to Bill Shauffer, 'What are we going to sing? Don't we need to practice or something?' 'Oh, we don't need to practice,' Bill said. 'We'll do "Spanish Cavalier" or "Down By the Old Mill Stream" or something like that.'

"Just then, through the open door of the church, I saw one of my milk trucks go by. I leapt out of that church as fast as I could go; I stopped the truck and said, 'Langklotz, will you do something for me for fifty dollars?' Langklotz said, 'Ron, I'd do anything for you for fifty dollars!' 'Then get in that church and sing in a quartet,' I said, and I headed off down the street in the milk truck to deliver milk, still in my tuxedo, and Langklotz in his route clothes went into the church."

Everybody's favorites of Daddy's dreams, though, are the Spring Brook ones.

Ronald is grown up. He's married, has children. But in his dream he's little again, maybe eight years old. He's down at the crick in the back pasture, dangling his feet over the bank. Fishing. It's the part of the crick that he and Trever have dammed up with rocks and clods of sod to make a swimming hole.

He looks up and sees a luminous figure gliding toward him across the water. The figure has a beard, a long, flowing robe, and a benign expression on his face. He looks like the Sunday School pictures of Jesus. Ronald knows that he is Jesus.

"Little boy," says Jesus, "is this the Sea of Galilee?"

"No, sir," says Ronald. "This is Spring Brook."

A puzzled expression crosses Jesus' face. "Then what in the world am I doing here?" he asks, and the dream is over.

The second Spring Brook dream comes a number of years later. Again he's down by the crick, but this time he seems to be his own age. Across the little stream, on the hillside, three figures are sitting on a bench. They are hooded and completely concealed. They are Green Bay Packers. But Ronald knows they are also the Trinity.

God says, "I started this world going."

The hoods of Jesus and the Holy Ghost nod agreement.

"And then I got busy with other things and forgot all about it," says God. The hoods nod.

"And now that I've remembered and stopped by, I see that things are a mess."

The other two nod again.

"I see three things I could do," God says. "I could just destroy everything and let it go as a bad job."

The two nod.

"Or I could roll everything back to the primordial ooze and let everything start evolving all over again."

The two nod.

"Or—" God gives a weary sigh, "—I could just watch it a while longer, see what develops."

All three hoods sit silent, brooding.

Finally one hood turns toward Ronald.

"Ronald," says Jesus, "what do you suggest?"

25 ⚹ CORN

When Daddy is growing up the fields on the farm are of three sorts. Pasture for the cows. Hay—some the just-being-developed alfalfa, some sweet clover and timothy (for horse feed), brome grass, other grasses. And grains for animal feed—corn, oats, and barley. Between Daddy's boyhood and when Jackie is near her teens in 1940, the land Daddy and Grampa are farming has been increased by the Hill Farm, Chez Nous, and rental land. While each of the farms still has open pasture, hayfields, oats, barley, and a little field corn, much of the land is now used to grow hybrid seed corn. This change is caused by the rapid development of hybrid corn, and Grampa and Daddy's involvement in that development.

By the time Europeans came to the New World and discovered a gold far more valuable than the metal they coveted, corn had been developed by the Indians from tiny, few-kerneled cobs into larger, many-rowed and kerneled ears. Primitive cobs, some twenty-five thousand excavated in a Mexican cave, were discovered by an archaeologist in the early sixties, and radio-carbon dated at 7,200 years old. It's generally accepted that corn cultivation made possible the high level of civilization of the Incas, Mayans, Aztecs, and earlier groups still being discovered and named, for civilization flowers only when it is resting on a stable food base, the securing of which doesn't take the total energy of a people. A pioneer in corn genetics, Paul Mangelsdorf of Harvard, has said, "No civilization worthy of the name has ever been founded on any agricultural basis other than the cereals." For the Americas, it was corn.

Studies of corn fill libraries. Writings abound on its every aspect. Besides the archaeological, there's the historical, scientific, mythological, and literary, in addition to research, scholarly, and popular treatises. A number of shelves are crowded with the debate among botanists on corn's ancestry, so passionate a quarrel that in the literature it's often referred to as "The Corn Wars." The participants have famous names and honor-studded careers, even Nobel prizes: Beadle, Manglesdorf, Wilkes, Galinat, Doebley, and more. At stormy conferences academic gauntlets were thrown down. The Corn Wars were no two-bit skirmishes.

The problem was this. Most domesticated plants have their identified wild ancestors, which have been adequately researched to establish their role in the development of the species. For example, a grain that sustained the ancient Fertile Crescent was emmer wheat, a forerunner of modern wheat, still in cultivation. Corn, however, was long a mystery. It's a grass, as are wheat, oats, barley, rice, rye, and other grains. But where is located the wild grass from which corn evolved? There were various theories but no absolute proof, although a wild grass from Mexico, an annual teosinte, had corn-like features and botanists—some very vigorously—fitted it in somewhere: if teosinte with its twenty chromosomes, like corn's twenty, was not an ancestor or descendent, it was at least a kissing cousin. By the end of the twentieth century, though, the arguments and evidence for the annual teosinte prevailed over its rivals. The mystery was essentially over.

How the actual descent came about, however, is still unresolved. Cobless teosinte has only two rows of several kernels each, while the Indian maize that the Europeans found had fully developed ears with many rows and hundreds of kernels. Furthermore, evidence from paintings, sculptures, and actual remains found in grave excavations show that maize was relatively unchanged for at least a thousand years.

The origin of modern corn may well always be a hypothesis, for there are no known parents. The accepted hypothesis at present, using modern DNA analyses and other methods, indicates that corn arose from a series of mutations affecting the female inflorescence that led to primitive maize, and from this, the growers' selection resulted in modern maize. Research done by John Doebley at the University of Wisconsin has established this.

Although the related teosinte can still be found wild in Mexico, modern corn is a plant that can't live long without human intervention, though this is also true for most annual grain crops. But consider modern corn in the wild. Do we see it escaped from cultivation, flourishing in empty fields and hedgerows as asparagus, hemp, and a number of other plants do? It's a poor competitor in the struggle for existence. If a ripened ear falls to the ground and its kernels make it through the thick husks to sprout, the young plants, clinging tightly to the ear, will crowd one another out. If a single kernel does manage to grow independently, its own fallen ears will have the same problem. The kernels also don't have the kind of husk that protects seeds from rot over the winter. And corn plants eventually need cross pollination.

Ron and grandsons Ricky and Bart examine a corn plant.

There is no natural way to ensure the continuation of modern corn. People have had to plant it, tend it, gather it, store it in dry places, and replant it the next year. Native Americans kept safe several years' supply of seed, in case of crop failure. Had they failed to plant corn for more than a few years in a row, there would have been no corn plants to amaze Columbus, nor hybrid corn today, spanning the globe in a million acres, the world's third major food crop (after rice and wheat), and in this hemisphere, the first.

The development and promotion of hybrid seed corn came about by research at the land grant universities of the Corn Belt. The land grant system was established by Lincoln in 1865; corn breeding programs began in the late nineteen-twenties and thirties at the midwestern institutions. Illinois, Indiana, Iowa, Michigan State, Minnesota, Nebraska, Ohio State, and Wisconsin all contributed to the development of inbreds. In order to utilize these materials, it was necessary to obtain growers. The extension services contacted seedsmen and interested farmers to produce these improved hybrids, and this contributed to the large number of small independent commercial corn companies that sprang up in the Midwest. Dougan Hybrids was among them.

Professor Norman Neal, a University of Wisconsin corn breeder and frequent guest at the Dougan dinner table, authored various University Extension booklets on corn that Jackie found interesting. In a 1949 booklet on corn history, he says that the first Europeans to see this remarkable plant were scouts sent by Columbus from his ships, in 1492, to explore Cuba. They returned with a report of a grain which was "well tasted baked, dried, and made into flour," and that they had seen fields of this crop eighteen miles long. The Jamestown settlers, arriving in 1607, found the Indians growing corn in "hills," fertilizing each hill with a dead fish. Captain John Smith of Virginia wrote in 1612 (here spelling is modernized):

> The greatest labor they take is in planting their corn, for the country naturally is overgrown with wood. To prepare the ground they bruise the bark of trees near the root, then do they scorch the roots with fire that they grow no more. The next year with a crooked piece of wood, they beat up the woods by the roots; and in these moulds they plant the corn. They make a hole in the earth with a stick and into it they put 4 grains and 2 of beans. These holes they make 4 foot one from another. Their women and children do continually keep it with weeding and when it is grown middle high, they hill it about like a hopyard.
>
> In April they begin to plant, but their chief plantation is in May, and so they continue till the midst of June. What they plant in April, they reap in August, for May in September, for June in October. Every stalk of their corn commonly bears 2 ears, some 3, seldom any 4, but many one, and some none. Every ear ordinarily has betwixt 200 and 500 grains. The stalk being green has a sweet juice in it, somewhat like a sugar cane, which is the cause that when they gather their corn green, they suck the stalks.

The booklet says that for newcomers as well as Indians, the method of selecting seed stock for the following year is the same, "show corn." Walking through the fields and choosing the best-looking ears to be shelled, saved, and planted. This selection by looks resulted in what development there has been in strains of corn over the centuries of cultivation, for corn is a plant of great variety. A tropical plant might grow to sixteen feet, with four or five ears to a stalk. Some stalks are as short as two to three feet, with only one ear. The plants also vary in color: from green, to purple-green, to red-green; and the kernels, as in Indian corn, can be as multicolored as autumn leaves.

By 1900, farmers using this method of seed selection had developed thousands of strains that no longer looked like Indian corn. Many were sold under commercial names such as Leaming White, Leaming Yellow Dent, Reid's Yellow Dent, Krug, Burr White.

Neal's booklet identifies these commercial strains as "dent" corns, one of seven main classes recognized at the time of his writing. Flint corn's kernels have a flinty, hard-starched endosperm, which make them resistant to insect damage. Sweet corn contains sugar instead of starch. Flour corn has all soft starch endosperm. Popcorn is flinty, and when heated at 12 to 13 percent

Harvesting corn planted in rows wide enough for horses.

moisture, bursts and turns inside out. With pod corn, single kernels on the ear are encased in their own glumes or little husks, giving the ear a brushy appearance. (Daddy keeps an ear of pod corn on his office desk; it's a lively conversation piece.) Waxy corn's starch is of a different chemical structure. Dent corn develops a dent in its crown when dried, and is the variety that makes up most of the commercial crop in North America: this is what is commonly called "field corn."

Neal and others have given descriptions of a typical corn plant, and how seed develops. In the corn belt of the Midwest, a plant usually grows about eight feet tall. It has a root system spreading below ground, with another system of brace roots slightly above ground. It has about fourteen long, broad leaves, each arising at a joint on the stalk, where the ear shoots also arise. As the ear shoots grow, they put forth pale green or reddish silk.

The male and female organs are in different flowers on the same plant. The male tassel, at the end of the stalk, by maturity has five to twenty branches, each bearing hundreds of little spikelets. These put out oblong sacs, about a fourth inch long, called anthers. Each anther contains pollen grains; when the plant is mature the pollen is released to drift on the wind. The number of grains from a single tassel is enormous, 14 to 18 million. Every grain carries the male germ. When a grain lands on the female flower—the tender silk hairs emerging from the ear shoot—it is trapped there. Each strand of silk—and there are eight hundred to a thousand per ear—is attached to its own small blister-like structure on the cob: this incipient kernel is the ovary which contains the ovule. The pollen grain—the sperm—now splits in two.

The corn harverster took only one row at a time.

One part forms a slender tube that grows down inside the silk. The other travels down this tube. When the tip of the tube reaches the ovary it penetrates and enters the ovule which contains two female cells, one the egg, the other, the endosperm mother cell. One of the sperm cells unites with the egg to form the cell from which the embryo (20 chromosomes) of the young plant develops, the other unites with the endosperm mother cell and the resultant cell develops into the endosperm (30 chromosomes) of the kernel, which supplies nutrients to the embryo during germination. The whole fertilization process, from pollen alighting on the silk to uniting of male and female cells, takes less than twenty-four hours. From fertilization to mature kernel is about fifty to sixty days.

Until hybrid corn sweeps the field, corn plants of all varieties are reproduced by cross pollination. Pollen from the tassel of a plant seldom pollinates more than a fraction of kernels of its own ears—one to two percent—for there is delayed timing: the silks usually emerge from two to four days after the pollen begins to shed, so that the air is filled with a potpourri of pollens from many plants. The resultant cross pollination makes each ear have hundreds of different male parents contributing to its kernels. This makes it a complex hybrid, but since there is no way of knowing the father of each kernel, it's not a controlled hybrid, not the hybrid corn that has revolutionized corn production all over the world, and pulled the Dougan fields into that revolution.

Omitting much of the richness and drama of hybrid corn development, the names of certain vital researchers, and some findings made independent

The horse-drawn harvester lifted entire stalks into a wagon.

of Mendel, the story picks up early in the twentieth century, when in the wake of Mendel's experiments and theories, the people working to improve corn wondered what would happen if pollination were controlled. One way would be if the silk were fertilized solely by the plant's own pollen—by inbreeding. Then all the kernels would have the same father and mother, from the one plant itself.

The experimenters tied a paper bag over each tassel; the ears had been covered before silking. When the silk emerged, they carefully dusted the pollen from the ear's own tassel over it. They then took the mature ear that developed and planted its kernels. In spite of all the kernels having the same parentage, the plants that grew from them had different characteristics. Some were freakish, growing like a vine on the ground or having ears at the ends of the tassels. Out of several hundred plants, the experimenters selected the best looking ears, planted the kernels, tied paper bags over the maturing tassels and ears again, and again bred each plant back onto itself. They planted this generation, discarded the less desirable ears, and inbred yet again. This they continued for seven or eight generations, until they arrived at a plant where every offspring in the row looked exactly alike. However, with each generation the plants had reduced vigor, now standing only two to three feet tall, with small ears. What the experimenters did have, though, was a pure genetic strain. They could plant a kernel and know exactly what the offspring would look like.

This inbreeding was being done with a large number of different plants, and resulted in many pure lines. At this point, the experimenters took two

A tractor took over for the horses pulling the harvester, but horses still worked the wagon.

parents of pure strains, two unrelated inbred lines, and crossed the pollen of one set with the silks of another. When they planted the resulting kernels, the outcome was dramatic. Tall plants, vigorous plants, showing heterosis or hybrid vigor. Each had a large ear. Every plant from the same parent cross was exactly the same, and with a higher yield than its parents or original stocks. The seed that resulted from these plants produced tall plants with large ears and a high yield. This corn was hybrid corn: the result of crossing two unrelated inbred strains.

Any one of these many inbred strains, crossed with another (and they tried it both directions: A as the male, B as the female, and vice versa) still might produce poor seed. So the experimenters made hundreds of these crosses, planting them out in plots, testing the results, and repeating the pedigrees that proved promising, while discarding those that did not.

It's obvious that to produce this sort of corn is expensive, since a grower must use the seed from the tiny inbred ears in order to cross inbred strain A (Pedigree A) onto inbred strain B (Pedigree B). However, the result of A x B is a large ear. Take two more inbred strains, C and D, cross them, and then cross the two resultant large ears (A x B) x (C x D) and the result is a quantity of very satisfactory seed, all of which has four parents.

Experiments were made with various combinations of strains. A x B is a "single cross" hybrid. (A x A1 [sisters]) x (B x B1 [sisters]) is a "modified single." (Though an irresponsible grower may take this seed and sell it as a more valuable single, Daddy reports.) (A x B) x C = a three-way hybrid; (A x B) x (C x D), described above, equals four parents, and is called a "doublecross."

These varieties of hybrid seed, grown by farmer-dealers, are now sold to farmers. This seed is more expensive by far than open pollinated seed, but the results in increased yield, standability, and uniformity make it well worth it. Farmers from all over the country buy seed from commercial hybrid seedcorn growers, who do the original crossing.

R.A. Dougan and his father W.J. are commercial seed growers. They purchase inbred strains from the University of Wisconsin, or two single hybrid strains, and raise them in their own fields, two rows of Pedigree A, six of Pedigree B. One strain, "A" (designated as the "male"), is allowed to tassel and pollinate; the other, "B," the "female," is detasseled so that it can't self-pollinate. Therefore all the corn in the field is pollinated by the "A" strain only. There are, of course, ears growing on the "A" male corn; these will be self pollinated, and the offspring inferior. Harvested separately, this corn is fed to livestock. (This cuts down the necessity of raising much field corn for the cows.) The corn on the female stalks, "B," will be dried, graded, bagged, certified, and sold to area farmers as Dougan Hybrid Seed Corn.

Once a farmer makes his original purchase of expensive hybrid seed, what's to keep him from planting the corn it produces and raising his own much cheaper seed from then on? If he does, he'll not get the same result. The seed breaks down, hereditarily. He'll probably lose a fourth of his previous year's yield. Therefore, if he wants to continue with hybrid corn, these crossings have to be made yearly, the seed bought yearly.

There are a number of things in a corn plant that universities, agricultural experimental stations, and commercial farmers who are developing their own pedigrees, are trying to develop. Some are:

1. High yield: increased number of bushels per acre.
2. Standability: strong stalks and roots: so that the plants won't break down, or "lodge" in the field.
3. Resistance: to disease and pests in seed, stalk, leaf, and ear.
4. Predictable maturity: corn that will ripen before frost. The farther north the corn is to be grown, the fewer days allowed between planting and harvesting.
5. And a more recent aim: to vary the nutritional content of the kernel to fit more nearly perceived human and animal needs.

There are additional goals for the growers of sweet corn. They want increased sweetness, a slower breakdown of sugar so that the corn will be less starchy when it arrives at the market, and an overall better flavor.

Sometimes in plants there are mutations, sports. A gene will change, producing a plant different from all others. This applies to corn in this way. A disease or fungus may come along that ruins a stalk. Perhaps somewhere in a blighted field an unaffected plant will be found. Breeders will take that plant, breed it back on the inbreds that are affected, select the next generation for unaffected stalks, and after about seven generations will have the original affected inbred with all its same hereditary factors, but with one new gene. They will have eliminated all the other genes that caused that particular blight. The same is true with insect pests: find the plants that resist certain pests, and breed their resistance into all corn. (Genetically modified corn — a genetically modified organism, or GMO — that creates a plant with pesticide in every cell by introducing a foreign gene into the original plant, and other GMO wonders prevalent by 2012, are beyond the scope of this story.)

There's danger, however, in narrowing a plant (or animal) to a few favored strains and discarding the rest. Genetic diversity is lost. Corn, for instance, is subject to a great many insect pests — corn borers and rootworms are well known. It also is afflicted by diseases — seed rot, stalk rot, smut. However resistant a plant is bred to be, it can become vulnerable to new or mutated insects and diseases. Uniformity can have bred out of a plant the very material that will prove resistant to a new pest, and that material might be lost if other plants containing it have not been maintained. If all the world were one strain of corn, corn might be wiped out in a season.

Jackie is witness to this the summer of 1970, the last summer Daddy is in the hybrid seedcorn business. The story begins earlier, however, with the development of a strain of corn with a male-sterile tassel, caused by male-sterile cytoplasm. This variety could be used as the female, and would require no expensive detasseling. The only problem was that the seed produced was also male sterile. This was met by introducing a fertility-restoring gene. The new hybrid was received with joy: by 1970 nearly all corn grown in this country had the cytoplasm in its genealogy. Detasseling was a thing of the past. But a new strain of southern corn leaf blight, highly virulent to this type of corn, hit the country in 1970 and destroyed 15 percent of the nation's corn crop. Jackie, now teaching in a new university out on the prairie of central Illinois, is surrounded, as she drives north to visit the family farm, by cornfield after withered cornfield. The cornfields don't appear normal till she's almost to Wisconsin.

Damage to the Dougan fields is slight, though some townships in Rock

County—mainly Newark and other southwest townships, and those areas that have practiced irrigation—have stronger evidence of blight. The *Badger Farm Bureau News* reports that the disease is present, to some extent, in practically every field in Wisconsin, spread on the wind by "spore showers" from the south, but that because the weather has been on the whole dry, it will not have much effect on overall corn production in the state. The *Beloit Daily News* runs an article about helicopter spraying of the Newark fields with Dithane M-45 (three applications needed, at about $3.25 an acre) and quotes county agent Hugh Alberts: "I've been in only one or two fields where there is absolutely no sign of the blight." He says that seed corn of the "T-cytoplasm" type appears to be most susceptible. Corn from a T and normal blend seed also has shown up with moderate blight, while most fields planted with "normal" hybrid seed are virtually free of the fungus. "The weather is the single most crucial factor right now. The fungus spreads rapidly in hot, humid, or rainy weather, while warm, dry weather appears to retard the rate of infestation. Spores of the fungus are wafted from field to field by the wind, and thrive on moisture and heat." Alberts goes on to describe the fungus and the progress of the disease in the kind of detail that Jackie's medieval history books reserved for the Black Death: "The fungus usually shows up first as quarter-to-half-inch lesions on lower leaves of the stalk. Then dark blotches appear on the shank, or stalk, and lastly they appear on the ear itself. Fungus infested ears of corn will ripen with large percentages of the ear blackened. The feed value of the discolored ears isn't significantly lowered, but the marketability of such corn is poor."

In retrospect, authorities agree that a difference in 1970 weather patterns or in the virulence of the new strain of southern leaf blight could have wiped out almost all the country's crop and turned a bad scene to catastrophe. As quickly as they could, using Florida, Hawaii and South America to provide an extra growing season, corn breeders began producing hybrid varieties which had normal cytoplasm, or from which the sterility-fertility cytoplasm had been eliminated, so that there would be some resistant seed for 1971, and plenty by 1972. Detasselers returned to the corn rows.

The National Academy of Sciences says, "The key lesson of 1970 is that genetic uniformity is the basis of vulnerability to epidemics." Henry Wallace, a pioneer in hybrid corn, once warned, "Neither corn nor man was meant to be completely uniform." Garrison Wilkes has said, "Quite literally, the genetic heritage of a millennium in a particular region can disappear in a single bowl of porridge," and from Walter Galinat, that unless genetic variability is treasured and carefully preserved, "we and our mutually symbiotic food plants may vanish like the dodo."

A corn geneticist, Professor R.L. Lambert of the University of Illinois, who talks to Jackie many years later, further explains the 1970 epidemic, and puts genetic diversity in present day perspective. "The epidemic was unusual," he says, "in that it resulted from a very specific series of events." He explains. First the DNA of the mitochondria of a corn cell had a lesion in a gene that made it susceptible to a new race of southern leaf blight that could attack plants with this form of cytoplasm—the so-called "Tms," Texas male sterile cytoplasm that Hugh Alberts describes in the *Beloit Daily News*. Because of the seed production system used at the time to produce hybrids without detasseling which involved this type of cytoplasm, most U.S. hybrids carried Tms. As a result a vast area of the country contained susceptible hybrids. These were a ready medium for the blight to infect plants widely. In terms of today (2012), single cross hybrids and individual plants of a hybrid are highly heterozygous, but all plants within a hybrid are highly homogeneous. However, there are a large number of different hybrids being grown so there is still genetic variation. At present most hybrids grown in the U.S. are considered to be of the B73 and Mo17 inbreds, which are used in hybrids that allow for genetic diversity among hybrids. In addition, since the widespread use of single cross hybrids by farmers early in the sixties, over fifty years have gone by during which no catastrophic pest outbreaks have occurred except for the 1970 southern leaf blight.

Jackie, an early detasseler in the Dougan fields, watches cornfields all her life, and regularly strays through them. She appreciates anew that during all her father's corn-growing career he was enthusiastically experimenting with new hybrid varieties, as well as growing everyone else's varieties in his test plots. She recognizes, too, that corn is as important to human existence as milk. They are both staffs of life. The farm's concerns cannot have been more basic.

26 ⚼ BAT

P at and Lew live in a house they've built on the edge of the dairy. Every afternoon Pat rests on the couch while her two small daughters are napping.

One day she hears the door open. She turns her head to see her father stealthily enter the living room. She watches as he tiptoes across it, reaches high on the picture window drapes and hangs up a sleeping bat. Without a glance at her Ron tiptoes back out and closes the door gently behind him.

Pat contemplates the bat for a few moments, then shuts her eyes again and joins the little creature in slumber.

27 ⨯ BEADLEVILLE

J ackie is a freshman at Beloit College. Her English teacher, Chad Walsh, assigns an essay. Jackie doesn't need to look far for a subject; she is surrounded by subjects. She writes:

BEADLEVILLE

Not very far from here there exists a thriving and prosperous community that is known by the name of Beadleville. You will not find it on any map; neither will the encyclopedia have a squib about its location, its population and its points of historical and scenic interest. But the residents of Beadleville do not mind this anonymity. Let us take a trip there and view them at their work and play.

A view of Taliesin North, by Spring Brook.

As we come over the hill we see Beadleville spread out ahead of us—or, rather, that section of Beadleville known as West Beadleville. The houses are lined up in orderly rows, and neat fences separate one from the other. The inhabitants are very much in evidence, going briskly about their individual businesses. Their tails are curled tightly against their backs, their ears flap with activity, their voices oink in eternal chorus, and their noses root in the soil. As we approach they crowd around the fence, grunting and squealing, in hopes that we may have brought with us a few ears of corn or a can of sour milk. West Beadleville is made up mainly of the younger set of the community—boars and gilts who can no longer be called piglets but now must be referred to as shoats. Their mothers live here too, although this is no longer necessary. These shoats are filled with the joy of existence, and spend their days in eating, sleeping, rooting, and fighting. The warm sun reflects from their burnished copper sides—they are Durocs—and each resembles an animated football with snout, four legs, and a tail.

Young Beadleville pigs are ready for lunch.

A quarter mile away is another section known as East Beadleville. This is built in a woodsy spot, and we must push through brush to get to it. Right now East Beadleville is a bachelor's retreat where young boars jostle and fight all day long. Later in the spring Bachelor's Retreat will be a lying-in hospital, and here the huge sows will bring forth their litters of ten and twelve.

After leaving East Beadleville we follow the bend in the road to the last section of town—Taliesin North. There is only one large building in Taliesin North, which serves as community center, living quarters, and farrowing house. The building is functional with large sheltering doorways. The beams of its construction blend artistically with the low overhanging eaves. The octagonal construction permits entrance from eight sides, and each interior room is wedge-shaped. The only furniture is a low rail about six inches off the floor to prevent the mother from lying on her prog-

Taliesin by the Big House, soon to be Taliesin South.

eny. Taliesin North is an architectural gem, sprung from the earth and yet not of it, breathing in each graceful line the essence of true art.

But, you ask, how did Beadleville get its name? Here comes the answer now. That tall, lean man with his face browned by wind and sun is Leonard Beadle. He is father, mother, mayor, arbitrator, attending physician, midwife, and God to the many inhabitants of Beadleville. He feeds them, tends them, breeds them, sends them to the fairs, and carries home their ribbons.

The pigs have learned through sad experience that Mr. Beadle's word is law. Take the case of the five-hundred pound sow who refused to walk up the ramp into a truck. Mr. Beadle turned her around, put a bushel basket over her head, and in trying to get it off she backed into the truck before she realized her mistake.

Early last spring when the population of Beadleville was increasing by leaps and bounds, I took home two of the smallest citizens who, due to their size, had been crowded off the cafeteria line. By a sad law of nature the small get smaller and the large get larger. These piglets were near death. After a few weeks of bottle-feeding every time they squealed (for the hunger of a pig varies directly as to the square root of its squeal) the two had passed their littermates, and now are as healthy as any hogs in town. Hamhocks is that big boar over there, and Twinkletoes is the little gilt whose ears seem to be on backward. You'll find them quite friendly.

If you come back next year, Beadleville will not be as you see it now. The community is mobile, and the sections move often. Taliesin may be down by the creek, its name changed to Taliesin South, and East Beadleville may be up the hill and known as North Beadleville. But no matter where the settlements are located, life will be going on as usual. The carefree adolescents will be trotting on tiptoe to bury their noses in the trough; the mothers will be placidly engorging their demanding offspring; and the young boars will be champing to get out of their monastic seclusion.

———

Chad Walsh gives Jackie a B+ on her essay. He likes the pun on "square root." He also writes, "A great deal of quiet charm and humor here. Watch your spelling. I like your feeling for the country and its varied inhabitants." Jackie likes the comments. Her cousin, fresh out of architecture school, thinks it deserves an A. "Your professor is new to Wisconsin," says Paul. "I bet he doesn't recognize your dad's joke in naming the octagon pig house after Frank Lloyd Wright's home at Spring Green! All that middle section is a spoof on Wright's architectural theories! Try sending it off to *Architectural Forum*. They'll print it!"

Jackie considers. She retypes it and sends it to *American Farm Youth*. They accept it and pay her five dollars. She's well pleased. It's her first publication, not counting "Molly the Maggot" and the long continued story that was printed in *The Galesburg Post* when she was ten. She shows the magazine with its story to Grampa, and to farm manager-pig potentate, Leonard Beadle. They are well pleased, too.

28 ⚔ RONALD PART 5 ⚔
KNOWING MY OWN MIND

A few letters may be missing from the box of Ronald's letters from France, but one is clearly absent. It's February 12, 1924, where he tells of his engagement. Small wonder the letter is gone. It must have been read and reread by Grama and Grampa, and then carefully considered, point by point, Grampa sitting late at his desk. When the news is out, it would have been passed from relative to relative. It probably ended in shreds. Whatever response W.J. makes, events in France are too rapid for the mails. Ronald's next-day letter says not to tell Trever or Esther yet, nor the relatives and hired men. Vera has written her mother. They have not told the Wadsworths.

"We are all treated like inmates of a girls' boarding school," says Ron, adding disparaging words about the Wadsworths, then goes on to farm matters. "What do you think of my going to the Guernsey Island for a week? Ought

Vera Wardner, left, and Mlle. Calais dance by the cannon in the Methodist Memorial courtyard.

to be worthwhile. My head is buzzing with plans for work—now that I have really decided that farming is to be my line, I'm excited about it. I'll be no more the typical farmer than you are, Dad."

W.J.'s reply to the engagement news is brief. It is dated March 6 but of course Ronald doesn't receive it till much later:

I do not like the tone of your letter regarding your people there. You youngsters are apt to get a little "heady." Their anxiety is for the success and influence of their work. Put yourself in the manager's position and you will see things differently. I have my time with the youngsters here who think they have eclipsed the boss in vision, ability, character, everything. Sometimes I take the trouble to show them where they are short. More frequently I quietly let them out.

Be careful. Above all do conscientious work. From your own statement of the lovelorn couples among the workers I can see how you are in danger of making your own affairs paramount.

Regarding your engagement: We are happy in it. We feel you should know your mind. You realize the great importance to yourself, the girl, and all concerned if a right choice. You may assure Vera we will receive her with true parental love, confident that we have not lost a son but have gained a daughter.

Bashful Vera is beseeched by a sailor suitor, in a play at the Memorial.

With no replies yet, Ronald continues to embroider on his consuming subjects. He's not keen for a long engagement. V has her degree, "and other sidelines that make her ability to think and talk rather exceptional, so it won't hurt me to study a bit longer." He expects the awaited letter will surely warn them to go slow. "Don't worry about my knowing my own mind. V is quite the sort of girl you have dreamed about for me." That she is his superior both mentally and spiritually, but he can catch up in the latter with her influence and his own home training; in the former with reading, study, school.

When it comes to farm possibilities, Ron writes as though he were already a partner:

How are the purebreds coming along? Do you think we would want to hit that end of the game together. Don't see why we couldn't by careful breeding and testing establish a reputation for purebred stock that would drag buyers to our place. I think the main thing in building up a high average is ruthless culling of stock. It means larger profits later on.

What sort of herdsman have you now? Is that part of the work giving you trouble? Mother says help turnover is pretty heavy. Hate to think of you in the milk room. What is the matter with help anyway? They surely must be satisfied with their living conditions, and they can save more money than in the city. Why this particular walkout?

Have you finished your books for last year? I'd be no end interested to know what they showed. How heavily did Trever and I come in? You will have to explain the figures because I don't know much about bookkeeping. I remember you told me once that the year after the war the place paid 8% on the investment and a managerial salary (money, living, etc.) of about five thousand. I don't imagine that with the fall of prices on farm products we have kept up to that, have we?

I don't believe my enthusiasm is of a passing nature. As I look back I realize farming is the life that has appealed to me most as something permanent. The summer I really worked at home was the happiest I have ever spent—although I did lie down on the job once in a while.

On a campout yesterday I found a barnful of white steers that smelled warm and cowy. They weren't cows but I wanted to put my arms around them just the same. You know I have always said that one of the most beautiful lines in the world is the straight back of a cow.

Lovingly, Ron

29 ⚹ HOWARD JOHNSON

Grampa takes pride in getting onto his land very early in the spring. The dairy's fields are flat and well-drained, and he prepares them carefully during the fall and winter, mulching and manuring, so that as soon as the weather allows he's able to plow and plant. His hay is always the first mown in June. His corn, which according to folk rhyme should be "knee-high by the Fourth of July," is always hip high.

Howard Johnson is a farmer near Shopiere who sells his milk to the dairy; he's one of the milk business's producers. One spring day he's just finished milking and is turning his cows out into the barnyard when he notices that a corn plant is growing in the manure pile. The pile has sat there all winter in a sheltered southern exposure between the silo and the barn, where it gets the full sun from morning to night. Howard goes over for a closer look. He finds the plant to be sturdy and already a foot high. It's been thriving in greenhouse conditions.

He grins, gets a shovel, and digs it up. He puts it into a cardboard box, and the box in the back of his pickup. Then he tends to his milking equipment, slings his cans on his truck, and drives over to Dougans.

At the dairy it's 6:45 a.m., just after breakfast. Everyone is bustling. Barn hands are sweeping down the barn. Milkhouse hands are already bottling. Farmhands are hitching up the horses, filling the tractors with gas, getting out plows, and checking equipment before they disperse to the fields. Other local farmers, like Howard, have driven in from the surrounding countryside and are unloading their milk cans. Grampa is in the thick of the three-ring circus, waving his arms like a ringleader.

Howard lifts the box with its little corn plant from his truck. He takes it over and puts it into Grampa's hands. He lifts the pad and pencil out of Grampa's overalls breast pocket and writes, "Mr. Dougan, is this corn ready to cultivate?"

Howard Johnson, left, shows pigs at a judging. His son Rex is on the right.

Grampa's eyes grow big as cowpies. He turns the box this way and that; he examines the plantling from all sides. "My, my!" he exclaims. "Look here! Where is Ronald? Where is Mr. Griffiths?"

He thrusts the box back to Howard Johnson and whirls around. "Men! Men!" he shouts, beckoning in all directions with wide sweeps of his arms. "Come quickly! Look at this! Come see how high Mr. Johnson's corn is already!"

The men hasten up, but Grampa is already off and away. "Hurry! Hurry!" he shouts over his shoulder, heading for the horse barn. "We haven't a minute to lose! Mr. Johnson has corn ready to cultivate, and we haven't even planted yet!"

Ronald saunters up, and Howard explains to him the reason for the plant's precocity. They have a good laugh. Then Ronald takes the box and plants the corn at the edge of the flower bed beside the Big House. It will remind Grampa, at least until he drives past Howard's farm and sees that the Johnson corn is no further along than his own, of the spring that he wasn't the first to get his seed in.

30 ⁂ JOE

Over the years Grampa and Daddy have hired handicapped workers. Maybe it's Grampa's deafness that has always made him and Daddy aware of other people's disabilities, and aware, too, of everyone's need for the self-respect and dignity of work.

Jackie grows up taking for granted such workers; she never hears the word "handicapped," only how Jim Howard, a herdsman who was on the place long before she was born, and who happened to have one leg much shorter than the other, could jump up and grab the manure trolley rail and swing himself all around the barn. She knows Charlie, the one-armed milkman. She knows Bill, in the milkhouse. He's big, clumsy, and somewhat retarded, as well as diabetic, so that his meals must be carefully prepared in the Big House. The farm is a sheltered home for him; he's able to have all his needs met and draw a salary besides. He shuffles around doing the routine jobs he's capable of. Daddy shakes his head over the minimum wage when it comes along. "What about a man like Bill?" he says at the table. "He's not worth the minimum wage to me; I can't afford to keep him if I have to pay him that much. But if I don't keep him he'll have to go to an institution—and that'll cost the government a whale of a lot more."

Then there's Joe. Joe is a Turtle Township neighbor. Jackie's first essay in her freshman writing class at Beloit College is about Joe. It begins, "The country is kind to its children," and goes on to tell how Joe's family moved away from town so that Joe would be able to do more things with less ridicule and pressures. Joe is severely brain-damaged and can't talk; he communicates with gestures and noises. He's had no schooling; there is no school set up yet for people like Joe. But as is the case with many cerebral palsied persons, he's bright. He can drive and repair a tractor; he's a fine mechanic. He can do many farm chores. He draws a regular paycheck at the dairy.

One summer a church member asks Daddy to hire her son. Daddy does, to do odd jobs and this and that. Raymond is retarded, but he has a more visible handicap — he has something wrong with his legs so that he can't walk in an ordinary fashion: he walks with bent knees. It's a strange gait, as if he's on springs, or marionette strings. He bobs along at a semi-crouch. Jackie is used to seeing Raymond at church, so that when she meets him on the farm she scarcely gives him a second glance.

But Joe has never seen Raymond, nor any person with Raymond's sort of handicap before, and Raymond has never seen a severe spastic. Joe drives his tractor into the farm one June morning, stops it, and lurches off the seat. He shambles along the drive toward the milkhouse, his head rolling, his mouth working, his arms jerking. Suddenly he spots Raymond, swinging up the walk from the round barn, bouncing from his knee springs like an anthropoid.

The two stop in astonishment and stare at each other. Joe is overcome. He screeches with glee, his head swivels and bobs, he points and slaps his thigh and stamps his foot. Raymond is the funniest sight he's ever seen.

But Raymond finds Joe equally amusing. He turns to a hired man nearby. "That guy better — watch — out," he says firmly. "If he don't watch out, he's gonna — screw — his — head — right — off!"

Joe Lentell is on the right in this group of seed corn laborers.

31 ⚹ DOUGAN HYBRIDS

I t's 1934. For almost nine years Daddy has been working alongside his father. While Grampa's jurisdiction is more the farm, and Daddy's the milk business, Daddy's passion is cows. He's intensely interested in breeding, in herd improvement, in cattle genetics, and indeed remains engrossed with herd improvement all his life. He feels proprietary about the dairy's cows. At the Little House one summer he asks Mother to take down the curtains from the dining room windows. They are obstructing his view of the East Twenty, currently in use as a pasture. "I want to be able to see my cows," he says.

So he's not as alert to what's going on in plant genetics. It's Grampa who hears the first news that there's something dramatic in that area, something called hybrid corn. When he tells his son about it, Daddy's ears prick up, too. He and his father hasten to Madison, and discover that for progressive farmers, they are johnny-come-latelys.

The University of Wisconsin, one of the land-grant universities established by Lincoln, had back in 1923 appointed Dr. R. A. Brink as Assistant Professor of Genetics. Brink was impressed with the work Dr. Donald Jones had been doing at the Connecticut Experiment Station, developing corn inbred lines and crossing them to produce hybrids. Both men had been students at Harvard of the great hybrid corn geneticist, Edward Murray East. Brink decided to initiate a program similar to Jones's in Wisconsin. By 1929 seed of over 150 experimental hybrids had been produced by hand pollination and tested the following year at six locations. Fifteen of the hybrids showed an increase of 20 percent yield over open pollinated varieties of corn. In 1931, eleven of the experimental hybrids yielded an increase of 50 percent or more. The university began demonstration trials to interest area farmers, and in 1933 the College of Agriculture decided to produce and distribute foundation seed stock, to make hybrid seed corn production a farmer enterprise. Seven farmers, that year, grew 450 bushels of seed on a little over fourteen acres.

The next year, 1934, twenty-two farms are growing seed. The Dougan

Grampa with Dougan Hybrid Seed Corn.

farm becomes one of these. Daddy and Grampa get crossing stock from the university. They plant only one small field, that first summer, two rows of male corn for every six of female. Grampa, Daddy, and a few of the farm-hands detassel the female corn. When the corn is ripe, they husk the female corn by hand into a blanket to protect the seed. The corn lives up to its prom-ise: though a poor summer for grain, the hybrid produces forty-five bushels an acre, as compared to twenty bushels for the non-hybrid corn.

For lack of heated space on the farm, Grampa and Daddy take the ears to town, to the furnace at Aunt Ida's on Bushnell Street. They dry the corn by hanging two parallel loops of binder twine from nails on a ceiling beam, then laying an ear of corn across the base of the loops so that the ear forms the seat of a double-roped swing. They then cross the twine above it and lay in another ear. Another cross, another ear, until the swing is ten ears deep, now looking more like a fat, yellow, nubbly Venetian blind. These racks of ten hang all over the basement, while the warm air circulates around them.

No ear is anonymous. Every rack has a number, and the ears on each rack are numbered from one to ten. This identification is necessary because each ear is going to be tested for germination. They do it this way: when the ears are judged dry enough, Daddy and Grampa take a few kernels from the first ear of Rack 1 and start a rag doll. They space the kernels on a strip of heavy cotton which has been marked off with a wax pencil into one hundred squares, each square numbered with the identification of that particular ear. They then proceed with the next ear, filling up more squares, and rolling the cotton into a cylinder as they go. They make a large rag doll, soak it in water, put it in a warm place, and allow the bundle to sit for several days.

Anticipation is high as they take the corn dolly to Aunt Ida's kitchen table to see how many kernels have sprouted. The percentage of sprouts from each ear will determine the germination of that ear. If nine of ten seeds grow, the germination is 90 percent.

Daddy starts unrolling the damp cotton carefully. The first row of kernels comes into sight, and Grampa and Daddy are delighted. Every single kernel on its marked square has sent out a pale little tail of root. The second row makes almost as fine a showing, with only one kernel failing to germinate. The third row is also satisfactory, and the fourth. But in a few moments their pleasure turns to puzzlement and then dismay. The proud rows begin to falter and then fail. They unroll incredulously. There is absolutely no germination at all on the center squares of the roll! They take their rag doll and hightail it up to the Agronomy Department to see what's ailing the Dougan cornfields.

Andy Wright takes one look and begins to laugh. "You've made too big a rag doll," he says. "The kernels need air to germinate!"

Grampa and Daddy return sheepishly, for this is something they should have been able to figure out. They make smaller bundles. This time they find, on the whole, excellent germination. Any ear that shows up weak, they discard.

Next they hand-shell the ears and grade the kernels. The grader is not much bigger than a breadbox. A batch of corn goes into a perforated cylinder which is turned by hand. The flat kernels shake out, the larger rounds and thicks are left behind. It's a crude machine. They have to keep changing the grids and sending the remaining kernels through again and again, before the corn is all properly graded. No size or shape of kernel is necessarily better than another. But the kernels must be sorted on account of the limitations of corn planters, whose plates will let through only three kernels of one size at a time. If smaller kernels are present, they'll crowd through with the larger ones and make too many stalks to a hill. If the kernels are too big or fat for the opening, they'll clog it and no corn will be planted at all. A farmer can change the plates on his planter to accommodate different sizes of seed, but it will be many years before a planter is developed that can handle mixed-size seed.

Finally Grampa and Daddy dust the seed with a fungicide, bag the seed by hand, stitch up the bags, and label them. The university makes its own germination tests, certifies the corn, and seals the bags with a little metal tag that is to be broken only by the buyer. This insures that the bag hasn't been tampered with between certification and purchase. Daddy and Grampa then sell the seed around Rock County, for seven dollars a bushel.

By now Daddy is definitely into the seed corn business, for open-pollinated seed is selling for less than two dollars a bushel. With hybrid seed bringing almost four times as much, and producing so much more per acre, too, this is a venture worth continuing for economic reasons as well as genetic interest.

The second season, 1935, seventy Wisconsin farmers raise hybrid seed corn, and the Dougan farm increases its production. A problem with hybrid seed is that it must not be grown close to any other variety of corn where it might chance cross pollination. There are strict rules from the university about how much isolation a field must have for certification, and if there is not quite enough space between, how many extra rows of male corn must border a field, in order to insure proper pollination. This means that as the Dougan hybrid corn acreage increases, if all the fields are not the same strain (and they aren't), there must be careful planning—and one must also always take into account what and where his neighbors are planting.

When detasseling time comes this year Daddy and Grampa recruit along Colley Road and in the Township for farm boys. Billy Beadle, Frank Moore, and Phil Holmes are Turtle neighbors; they've known and respected Daddy Dougan all their lives. They do a responsible job. But at twelve and thirteen years old they are not above pranks. When Grampa drives them from one field to another in an old milk truck, they rock it in rhythm. Grampa is unable to see the trick going on behind him. He hangs on, driving, thinking the problem lies with the truck or the rough surface of the field he's traversing.

The boys have, or borrow, horses, and discover that detasseling from horseback eliminates much of the job's discomfort. Frank, the youngest, is pudgy, and Grampa is solicitous toward him. "Get up there, Stubby," he cries, helping him onto his horse.

At the end of the season Grampa, always the educator, invites the local farmers and members of the Clinton High School agricultural class to a hybrid corn demonstration. This is his and Daddy's first Corn Yield Field Test Trials, which becomes an annual affair.

This season there is much more corn; Daddy and Grampa fix up the cellar of the Big House and use it for drying space around the octopus-armed furnace. They do this the next year, too. By the fall of 1937, Ronald and Vera

Ron stands before the "corn room" in his remodeled farmhouse. The sack reads "Wisbred"—he and Gramp started selling with that consortium.

have bought a nearby farm that Daddy and Grampa have been renting, a mile and a half up the road from the dairy. Mark Kellor remodels the back sheds into a corn dryer. After the corn buildings, the house, too, is remodeled and the family moves into Chez Nous at the end of August, 1938. Now the corn dryer is just beyond the back door, and Jackie and her sisters and brother find it intensely interesting.

The corn ears are placed in several bins whose floors are open-slatted with a space beneath. Air is heated in a shell around a furnace, and driven by a fan under the bins. The hot air rises through the ears and out an opening at the top. Vents can be adjusted to drive the hot air down though the bins. The small room adjacent to the bin area is not yet completely enclosed. Daddy fixes up an old arm chair with plenty of blankets and spends the nippy fall nights there, dozing and reading in front of the furnace. Every so often he stokes it with logs. Daytimes, Patsy, Jackie, and Craig creep through the sliding door of the hot air tunnel behind the bins and squirm on their stomachs down the long secret passageway. They are careful not to jostle the vents into the bins. When they've had enough of the mystery, and of the rush of warm, grain-heavy air saturating their lungs, they have to wriggle out backwards. There's no room to turn around.

In the basement Daddy has a little still for determining the moisture content of the drying grain. A given weight of corn is poured into a flask of oil and boiled until all the water in the sample is expressed and collected into a calibrated tubular container, from which can be read the percentage of moisture still in the corn. It has to be 12 percent or below before it meets university certification standards. The smell of the boiling corn permeates the house with a redolence not unlike popcorn, and the corn residue, though just as hard on the teeth, is tastier than old-maid popcorn kernels.

This distillery is in operation only a few seasons, for before long a moisture tester comes into general use that depends on the resistance of a given weight of corn through which an electric current is directed. The moisture of the sample is then translated into percentage on a scale. This gives instant results, without mess or smell. The little still is relegated to a back corner of the basement, alongside an ox yoke that was a relic when Daddy was a boy.

The grading is also now done with more sophistication. The kernels spill down onto a shaking, slightly inclined grid. A strong blast of air rises through the grid so that the corn floats a fraction of an inch above its surface. All the chaff and light, undeveloped kernels jig swiftly down the incline and are funneled off, while the rest of the corn is cycled into another grader which successively sorts it into a dozen variations which rain down into a dozen bags. Daddy has a trick that everyone likes to watch. He sets his hat over the initial grid and there it floats, held up by magic.

When the fifty-six pound cloth sacks—one bushel each—are finally stitched and certified, there's no adequate warehouse in which to store them until they're sold. After strengthening the basement beams underneath a large room off the front hall, Daddy moves all the sacks into his newly remodeled house. Only a small crawl space is left under the ceiling, brightly illuminated by an overhead bulb. Craig, Jackie, and Patsy find this an inviting place to play. They clamber up with books and blankets and graham crackers and chocolate milk and establish their territories. They creep back and forth to one another's houses. Town friends, when they come out, gawk at a room filled floor to ceiling with corn.

Ron displays one of his own hybrid crosses.

At some point the three notice the little metal tags on the sacks. They pry one open and it breaks with a satisfying snap. They search around and open all the accessible tabs. When Daddy discovers this he turns the air blue with French profanities. The three insist tearfully that they had no idea they were doing anything wrong. Daddy has to have the university recertify the tampered bags, and everyone is forbidden to play there any more.

By the next year farm space has been made for storage—a long, low building at the end of the sheds, with a gigantic concrete floor perfect for roller skating until it becomes filled with corn bags and grit from farm boots and spilled seed. A year later some circular bins with raised cement floors are built; when the platforms have been poured but the corrugated metal walls not yet erected, Jackie roller skates round and round on the smooth concrete, sometimes in the moonlight, risking a three-foot drop if she goes over an edge. Mother reclaims the storage room in the house, but no matter how many years it functions as her office, it never loses its original name, "The Corn Room."

The following year, production increases again. When detasseling time comes, the Turtle boys aren't a large enough crew. Daddy puts an ad in the *Beloit Daily News*, saying that any fourteen or fifteen year old, sufficiently tall, who wants to detassel corn should be on the Big House lawn at the dairy by seven o'clock the next morning. The pay will be twenty five cents an hour.

The next day, shortly before seven, Daddy is startled to find forty or fifty kids, girls as well as boys, milling around on Grampa and Grama's front lawn, with bicyclers still streaming out Colley Road as far as the eye can see. About seventy-five eager workers are finally assembled. Daddy organizes the hordes into teams. He allows groups of friends to work together. He explains how to do the job, and why it's important to get all the showing tassels. He starts them out in the fields and then, like a border collie, races back and forth all morning to meet each lot as they emerge from their rows and to start them on fresh sections.

The day is a hot one. What breeze there is can't penetrate the tall corn. Before long, the detasselers stumbling out are sweaty, thirsty, and drooping. Daddy keeps water and orange drink flowing. He shouts encouragement.

There's one section where no one stumbles out. Daddy keeps doubling back, checking at the fence to see whether any detasselers have emerged yet. He begins to wonder if the job has proved too much for them, if they've gone back to town. Finally he goes in to see.

He finds the group of boys in a clearing in the middle of the field. They've made the clearing by knocking down corn stalks in order to let the breeze in. They are sitting in a circle, playing cards. They'd gotten tired, they explain, and are taking a little rest. Daddy is dumbfounded. He fires the lot, and doesn't give them any pay for the work they've already done, although one boy has the cheek to ask for it.

Next morning at seven the ranks have considerably thinned. Many of the town kids fail to show up. The thirty-odd that are left form an efficient, workable crew.

Detasseling continues every summer, and as soon as Jackie and Craig are tall enough they join the work force. Around the country, methods are tried here and there to eliminate hand detasseling: a machine is developed, for instance, that cuts the tassel right off. This turns out to be chancy. Too many short stalks are missed, or the whole tassel not chopped far enough down so that its branches grow out again, and can produce enough pollen to condemn a field. The machine is not generally adopted.

At intervals during the tasseling season inspectors show up and check the fields. Nobody knows when this will happen. If a field has tassels in excess of the permitted limit, that field will be condemned. It pays to have able and conscientious detasselers, and a competent detasseler boss.

Considerably later in the history of hybrid corn there's a hiatus in detasseling. Those working with corn genetics develop a male-sterile cytoplasm—the tassel does not produce pollen. This is hailed by seed growers, for having to remove the tassel has always added to the difficulty of the process and the expense of the seed, while failures in detasseling result in economic loss. Indeed, Dougans lose a field once, when a corn boss completely forgets about a remote field and it tassels out before he remembers. The new process isn't without cost to the grower, however, who must pay royalties on every bushel produced by the sterile tassel method. Nonetheless this new corn sweeps away the old.

Unfortunately, there's a genetic flaw. The sterile cross has a linked characteristic: the corn grown from this seed turns out to be susceptible to a mutation of a fungus called southern corn leaf blight. In 1970, all over the Midwest, the corn crop browns, withers, and fails. Southern Wisconsin is not too hard hit, and Daddy does not lose much corn, but the corridor Jackie frequently travels, between her home in south central Illinois, and the farm, is a wasteland. The seed growers are forced to go back to strains that require detasseling. They compensate by speeding the job—a detasseling contraption is invented that fits on the front of a special high-wheeled tractor that spiders through the fields, over the corn. A crossbar has a series of rigid platforms that hang down between the rows. Detasselers stand on the platforms and are carried along at a uniform pace and at a level where tassels are easy to remove. Jackie compares this to the discomforts of her own detasseling days.

Over the years, the Dougan farm is one of thirteen farms in the state which grow university experimental strains in test plots each summer, under university supervision. In addition, Daddy grows seed from Indiana and

In the new seed house at Chez Nous, Ron holds a half-bushel sack of DOUGAN HYBRIDS.

Minnesota experimental stations, and seed from other commercial dealers. Every fall he holds Corn Yield Trial Days, where farmers and other dealers come and compare the various strains. It's always a festive occasion, with the farm spruced up, a food tent provided by the Grange, the university down in force, and also a number of non-rural visitors. Daddy always has a handsome brochure printed up, describing the different hybrids. One year in his brochure he prints comparisons of all the seeds tested. His own varieties do very well overall but here and there another dealer's strains do better on this particular trait or that, and the triumphant dealer immediately publicizes the success. Daddy loses business to competitors. He decides that from then on he'll just print and advertise his own results; let the other fellow do his own comparisons.

In the genetic area Daddy works to develop his own strains, calling them "Doc D," after Craig, now a medical doctor; "Roy V," after Roy Veihman, his head of corn sales, and "Bob G," after Bob George, his farm manager. He tells Mommy, regretfully, that he'd like to name a strain after her, but that her initials, "Vee D," might not adapt well to the selling of corn.

Daddy continues promoting his own popular strains, while experimenting with and developing others, until he retires from the hybrid seed corn business, and from farming, in 1972.

He writes a letter of thanks and regret to his seventy-five corn dealers, starting, "How does a kid get to be 70?" The breeding of cattle has been Daddy's lifelong passion, but hybrid seed corn proves to be a passion fully its equal.

A coda. Had Daddy been younger, not retired but continuing in seed corn production, or had Craig chosen to be a farmer and to carry on the seed business, the operation would probably not have lasted many more years. For though his father would have left Craig a strong base of faithful salesmen, and Craig himself had had a lot of experience in raising and marketing corn, there was beginning a gradual decline of the small and medium companies which Daddy was a part of. In 2000, in the Corn Belt, perhaps less than 50 percent of the hybrid seed corn companies still existed that were operating in the fifties. This follows the pattern of consolidation of smaller companies into larger conglomerates in all sorts of farm businesses; the rise of agribusiness. There are reasons for this. In the seed corn arena, there has been a lack of production of public inbreds by universities, and the necessity for greater production and processing of single cross seed. This has caused the exchange of breeding materials by private companies and breeders to diminish. Along with this, commercial corn hybrids have been patented, which prevents other companies from selfing in them to develop improved inbreds. An increased cost of advertising — radio, TV, newspapers, glossy brochures — also reduces profits.

And then, the application of biotechnology producers — transformation with DNA, molecular markers, and other scientific innovations — has greatly increased the cost of development of new inbreds. Smaller companies, like Dougan Hybrids, would not have been able to cover the cost of research labs, personnel, equipment, and other necessities, no matter how interested and dedicated the owners were, nor how knowledgeable they became.

The thirties through the sixties, when Grampa and Daddy were operating, was a lovely time to be in on the excitement of the development of corn. But for the small grower, it became increasingly lonely, and today, 2012, it is very lonely indeed.

32 ⚭ P C

It's a sunny June day. Craig is eighteen, Grampa is seventy-nine. Grampa has retired, but still works all day, every day, on the farm. Craig is working on the farm, too, before starting Beloit College in the fall. Daddy has teamed him up with Grampa, to be Grampa's Man Friday on whatever project Grampa wants to do. Today Grampa's project is to make water run uphill.

They are down in the pasture by the tracks of the Chicago, Milwaukee, St. Paul and Pacific Railroad. Alongside the railroad bridge over the crick there is a concrete underpass in the embankment, for cows and machinery to go through to the fields beyond. The floor of this underpass has filled with water and sludge. When the cows come through it, they get muck halfway up their legs. Grampa does not like his cows coming up to the barn with dirty legs.

He's hitched a long scoop bucket called a slip to the one horse left on the farm, Barney. Barney is old, too, and blind, and retired, except when Grampa finds a job for him.

Grampa and Craig position the bucket in the muck. Each holds onto and presses down a handle; there is one on either side. Grampa speaks to the horse, old Barney plods, Grampa grunts, Craig wrinkles his nose, and mud and water are scooped uphill. But the grade is a long one, and when they dump the bucket, midway up, muddy water flows back down into the underpass.

Craig can't see how they are any ahead. The next rain will fill the underpass up again anyhow, no matter how clear they get it now. He can think up a dozen ways of doing the job better than Grampa's way, most of them more ambitious than he feels: siphons, drains, canals. His main thought is, why do the job at all, why not just let the cows have dirty legs? He and Grampa, after several hours at this job, have much more than legs that are dirty.

Gradually, however, the underpass clears. Enough water soaks into the hill that after repeated trips the end of the job is in sight. Craig and Grampa sit down on the bank of the crick for a well-deserved break. Barney lowers

Grampa prepares a field for planting.

his head and crops grass. Grampa takes out his blue farm bandana and wipes his face. The sun shines warm. The crick swirls and eddies beneath their feet.

Craig has been thinking ahead to college, to life. He's been active in the Methodist Youth Fellowship at church. Now Reverend Krussell has been urging the ministry. Craig motions for Grampa to hand him his pencil and paper.

"I have often heard," Craig writes, "how you left the ministry for the farm, but I've never heard how you decided to be a minister in the first place."

Grampa studies the paper. Craig rolls onto his elbow and nibbles a grass stem. Grampa folds the paper and puts it back in his pocket. He ponders before he talks.

"My family were religious people," he says, "and I was raised to be God-fearing and Bible-reading and church-going." He goes on, telling Craig about what it was like to be a boy on the farm at Lowell, about his father's death, and his mother's hopes for him. He tells how he felt drawn to the service of the Lord, but that he was uncertain that this was God's plan for him. He had had to drop out of high school, and already he was older than other college students. He spent much time in thought and prayer as he worked the land, wrestling with the problem.

"And finally one evening," says Grampa, turning and twinkling at Craig, "I went up on a hill, and I stood there, looking at the sky, communing with the Lord. And I shouted out loud, 'Lord, what am I to do? Give me a sign!'"

Craig is strongly interested. He indicates this by his face and eyebrows, and asks with his voice, "And did He?"

Grampa nods and chuckles. "He did. There in the clouds I made out the letters P C — 'Preach Christ!' That was my sign. I knew now what it was that the Lord wanted me to do. And so I left the farm and went to the university."

Craig sits up and reaches for the paper again.

"How awful for you, then," he writes, "when you finally got to be a minister, to lose your hearing and have to leave. For the Lord to take away from you the very thing he'd told you to do. Didn't it make you doubt Him?"

Grampa studies Craig's words, almost imperceptibly nodding and nodding his head.

"Yes, it was hard," he says at last. "And I spent many months thinking and praying and agonizing. And finally in great torment I went up on another hill, and I stood there looking at the sky, and I shouted out, 'Lord, what am I to do? Give me a sign!' And there, in the clouds, I again made out the letters P C!"

Craig looks puzzled at Grampa. Grampa's face breaks into laughter. He laughs so hard he can hardly talk; his eyes disappear.

"And it came to me," laughs Grampa, "it came to me, that I'd perhaps misunderstood the Lord the first time, and that all along He'd been saying to me, 'Plant Corn!'"

Craig and Grampa whoop. Grampa rolls back on the bank and kicks his feet in the air like a colt.

33 ✦ RONALD PART 6 ✦ SHE TOUCHES ALL MY INTERESTS

It is not until March 4, 1924 that the long awaited letter from W.J. finally arrives. It's in response to Ronald's letter of January 30, where his son first talks openly about Vera Wardner. Ronald's answer is immediate.

Dear Dad,

Wish I could tell you how much I appreciate your answer to my "girl letter." It is remarkable that you should be able to tell the minute I began talking absolutely seriously. It tickled me that you didn't warn me to watch my step. Mother's note is awfully dear—"Oh yes, can she cook?" and "I'm glad she isn't a French Catholic." I've answered most of your questions in other letters, but here is more.

Vera is small, with brown (almost black) eyes, good color, high cheek bones, a delicate mouth, brown hair that is hazy with grey—she had flu during the war. She is twenty-eight years old—sounds bad on paper, but knowing her, the difference doesn't mean a thing.

After high school she went to Physical Education School in Chicago. She is of an athletic turn of mind without losing her delightful femininity. Her dancing must be mighty good, for in a city-wide exposition a few years ago, she was chosen to represent that line of work. After her Phys Ed work, she spent a couple of years in religious work, playing the piano, etc. She has a beautiful workable faith.

Vera Wardner on the ship to France.

She felt she needed more schooling, though, and went to Illinois Women's College in Jacksonville, a school of perhaps 500 girls. She swept everything before her—not that she has told me, but I know enough about schools to know that she had the school at her feet. She taught gym part time and laid into student activities. She made a Phi Beta Kappa average. Her major was French. After graduating she was elected President of the Alumnae Association. Before coming here she was teaching French and English, and directing girls' physical work at the high school in Winchester, Illinois. They want her back, and her college wants her in physical work there, also. Her mother is alone now, though, so V thinks she will get a job for the winter in the Chicago schools and live with her mother.

She is wonderfully sympathetic without making it evident—one knows of her interest and understanding without talking about it. She is a highly complex being—half the time one would think her sixteen because of her delight in play, and her exercise in imaginative things. The rest of the time one knows that she is unfathomably deep and has solidity of character on which one can rely. She continuously sparkles—but it isn't at all a surface sparkle. It is her clean character, her delight in good things, her love of people that shows itself in her eyes and laugh. She touches all my interests—only in places where I have but a hazy turn in the right direction, she has thought things out. I never feel that I have to help her along with a crutch in any topic—and still

Vera, on left, in a play at the Memorial, where she taught music, dance, piano, and English, and created dramas and other events with the young people of the town.

I know that I satisfy her as wholly. I will grow all my life in keeping step with her.

You credited me with a level head because of my first letter. If that reputation isn't gone by now, this letter ought to shatter it. Know that while I see depth and all, I also have the urge to rave. Oh well, you will too, Dad. You will twinkle all over as you show her off. You and Mother will practically live at our house. You will find depth to her, and at the same time you'll get a kick out of bringing in baby rabbits to show her.

Vera poses, in the same costume.

Ronald then outlines an "astounding plan that will leave you gasping." His contract with the Memorial ends in June. Vera's ends in July. Dr. Harker, the president of Vera's college, "who has been almost a father to her for six years," will be in France: they have just found this out. Why shouldn't he marry them? They could then pool their resources, honeymoon for a month in France, Switzerland, and Italy, and return in time for school.

Ronald regrets this plan omits a home wedding, but points out the savings: dress suits, showers, bachelor dinners. It would save Vera and her family even more. In Evanston, with Ronald's school money and Vera's earnings, they could make it until he graduates and is ready for the farm. This is his idea alone, he insists, but he has talked it over with V and the plan appeals to her.

Ronald posts his letter with hope and trepidation, and continues waiting.

34 ⚹ DETASSELING CORN

Craig is in Beloit High. He has to write a theme for his English class. He thinks back over the summer of working on the farm.

THE DETASSELER

On the hairy surface of the quack grass and velvet weed, the early morning globules of dew cling, glistening in the sun. The earth is a richer black than usual, made so by a recent shower, and the head-high corn stands silently in the windless July morning.

Into this lovely setting steps the detasseler. His orders are to pick all the showing tassels from the cornstalks as he walks between the corn rows. At sixty cents an hour, what could be easier? With a light heart the novice enters the half-mile-long field and slowly bobs out of sight, leaving a trail of soft yellow tassels behind him.

An hour later our hero appears. His countenance no longer bears the smug smile it possessed a while ago, and his pants are saturated to the knees with dew. His arms and neck are crisscrossed with welts obtained from the sharp thin leaves of the corn plant. His shoes are now samples of good Wisconsin earth, coated an inch thick in most places.

After considerable thought on the subject—and there has been much time for thinking in the corn row—he realizes that the job is more difficult than he'd anticipated. The foreman assigns him to a new section, telling him that he is leaving too many tassels, and after all, what is he getting paid to do? Fine thing, our hero glowers, but says nothing and begins once again.

The corn seems higher than before, and the sun's heat is emphasized by the lack of wind. "Gee, it's hot," he mutters over and over again. His hand closes on a tassel. He pulls. There is a sticky feeling when he lets go. Careful scrutiny shows him that this particular tassel was the pasture for an ant colony's aphids, or cows, and he has wiped it out. He rubs his hand on his trousers, but streaks of green remain embedded in his pores. "How the heck did I get into this job?" he wonders, raising his eyes heavenward.

Suddenly he appears at the row's end. His glazed eyes spot the water jug. He stumbles over to it and sends the lukewarm liquid into and around his mouth. It mingles with the sweat and dirt on his neck and makes little rivulets around his Adam's apple.

By the end of the day, the detasseler is no longer a novice. He has learned many things about corn he has never known before. He wishes he had never discovered these things.

How important! A corn tassel.

He teeters to his bike and slowly pedals home, eats, and drops into bed.

The early morning dew glistens in the sun. The head-high corn stands silent in the hot, windless morning. Into this lovely setting steps the detasseler foreman. "Anybody know why that west-side kid didn't come today?" he asks. No one knows. "Damn kids—can't count on them," he mutters and hurries off to tell the boss.

Craig gets his paper back. On it his teacher has written, "A pleasure to read!" Craig glows. He takes it to show Daddy and Mother and Grampa.

Jackie likes Craig's story. She, too, has spent summers on the crew, starting when she was tall enough. She knows Craig's descriptions are accurate. There are details, though, that he has missed.

When it rains, for instance. She welcomes a shower on a blistering day. But the rain pelts her lifted face and blinds her. Her glasses are scant protection, and in addition they steam up with her body heat, and stream with rain. With or without them, she can't see the tassels. Corn cuts, too, are somehow sharper in the rain; the wet seems to hone the leaf edges. And the mud that

A detasseled field of Dougan corn, a detasseler in its midst.

sticks to her shoes quickly becomes a heavy boot. Each foot must be slung forward with conscious effort. It does no good to go barefoot for then the mud clings over her ankles and up her legs, heavier by the step.

But in the early morning, on a fresh summer day, when the dew glistens on the hairy sides of the velvet weed, it's joyful to start off down a row. She is doing a vital job and being paid for it. The sun is not high yet. Its rays filter through the corn stalks. The air is cool. There is friendly shouting back and forth between the rows with the other crew members. Sometimes they throw tassels high in the air in an exuberance of good spirits. Then the individual paces of the other detasselers gradually leave her alone in the green world. Sometimes she stops detasseling and stands very still, to experience the solitude. Sometimes she makes up cheerful songs and sings them at the top of her lungs:

> Here we go a-tasseling, a-tasseling, a-tasseling,
> Here we go a-tasseling, all on a summer's morn.
> We tassel fast, we tassel slow,
> We tassel every female row,
> So hardly any tassels show
> Out in the Dougan corn.

Or she sings,

> Stand up, stand up for Dougan,
> You Hybrid 6-0-2!
> Stand up, stand up for Dougan
> And show what you can do!

She sings, like Robert Frost's scyther, from sheer morning gladness at the brim.

After a while, of course, discomfort sets in. The sun rises above the cornstalks and pours down heat. No wind can penetrate the rows down where she is. Her clothes, saturated with dew, steam dry. So much sweat trickles down from her hair that it runs into her eyes if she's forgotten to wear her sweatband. And she develops her personal detasseling malady, a stomachache.

The reason is this. A tassel has many pollen-bearing fronds sprouting from a common base. To pull it, one must part the top leaves and grasp it firmly at the base. Then it must be pulled up, with a sharp wrench, which snaps it. If the tassel is pulled down, it usually breaks off short, leaving the base and the start of the fronds hidden inside. These then are a time bomb. They will tassel out after the field is supposedly picked clean. Because she's short, Jackie's upward thrusts are not made with her arm muscles only. They also involve a tightening and jerking of her diaphragm and stomach muscles. One or two rows of work don't bother her. But as the hours of the morning go by, her stomach hurts worse and worse from the repeated jerking.

Added to this is the ache of her arms. The tassels are over her head. She progresses down the rows with her arms up so that her hands are ready for business. But hours of upraised arms is excruciating. Still, if she drops her arms between pulls, it takes forever to finish a row. Worst of all is when there's a field of very tall corn, too high even for tiptoes. Then she must not only jump for the tassel, but pull it out on the upward thrust.

Detasseling sections vary in difficulty. If the person the day before did a good job, the one who follows is lucky. If the predecessor was careless, it's another story. Hardest is when a new field comes into tassel all at once. Then there's a tassel to every stalk, three stalks to a hill, on both sides—for the detasseler covers two rows at once. Jackie can't just walk along, pulling here, pulling there. She must stop, make three individual jerks, swivel, make three more jerks, take a few steps forward to the next set of hills, jerk, jerk, jerk, turn, jerk, jerk, jerk. The tassels form a pale yellow carpet behind her, and the gray path ahead is interminable. Its end, with the milk can of tepid water, is the Holy Grail. As she tassels on and on she feels her stomach cannot last. She will lie down and die between the rows.

Compensation comes the next day, if she can manage to get a section she has thoroughly picked. Then she can gallop along the rows, catching the stray tassel here and there. This is the way it is at the end of the season, too. The crew is down to only a few workers, and they romp though the fields, finishing the day's work by nine or ten in the morning.

The west-side detasseler in Craig's story is afflicted with painful corn burns. Jackie is too, until she learns always to wear a long-sleeved shirt, no matter how tempting it is to take it off and let the air in. Otherwise corn leaves, slashing at the same angle at the insides of her upraised arms, first redden the skin, then make it raw, and finally bring out thin lines of blood.

In the depth of a field there is no way to tell how far she's come, or has yet to go. She can only pray for deliverance. But at last she glimpses the fence, beyond the last two hills, and tumbles out onto the grass. She sprawls there for a few moments — water is only at the starting end — then gets slowly to her feet, takes her bearings, and starts back along two fresh rows. The bearings are important. Detasselers have been known to get mixed up and detassel the necessary male rows or to return in a wrong lane, leaving a female row in full tassel.

While she's detasseling, the crew foreman is policing the field, checking on the efficiency of each worker. Some years he rides the horse, and Jeff wears a muzzle like a kitchen strainer without a handle. It's ignominious to Jackie to have Frank Moore come up behind her and cast down an armload of tassels she's missed. She not only feels chagrin to be doing a mediocre job, she also knows what missing tassels means. To the kids who bicycle out from town, detasseling is just a job. If they're careless, so what? But Jackie has a vested interest in the work. If the state inspector finds more than a tiny percentage of female tassels pollinating in a field, that field is condemned. The work and cost that went into it is not quite for nothing — the corn can be fed to the cows and pigs, as the male corn is — but it's worthless as hybrid seedcorn. Maybe Daddy should give everyone a simple lecture: That a corn plant is both sexes, the tassel male, and the ear with its silk hanging out to catch the pollen, female. Therefore a plant can self-pollinate. But if you plant a field with two different sorts of corn, and pull the tassels off just one sort, then that sort becomes female only, and is pollinated by the tassels of the other sort. The ears that are cross-pollinated result in hybrid vigor, result in much better corn, and that's because ....

Jackie shakes her head. There's so much more to it; even the start isn't that simple. Better just to keep telling all the detasselers that a lost field is a major disaster for the farm, and they better not be the cause of it.

But, in her telling, she has left herself still in the cornfield, on the return trip. She tassels back down the section with dogged determination until finally she bursts forth near the spot she started. There sits the blessed water can, or occasionally a case of cold orange or chocolate, just brought from the dairy. She can empty a half-pint of orange in one long breath. Sometimes the foreman is waiting for her, to direct her to a new section. Sometimes the rest of the crew is lounging there waiting for the stragglers before they all head for another field. If the field is on one of the other farms, they pile into the back of the farm truck. Then the ride is a gratefully received rest, with the wind blowing through Jackie's hair.

And finally, when all the fields have been covered and the job is done for the day, comes the delicious shower in the back hall washroom, which rinses all the grime and sweat and tiredness away.

From the knoll of the Chez Nous yard, Jackie has a view of the detasseled fields. The plumed male corn stands out clearly from the detasseled female. The even pattern of six green rows and two tawny, six green, two tawny, combs over the land. She takes pleasure in the sight. It's a satisfying job, she thinks, detasseling. She knows Craig thinks so, too.

35 ⚔ DON KING

Don King is Jackie's major professor at Beloit College. He grew up on a farm in Connecticut, so that he knows farm work as well as he knows the classics and ancient history and philosophy.

Through Jackie he learns about the farm. He meets Mother and Daddy, and they, with Don's wife Louise, become fast friends. For many summers Don works on the farm as Daddy's corn boss. In all the interstices of work, and often during the work itself, he and Daddy discuss and argue many subjects. They appreciate each other's knowledge, each other's stories, each other's humor.

During Don's first summer on the farm, in 1948, Daddy writes to Jackie who is away:

> Don King is nice to have around. Craig is working with him some. I had him worried the other day. He made some derogatory remark about a truck that was out of condition — "like most things around here." I jumped on him and told him that wasn't the spirit. If more men would hook up a wire instead of letting it flop, etc., if more men would say, I'll fix that instead of cussing those other guys that were always breaking things, everything would be smoother. He came around the next day and said maybe he was out of line, but … which is about as close to admitting himself wrong that he will ever come. In that he's like me — I don't like to admit myself wrong, either.

Fall and spring, Don's small Latin or Greek classes sometimes adjourn to the farm and go through their lessons sitting on hay bales. On his desk in Morse-Ingersoll Hall there's always an ear of hybrid corn, and all the students, along with their professor, keep a kernel of corn softening in a cheek and from time to time worry it with their teeth. It becomes part of a Beloit education in Classics.

Don shakes his head over Daddy's idiosyncrasies. "Roads are for other

Ron Dougan with Don King, Beloit College professor and corn boss.

people to drive on, not Ron," he says. "He drives through fields. It's part of his general disregard for regulations. You learn to be nimble, leaping into a car. He starts when he's ready, even if you're only half in. It's worth your life."

Don is a devout and knowledgeable Roman Catholic, and has the greatest respect for Grampa. "Your grandfather's table blessings are fantastic," he tells Jackie and Craig, for Craig is also his student as well as his comrade in the corn. "Grampa quotes from the Psalms, from the Old Testament and New Testament, for several minutes at a time. You're listening to great literature, yet it's a blessing with emotional sincerity. There is real gratitude to God."

Grampa knows Don King only as a college professor, when Don first comes to the farm. Other Beloit faculty have occasionally worked summers; Grampa has not been impressed with their sinew or their sweat. He takes Don with him to pick sweet corn. Picking corn is something Don grew up doing. He and Grampa pick side by side. Don slows the pace of his picking to keep even with Grampa. After a while Grampa suddenly looks up. "You're the man, and I'm the boy here!" he exclaims.

Don takes this as a compliment. Later he wonders. "I'm thirty-nine," he tells Ron. "Do you suppose that up till now he's thought of me as a boy?"

Daddy says, "Don, at Gramp's age, we're all boys!"

36 ⚹ BARLEY BEARDS

Grampa is 21 when he starts his freshman year at the University of Wisconsin. He's accepted on probation, for in spite of rapid progress at Wayland Academy, he hasn't completed all his high school credits.

A beginning class is Freshman Rhetoric. His professor assigns an essay, "Work—Agreeable or Disagreeable?"

DISAGREEABLE WORK IN BARLEY CULTURE

The enormous amount of barley raised yearly in the United States represents a great deal of disagreeable work, when we realize what a large part of the labor in producing a crop is of the most disagreeable nature.

Let us first consider the grain in the bin, about the last of March, when the farmer begins to get his grain ready for sowing. The grain has to be cleaned through a fanning-mill in order to get all the straws and coarse dirt out so that they will not clog the drill or seeder.

This is not particularly disagreeable. However, after one has worked in the barley dust all day, he will find his head and lungs stopped up and irritated by the dust, which is very injurious to the mucus membrane. Then about the middle or last of April the seeding begins. This is the only work in the entire process that is not dreaded by the farmer.

About three and a half months after the seed is sown the ripe grain is ready for harvesting. Then the really disagreeable work begins. The heads of the golden grain are beautiful with their long beards, but oh! how they feel when the poor laborer gets a head started up the leg of his pantaloons or his sleeve, and in his frantic efforts to stop the seemingly animate creature, crushes it—whereupon thousands of these pieces of beards begin to scratch and prick. Some of them fall down into his shoe and there keep his ankle warm by a continual scratching. Before he has worked long his clothes are filled with these pieces of beards which harass him the rest of the day. By the time harvest is over, which lasts from two to three weeks, the farmer and his help are chafed and scratched from head to foot.

These wounds are hardly healed when the barley has been in the shock long enough to dry and must be put into the barn or stack. The beards crumble worse now because they are dry and more brittle. During the drawing in of the barley everyone has to eat and sleep in beards as they are everywhere, in their clothes, in their hair, ears, and even in their mouth and eyes. However there has to be something done when a beard gets into an eye, as it can become very serious if not attended to at once.

There is no more trouble with the terrible barley until it is time to thresh it. This "caps the climax" as the grain is dry and dusty. The threshing machine breaks the beards up very fine and all the hands around the job have to inhale this dust. Also it finds its way into ones ears and eyes. In the eyes it can cause inflammation and sometimes blindness.

The next time the barley has to be handled is for selling. This is a dusty and disagreeable task but as the money is so near the farmer does not feel this very badly. However, it does make him rather gloomy when he is obliged to go through all these hardships and hard work, then receive only 35 or 40 cents a bushel for his barley. For it is as low and even lower than this, some seasons.

Jackie finds this essay heartfelt. She would suggest only one addition. What makes a barley beard so animate, so lethal? She knows from personal experience. One once got inside her shorts, and worked its way into a tender and unmentionable place. And Daddy had to have an operation on a salivary gland; instead of the suspected tumor they found a barley seed. For barley operates like a porcupine quill — every grain ends in a whisker with a tiny barb on it, and that barb causes the kernel to creep forward, indeed like a living creature. It's nature's way of spreading the seed. But perhaps Grampa's professor didn't miss an explanation; most likely everyone then, city or country, was familiar with barley.

Grampa's professor gives him a B on his essay; later he receives an A in the class. That, and other good grades in other classes, take him off probation. He does well in his whole college career — so well that at its finish he is chosen to be one of the graduation speakers for the class of 1895. He speaks on the wonders of the earth, but not on barley. And he remains devoted to the university, and working with it, for his entire life.

37 ⚜ SUCKERS

Patsy is thirteen, Jackie twelve, Craig ten. It's a hot summer day and Grampa needs help. He and Daddy have discovered one of the fields of hybrid seed corn is full of suckers. A sucker is a superfluous stalk that grows up from the root of a corn plant. Suckers don't usually get tall. In corn destined for silage, a sucker here and there doesn't matter, but in a field of hybrid seed, suckers can be time bombs.

For hybrid vigor depends on cross fertilization. The tassels are removed from all corn plants designated female. They cannot self-pollinate; every kernel on every ear must be pollinated by the corn planted alongside that has been designated male, and bears a tassel. But if the female plants have suckers, the stunted suckers can grow unnoticed in a field, achieve maturity, tassel out, and pollinate their own female corn. The field will be ruined for seed purposes. A great deal of money will be lost.

In the field Grampa has discovered, the corn is not yet very tall. The suckers are short, but he wants to be rid of them at once. He's reluctant to take men off other jobs. He seeks out his grandchildren.

Two of Craig's friends have ridden their bikes from town. The three boys and Patsy and Jackie listen to Grampa's plight and agree to pull suckers.

"This is a paying job, isn't it?" asks Ed Grutzner.

"It ought to be," says John Eldred.

Craig relays the question to Grampa.

Grampa nods. "When the field is clean, I'll pay you what you're worth," he tells his recruits. He leads them to the corn rows, shows them what a sucker is and how to pull it, and stresses the importance of getting all of every sucker. Then he leaves them.

The five get to work, and quickly discover that pulling suckers is not easy. They have to examine every stalk of each three-stalk hill, remove any suckers by snapping them sharply at the base, then go on to the next hill. At first they stand and bend, but before long that proves too back-breaking. They kneel, and crawl from hill to hill. The sun beats down. There is no shade. Sweat pours into their ears; their clothes stick to them. They are plagued by flies and by tiny midges that go straight for their eyes; once in a while there is even a horsefly. Their knees become bruised and black.

The field is endless. The hours go by. But at last the final sucker has been eliminated, and they wearily report to Grampa. He leads them all back and checks their work. "You have done a thorough job," he says approvingly. "Hold out your hands." He reaches in his pocket and pulls out a fistful of quarters.

Grampa looking for suckers?

He places a quarter in each grimy palm. The troop wait expectantly for Grampa to go around again, and again, doling out quarters, but he doesn't. He puts the rest back in his pocket, twinkles at them, and says, "Thank you, cubbies! Go help yourselves to chocolate milk." Then he departs to continue supervising other workers.

The five stare at their quarters. They look at each other in disbelief. Then the sweaty, disheveled crew storms the office. Daddy is there. He stops his work to listen to their outrage. His own children do the talking; John and Ed stand aloof, but look aggrieved.

"Four hours!" Patsy cries. "We worked four hours in the hot sun, and we got every single sucker!"

"For only a quarter!" Jackie adds.

"He said he'd pay us what we were worth," Craig says witheringly.

"Maybe that is all you're worth," Daddy says, but he's laughing. "There were still five suckers in that field." He grins at his own joke, but no one else finds it funny.

Daddy reaches into a desk drawer and gives them each another quarter, and then a dollar. "There," he says. "Detasseling wages, slightly over. Your grampa is a Scotsman, remember. He squeezes a buffalo nickel so hard it needs a laxative."

Craig and his friends and Jackie are mollified, and go for chocolate milk. Patsy goes too, but she's not about to forgive. Grampa's words have struck her to the core.

"So that's what he thinks I'm worth," she glowers. Every time she re-members, her mood darkens all over again. She takes it personally. She feels diminished.

She stays mad at Grampa for a long, long time until she is old enough to realize that it is a generational thing — that when Grampa was a boy, he'd have been paid a quarter for a whole day's work, and when Daddy was a boy, hired on as Assistant Herdsman, he'd earned a man's wages, a dollar a day, even though that was probably not what he was worth — especially once he broke his heels and couldn't work at all. With this perspective, Patsy is at last able to feel charitable toward Grampa. He must have thought that he was be-ing generous, that she and all of them were being paid well. And you do have to make allowances, too, for buffalo squeezers.

38 ⚜ KILDEER

Craig is sixteen. Daddy has pulled him off the detasselling crew to mow hay. Craig is happy with the switch. He loves to drive the horses, Buck and Barney. They are the final team on the farm, and Grampa likes to keep them busy. Craig enjoys sitting on the cupped seat balanced between the large light wheels of the little mower. He likes managing the long mower arm. It sticks off to the side at a right angle a few inches above the ground. On its forward edge are two staggered rows of sharp steel teeth. The motion of the mower activates the cogs that activate the teeth to move rapidly back and forth, so that the hay, and anything else unfortunate enough to be in the pathway, is instantly severed.

Craig keeps a careful eye on the arm so that it fells a continuous swath and leaves no wispy edges behind. At the end of the row he raises the arm almost straight up, turns the team, lines them up, and starts them along the next side of the square. The noise is no more than the plodding of the horses, the clickety-clickety of the mower, and the sigh of the falling grass. Bees hum, butterflies hover, and in the sunny sky the kildeer cry, "Kildee! Kildee! Kildee!" The uncut hay smells fresh, while the cut hay shriveling in the sun is already sending up the most exquisite of scents found on any farm; found, indeed, anywhere. It's a pleasant job, and one that requires skill. Craig takes pride in how well he mows.

Ahead of the horses a bird suddenly stumbles out of the alfalfa. It's brown and white, with two black bands on its white throat. It staggers and flutters across the cut rows, dragging one useless wing and crying piteously.

"Whoa!" yells Craig.

The horses stop obediently. He climbs off the little seat and walks ahead. He peers into the alfalfa from whence the bird sprang, carefully parting the foliage here and there. In a moment he finds what he's looking for, a kildeer nest. It's in a slight depression on the ground and has four buff-colored, blotched eggs in it. Off across the stubble the mother is still putting on an excellent crippled-bird act.

Craig returns to the mower. He backs the team, detours past the nest, and slants back into the standing hay beyond it. When he returns on the next round the kildeer again leaps and staggers from her nest. Again Craig detours. The next trip he veers to the other side, so that a small uneven island of alfalfa is left surrounding the nest. He continues mowing the field. One side of it, with its island and its raggedy edge, makes a messy-looking job.

At noon he drives back to the round barn. Grampa and Daddy are coming from the milkhouse. They have a view of Craig's distant hayfield, for the land between slopes down to the crick. Craig stops in time to hear Grampa say, "Ronald, if Craig can't mow any better than that, you'd best put him back onto detasselling. We can always find a man."

Daddy cocks his head at Craig. Craig climbs down from the mower and explains about the nest.

"You know that gully area across the tracks?" Daddy asks. "Where the soil is shallow and some rocks come to the surface?"

Craig nods.

"Well, I was about your age, bouncing along on some machine or other, when I saw a kildeer acting peculiar. So I got off and found the nest. I was so surprised—it wasn't in any vegetation or camouflaged, but the eggs lay there on the gravel looking just like pebbles. I went back and got my new box camera and took a picture. I was so proud of that little black and white print when it came back!" He spells Craig's explanation to Grampa.

"Let's go see," says Grampa.

The three walk down the lane, splash across the crick, and go up the rise to the hayfield. As they approach the island the kildeer staggers out across the cut hay, dragging her injured wing and crying. Craig parts the stems and shows Grampa and Daddy the clutch of speckled eggs.

"Poor little frightened mother!" croons Grampa. "Doing your best to protect your eggs!"

Craig doesn't lose his job as mower.

39 ⚜ RONALD PART 7 ⚜
PRACTICALITIES

Ronald's letter describing Vera, and proposing a French wedding is in the mail. Wesson, meanwhile, is answering an earlier letter, pushing Ag School with all his rhetorical ability.

In regard to your growing impatience to get at the actual job of living and doing I will say: "Steady, boy." I am as deeply interested in these problems of yours as you are. However, I am taking a long view.

Your B.A. or a B.S. even an M.S. will not be of much worth. The world seldom asks what degree you have but is constantly putting the question, "What can you do?" and "What do you know?" Only the knowledge and efficiency that is acquired in getting the degree counts.

To put in a year at miscellaneous studies to get a degree would not pay. But two more years at studies that will quicken your mind, broaden your vision, give principles upon which to act, and bring you into touch with the minds that are leading in agricultural development, would be well spent. The agricultural field is so big, opportunities so varied and rewards so great to the men who are thoroughly prepared that I feel you cannot put too much emphasis upon preparation. All of this need not, indeed cannot, be gotten in school—but the foundation in schooling is essential.

It would be a calamity for you to plunge into actual farming and breeding without more school. Your plan of finishing at N.W. then after a few years take superficial work at Madison is no good. Here is a program both work-able and valuable, but let us first put aside the question of long engagements. One kind is where the parties want to play around a little longer without the responsibility of married life—or where they are not sure of their choice. The other kind is where the engaged parties know their choice is right and realize the great responsibilities of life together. They clearly see their future and the need of thorough preparation. Such long engagements are enjoyable. You can enjoy each other's work and come to your life with happy confidence.

For now your program should be: (1) Spend the entire summer traveling in Europe. I am getting letters of introduction for you. You have second cousins in England a plenty. I do not know how you would fare in Scotland or Ireland. Hardly think they would own you. (2) Return in time to get into the Agricultural School. Major in Economics, minor in Animal Husbandry. I would not be surprised if you could finish in $1^1/2$ years.

But that, continues his father, isn't important. What is, is that two years of Ag School would contribute more to his son's start in farming than five years without further school. The two of them could fix definite plans for herd development, the school would help them. Ron, nearby, would be in close touch with the work — keeping records, selecting families, etc. He could keep the books of the farm, and apply the economic principles he learns in school to the farm's problems. "Your close touch with the practical, the incentive of working toward a real home, and the inspiration that V is watching your work and progress would make you an outstanding student. This training and prestige would put you in line to be not only a noted breeder and successful milk producer but a famous judge of stock and an authority on economic problems."

W.J. projects a fantasy:

This statement could appear as a news item. "Congress has authorized a commission to study world problems in agriculture. It is to be composed of experts and practical farmers. The selection on this commission of R.A. Dougan of the Dougan Guernsey Farm, Beloit, Wis. is especially fitting. Mr. Dougan is preeminently fitted to render this service. His academic work was taken at N.W. and the University of Wisconsin. He has lived and worked in France and traveled throughout Europe. He is a thorough student, a keen observer, and above all a practical, successful farmer."

He adds, "Then there are opportunities in everyday experiences that can come only to the thoroughly prepared." He makes a family comparison: "Your cousin Roger was to take a course at Ames, then get married. On the spur of the moment he married and plunged into farming. He has made a failure — spent lots of money and made none. He is short in training and education. You stand little better chance if you do not hold down to getting prepared. These two years will glide by very fast if the life is full and satisfying and with so large a prospect in the future."

And returning to his fantasy:

> I forgot an important part of that news item, i.e., "The purpose of this commission is to coordinate and regulate world agriculture so as to ensure an adequate food supply and better the conditions of all tillers of the soil. The American committee will cooperate with similar committees from all leading nations. They will visit and study China, India, S. Africa, Australia and Europe as well as N. and S. America. It is expected the work will require two years."
>
> This is fanciful, but movements of this nature are sure to be necessary. The difficulty is going to be to find big enough men to do the work.
>
> On the practical side: the finances of the farm are still holding good. If they were not, I could not give my family what I am giving them. You and Trever called pretty heavily on me last year. I only saved $500. It was a very good year so far as the farm was concerned but my personal expenses were big. I am enclosing a statement for you to study. Note that the nominal salary allowed is arbitrary. I have actually had from the farm this year over $4000: that includes cash, living, etc. Besides this I have had the interest on the money invested in the place.
>
> Here is what we may expect of the farm year after year:
> 1. It can pay a normal interest on investment of 6%.
> 2. Pay all expenses for supplies, repairs, feed necessary to balance rations and upkeep of soil and buildings.
> 3. Pay $7000 to $8000 for labor.
> 4. Pay one manager $3000 to $4000 for his cash salary.
> 5. Furnish a considerable portion of the living for help and manager.
> Now you see as we increase the managerial expense we must decrease the labor expense for the place cannot stand more than $12,000 for the whole labor and management.

"You ask what is the matter with labor! It is the fool age that pays for trash rather than for things of value." W.J. cites brothers who left his employ for a dance band, at four times his salary, and a fraction of labor hours. "No wonder such boys are discontent with farm work when any fool can do things like they do and the fool public thinks they are getting their money's worth."

This is not the letter Ron wanted, but then, his father has not yet caught up to what is happening in France.

40 ⚹ GARY WALLACE

I t's early afternoon on a July day in 1939. Gary Wallace, thirteen years old and a Beloit boy, is trudging along Colley Road toward town. He's put in a seven-hour morning in the Dougan cornfields.

Today has been an especially rough one. The boys were instructed to bring along any sort of sharp knife, and after detasseling they went through the fields cutting suckers. Gary doesn't really understand why these short stalks must be removed, but Ron Dougan says they are dangerous and can contaminate a whole field. So suckers must go.

Gary has to lean over to cut them. The constant bending becomes so difficult that he tries staying permanently bent. But in a very short time this makes his back feel as though it were breaking in two. Before the job is done he's crawling on all fours and gibbering to himself.

Now, going home, he's hot, dirty, kneesore, footsore, and corn-burned on both arms. His shoulders droop with weariness. He scuffs gravel, not for fun but because it's too much effort to pick up his feet. He doesn't care if he sees another corn stalk ever again.

A pickup truck spits to a stop beside him. "Going to town, sonny?" calls a stranger. "I'll give you a lift."

Gary eyes the truck. It has ladders and pressure painting equipment in the back, and appears to be local. The man is not a farmer.

"Okay," says Gary, and climbs in gratefully. The truck roars off.

"Say," says the man, "I need a helper. I'm doing a paint job down on Broad Street. I'll pay you three dollars an hour."

Three dollars an hour! Gary's heart leaps. That's undreampt of riches. He's only getting thirty-five cents an hour from Dougans. There must be a catch.

"What do I have to do?" he asks warily.

"It's a breeze—just move the hoses and ladders for me, and generally be my assistant. Do you need to go home first? You can start right now."

"Okay," says Gary, dazzled.

The man drives to the spot, a group of tanks next to Burman's used car lot. Gary helps the man get his equipment out and ready. Then they start to spray paint the tanks silver. There's a high wind out and the paint blows. Gary thinks this isn't a very economical way to paint; too much is lost between the nozzle and the surface. His boss really ought to wait for a still day. But his not to reason why; three dollars is three dollars. And it's easy work. He rejoices in his new employment and frequently estimates his earnings.

Several hours go by. A thought strikes him. "Is this job just for this afternoon?" he asks. "Or is it permanent?"

"As permanent as you want to make it," grins the man. "You're doing fine."

Just then a squad car pulls up. Two policemen climb out. "Okay, Tip," says one. "We've caught up with you again. Come on."

"You guys keep harassing me!" protests Gary's employer. "This is a legit job! What've I done? Just tell me, what've I done?"

"Lately?" says the other cop. "Look at those cars, for starters."

Gary looks too. There's a film of silver paint on the windward side of every car in the adjacent used car lot.

"So let's get on down to the station," says the first cop.

"What about me?" Gary manages to croak.

"You run on home," the cop says. "This is between us and Tip here."

Gary hurries off. At first he's relieved that as one of the guilty painters he's not being held. But the closer he gets to home, the madder he gets. He's worked almost four hours. Tip owes him twelve dollars. He wants his pay! He'll track Tip to the ends of the earth and demand it!

He bursts into the house but before he can open his mouth his mother gasps. "Look at you! What in heaven's name have they been having you do, out there at the farm? Even your hair!"

Gary looks in a mirror. He hadn't realized it was happening at all, but he's coated from head to toe with silver paint. He resembles the Tin Woodman.

He blurts out his injustices to his family. They all advise him not to pursue his vanished wages.

"Be thankful you didn't get hauled in, too," says his mother.

"Chalk it up to experience," says his father. "And watch out for operators."

"The turpentine's in the basement," says his older brother.

Gary seethes as he wipes silver paint off his skin, but decides he'd be wise to take his father's advice.

The next morning he walks out to the Dougan Farm again. The breeze ruffles his still-silvery hair. He knows there are no suckers to cut today, they've all been cut. There's often orange drink or chocolate milk at the end of a section. And in the rows there's plenty of time to think. He can think about something he'll invent, a big machine on which a line of detasselers can just ride though the fields in comfort, pulling tassels at waist level while they joke back and forth.

He whistles. Detasseling at thirty-five cents an hour doesn't seem such a bad job after all.

41 ⚜ WELL

The whole life of the farm depends on a one-hundred foot well that goes down into limestone and yields about five gallons a minute. The well is adjacent to the Big House kitchen. It has been faithful since Grampa bought the farm, but for a long time it's been inadequate. Now, in 1934, with business increasing in spite of the Depression, Grampa and Daddy decide to dig a new well.

The site is on the other side of the Big House, the west side. The well-digging company brings in its huge equipment, and the drilling begins. They are putting in a six-inch pipe.

Jackie and her siblings are fascinated. Children aren't allowed close, but standing on Grama's lawn they can watch the big drill rising and falling, and hear the regular muffled thump. They can see the auger, and glimpse what it brings up. At first it is soil, and Daddy keeps samples in glass bottles, in a row on the sill of the Big House porch, each with the depth of where it was found, and the date. Then limestone starts coming up.

At mealtimes in the Little House Daddy reports on the progress. The well has gone down a hundred feet, and is into the limestone. It has gone down 150 feet, 160, 170. It's still in limestone. Daddy and Grampa start to worry. How deep must they go? The bit keeps pounding.

Finally at two-hundred feet the bit breaks through the limestone into the St. Peter sandstone. The drill goes down another thirty feet, and there is a gush of water beyond everyone's wildest expectations. Daddy sets up a pump on the side of the well. Pumping as fast as it can, it pumps out 200 gallons per minute, with no appreciable lowering of the water table. They have tapped into one of the finest aquifers in the area. The farm now has a permanent, plentiful supply of excellent water.

Al Capps, a farmhand, reports later to Jackie, that the well pumped water into a pressure tank under the house. "At the changeover to the new well, we had to fill every container up before they pulled the pipe, and then work all night to get things reconnected!"

Daddy and Grampa install a submersible pump in the new well, with the motor to run the pump at the top. Any time the pressure in the pump tank falls to below thirty pounds, the motor kicks on. They keep the old well complete with its motor and pump as an auxiliary, in case anything goes wrong with the pumping equipment of the new well. But they rarely have to use it.

Grama clucks over the torn up ground around the new well. She beautifies it with a willow tree and bushes and petunias. But Butter gets loose and nibbles everything down to the nub. This is the last straw for the pet goat, whose previous sins have been legion. She's removed to a farm that has other goats. Jackie regrets losing her, but has known for a long time that another misstep would lead to Butter's expulsion. Eating Grama's well-garden is a major misstep. But Butter is happy in her new home and eventually has triplets. Jackie and her sibs visit her and her babies.

Daddy tries, but is unsuccessful in getting a complete set of core samples. However, the auger has brought up enough pure white sandstone to make the most splendid sandpile the Dougan kids have ever had. It looks like sugar heaped alongside the sidewalk where the walk passes the milkhouse, and is shaded by a lilac bush. The four spend many hours playing there, occasionally tossing out a sandy cat dropping, for the farm cats find the new sand attractive, too.

Some time later, word comes that such sand is perhaps dangerous — the grains are sharp silica and might damage lungs. But by then, sandpile play is over, with lungs none the worse. As to the old well, various machineries for refrigeration and power are installed in its well head, and used until they are outdated or replaced elsewhere. Then it's covered over and its machinery, and all the pumps and generators that were added over the years, are forgotten.

42 ⚹ THREE MOLDY CHEERS

It's late on a blistering July morning. Daddy is the corn detasseling boss; he's following behind the crew to make sure they aren't missing any tassels. He emerges from the end of a section to find Nordy Gage, son of the Beloit College treasurer, and six other town boys collapsed on the grass beside the fence.

Nordy, who will grow up to become a prosperous pig farmer on Majorca, turns his head and half opens his eyes. "Let's give three moldy cheers for Ron Dougan," he murmurs feebly, and the boys faintly echo, "Hurrah. Hurrah. Hurrah."

Ronald can't recall a time he ever was cheered before. He's not sure this is one to take home and brag about.

43 ❈ RONALD PART 8 ❈
DAD, I AM A MAN

In Ronald's next letter, three days after his thunderbolt of March 4, 1924, he puts himself in his parents' place:

> I imagine myself with a boy half a world away making such important steps, and am wondering how I'd feel. I'd wonder if I knew the boy well enough to have confidence in his good judgment and his ability to direct his course for his future happiness. I'd wonder what affect being away from home, perhaps loneliness, would have upon him. I'd wonder if he were not letting circumstances and proximity run away with him. I'd wonder if it were the girl, or the sympathy and companionship that had captivated him.
>
> Of course you are thinking about me. You are balancing what you know about my level headedness against my known changeableness and boyishness. You have your hopes and fears about V. I wish I could reassure you—if we only had a few days together! I'm not thinking only of the present, Dad. I have absolutely no fear. I have found what I want. The happiness of the future will be our work and play together.
>
> Know that it isn't proximity, or loneliness, or impulsiveness that has directed my course. Know that I could have followed every precept you or Mother have laid down, and in no single instance would V have fallen short. My ideal for a wife has slowly evolved, based on your teachings. Nearly every girl I have known has added something. V exceeds my dreams of the composite girl. That sounds pretty flowery, but I am sure I shall always think so—you wouldn't have me feel differently, would you?
>
> But as to my plans—I want your full approval of what I have about decided to do, of course. I know I have it.

At this point in the letter, Ronald's tone changes:

> First, I can't go on preparing for my work by more education if it means I have

to do it alone. The idea of fraternity or boarding house life for another year is unthinkable. Still, I feel the need of more methodical preparation. If that means delaying starting my home, I am ready to go to work immediately and get my future education from reading and study on my own.

As to time, we save the expected and necessary preparations. V's family would want a church wedding. I'd need to entertain my school friends—more expense and time. I'd much rather get back after the shouting had died down, and be ready to hit my work.

I have practically decided that we will be married this summer. My thinking is sound. I want you to di-

Dad, I am a man.

rect me as you think best about school or work. You can count on me to hit either for everything there is in me. Dad, I am a man. I'm thinking as a man, and I appreciate it that you realize it, and treat me as such.

Lovingly, Ron

Now it is March 13:

Your good letter in answer to my first one about farming arrived Sunday. I read it to Vera before I had read it over to myself. Don't think there are many sons who would feel sure of their Dad's understanding of their situation and of dealing with it so perfectly that they would feel safe to do that. As it is, you grow in my estimation every day—maybe because I am beginning to see more fully what a man you are. You put things so clearly—it makes me ashamed to attempt to write. Your ideas flow smoothly. Mine are a staccato type written best in broken sentences.

I am very sure, Dad, that farming is what I want to do. About having the tenacity to stick it out—I am tired of doing things by halves. I want to work at the dirtiest end of everything on the farm. I will stick to it until I have the knowledge and ability to take any job and do it expertly.

"V exceeds my dreams of the composite girl."

As to his school, "Just as three years of Liberal Arts seems foolish to the average farmer, so would a continuation along that line after I've decided to farm, strike him as abysmally dumb." But, he reasons, the training won't harm, he'll be able to converse with scholarly men, and his father's liberal college work and ministry have made him more than the average farmer. For his own self respect, and to keep pace with V, he needs the world of thought, of literature. And it fits with farming—he names leaders in agriculture with broad backgrounds behind their farming.

Ronald gives a final thought. He made a reasonable record at Northwestern, but left with quite a blot. For his own satisfaction he wants to carry a stiff program successfully. He also thinks he'll be able to pick up nearly a semester of lame credit.

> About Madison—don't you think my work there better come after I have formed some ideas about farming and cattle? Now I would go as a sponge. After a year or two of the practical, under your tutelage, I could take work there and accept the professors as colleagues. I would have ideas to talk over with them, and by keeping my mind open to truth, be able to rearrange my thinking, cull, and make additions to a structure that was already scaffolded.

But now, W.J. has received the letter of March 4. He writes in the margins. His remark on Vera's approving the plan is, "What about her people?" and on the pooling of resources, "You can't do it and maintain your self respect. If you were both in school and of the same age it might be worked. This way, she would be the breadwinner." And on March 22 he sends a chilling cablegram:

PLAN NOT APPROVED DAD

44 ❧ I WISHT I WAS A LITTLE ROCK

Grampa has a little poem he recites every now and then. Jackie and Craig and Patsy and Joan always laugh, no matter how many times they hear it. It's one of the rituals. Grampa shouts, his face creased with merriment:

> I wisht I was a little rock
> A-settin' on a hill,
> A-doin' nothin' all day long
> 'Cept jest a-settin' still.
> I wouldn't sleep, I wouldn't eat,
> I wouldn't even wash.
> I'd jest set there a hundred years
> An' rest myself, b'gosh!

Does Wesson want his son to join in farming with him, or to stand alone?

And then Grampa shakes with silent laughter.

Grampa doesn't rest very much, himself, which may be why he recites the poem. Sometimes he gets discouraged about the constant work and worries. Back in 1926 he writes to Trever, on the track team at the University of Wisconsin:

> We have a close year ahead of us. The running expenses are continually getting higher and the income is shrinking, so it is nip and tuck to make ends meet. With any reverse it would put us in bad shape. You see I am needing to apply the very principle to my business I preach to you in your races. I believe I can win but it is hard to keep myself in training on a 20 year stretch and then for another 20 years. There can be no let up in training in life's game. Should I relax for a single month my business would feel it and should I grow careless for a year I would be busted.

And a year later, he writes, after telling Trever how interested he is in his track work:

> I am going to start training soon, tomorrow or next day. I am going to put in 11 hours a day at straight work. Not allow myself to loiter or loaf. We fall down a lot in the winter. We get careless and let things go. I have not done regular work for months. I will be as sore as you are when I start training.

All the years of Daddy and Grampa's partnership are harmonious ones. Grampa is in charge of the farm business, with help and advice from his son. Ronald is in charge of the milk business, with help and advice from his father. Ronald overcomes his father's conservatism somewhat, and Grampa, in turn, is able to curb somewhat his son's enthusiasm for plunging into things. They are a good balance. In a 1937 note to W.J., in discussing some farm policy or action, Ronald tells his father that whatever he plans to do is okay with him, and he supports him. He says, "I feel much the same about you as I do about Vera. A while ago she read me about a contest where men were supposed to write, in 200 words or less, what they liked in a wife. I said, 'That's too many words,' and she bristled, 'Couldn't you write 200 words about me?' I said, 'I need only five—I like what I got!'"

When Grampa retires and moves to the edge of town, he doesn't really retire. He comes out every day and is a trial to his farm manager, by still deciding what should be done, and countermanding orders. He works as hard as ever. He quotes to Ronald from the Book of John, about the two of them: "You must increase, but I must decrease," but he never really accepts or believes in his heart that he is going to be decreasing.

There's only one time Daddy gets angry at Grampa, and that is about Grampa's overexerting. It's in the summer of 1948; Grampa is almost eighty; the temperature is in the nineties. Daddy has been working in the Chez Nous seed house. There are several huge heaps of grass seed on the concrete floor; he's been inoculating and mixing the seed, turning it over and over with a shovel. He leaves for a short while; when he returns Grampa is there. He has stripped down to his summer cotton long underwear, sweat is streaming from his red face, and he is turning over seed with the heavy grain shovel. When he sees his son he straightens up, leans on the handle and says, "Ronald, I don't think I should be working so hard anymore."

Daddy blows up. He wrests the shovel from Grampa, makes him sit down on a pile of feed sacks, slams out a series of exasperated notes on whatever paper bags and scraps are lying around. His handwriting is so large and heavy it scores the paper beneath. The dots on the i's pierce right through the paper. Daddy's side of the conversation is, "You are a hard man to handle!" "Nobody's making you overdo!" "You won't let me lighten things up for you!" "You are no good to any of us dead and not to take a noon break at your age in this heat is just poor sense!" "Leave things to me!" "Go in the house and get some dinner and rest!" "By 2:30 we'll have some of the snarl out of the job. I'll send Pete up. You can do with him as you please!"

Grampa, shaken, puts on his clothes and goes meekly into the house. He lets Mother give him a cool drink and lunch. He lies down a while, then sits and chats. Refreshed, he returns to the seed house mid-afternoon. By that time several workers are there, Daddy is long done stamping and storming around, and all is serene. Daddy writes to his father in a gentler hand, "I didn't mean to upset you. But you are so infernally on the go!" Grampa laughs and shakes his head.

For Grampa is always on the go. He has a fast shamble that's unmistakably Grampa. You can tell it's him no matter how far away he is. Besides walking so fast, he walks at an angle, leaning forward, as into a strong gale.

Once, many years before the angry day, Ronald asks his father, "Daddy, why do you walk so fast?"

Jackie overhears the answer.

"Why, I have to, Ronald! If I didn't, I'd fall over!"

45 ⚜ GOD'S FOOTSTOOL

The worst thing Jackie ever sees with her own eyes, and which will haunt her to the end of her life, is the dog.

Town people are always leaving things in the country. They are always leaving garbage in the ditches, and old washing machines. They are always leaving animals: well animals, sick animals, baby animals—especially sick and baby animals. They drive out to the country and leave cats in the ditch, boxes of kittens in the ditch. They leave litters of puppies. They drive slow and open a door and shove a dog out of the car and drive away fast while the dog runs and runs after them till it can't run anymore. They don't care if the dog or the kittens or the pups die, they just want to be rid of them. Those that care a little bit make the drop near a farm, so that the kittens might be found. So that the dog will show up whimpering and wagging its tail at the back door. The town people must figure, "Any farm can use another dog or cat. Cats and dogs are no trouble on a farm." Once, in the night, somebody had driven right into the dairy and closed a dog inside Grampa and Grama's screen porch. They'd found it there the next morning, curled up on the mat. It had thumped its tail tentatively, had looked up with beseeching eyes. But that isn't the dog that is the worst thing Jackie ever sees.

She's eight. The family has a dog, Jip. Jip is a mongrel, tan and white. They all love Jip. Jip likes to lie under Daddy's feet at night when he reads, and have Daddy use him for a footstool. Grampa and Grama have a dog, too. Bounce is a rat terrier. Maybe Grama loves Bounce, but Bounce is not an easy dog to love.

One day Jackie and Craig are up on the flat part of the milkhouse roof. They notice a dog out on the road. It's walking strangely, in a weaving, erratic pattern. Its head hangs down. It's far away but even at a distance Jackie can tell it's just skin and bones. It seems to have something very wrong with it. A car comes by; the dog is near the middle of the road but doesn't shy away. The car swerves around it. The dog stumbles on.

"Let's go see what's the matter with it," Craig says.

Jackie feels uneasy. "Let's find somebody," she says.

They climb from the roof and go down the stairs. The dairy office is a room at the end of the Big House. Daddy is at his desk, working the adding machine. Jackie watches his fingers skip around on the numbers till he comes to the end of a column, gives a large crank for the adding up, and pauses.

"Daddy," says Jackie, "there's a dog in the road and something's wrong with it."

"It acts like it can't see and can't hear," says Craig.

"It's terribly skinny," says Jackie.

Daddy puts down his pencil and pushes back his chair. "Let's go have a look," he says. "Somebody's probably dumped it and it's sick."

They go outside. Grampa is just coming along the sidewalk to the office. He's in a hurry about something. Daddy spells to him, and he looks to the road, where the dog is still stumbling. He joins them. The four of them approach the dog.

Daddy keeps up a quiet conversation with the animal as they get closer. The dog stops, stands still, as if he hears the gentle words, as if he's waiting.

"He at least can hear," whispers Craig.

"Stay back, cubbies," Grampa says to Craig and Jackie. "The poor beast may have rabies. He may bite."

They get closer yet.

"Jackie, Craig, get back to the house!" Daddy orders suddenly. But it's too late. Jackie stands rigid. She has seen, too. There's no danger from this dog. This dog won't bite. This dog can't bite. His jaws have been sewn together with a thick cord, from lip to lip, all around his mouth. He can't open his mouth to eat, to drink, to pant, to bark. The holes in the dog's lips are lacerated and loose where the cord goes through, but the cord is tight. The holes aren't bloody. The cord has been in too long.

Grampa and Daddy don't send them away. Daddy kneels by the dog and strokes its head. Grampa stands with one arm tight around Jackie's shoulder, with his other arm tight around Craig's. Jackie is shaking against Grampa's body.

"Poor, poor little fellow," Grampa says. "Poor, poor little cubbies." His voice is stranger than Jackie has ever heard it.

Daddy cradles the dog's head in his hands, gazes into his face. "Look," says Daddy without turning around. His voice is as strange as Grampa's. "You can both look. Look at his eyes." With one hand he spells over his shoulder to

Grampa.

They come very close. They kneel and look into the dog's eyes. Jackie sees the dog's pupils. There is a hole right in the center of each one. It must have been made by a pin or a needle. She feels vomit rise in her throat, and swallows hard.

Grampa's grip on Jackie's shoulder is even tighter. "He's been blinded, too," Grampa says.

"There are some people that slow torture is not good enough for," says Daddy softly. "I'm sorry that you children had to see this. But since you did, I wanted you to see it all."

Craig is crying. "We can save him, can't we, Daddy? You'll cut the string, won't you?"

Daddy shakes his head. "He's too far gone. And he's so hurt he may bite if I do that. I'll take him and give him a drink; I think I can do it with a straw. And then I'll drive him up to Janesville. Doctor Knilans will put him out of his misery. He won't have much longer to suffer."

He stands up, spells to Grampa. The dog stands with his head down.

"I'll take the cubbies," Grampa says. Daddy leads the dog by the loose hair on his neck to the dairy. Grampa takes Jackie and Craig across the road, alongside the garden beside the currant bushes, into the orchard. They sit down under an apple tree, one on each side of Grampa. Grampa keeps his arms around them. Craig cries and cries against Grampa's side. Jackie's horror is too deep for tears. She keeps shaking convulsively, pressed close to Grampa's work shirt.

Grampa croons to them, making little comforting noises. After a while he starts talking. He tells them about kind people and cruel people. He says cruelty to animals is one of the worst kinds of cruelty because animals are dumb creatures and are at the mercy of their owners. He says cruel people are usually that way because others have been cruel to them.

"But you'll be the sort who will hate cruelty and help cruel people to learn to be kind," Grampa says. "Because you are treated kindly, and loved, and every day you see animals being treated kindly."

Grampa's talking helps. Craig gradually stops crying. Jackie gradually stops shaking. Grampa says, "Yes, ours is a special responsibility. Those of us who have been given so much have a responsibility to give much."

He gets up. He finds three windfalls in the grass. "Here," he says, giving them each an apple and biting into one himself. Together they go through the garden to the Big House, get sugar cookies from the cookie jar, and go to the milkhouse for chocolate milk. They sit on the old well lid outside the milkhouse to drink their milk.

Craig takes Grampa's pencil and paper out of his work shirt pocket and writes, "Are there dogs in heaven?"

Jackie waits anxiously for the answer.

Grampa ponders the paper for a long time. Then his eyes crinkle and he laughs silently.

"Do you know what I think?" Grampa says. "I think that dog will trot right up to God's throne. And then he'll curl up—just like Jip does with your daddy—and let God use him for a footstool."

Joan, Patsy, Jackie, and Craig wait with Jip for the school cab.

46 ⚔ WHEN MY COUNTRY CALLS

In the early sixties, near the start of the Kennedy administration, Daddy sits in his office and types a joint letter to his far-flung children — two of whom are Republicans and two Democrats — and to his friend, Don King. Don, a Democrat, had many a long and good natured political discussion with Daddy when Don was at Beloit College as a professor and, in the summer, when he was Daddy's corn boss. Daddy writes:

Dear Joan, Patsy, Jackie, Craig, ancillary connections, issue, and my spiritual son, Don King — Hail!

I wanted you all to know that your paternal ancestor yields in patriotism to no man, and wanted to get it on the record. When it comes to what I can do for my country I am in the front rank, volunteering my all in response to her urgent requests. (Of course I am a little apprehensive about what my country is doing TO me.)

When that great Boston agriculturalist [John F. Kennedy] picked a Secretary of Agriculture who claimed to know nothing about agriculture, and who did not want the job, having several druthers as a reward for being rejected by the electorate of his home state [Orville L. Freeman], I pulled in my belt, pulled down my hat, pulled up my pants, and got ready to go for the ride.

Back to my heart-warming patriotism: The Department of Agriculture, which has the avowed intention, as you have read, of having one employee for every farmer in the United States, has come up with a feed grain program by which farmers are encouraged to retire 20 percent of their corn land from production for one year, and for which they are paid varying amounts depending on the past history of productivity of the land.

Since in 1906 Professor Moore of the University of Wisconsin collaborated with Grampa Dougan in finding the finest land the Lord ever created, we are to receive $80.00 per acre for not raising corn on 28.3 acres. Well, the cheese smells so delicious that my natural cupidity has overcome my

Ron and Vera doing their civic duty in the Shopiere-Tiffany Fourth of July parade.

principles and we have signed up. One of the compensations of signing up, of course, is the lovely girls who seem to staff all the Agricultural Stabilization and Conservation Service offices. It is a pleasure to put one's problems in their hands. If they don't know the answers, they have a little book, and if the book is obscure, there is always the director (in our office named Claude), and if he is afraid of committing himself, there is a man in Madison.

Two of our employees just came in. They own small farms as well as work here, and the burden of their lament is "What is the sense of paying farmers to cut back on growing crops while at the same time pushing forward reclamation projects, and pay farmers for draining marshes, often in the same county?" But that is another subject.

I started this letter to let you know I am patriotically doing my duty. When my country calls I am ready.

Ron ends his letter with love, and adds, "I only regret that I have but one farm to give (for a consideration) to my country!"

This letter brings to mind an earlier letter of Uncle Bert, head of the History Department of Lawrence College, now Lawrence University: He wrote Grampa, "I mean to apply for the cabinet post of Secretary in Charge of Not Raising Pigs."

47 ⚔ ICE

After the cans of warm milk from the barn are pushed to the milkhouse on the two-wheeled gladiator-style carts, the milk is rippled down over coils filled with running water from the well, and in a matter of minutes is cooled to 51 degrees. It is bottled immediately and depending on the time of day or night, sent out on the routes or put into the walk-in cooler where it's refrigerated until next delivery time. This is the farm's raw milk, sold until a state law in 1950 prohibits it. The farm has had a pasteurized grade of milk since the thirties; milk to be pasteurized goes into vats, where it's heated to 144 degrees, held there for 30 minutes while large paddles slowly circulate it, then cooled on the coils, bottled, and refrigerated.

When milk goes out on the routes in winter, its only danger is freezing. But in the warm months milk heats up during delivery. Ice is necessary.

There was an icehouse on the dairy when Grampa bought the farm. It's a high-ceilinged, thickly insulated, windowless space filled with fine sawdust and is located above a granary, north of the milkhouse. It's reached from the outside by a wooden ladder fastened upright against the building. When Daddy was a boy this is where he and Trever kept the Baker's cocoa cans they peed into for their peeing competitions. Daddy's children don't know about the contests till they're grown; their pleasure is to climb into the icehouse, pull the door shut, and sit in the dark telling ghost stories. While listening they can burrow their fingers into the sawdust till they find a cake of ice, scrape the damp sawdust off its surface—there's always a very thin casing of damp sawdust surrounding every cake—and lick the ice. They are careful to cover the ice again when they leave.

In the early years ice comes from Rock River, above the dam in the center of Beloit. Conditions must be just right: a long enough spell of freezing weather to thicken the ice, and deep enough snow for the bobsleds, but not too deep on top of the ice. The ice can't be mushy. Nor can the temperature be so cold that water in a cut refreezes before the block can be dislodged and extracted.

When the time seems ripe, Grampa and the men drill a hole in the ice. If it's close to two feet thick, they bring teams and bobsleds. They sweep off any snow and score the ice. They cut down into it with big-toothed hand saws almost six feet long. They cut blocks a yard long and a foot and a half wide and with poles and tongs wrestle them up onto the ice until they establish a waterway. Once that is finished they can float a block to shore, hook an ice prong into it, and a horse drags it up the bank and onto the sleds.

Ed Branigan has an icehouse on the east side of the river, by the Portland Avenue Bridge. His men harvest ice all winter long and pack it in his ice- house. He charges a fee to others to do their preliminary work. Sometimes Grampa avails himself of this service. Then it's the Branigan men who cut down into the ice while the Dougan men cut the blocks into smaller sizes and load up the bobsleds that have been driven out onto the ice. They pack the cakes like children's blocks. When a sled is full the horses pull it through town, out Colley road, to the icehouse on the farm.

There, a tall slanting metal ramp, an elevator, goes from the ground to the icehouse door. It has a rotating chain with parallel cleats. A block is pulled onto the ramp with tongs, the horses strain at the pulleys, and the ice moves up the narrow track, guided and guarded by men on the ground and also by men at the doorway above. It's a dangerous arrangement, for if a block were to slip off, it is heavy enough to kill a man underneath. Once at the doorway

The elevator lifts ice blocks into the icehouse.

the ice blocks topple into the sawdust bed, are set in orderly rows, and when there's a full layer of ice, sawdust is spread generously on top, in preparation for the next layer. The icehouse door is arranged like the silo's vertical aperture, with slats, so that the enclosed space can be slatted higher and higher, while the height of the door gets shallower. By the time the icehouse is full, the ice is being elevated over twenty feet. Inside, the blocks are stacked twelve or more feet deep. Then during the warm months, ice is lowered from the icehouse, chopped up, and the milkmen shovel it over their loads, adding a thick quilted blanket on top to retard melting. They usually carry a small block of ice with them, too, and always an icepick.

Cutting ice and filling the icehouse is one of the most grueling tasks of the winter. It's backbreaking toil in frigid weather. If winter conditions are unfavorable some particular year and the icehouse doesn't get full enough, or if a summer proves exceptionally hot, exhausting the supply, then ice can be bought from Branigan. But the farm's margin of profit is so narrow that it is better for Grampa to cut as much of his own as possible. Also, there is a corps of permanent hired men, and these who in other seasons are busy with planting, haying, and harvesting, are a monetary loss if they're idle in winter. And idle horses go right on eating hay and grain.

A blow falls in 1920 when Fairbanks-Morse upriver begins discharging sludge into the water. Oil freezes into the ice; the oily ice on the milkmen's loads melts onto the bottles; and no customer wants a bottle streaked with greasy black. At first the farm goes above the factory, but soon time and access make this impractical. Grampa discontinues using river ice early in the twenties. Branigan's and Lindall's icehouses are hardest hit. They too must quit cutting river ice, and start freezing it by mechanical means. This raises their costs, and the cost of ice to the consumer. It isn't many years, either, before consumers start to abandon iceboxes in favor of refrigerators. The icehouses eventually shut down.

The loss of Rock River ice comes at a time when the farm is needing more ice, and has been having to supplement its supply by buying downtown. The number of customers is increasing. Also, delivery hours are edging later. When the trucks went out at two in the morning, and routes were finished by eight or nine, not as much ice was needed as when delivery moved to later in the day.

Grampa decides to manufacture his own ice. The biggest dairy in town has already built an ice plant. He buys a Lipman Ice Machine, and installs it in the now unused milk room at the end of the Big House. The machine uses an ammonia gas compressant. The ice it manufactures is also in the old milk room; all activity is set into the floor. There are rows and rows of metal lids. A man grasps a lid with two hooks and hauls a heavy metal container out of the floor. He takes it outside and hoses it down, then whacks it and the cake of ice, shaped like a giant Popsicle, drops out. He refills the container with the hose, replaces the lid, and drops the container back into the floor cavity to refreeze.

Jackie is not aware of the workings of the Lipman ice machine. But it's clear that below the cement floor there are mysterious forces at work. At age five or six she's fascinated when the cakes are pulled up, but always a bit uneasy when she tiptoes past this dimly lit area. Floors are meant to be walked on; there is no walking on this floorway of metal lids receding into the gloom. And even though it is covered, this is a floor that she knows is riddled with ominous holes. She prefers the icehouse, which works in tandem with the Lipman ice machine, for the Lipman does not always manufacture sufficient ice for the demand. Grampa likes to have plenty of ice.

The farm does harvest Rock River ice a final time, early in February, 1935, and it makes the newspaper as an historical item:

ICE HARVESTING AGAIN HAS ITS INTERESTED SPECTATORS
Hundreds of Men Once Found Work During Winter
Storing Ice for Use in Summer
on Swelteringly Hot Days

It was a familiar sight to a number of "old timers" as they drove along Riverside Drive this week and saw a group of workmen taking ice from the river, but to a large number of children who stopped their skating to watch, harvesting ice was something new and exciting.

Since the middle of the week a half dozen employees of the Dougan farm have been working in Rock River just below the Fairbanks, Morse & Co. golf course, cutting ice and hauling it to the farm. The harvesting was done on a small scale, but it was reminiscent of a few years back when hundreds of tons of ice were cut during below-zero weather to be used when the mercury soared on hot summer days.

Approximately 400 cakes were taken from the river this week by the Dougan men. The ice was about 18 inches thick and the cakes were 22 by 41 inches square. The men working were Henry Duerst, John Dummer, Alfred Gerue, George Taber, and Tom Capps.

The men used a horse and marker to lay out the cakes and then took turns sawing out the blocks. A trough was set up from the hole in the ice to a loading platform and the cakes were snaked to the platform up the trough by a cable and team.

The account continues by telling of the former icehouses and the hundreds of men with pike-poles who were employed as harvesters. It describes daring workmen riding blocks of cakes down the trough to the icehouse; the machine that carried the blocks up to the various floors of the building; and the men inside lining up the blocks and "salting" each row with sawdust. The article finishes, "Then, too, there was something else about cutting ice in cold weather that earlier kids liked. That was the glass-like surface which froze over the places where the ice had been cut. That ice was always the best on the river, and the river club which got possession of such a strip had the edge on the other kids."

The Lipman ice machine works well enough, although Daddy sometimes has to lean down into a hole and do something with a monkey wrench. The area is in use till the late forties, when a snow-making room is constructed beside the boiler room of the milkhouse, out by the cooler's loading dock. A small amount of water constantly squirts through an aperture in the ceiling, is frozen immediately, and shaved off by a rotating blade. The shaved snow falls to the floor. Every morning there is a vast snowdrift to fill the milkmen's trucks, for the machine can produce a ton of flaked snow a day. And when in the early fifties all the first grade classes in the city (and some kindergartens) start visiting the farm every spring and fall, a snowball fight becomes a popular staple on the agenda. Beloit Hospital uses the snow machine, too. When they have an amputation, they send out a truck for a load of snow.

This room continues producing until the last milkman loads his last load, when the bottom falls out of retail home delivery. Two of the milkmen do continue city routes; they buy their milk from Mueller's Dairy in Rockford, and utilize the advanced technology of refrigerated trucks. They no longer need ice.

There is one other noteworthy story of harvesting river ice. It's 1928, and the river is not Rock River, but nearby Turtle Creek. The crick has flooded, then frozen so hard that it's perfect for harvesting. The men take bobsleds and a flatbed hay rack with runners through the back pasture, under the railroad tracks, and on through the fields to where there is a slow place in the stream, a kind of pond. The ice there is more than a foot thick. DeWitt Griffiths scores the ice, men ply the two large saws, and soon a four hundred pound block is free and floating. With tongs and planks and ropes and crowbars, it's jimmied up onto the ice, sawn lengthwise and into smaller cakes. Each cake is skidded to a bobsled, roped, and pulled by a horse up an inclined plank onto the sled.

Back at the farm several bobsleds sit around the yard by the icehouse, waiting to be unloaded. Grampa is up in the icehouse with the pulley; a horse below provides the power to skid the blocks up. Grampa intermittently stops the progress of the cakes while those that have

Through deep snow and ice, the milk must get through. Here, Roy Viehman stands by his delivery truck.

already tumbled in are arranged and packed in sawdust. When he's ready to go again he hollers down. At one point he loses his balance just as he hollers and grabs hold of the rope. The men giddyap the horse. The rope jerks his hand into the pulley and lacerates it. Grampa has to leave the job, get bandaged, and take the rest of the afternoon off.

He's ready for supper, though, when the cold and tired men troop in. Not just Dougans have been farming the crick; the neighbors have brought their teams and sleds, too, and have been helping fill the Dougan icehouse. Then the Dougan men will help fill the other icehouses. It's a neighborhood "ice bee." The table is crowded.

Grama has prepared a huge oyster stew for everybody, thick with cream and rich with plump oysters, the humps of their gray backs and the lace of their ruffled edges bobbing above the surface. Butter globules rise and spread out into yellow puddles on top. The aroma curls up with the steam and makes misty the bright chandelier. Grama ladles stew out of the tureen into broad, slant-lipped soup bowls. Several baskets of oyster crackers are on the table, and homemade bread and butter. Wedges of cherry pie wait on the sideboard.

Grampa sits at his place in the middle of the large dining room table, resting his bandaged hand carefully on the tablecloth. He watches the hungry men, their heads lowered, downing the savory stew. His eyes are merry.

"There was a fellow once," says Grampa, "who went into a restaurant and ordered some oysters."

The men look up to listen to Grampa's story.

"They brought them to him," Grampa continues, "and the waiter comes back after a while and the fellow is staring at the oysters, they are still all on his plate. The waiter says, 'Is something wrong?' 'I don't know,' says the man. 'Here, taste one of these for me.' So the waiter downs an oyster." Grampa pauses and downs an oyster himself. "'Here, try another one,'" Grampa goes on, "so the waiter downs another one, downs three or four. 'They seem all right to me,' the waiter says. The fellow replies, 'That's sure funny, I've swallowed these four times already, and I can't keep them down!'"

Grampa laughs. So does everyone else, but less heartily than usual with Grampa's stories. He, of course, can't hear the difference. With gusto he spoons into his stew again and captures another floating oyster.

48 ⋇ ERV FONDA

It's 1948, February. Ervin Fonda, a mechanic, needs a job. He goes into the seed house at Chez Nous, looking for Ron Dougan. There are several men at work in there. Erv glances at one and thinks, "Who the hell is that bum?" It turns out the bum, in shapeless hat and tattered leather jacket, is the boss.

Ron says, "Wait a minute. I have to go to the office but I've got to change clothes first. Give me a ride down to the dairy."

Erv waits, and Ron comes out of the house in his office clothes. He now looks more like a boss.

"I don't know if I need a man or not," Ron says, on the way to the dairy.

"I have to get my house trailer off the street. It's parked in town," Erv says.

"Well, drag it out here. If you like it, okay. If not, you can pull out."

Erv isn't sure that mean's he hired, but he brings the trailer and settles in by the garage. The next day it snows. Johnny Sapp, hauling milk from farm producers, calls in stuck. Erv takes an old spare routetruck and gets Johnny back on the road. He still doesn't know whether he's hired, but he stays twenty-one years.

Erv does everything that needs doing. He can build anything, fix anything, improvise anything. Grampa brings him something to be welded. Erv welds it. Grampa, who now lives on the edge of town and is supposedly retired, says, "Erv, I want to give you a twenty dollar a month raise. Go tell Ron." Erv does. A couple of weeks later Grampa comes into the garage again and says, "I want to give you another raise. You deserve it. Go see Ron and tell him."

The second or third time Erv comes to see Ron, Ron asks, "Who are you working for, anyway?"

"I'd just as soon work for Grampa," Erv says. "He pays better!"

The big garage was built the year before Erv comes. It's a long cement-block rectangle, with no redeeming characteristics, located east of the round barn across the lane that goes down to the crick. It's a combination garage-shop, and has been needed for a long time. There's never been space to put all the milk trucks inside, and over the years winter mornings have regularly been harrowing: uncovering trucks from snow, plowing them out, and getting them to start. A truck is usually backed up the barn ramp the night before, in hopes that it will cough into life when it is rolled down the following morning. Covered space for repairs and construction has been at a premium.

The earliest garage Jackie remembers was a cramped, roofed-over space adjacent to the milkhouse, filling a gap between it and the tool house that stood close to the north. It apparently became a garage by default. Trucks usually entered from the Big House end, were loaded inside, and exited from the farther end, close to the gas pump and the Little House. It had an oily cement floor and its chief interest lay in a room, one side of which opened into the garage's north wall. This space was originally part of the tool house but was now closed off from it. You climbed up two steps and were in a shadowy black cubicle, everything permeated with oil and smelling of it. It had work shelves on its three sides, but not enough space to do any work because of the clutter. Drawers and shelves were under the work shelves, and myriad smaller shelves and drawers and cubby holes and hooks above. In this room, after you'd pulled the lightbulb string, you could find whatever you wanted if you rummaged long enough. Or if you had nothing in mind, you soon found something useful to go do something with. The room was crammed with nails, screws, bolts, nuts and washers of whatever size; buckles, leather straps and belts, little rolls of copper wire, covered wire, plain wire, electrical tape black and sticky; oil cans, some that spurted when you pressed their bottoms, others with a tab you could squirt with your thumb; jars and bottles of various pastes and liquids, and a thousand bits of nameless hardware, plus the smaller tools, the pliers and screwdrivers and planes, hammers, hacksaws, awls. (The larger tools—shovels, rakes, hoes, scythes and such—hung in their places in the tool house.)

But a true garage and shop has been sorely needed, and shortly after it's built, Erv steps into it. It has a large work area at one end, and then space for many trucks and tractors. Erv equips the shop lavishly. It's his domain and there he is king. Even Grampa bows to him; he's the first employee ever allowed to smoke on the place.

"Grampa," he writes on Grampa's pad, "I can't work if I can't smoke."

Grampa ponders the words, and Erv's value. "Very well," he says. "But only in the garage. If you smoke in the yards or around the other buildings, you'll have to leave. And the other men mustn't come in and smoke with you."

Erv is on hand when the inner silo develops a sudden crack, due to more lateral pressure from wet silage than the concrete can bear. The silage, residue from the Libby canning plant at Janesville, has just been offered free to area farmers. But the processing has left it drenched and heavy. No one realized the danger. The silo could well split. If it does, it will bring the entire round barn down with it. To empty the silo would solve the problem, but there's no way to get the silage out in a hurry.

Everyone is acutely concerned. Something has to be done, and quickly. Daddy has an idea: to belt the silo with steel bands from an old stave silo he knows of. Can Erv handle that?

"Easy," Erv says, and spits.

The bands are immediately fetched. They are too short, but Erv has anticipated this. When one has been fitted around the circumference he bends the ends out, drills a hole in either end, and bolts in a double-threaded iron rod that he has ready. It bridges the gap, and when twisted it tightens the belt. He puts thirteen belts around the silo, starting in the lower barn. The structure does not crack any further.

After Grampa buys a new Dodge and throws all the rods by stepping too hard on the foot feed, Erv overhauls the whole motor and puts in a governor. He has to repair the car again when Grampa drives all the way to Janesville and back in low gear. "He said to me," Erv reports, "'I don't know what's

Erv Fonda (left) and Ralph Anderson.

wrong with this car. It's heating up terrible.' I checked it and couldn't find anything wrong, until I questioned him and found he hadn't pushed it up into fluid drive. He couldn't hear how the car was racing."

Erv is kept busy repairing Ron's cars, too. Mufflers are routine. Daddy has a red Buick with a switch on the dash that will raise the frame eighteen inches. It means he can push the switch and head out across any field, bouncing through ditches and over contours, with the car's skirts, so to speak, held high. "It's a great toy, but hell on mufflers," Erv remarks.

Ron, cleaning his shotgun out in North Dakota on a pheasant hunting trip, gives his muffler a different insult. The gun accidentally discharges, and after Daddy has got over his quaking thanks that he hasn't hit himself or anybody else, he examines what he did hit. He finds he's shot out his muffler. He rackets back to Wisconsin, "like a homing pigeon," says Erv, where his mechanic discovers further damage — his boss also shot through the transmission up by the bell housing. It's a miracle he managed the trip home. The pipes are all knocked to pieces, and Ron does penance by searching all the neighboring towns for replacement parts.

After Grampa's death, Erv, his wife Olive, and little Ervie, move from their trailer into the Big House, replacing the Ulliuses who had been in charge. Olive takes over the job of cooking and cleaning for the hired men. She likes the sociability, but the Big House has its trials. The routine is demanding. Her cooking is half-hearted at best. This is somewhat ameliorated by her mother, who likes to come out and lend a hand, especially in the making of apple pies for which she gathers the Marstons' windfalls.

The men enjoy baby Ervie. He shrieks with delight when they toss him from one to another like a beach ball. They hang him by the drop seat of his coveralls from a cabinet knob in the kitchen, and Olive doesn't discover this till she sees it in a photograph. But strong arms, raised to catch the baby if he falls, are also visible.

Upstairs, a Dane has the room over the kitchen, and he can't be made to understand that the register — he's had nothing like it at home — doesn't go direct to the furnace but is merely an air vent, a "cold air register," to allow heat to rise into the upstairs rooms. He empties his cuffs and boots over the grill; oats, corn, and chaff rain down onto the cooking below.

George Schreiber, who works in the milkhouse, comes home drunk one night and falls into a bushel of ripe tomatoes in the back room. That's the last straw.

Erv moves his family to town. He starts to build a house, though, on the west end of the farm, across from Marstons. The tending of the Big House goes to a widow, Pat Gehrke, who happily moves in with her three children.

The men covet an elevator. In a farm magazine it's priced at $1400, more than the farm can afford. Erv visits a farm machinery store, studies the elevator, then builds one from materials around the place. The most expensive part is the belt; there's nothing on the farm long and wide enough in one piece. The Northern Belt Company in Janesville makes one for $60. That, plus a few odd expenses, is the total cost of the new elevator.

The elevator has many uses. It eliminates much lifting and heaving. At the seed house, it stacks feed bags. Also, sacks of corn or oats to be delivered are laid on it, end to end, and lifted to the truck bed. Out in the field, hay bales are raised to the flatbed wagons. This is especially helpful in early morning or evening, when moisture has soaked into the bales making them excruciatingly heavy.

When a baler is invented that kicks bales up into a wagon, Erv makes the special wagon tops, with their high sides and the curved backstop that a bale bounces against instead of sailing right over the wagon and reducing the tractor driver to a grease spot.

The milkhouse gets a new bottle washer. Erv sees the need for a milk case washer and builds one by remodeling parts from the old washer. And when he isn't repairing or improvising, he's busy with construction, especially shingling. He, Craig, Steve Ferguson, and Gilbert Gjestvang shingle the barn at Chez Nous. They bring up eggs and fry them on the shingles, and Craig memorializes the event in a movie. When Erv later shingles the roof of the new seed processing building at Chez Nous, the pitch is so steep that he ties a rope around himself that goes over the peak and is fastened to a truck on the other side.

Using university advice, Erv designs and builds the Ladies' Lounge at the dairy. There are too many cows for the round barn, and the latest dairy science says it's healthier to leave animals outside, anyway. The buildup of manure and straw in a shelter will keep the cows warm.

The Lounge is built at the edge of the barnyard; its long front side, facing the barn, is entirely open. The size of the building, 160 by 44 feet, is arrived at by allotting each cow so many square feet. Erv, Harry Wellnitz, and Lawrence Langklotz shingle the huge roof of the shelter as well as the end of the adjacent horse barn. The men labor till dark day after day on the vast expanses. "Shingling these roofs is like peeing into the ocean," Erv remarks.

The Ladies' Lounge basically works well, but it has a serious flaw. By the time it's ready for occupancy, it's already overcrowded, and the dominant cows are not ladies. A newly freshened heifer will join the herd, and the older cows, crowding into the middle, won't give her space inside, forcing her out into the cold, where she can freeze a tit or tail. Erv can't see how the Lounge can be expanded any more; even if it could be, it would probably soon become overcrowded again.

Dick Knilans, the vet, ponders the situation with Daddy, with Erv, with the herdmen who tend the cows. The Ladies' Lounge isn't the only shelter where there's this problem.

"After you milk the cows and wash their tits, and they go outside in the cold again, their tits—particularly if they're wet—can freeze," Dick says. "Especially your younger cows who have smaller tits that produce a lot of milk, because the udder is tight and the circulation isn't too good. The ends freeze and the tits freeze, they turn black, and, as you know, that can end a cow's productive life. It's your young cows that are getting squeezed out into the cold. You didn't have this problem when all your cows were inside in their stalls and only went outside to drink."

Dick's solution is threefold. Be sure the tits are dry on all the cows before they're turned outside, even if it means holding them in the barn a little longer. Apply a freeze-guard cream on the tits of the younger, more susceptible cows. Or, keep those younger cows in the barn during the freezing weather, and let the older cows have the shelter to themselves.

Erv goes from constructing the Lounge to directing the building of an extension on the garage for the Turtle Volunteer Fire Department. Almost from the garage's start, the Turtle fire engine has been housed in the last parking slot. The siren is on top of the milkhouse and is tested every noon. When a real fire occurs, the call goes to seven phones on the network, including one at the Big House. Gilbert Gjestvang, who is living over the milkhouse with his wife and baby, isn't allowed to be on the network, and it's too bad, for he is right there and enthusiastic. But it's against the rules; he isn't a United States citizen. As the alarm spreads, firemen from all over Turtle rush up with the red lights on their car roofs pivoting.

When Turtle wants to expand to another engine, Ron balks at losing more garage space. He says it's okay to add an extension. The volunteers do the building. There is a party every night, laying blocks and filling the holes with beer cans. "If we ever tear that building down," Erv says years later, "it will be a beer can collector's paradise. There are more cans in those walls than cement blocks!"

Erv had not yet moved onto the farm when Ed Pfaff returned a load of garbage to the townies who dumped it in a ditch near the dairy. But he has his own satisfying story. He, Olive, and his children are now into the house he has built, on the edge of the farm property and just across from Marstons. He's returning at night from a fire when just beyond his driveway he sees a woman climb out of a brand new car and throw a sack of trash into the ditch. He turns on his siren and flasher, swings in behind her, and trains his light on her car. He jumps out. "Lady," he says, "you either pick up that stuff and clean the rest of the ditch or I'm turning you in. I've got your license number!"

The woman is frightened. She thinks he's police. She clears the ditches on both sides of the road all the way to the dairy; they have not been so litter free in a long time. When she finally leaves for town her trunk lid is up. The trunk is too full of refuse to close.

In most ways Erv is an ideal employee. But there's at least one problem. As farm mechanic and fixer of everything, he's in charge of keeping an eye out for what the farm needs in the way of tools and building supplies, and of ordering these necessities. However, many things, by a kind of osmosis, gradually become his. This is most evident when he's building his house, a quarter mile down Colley Road on a portion of Dougan land that Ron has sold him. He orders more two-by-fours, more eaves troughs, more anything than the farm needs or even wants, and then carries the extras home. Once, after he's salvaged a load of nail-filled lumber, he asks a farmhand to add a nail-puller to the list of items he's being sent to town for. The farmhand does, and at the hardware store goes to some pains to charge the nail-puller to Erv's account.

"What did you do that for?" Erv snarls when he sees the bill.

"You're the one that wanted it, and is going to use it," replies Ralph Anderson, who has uncomfortably been watching Erv's buying proclivities.

Erv goes to the store and switches the nail-puller to the farm's account.

"Your dad just closes his eyes," Ralph tells Jackie when she's home on a visit. "Everybody knows it. George Schreiber's told Ron more than once that 'people' are stealing him blind! And Ron just shrugs."

Jackie knows that Daddy is aware, but loath to do anything. The mechanic is skilled, hardworking, and good natured. He's a genius when it comes to improvising. Such a combination is hard to come by for farm work. In the balance, his pilfering is probably not harming the business much.

But when the house is finally finished, Daddy does speak up. He says to Erv in passing, "Erv, I hope you never plan to move. I don't think I can afford to build you another house."

Erv grins at Daddy. They understand each other.

49 ⚹ RONALD PART 9 ⚹ PLANS AND PLEADINGS

Ronald's response to the PLAN NOT APPROVED cable is urgent.

> Whew, Dad, talk about the long arm of the law—it is nothing compared
> with the reach of a cablegram. It came Saturday. Your letter with the financial
> report followed. It took the ache out of the cable and gave me much to think
> about. I read it to V right after dinner.
>
> What I am thinking about most I tremble to write, because whereas in a
> conversation, light touches have no effect on the deep trend, in letters they
> are down in black and white to be weighed and balanced. I think Emerson
> says, regarding friends, that one can talk freely and know that the real will be
> sifted out and treasured and the chaff will be blown away by a kind breath
> and forgotten. That would be the ideal correspondence, but I'm afraid it is
> next to impossible.

Ron is emphatic about two things. That neither he nor V wish to do
anything that doesn't meet with his father's approval. His cooperation, intimate interest, fathering, is essential. And that in all the planning of their life
together, he, Ronald, has taken the lead. He adds a third. "You and I have
not seen a great deal of each other for several years. You cannot know how I
have matured. The day I was twenty-one I looked in the glass and grinned at
myself. The birthday didn't mean a thing but the sense of values, the maturing
judgments gained from the experience of living, had changed me from the
wide eyed kid who entered Northwestern three years before into a man who
thought for himself, and was ready to accept life's responsibilities."

He says that Louis Aubere's death had steadied him, and this year away has
given his thoughts on life a solid basis. "No, Dad, we aren't a pair of heady
youngsters carried away by proximity and environment. We both realize the
responsibilities marriage will mean, but we are fearless in facing them."

The letter spends several pages figuring expenses of school and marriage. It includes $5 a week apiece for food. Tuition and books should be $280. The house would be the greatest expense.

> We would save, however, on the continued dribble a fellow spends socially. Fraternity, parties, eating out. We aren't strong for that life—V would be a check on me, I'm sure—even the practical me that emerged last year, realizing that most of the things a student counts as life are merely froth, and give no permanent value. V's music, plus her schoolwork, plus the interest we both would have in my Economic work, plus our reading together, in both French and English, will furnish us a full life without going outside our little sphere. There is the matter of kiddies. We would, of course, wait.

Ronald repeats his post-degree hopes, that since he hasn't spent time in recent years talking to neighbors, reading farm journals, etc., that it would be better to delay Madison and work on the farm. "As things stand now, books and language are my background. To get the most out of crop rotation study, for example, I must know how the farmers of my section plan, and why. Other ideas would have something to balance against. The same with feeding cows, or plowing, or anything. I can study farm movements better after I know the psychology of farmers, just as now a study of foreign exchange would mean a great deal more to me than before I saw it in operation." He adds, "My ability to meet and hold my own with leaders would be infinitely greater, inasmuch as I would have real work back of me."

He's pleased that Vera has volunteered to teach or tutor in Madison, give music lessons, "but after our Evanston year I would want to assume all responsibility. She will have her hands full with babies, and our home." He can earn, save, borrow, and after Trever's schooling is finished, W.J. might be able to help. "No, Dad, I have no illusions about my ability to hew out my place in the world without adequate preparation. That I am resolved to get."

He points out again their unusual courtship:

> Having lived here together is going to make it difficult for us, if next year we have to manage with a less complete companionship. We are seeing each other a hundred times a day, watching the changing expressions chasing across our faces, making things easier for each other, working out plays and programs together, seeing each other the last thing at night when we all go into the library after the French village people have left, and the first thing in the morning as we go down to breakfast. Put yourself in our places, Dad.

We are absolutely sure of ourselves and our ability to make each other happy. Marriage will not interfere with my plans for fitting myself to play my fullest role in life. It will make my preparation more real, more thorough.

Ronald details wedding and travel plans again, and adds that he is assured of a job working home on the Leviathan. Or he might arrange, through some breed journal, to accompany a shipment of cattle from Guernsey, Jersey, or Holland, and in that way earn something. But he returns to his major theme with a note of desperation:

I want your approval. Of course there are objections, but half the joy of the next few years will come from meeting and surmounting our difficulties. I so want you to see things as I do, to realize my steadiness in planning, that I absolutely want to make a go of farming, that we are ready to sacrifice to make a go of our home. I want you to know how much of beauty I have found in V's life, how inseparably our future must be together. We can find happiness, Dad. We have found it.

Do you know what you can do for me for an engagement present, and what will most thoroughly set the world at rights? Go to Western Union and send this cablegram: PLAN APPROVED—LOVE—DAD.

PS: I am enclosing a picture of V and Mlle. Callais in dance costumes. The picture is almost precious, in the sense of exquisite. It is a good likeness of V, but not the same type that I've taken in big sweater, full skirt and stubby shoes.

At the moment that Ronald is writing this letter, his father is outlining why he disapproves the plan, and alternately suggesting several of his own. He has not yet received the letters of March 7 and 13, to know how events have galloped forward.

He is unwilling to take away Ronald's initiative, nor to dictate, but wishes him to see things in a true sober light. What about Ron's "financially sound" budget—Vera having a regular income, and his $800 or $1,000 from home. This is ethically and financially unsound. Ethically, "It may be the modern way for brides to share the expense of home and honeymoon but I have always felt it belittling to the man. Also it makes his marriage vows a farce. He promises to love, protect, and keep her. The words, 'With this ring I thee wed, with my earthly goods I thee endow,' become a mockery."

Wesson tells his own story:

You compare your financial condition favorably to that of ourselves when we started. I will tell you of our start. We had been engaged over three years. Your mother had taught, mostly paid back her school debt, and provided herself with a modest outfit. I had my degree and was established in my life work, where I was guaranteed a regular job, a place to live, and a cash salary sufficient to secure the basic necessities of life. Besides this I had a nugget in the bank, $2000 to fall back upon in case of any unforeseen setback.

My salary during those years in the ministry was as good in buying power as three times that salary now in the same environment and as good as six times my salary in the environment you will be in. Some years we were able to save. Only one year did I have to draw on my bank account.

Wesson appreciates Ron's enthusiasm over the romance, and the "kick" he will get in touring together, "but I cannot quite get the vision of your boat

Wesson Dougan in his first parsonage office.

trip home. Will your job be coal heaving, dish washing, or deck work? What chance will you have together? Don't let me discourage you, that job is a necessity, but would it not be better without a wife on board?"

He continues that in Ronald's first "girl letter" he was sensible. He still thinks so, and that the pair will reconsider and wait. He repeats his own plan, that Ron put in a hard year at Madison, be married summer of 1925, then both go back for his second year. "V could take some post-graduate work and you finish a strong course. You may say this will be a heavier financial burden but I am sure it will not. Also, it will have been deferred a year and will give us time to adjust."

This, he warns, is a crisis in Ron's life. "The step you take now will in large measure determine your place for the rest of your life." Wesson then moves to the farm proposition:

> There is one thought we must keep in mind. We must make money before we can spend it. We cannot plunge into purebreds, buildings, equipment, etc. One expression in your letter relative to 'working' on the farm I wish to correct. Your first expression was right, you must actually do the work. I do not need help to spend. Goodness! I could spend $20,000 in a week just in carrying out some of my cherished plans, plans I have been thinking out for years. But I realize I must first make the place as it is earn the money to complete these plans. That means I must work.

He repeats he would be glad to say go ahead, and back him in his romantic scheme, but he cannot afford the risk. "Under the circumstances, I feel you should go slow."

Even as he writes, W.J. realizes that Ronald may go ahead in spite of his father's disapproval: "I agree that your marriage there would be desirable from many viewpoints: especially the showers and dinners and church wedding, etc., and then it would be romantic. I do not know but even the boat trip home with the bride in the cabin and the groom heroically heaving coal would add to the picture and be a great story to tell your grandchildren."

He refers to Ronald's earlier dreams: "I have realized for some time that you were growing and would soon drop the toys and play, and find delight in tasks and difficulties and service. I imagine that lazy sailboat trip around the world has lost its glamour or even building a little boat, steaming to Chicago, and selling for a great price does not seem so attractive now."

Wesson could write pages about his own work and worries. "Sufficient to say—I am on the job and trying to 'carry on.' Am getting a pretty good bunch of help together. 'Fired' one man and hired another last week. It is 11 p.m. and I am getting up now at 4 a.m., so must say good night."

But W.J. receives Ronald's March 7 letter before he mails his own. He adds a supplement the next day. The tone has changed. "Good morning my lad: or I mean *my man*. Yes, you are right. You are at the responsible age and from all your statements you are assuming the responsibility of manhood." The rest of the letter reiterates the need for purposeful schooling to become an educated man. "Without it you will be just ordinary."

He gives farm salary and status expectations, saying that two years of school would give him the same entry salary as he would get by working those two years, because his studies and vacation work would fit him for this immediate job:

> That is, if you put in vacations at real work with the herd and on the farm. Of course the expense of those two years in school would have to be figured against ultimate earning capacity for whole life. I have little question but it would pay in dollars, to say nothing of satisfaction in life.
>
> I anticipate your reaction to this thought. It puts off your independence two years, and will burden me to carry you that long. I feel a little uncertain in advising it; however the reward is so far reaching in your life, I feel you should start in this line. If unforeseen disaster interferes, then you can change to the work plan. To deliberately drop schooling now would be wrong.

And then W.J's sweetness shines through. "Now my boy whatever plan you adopt for your home and your school I will do my best to help you. I am willing to sacrifice much and work hard to give my boys a start. I realize that a little help at the right time is valuable in a boy's life."

He sums up how Ronald can round out his education:

> (1) You have a good start in English and some language. You can write. Aim to get some platform work. Get to talking. Stump speeches. Next year will be a good chance. Then get into oratorical contests and debates at school.
>
> 2) Add to your science studies enough at least to have the mystery taken out of the common and natural phenomena about you.
>
> (3) Study commerce. How the world is financed and fed and clothed. Not neglecting the simple but necessary factor of common accounting.
>
> When you have a working and thinking knowledge in these three lines

you are approaching a practical education. I think you could do this next year at N.W. if no circumstance arises to call you away. It is worth starting and striving for.

Please write me at once just how much money you will have to have and when.

Your loving father

Ronald's next letter, after responding to the cable, though not yet receiving his father's followup, is to his mother. He outlines travel plans and expenses. He interjects, "Jimminy, Mother, I surely appreciate how overwhelmingly this has come to you. It has worked out so gradually for me, that I have to put myself in your place to recognize the turmoil it has thrown your thinking into. My decisions, however, haven't been made rapidly."

He mainly reiterates how marriage will not interfere with his goals. He gives newsy items of the Memorial, and that the Applebys of Vera's college are standing in for the vacationing Wadsworths. "We told them of our engagement. They are enthusiastic, thinking our plans practical and logical."

He awaits his father's post-cable letter: "It will be a stiff one," though how can it bring up any eventuality that hasn't been considered and satisfied? "I get more angry with correspondence every day. One evening beside Dad's desk would bring everything into line. Mrs. Appleby was talking about the suddenness to our families. Of course it is sudden, but she said as far as our knowing each other, and being sure of our ability to meet our problems together, we have gained more understanding in our half year living in the same house, than in three years, meeting in the ordinary fashion."

Ron says they have stopped all June preparations until letters could make things more clear. They do want definite sanction. "But there is much to be done if it is June. Arrangements with Dr. Harker who will perform the ceremony, and invitations printed in time for our relatives to know. V has started a little white dress. My wardrobe is depleted." He finishes:

I know along what course lies my happiness. Please do tell me you know me and love me, and that our plans can continue as I have outlined.

I'm still craving to talk things over with you, Dad. You never did tell me how you and Mother scheduled to make a go of it. It's funny how my life has become so absorbed in planning for work and a home. Everything else is secondary.

Ron also writes his brother, about Trever's fraternity initiation. He outlines marrying, finishing school, settling on the farm, and going on to Madison in a year or two. "You will love V, and we will plan to be together a lot—you and I. The engagement will be announced in the *Tribune* by the time you read this. What a surprise at school! Can't you hear the boys whoop when they learn about it?"

Eunice, though, writes of Trever, "He feels pretty disappointed. He was expecting a few years of good old times with you. Now he feels he has lost you just when you were be-ginning to know each other. I felt bad at first—you are so young and not prepared for marriage. Well, maybe it will be all right."

And then, on April 8, W.J.'s post-cable letter ar-rives. As Ronald predicted, it is stiff. "Your objections are real," Ron says, "but they can be met by practical solutions."

He answers point by point. About V's working: not married, she'd be work-ing anyway. By pooling their budgets and time they save

Vera performs an angelic dance at the Memorial.

on both. As to the ethics of a working wife, how is it different from a house-wife helping the family budget by making her own clothes, raising chickens? "Unless a woman does absolutely nothing except her reading, her clubs, her friends, she is doing her share to keep the home running—yes, in a financial way." This is an argument his father can hardly refute, for Eunice receives a salary, if only on paper, for boarding men in the Big House. Ronald also adds, "Even had I a great deal of money and V's teaching unnecessary, she's not the type to sit around. Her teaching gives her something definite to do, and a congenial outlet for her energies."

Ronald agrees that their budget would not cover the unexpected. He rec-ognizes his father's financial position and will not call on him for more than he would be able to contribute easily were Ronald alone.

He counters the suggestion that he transfer to the Ag School in Madison: he's nearing graduation at Northwestern, and would lose credits. He should finish in a year.

He says yes, they could cut out a honeymoon, but travel is inexpensive. It seems foolish not to see more of Europe before returning home.

Ronald speaks of the impending marriage as a *fait accompli*. He is seeing the American consul in Paris about birth certificates and other necessities of French law. His father may need to send a notarized letter, giving consent. There has been an announcement dinner, hosted by the Applebys, with the Harkers in attendance. The village has been congratulating them for two days. An announcement has been sent to the *Tribune*.

He takes his mother to task on the age difference. "V continually reminded me our people might object. You will be reassured when you see us together. I have known girls of sixteen with less vitality and snap. Except when you bring it up, it never enters my head. Just the same, I suggest you not tell anyone, even Aunt Ida, our true ages. They know mine, so trim a few years from Vera's. She is infinitely younger than she really is, and what people don't know doesn't hurt them. At least, not knowing, they can't talk."

The letter ends with a promise to write Helen Burnette; his mother wants her to hear the news directly from him. He says, ingenuously, "You never had any desires for me along that line, did you? She is wonderfully nice, I know. It is rather funny, because V's family has been pushing her to marry this Theodore chap. She ran away from Chicago largely to make up her mind. Her mother is all for us, but in her first letters, before she knew we were sure of ourselves, she let a note of sadness creep in for Theodore."

This letter of further reinforcement turns out to be superfluous. Wesson and Eunice have at last been persuaded by the earlier letters, or if not persuaded, have realized that momentum and inevitability are against them. They recognize their son's overwhelming need for their blessing. They cable on April 13,

WE LOVE TRUST APPROVE DAD AND MOTHER

Ronald's response is a paean of ecstasy:

> Today has been so perfect I must tell you about it! The sun is shining for the first time in weeks. Mlle. Duvillers and I played with the children all morning on the chateau grounds, and this afternoon V and I took forty more to

play there. It is on a high mound over the river valley. Today the low rolling hills were bathed in a hazy purple mist of sunlight and spring smoke. And the flowers! Violets, great golden buttercups, others I do not know in English. The dog went wild, tearing around in the new grass and showing off to another dog that wagged and grinned his approval. I ran and shouted and tossed babies around, and chewed violets and laughed with V. Oh, it's so good to be alive. So much of beauty almost hurts me.

It is light now, the after supper twilight. Sometimes I think this is the best part of the day. But then there are breakfasts, with coffee and good bread, and everyone ready for the day, and the morning sunlight at ten o'clock. I like late afternoons, too, with its calm sun and people hurrying home to supper. When I try to decide what part of the day I like best it is impossible. The quiet of my room at night, after I have locked up, is satisfying. I like the feeling of a day finished with nothing to do but clean up, and maybe read or write until I am sleepy. I must be a sensualist in the fullest sense of the word. The little delights of every day give me the keenest satisfaction and well being.

But you want to know what I am thinking and what the last few days have brought forth, don't you? Sunday morning, just as I was starting out to find a camping place for next Sunday, a cable came that made V and me nearly jump out of our skins.

This should be the letter's conclusion. But there is a final thunderbolt. "Harkers have left but will return in two weeks, before departing for the States. Dr. Harker grinned and said, 'It will hurry you children, but why don't you get things in shape for me to marry you when I get back?' Whew! But the Applebys are enthusiastic."

The upshot is, the late June wedding is set forward to Saturday, May 3. It will be at the Memorial, with the required town hall civil ceremony in the morning. They will have a few days in Paris, then return to their jobs till their contracts are up. The necessary affidavits will come promptly. Announcements will be made in the village for the required ten days. They are buying the remaining material for V's dress on Monday.

"This is the last time, positively," writes Ronald, "that I'll take your breath away. I do want to talk more about our travel plans, getting home, school, work, but if I mail this now it will go out tonight."

The young couple is well aware of the time mail takes to arrive at the farm. Ronald's parents will learn of the wedding only two, possibly three days before its actuality. But that is time enough.

50 ⚹ STANLEY OTIS

Stanley Otis's father Dan is a professor at the University of Wisconsin. His specialty is Farm Management, and he sends several Master's students to the Dougan farm to work and do research for their theses in the area of Farm Economics. For a while he's head of the university's Short Course for farm boys. He also spends time as an assistant dean, and promotes Extension work. He's an officer in the Banker Farmer organization, and on the editorial board of their magazine.

Professor Otis develops a form of farm bookkeeping called the Otis Method. He and Grampa go all around the state, traveling by train, staying overnight at hotels in towns large and small, holding meetings with county agents, who are in turn in touch with all the area farmers. Dan Otis explains his system of record keeping and W.J. speaks about efficient farm management, and how his own efficiency is aided by the Otis Method. The two are a symbiotic team.

Dan Otis gets an idea that city boys, who are at loose ends all summer, would profit in many ways from exposure to life on a farm. He organizes a pilot Extension program to place city boys on farms. Three boys start the program. One of them is his own twelve-year-old son. He sends Stanley to the Dougan Farm, the summer of 1925.

Daddy Dougan speaks to Stanley on the red rug before his desk, just as he does any new employee. He says the program is an experiment and that Stanley has a responsibility as one of the first boys picked. He will receive room and board plus a small wage, but his main payment will be in experience and the wholesome atmosphere of the farm. He then outlines Stanley's chores. Stanley listens cheerfully and not greatly concerned.

His day begins by riding Prince to the pasture and bringing in all the horses. He curries them, brushes them, harnesses them, and gets them ready for work. After that he splits kindling behind the Big House and fills the kitchen woodbox. Then comes a bountiful breakfast, and the rest of the day is spent with the men in the fields, or doing whatever work or chores transpire.

A week after his arrival Daddy Dougan calls him again to the red rug. "Now Stanley," he says, "when your father asked me if you could come for the summer I was very hesitant because I didn't really know whether it would work out. But I was ready to take the chance because I know your father so well. Now—I notice that you're not always getting the horses ready like you should. And Mrs. Dougan says that the woodbox isn't always full. And I notice that when you're asked to pick strawberries you're not very anxious to do that, but when you sit down at the table to eat you're very good at eating strawberries. In fact, you can beat two hired men at that."

Stanley gets the message. He hadn't realized he was supposed to be quite so devoted to his duties. He promises to try harder.

He learns some things about farm life. One of the horses, King, will aim a terrific kick at Prince if Prince gets too close, and he himself might get caught by a hoof. He learns not to be careless in tightening the cinch strap, after the saddle slips to a forty-five degree angle while he's riding and he's nearly bucked off. He witnesses twin calves being born in the pasture, one on the ground and one half out, and rushes to tell Jim Howard, the herdsman. He learns not to challenge a spindly looking neighbor boy, one of the Mackies, to a wrestling match, and that it's not really wise to challenge any farm boy. He comes to recognize a potato bug. He accepts the herdsman's suggestion, when they are standing by the calf exercise yard out back of the round barn, watch-

It was Stanley Otis's job to groom the horses every morning.

ing half-grown calves frisk about, and Jim says, "Why don't you try to ride one of those?" He is thrown onto the concrete so fast that he can't remember being thrown, only that the sky is very, very blue.

He learns to mow, behind the bay team, Pat and King, or behind Kit and Prince. He pitches bundles, and watches how a top-notch loader arranges them with the butts out, layering them to lock them on the flatbed wagon so the load won't fall off. He's fascinated by the steam and by the rotating belts of the threshing machine, and how the cutter bar cuts the twine as the grain to be thrashed feeds into the jaws. During thrashing he breaks a tine on one of the brand new three-tined pitchforks by tossing it into an empty wagon. He never tells anyone he did it, but suspects that his employer knows who's responsible.

In the back of the barn he finds an old buggy with a broken shaft. He's not been close to a buggy before. He gets permission from W.J. to try to repair it. Somehow or other he gets the shaft to hold together, cleans up the buggy, and drives it to church with Prince pulling. He's self-conscious; there are no buggies on the streets, only Model T's and such. People smile as he goes by. He ties the horse to a drainpipe behind the church. W.J. compliments him for managing the trip down and back.

Stanley enjoys the social life of the farm. The mealtimes, with the family and help sitting together. Listening to visitors chat on the Big House porch. The music evenings in the parlor that Ron's wife organizes, with Esther singing while Vera accompanies her, and then all of them gathering around the piano and singing. Noon hours, joining the men pitching horseshoes in the driveway. Evenings, sometimes a ball game. Helping turn the crank on the ice cream freezer, on the lawn after supper.

He's fascinated by how Ron and Mother Dougan talk to W.J. with their flying fingers. When he goes to church, he watches Mother Dougan translate the sermon just as fast as the preacher is talking. He learns the deaf alphabet, and even though he goes too slowly between letters for Daddy Dougan to get his words, he feels it an accomplishment.

All in all, the summer is a success, measured in weight gained, muscles hardened, new skills learned, and responsibility accepted. Professor Otis's program fizzles, however, because the city boys on the other two farms get tired and go home.

But Stanley Otis comes back and spends his thirteenth summer on the Dougan Farm. That summer he learns to plow well enough with a three bottom plow that Daddy Dougan shows his city lad off to visitors.

51 ⚹ HAYSTACK

P aul Herried is fifteen when he comes, for summer vacation, to work on the farm. It's during World War II and help is hard to get. Grampa has given him a job.

His first morning he spends doing odd jobs around the place at Grampa's bidding. At noon, he sits under a tree and eats the sack lunch his mother has packed, and drinks a pint of chocolate milk. Afternoon comes, and Grampa sends him up to Ron's place, with another hired man, to bring back a load of hay from a haystack out in a field.

The hired man is a regular employee, and about five years older than Paul. His name is Leland. While driving the horses to the haystack, Leland discovers that Paul knows Ron's family, that he is in the same class at high school with Patsy. Leland's eyes brighten; he questions him. There is a country dance

Pitching hay.

coming up, and does Paul think that Joan, seventeen and the eldest of Ron's girls, would dance with him? Paul hasn't the faintest idea whether Joan ever even goes to country dances, and if she did, whether she would dance with Leland. Personally, if he were Joan, he wouldn't. He doesn't find the fellow much to his liking. Paul pleads ignorance—how could he be expected to know? Leland persists until he realizes what a useless source of information his partner is, and then falls silent the rest of the way.

They arrive at the field and the haystack. Leland parks the flatbed wagon right next to the stack, climbs down under the edge of it, and goes to sleep in the shade. Paul is surprised. But he gets busy at the job, struggling to load the hay on the wagon. It's hard going for the hay is badly twisted. Eventually Leland wakes up, yawns, stretches, and begins to help. The two pitch hay for the next hour and a half, till the wagon is loaded. They then return to the barn and unload the hay.

At the end of the job, Grampa pulls Paul aside. "I find it incredible, laddie," he says, "that it has taken two men four hours to get in a load of hay. You needn't come back tomorrow."

He is right, Paul agrees, and says nothing. That is the last he ever sees of Grampa, or of his partner. But a very many years later Paul, now the head of a large firm in Ohio, says to Jackie, "Some poor misguided souls have since paid me more than five hundred thousand dollars a year for my services, but that is the only time in my life that I was ever fired."

52 ⚔ RONALD CULTIVATES

Ronald is sixteen. He's learned to drive this past year—the farm's first automobile, a seven passenger Overland. He asks his father to let him take the car to an all-day Fourth of July picnic at Yost Park on the River Road. Grampa agrees, but only if Ronald leaves promptly at noon in order to come back and cultivate corn. Ronald agrees. He goes to his picnic and thoroughly enjoys his hours there, but fudges a little on the time of leaving. Back at the farm he hitches his team to the cultivator and starts on the field west of the buildings.

The horses plod down the rows between the young corn. The cultivator, behind, has two shoes, each with four cultivator shovels. The shovels are hung on a frame so they can swing sideways, to miss the plants. The shovels run on both sides of a row, halfway to the next row. They uproot and turn under the myriad young weeds—pigweed, mustard, velvetweed—that are hogging the nutrients in the soil. Unchecked, a velvetweed can grow to six feet, with broad and velvety leaves and shiny black seeds in the fluted bowl of its segmented seedpod.

Ronald sits on a light metal seat between the shovels, guiding them with his bare feet. He can cultivate two rows at once. He's a careful worker, and leaves clean aisles behind him.

It's a drowsy afternoon. The sun shines, a breeze barely stirs the young corn leaves. Flies drone, causing Barney and Bess to flick their tails. Ronald, jog-gling slightly on the seat, goes from south to north, starts the next lap from north to south, then south to north again. His feet on the cultivator shoes swish through the dust.

Near the end of a row, on his way back south, he glances up from watching the shovels and sees a squad car pulled up at the side of the road. Two policemen are beside the fence, and his father is with them. W.J. looks grave. They appear to be waiting for him. At the end of the row he stops the horses, climbs off the cultivator and comes to the fence.

Ron is cultivating.

"Your name is Ronald Dougan?" asks one policeman. Ronald nods.

"You were driving an Overland shortly after noon today?"

Ronald nods again.

Grampa says, "These officers clocked you speeding on the River Road. You were going forty miles an hour."

Ronald can't deny it. The officers are serious, his father is serious, Ronald is serious, too, for there will be a court appearance, and almost certainly a fine he'll have to pay. Equally bad, perhaps worse, is his father's disappointment in him. He returns to his cultivating. The afternoon has lost its bloom.

In a few days he and Grampa go to court. They see Judge Clark in his chambers. The judge gives a lecture on the gravity of the offense, and how speeding endangers the life and limb not only of the driver, but also of innocent bystanders. Ronald wilts inside.

Then Judge Clark says, "Ronald, how old are you?"

"Sixteen, sir," Ronald replies.

"Have you ever been before me before?"

"No, sir."

"Well, I tell you. I won't fine you on this if you'll promise not to appear before me during the next sixteen years."

Ronald promises.

In 1934 Ron Dougan runs a red light and pays a small fine. It's a few months short of sixteen years, but Judge Clark isn't presiding.

In 1960 Ron Dougan again gets a traffic ticket. He appears before his friend and chess partner, Judge Arthur Luebke. Ron expects to be fined, for Art Luebke is nothing if not scrupulously fair. This is as it should be. And sure enough, he is fined the maximum for his offense.

But then Judge Luebke asks, "Is there any previous record on this individual?" He stares through Ronald as though he were a stranger.

A clerk checks the records. "There's a speeding charge from 1918 and a red light violation in 1934."

On account of the earlier infractions, Judge Luebke adds ten dollars to the fine.

The two men never mention the court appearance. But a few months later, at a chess club meeting, Ronald takes malicious satisfaction in beating the Judge; it is always a red-letter evening for anyone who succeeds in that.

53 ⊀ RONALD PART 10 ⊁
WE ARE ENTIRELY HAPPY

G rama is beside herself on May 2, 1924, the day before Ronald's wedding in France. She wrings her hands, wails, "Oh, he's so young, so young!" and, "He's way over there all alone, getting married all by himself!" She says, "It's just not possible my little boy is old enough to be married!" She repeats to everyone the lovely things she's heard about her son's bride, but always with the refrain, "But he's so young!"

She goes to an afternoon church affair. A friend presents a stranger to Eunice and says, "This young lady knows the girl your Ronald is marrying." Grama listens eagerly as the stranger gives glowing praise of Vera—so artistic, so talented, so sensitive. Eunice returns to the farm mollified.

In an April 13 letter to Ronald, the day of the "We Approve" cable, she says, "Things have moved so fast I have been in a daze but am coming out now and feeling better. With Vera having right ideals and a Christian makes it easy. I know I shall love her. You have written some wonderful letters."

She reports Trever's remark, "Ron is an idealist. I hope he is not looking at things from across the ocean under romantic conditions, and when he gets into the actual, he'll have a tumble." But she reassures, "You are looking at the situation from all sides, but it's the every day perplexities, grind, and disappointments that try one's character. I know however, you will be able to face anything with the love of a devoted wife, and if you put your trust in your Heavenly Father."

Two things missing in Ron's letters have distressed her. She'd prayed that this work and year abroad would set his soul on fire, "but you have never mentioned Him and your life service dedicated to Him." And then there is the habit from college. "We cannot think you have smoked over there, but one little word of assurance would give us such joy."

> We are glad Vera is sensible. How much more satisfied than we could be with
> a frivolous girl without ideals. She will be an inspiration and perhaps show

you easily what I have been trying blindly to show you all these years.

I had a good time with Trev this vacation. He is a dear, but does have such wrong ideas of Christianity. He won't go to church, though promised to go Easter and Mother's Day. If he could only see the truth how gladly he would accept it.

I sent the cablegram with Dad's sanction. It is all you asked for an engagement present. God bless you. He must be leading you for I have always prayed that He would.

Eunice writes again on May 2, having just learned the marriage will be the next day. "It did take the breath away but we feel it is all right under the circumstances. We surely wish you a contented life together. You will not have all roses but if you are of one mind and are patient with each other, you will have a fine home."

She reports that Esther has washed and polished the car. In Madison next day they'll celebrate the wedding with Trever. "We can't have you, but the rest of us will be together thinking of you. By the time you get this note Vera will be our daughter. She will take the place of my first little girl. Aunt Ida was so shocked, but is resigned now. I think you have missed your calling—you should be a lawyer. You can win your case whatever you are trying to present." She ends with bushels of love to both their dear children.

Ronald writes April 30, three days before their marriage, how busy they are. V is finishing her dress, he is tending odds and ends. They'll make the bouquets themselves, of white lilacs, margaretes, and daisies. It will be bundles of fun. Their names are published in the town hall, where they'll go for the civil service Saturday

The wedding ceremony at the Methodist Memorial.

noon—the same as getting a license at home, but one must have a ceremony. The religious one, that afternoon, is optional, but he wouldn't feel married without it.

> At 5:30 we shall take a train to Paris. I have theater tickets. Sunday we may go to Versailles, the fountains will play that day. This happens only a few times a summer, as it costs the state too much. However, we might stay in Paris and hear Bonnet play the organ at Notre Dame.
>
> I've never seen the world more beautiful. The other day we passed an open garden gate. Gardens have high stone walls around them, so this was unusual. We looked in and were getting a big kick out of the flowering pear trees, the low, branching apple trees strung on wires, and the grass sprinkled with great double margaretes when we saw a little old man coming. He apologized for the garden but jimminy, it is a little paradise. He took us through the house, showed us chickens, birds, the view of the town from his attic windows. He begged us to come back when Madamoiselle was Madam.

Ronald gives his mother some assurance on one matter of her concern. He says he believes in God's goodness, that it is hard not to know V and catch something of her surety. He says nothing about smoking. "This letter is choppy but what can you expect from a chap who will be married in three days? Bet Dad didn't do much sitting around before his wedding!"

The cable to Vera Wardner and Ronald Dougan arrives in time:

CONGRATULATIONS ALL HOME FOLKS

After the wedding and brief Paris trip, Ronald and Vera write an antiphonal letter describing the wedding. Ron writes, "When Vera appeared, walking toward me, following her little flower girl and her maids of honor, the satin of her dress holding the light a bit, and her veil flowing back from her sensitive little face, she was absolutely lovely." Vera takes her turn. "Ron, tall and handsome in his tuxedo, was waiting for me. He looked so dear and fine—and when our eyes met and he smiled at me, something welled up in my heart and I wasn't afraid, just awed."

Dr. Harker talks of the joys, responsibilities, and possibilities of marriage. The service is not long. At the finish, he introduces the couple as "Mr. and Mrs. Dougan," and in Vera's words "there followed the usual kissing of the bride, led off by a certain R.A. Dougan. I understand Mr. Plut, the janitor, had been looking forward to this part of the ceremony for three weeks. He gave me resounding smacks on both cheeks, French fashion." She describes the wedding cake, "a huge pyramid of French culinary skill," throwing the bouquet, the changing into traveling suits and the running for a taxi amid showers of shoes and confetti. Ronald takes up the tale, describing Versailles (they ate in Louis XIV's dining room — a chocolate bar) and travels near Paris; Vera describes a boatride down the Seine, and finishes the letter by saying how very happy the cable made them. "It was so

In the courtyard, with Dr. and Mrs. Harker.

satisfying to know that you all were thinking of us and loving us, at this biggest moment of our lives."

Ronald's contract with the Memorial ends before Vera's does, but he continues working part-time for his board and room. By chauffeuring American tourists to the war sites and Rheims he earns 20 francs a day. He never reveals his nationality and that he can understand English; and enjoys his passengers' comments about their handsome young driver. He books passage for Vera on the Leviathan sailing out of England. He himself has been promised a crew job. But the company changes hands and ignores previous commitments. Vera is glad, for the Leviathan is considered a dangerous scow. They plan now to go to Switzerland and Italy, and sail from Naples on July 19.

Ronald visits the Channel Islands. With his letters of introduction from important Guernsey breeders in Wisconsin, he's given royal treatment. On June 23, from a hotel in Jersey, he writes home:

> Today I have seen this island from end to end. Our Jersey-breeder friend, Mr. Peredes, had us out in his auto since ten this morning. We saw all the best herds and then came back for lunch. The cows are beautiful, although I'm sure our breed has the edge. They are wonderfully well formed. I haven't seen a bad back today.

You know their farming methods—inadequate for us, but the only possible way here. They have no land to grow corn and grain, but can graze almost all year round. There is a little of the smaller variety of clover, mixed with a ranker grass that is but little tenderer than our timothy. They are afraid to graze alfalfa, they fear bloat. Of course, America is their life saver. It has turned average farmers into men with an idea of world markets, and provided some with more than comfortable livings. Jersey hires a great many French peasants from Brittany for the potato season. I think the Isle of Guernsey is better cared for—I like the town better, and the farms are neater. The Jersey men think no good ever came out of Guernsey, and vice versa.

As to cattle, they are great. They make me homesick. Just the same, considering the prices, I'm sure we can get better at home, and really, I think our records are worth more, inasmuch as everyone understands ours perfectly, while the average man shies a little at these. They are stricter than we are about TB, and they test for butterfat oftener. The cows are crowded by our standards. The Jerseymen have been having a record scandal, something like the Holstein scandal of a few years back. They have thrown out no cows though, and are hushing it up. Fifty farmers have quit testing, because they think something crooked has happened, and they are leery of the whole business.

He writes several pages on his impressions of the Channel Islands, and finishes, "PS: In reading this over I find perhaps it is the most 'descriptive' letter you shall ever get from me!"

A letter W.J. writes "To My Dear Children" on June 16 arrives just as they leave Chateau-Thierry. He, too, writes a descriptive letter:

This is Monday morning 5 a.m. The dairy work is moving strong, every man at his post. The field man getting teams ready for a strong pull. Mother is making breakfast and getting the wash started. The fields, garden, and yard are very pretty just now. The alfalfa fields are ready to cut, a rich dark green. The oats and barley fields are a delicate pale green and the corn fields a black surface studded with spots of light green all in regular checks. Any way you look across a field, the hills fall into line and give a perfect row.

You know how I love the fields at this season. All is promise of an abundant harvest which we begin to see, not by faith alone as we did a few weeks ago, but in reality. Our senses can begin to touch the material and again be assured of God's love and care. His promise is sure: There shall be the seed time and the harvest. We have begun cutting alfalfa. There will now be almost a constant ingathering until the last potato is stored in October.

He says he's given Ron this home scene, written on farm paper, so Ron may not forget and lose spirit for the farm.

He and Mother feel it's not practical nor for the greatest pleasure to meet the boat in New York. "We will be at home when you arrive with everything in readiness to give you the paternal welcome, even to the fatted calf."

He encloses a draft for $250. "You may count the whole $450 as a wedding present. We will make no account of this. When you start school we will loan you the necessary funds or help you secure the loan."

W.J. tells of accepting several Institute talks in Illinois. "I am arranging to have Mother give talks on the farm home. She has the knowledge and has done the work. I am sure she will do well." He signs off, "Write often for we want to follow your course and enter into your plans. With tenderest affection, your "Dad."

Ronald replies from a Paris hotel, for he and Vera have just left Chateau-Thierry. "We packed in an awful hurry—about a day and a half—finished our three trunks last night at eleven. We then crept stealthily down to the Marne and threw in an undesirable wedding present."

The promised money comes a few days before they leave. "Gee, Dad, you are good to us. I only hope I can do for my sons what you have always done for me. This year has broadened me in every way. I am beginning to think

Boats on the Marne, where Ron and Vera sank an unwanted wedding gift in the middle of the night. The Memorial is the large white building on the bank.

in world terms, and every line of study has become vitalized. Here is one change in me. I used to discount as ignorant anyone who didn't speak perfect English. Now, I find those that don't, have different ideas, and are vastly interesting. Then my year of listening to broken English has also taught me patience."

He gives a last description of Paris, including leaning over the embankment of the Seine and watching fishermen:

> The sidewalk is lined with little book stalls. We browsed along until dinnertime, then found a place for less than a dollar. We are now at the hotel, happy as larks. V is writing her mother, so we write a bit, talk a bit. The room is perfect, even the ornate clock under a glass case — none of these old clocks ever go — and the great wardrobe with the mirror front.
>
> We are entirely happy. Our life in the single room at the Memorial didn't create a ripple, and even our frantic packing didn't cause scowls. It seems perfectly natural, this life together.

Vera finishes the letter:

> We've had such a splendid day, getting off early, finding our comfortable hotel, and doing just as we pleased the rest of the time. Perfect as it all is, we are more anxious than ever to get home, to see you, and start to work. We are ever so grateful for the wonderful wedding present. *Mille remerciements.* A million thanks!

54 ⚔ ART RASCHKE

A rt Raschke is a small, tow-headed man, badly crippled with a twisted
body and a hunch back. He works as a cow tester. Ron Dougan, in
1939, writes a letter about him to an official at the Department of Farm Accounts and Dairy Records in Madison. He says he isn't very happy about the
status of their local Dairy Herd Inoculation Association. "We have a good
tester in Arthur Raschke—possibly as good as we have ever had. The Association work has come to only part time this year, and he has gone home in his
spare time and helped an overworked tester in his neighborhood, thus giving
him a better income. He is a good man, accurate in figures and only needs
to be told once what is expected of him." The letter continues by saying that
the Association really needs about ten new farms in order to give Raschke full
time employment, an increase that isn't likely:

> This tester, as you know, is handicapped with a bad back, which unfits him
> for heavy work. I am wondering if we were able to make a place for him
> here at the farm, doing clerical work, checking loads in and out of the plant,
> helping get out statements, etc., if he would be able to continue his part-time
> testing for our association. Would the fact that he looked to us for part of his
> income disqualify him to test our herd—you know we are doing some work
> for Prentice's club. I've said nothing to him about this idea, or to my father.
> We might not be able to use him at all as far as that goes. The fact that he
> would have to be away entirely for about two weeks at a time would make it
> difficult to work out a schedule of office work for him. The last thing I want
> to do is take him away from testing work because he is a natural at this job. If
> we could get him a full association that would be the best solution. Neverthe-
> less I would like your opinion on our hiring him part time.

The state gives its blessing, and after a bit Ron works it out with his father
and Raschke that the cow tester be employed by the milk business in the dairy

"He was always kind with US!"

office. He works intermittently there for a number of years. He proves, unfortunately, to have an irascible temperament.

In the forties the government starts to become concerned about water pollution. The agent in charge of Rock River Basin asks the farm how its waste water is disposed of. Ron Dougan tells him that the water discharge from the dairy milkhouse goes into a holding pit below the barnyard. The overflow is piped down to the pasture where what isn't absorbed into the soil runs on into Spring Brook. This isn't sufficient, the agent says; the farm must come up with a better solution. At the very least, it needs a settling basin. Ron Dougan consults the university, lays some plans, begins work on a settling basin. In the early excavation he breaks the water line, and the job comes temporarily to a halt. After a few weeks the agent comes back. Ron isn't in the office. The agent asks Art Raschke what Mr. Dougan is doing about his waste water treatment.

"Not a goddam thing," snarls Art.

"Well, I better come back," says the agent.

When he does, he asks to see what's been done. Ron explains about the broken water line that has held up progress, and leads him down to the pasture to see the outlet pipe and the start of the settling basin. It's been a very dry summer; there is no water in the creek at all.

The agent looks at the cracked and dry bed. "But this is an intermittent stream!" he exclaims. "Intermittent streams don't come under my jurisdiction!"

He and Daddy both forget the whole matter.

Art Raschke's handicap contributes to his death a number of years later. He's at the 4-H Fair in Janesville, testing a cow, when the heavy animal turns suddenly in the chute, pinning him against the side of it. He hasn't the strength to push her off, and her bulk crushes him. In spite of his often ill-mannered ways, the farm mourns. And the area loses the best cow tester it's ever had.

55 ✎ ASSISTANT PIGMAN

Ed Grutzner and Craig are buddies from Todd School kindergarten. Over the grade school years, Ed often rides his bike to the farm to play. By the time he and Craig are thirteen, in 1943, they are old enough and big enough to apply for summer jobs. Grampa hires them.

They spend some time in the fields, pulling mustard weed from the alfalfa and clover. When detasseling season starts, they are on the detasseling crew. During haying, Ed drives a tractor, and helps fork hay into the round barn. One morning he is given the unenviable job of cleaning the barn cesspool.

Grampa, never one to tolerate someone standing idle and distracting the farm help, also assigns Whitey to this job. Whitey is a lippy town kid who is always underfoot. He's a sort of adopted nephew of George Schreiber, a bachelor who works in the milkhouse. Ed and Whitey, sharing the ladder into the foul pit, and passing up the buckets of liquified manure to each other, get into an undeclared contest to see who can accidentally slop the most verdure down on the one in the lower position. At noon, none of the day workers who carry a lunch will sit anywhere near them.

When Ed gets his driver's license, he's able to drive the truck to collect the ten-gallon cans of milk from neighboring farms, a job he enjoys. He also enjoys working in the milkhouse, washing bottles and cans. Not so enjoyable is hoeing around young corn in the hot sun, and even hotter, threshing. In his years of summer work, he covers all the necessary farm chores.

In his final year, when he's seventeen and has been diligent in all the minor chores, advancement comes with a burst: he's promoted to the position of assistant to the head pig man.

This man is Leonard Beadle, farm manager, formerly the Ag teacher at Clinton High, a man passionate about pigs, and as knowledgeable as anyone in the state. Daddy and Grampa have given him his head when it comes to raising pigs, and he is joyfully developing and enlarging the Dougan herd of Durocs into show animals. The farm workers joke about Leonard Beadle.

When he has to take a trip anywhere he loads a few pigs into the pickup truck, and often sells them on the way, but the men say he takes them along for company.

Mr. Beadle is glad to have an assistant. Ed learns that adult pigs are boars and sows, young pigs are boars and gilts—collectively, shoats—and then, of course the babies, the piglets. He enjoys feeding the pigs, their frenzied squealing and pushing and actually scrambling into the trough.

And he learns that pigpens must be moved each year to a new lot; this puts the pigs on fresh ground, which reduces the danger of parasites and disease. For the new lot, he and Mr. Beadle dig postholes and install stout wooden corner posts. They drive intermediate metal posts into the ground and string the bob wire by pulling it tight with a tractor. They hammer together a wooden gate, and install it. With the tractor they pull the pig houses and troughs to the new lot.

All this is hard work. It turns out to be minor, though, compared with moving the pigs themselves. They like it fine where they are. The head pig man and his assistant push, pull, and pummel, to no avail. Mr. Beadle smacks one on the snout with a 2 x 4; the pig's nose is a little bloodied but he doesn't budge an inch. The two pick up a pig by head and tail to carry it, but it's far too heavy. Mr. Beadle tries a trick that works with getting a pig into a truck: no pig, of course, will willingly climb aboard. But put a bushel basket over its head, and in trying to get rid of it, it will back up the enclosed ramp. On the open ground of the back pasture, though, the basketed pig, its squeals muffled, just backs rapidly in an erratic circle—there is no guiding it anywhere. Finally, man and boy drag the protesting pigs by their ears and tails, one by one, to the new pen.

Mr. Beadle, wiping his streaming brow, shares a bit of philosophy with his panting assistant. "People are a lot like pigs. If you want a pig to run south, make it believe that you want it to run north. With people, don't tell 'em what to do. Make 'em believe that it's their idea in the first place."

Ed stows away this wisdom—he will find it useful in later life—though it hasn't worked 100 percent well today. And again, no one wants to sit near him at lunch.

The Assistant Pig Man is chosen to accompany the pick of the pigs to the State Fair. He refuses. Mr. Beadle is upset. Ron Dougan remonstrates with Ed, but he is firm. "All those kids who take animals to the fair have to sleep in the pens with them. I live with pigs all day! I won't go sleep with them!"

Ron shakes his head. "Alas, you're still a city boy," he says, and sends Craig to sleep with the pigs. Ed follows his old routine, tending the porcine population that is left behind.

When the time comes for him to apply to college, Ed chooses Harvard; he wants to become a lawyer. On the application blank he is

Ed Pfaff astride—another way to move pigs!

asked his work experience. He states that he has been First Assistant to the Head Pigman on the Dougan Farm. He also lists Ron Dougan as a reference.

Nobody knows what Ron writes in his letter, or what the confidential records of Harvard might contain. But Ed Grutzner is accepted. He graduates, goes on to law school, and comes back to practice successfully in Beloit.

Many years later, the *Wall Street Journal* runs an article on college admissions. One paragraph states, "The more exotic or diverse the student's experiences, the greater the chances of catching an admission officer's eye. 'One could argue that the experience a student gets may help refine a particular kind of expertise or set of accomplishments that could be very valuable in a seminar or in a classroom discussion,' says William Fitzsimmons, Harvard's dean of admissions and financial aid."

Ed takes the article out to the farm and shows it to Ron Dougan, now nearing his nineties. He tells Ron that the inference is strong that in its search for diversity, even as early as 1948, Harvard College gave preference to the First Assistant to the Head Pig Man from Wisconsin. He suspects he is the only Assistant Pig Man ever admitted to that prestigious institution.

"Well," says Ron, "they do say you can judge a man by the company he keeps."

"I can't remember that my particular expertise or accomplishments ever 'refined' anything in a Harvard seminar or classroom discussion!" Ed says. "But I've never forgotten my lessons from the farm—especially that people are a lot like pigs."

"And in your law practice," Ron Dougan says, "you've probably had an occasional client where a pig might have been preferable!"

56 ❧ SLEEP LITTLE BABY

When Mother and Daddy get off the boat in New York in early August, 1924, it's shortly after noon. They loiter around the train station until 2 p.m. before they wire the farm of their safe arrival and the time they'll be coming into Beloit. They've forgotten that all businesses in the United States don't close down for two hours in the afternoon. They have practically no cash, though a year later Mother, getting Daddy's overcoat ready to send to the cleaners, discovers a twenty dollar bill in an inner pocket.

Aside from short rations, the trip is uneventful. The high point is trading berths with an overweight couple who look with dismay at the more narrow upper berth to which they've been assigned. Ron and Vera are glad to make the switch—they were feeling some apprehension themselves, having the couple over them.

As they approach Beloit they are excited and eager to see Grama and Grampa. They're also both a little nervous. Vera has on a brown silk dress with fur trim. She wants to look her best for the in-laws she's not yet met. As the train pulls into the station, Ronald gets her a glass of water. The train lurches; water spills all over her. She arrives stained and streaky. But it makes no difference. Grama and Grampa welcome her and love her, wet or dry.

At Northwestern, Ronald talks to his former professors. They all agree to let him finish his work and take the final exams. All but one. The Professor of Russian History listens to his tale, then barks, "Young man, I have never seen you in my life!" Ronald loses his two credits in Russian History.

Grampa and Ronald agree it will be best for Ronald to take his senior year at Beloit College, an option not considered before. Rent for two rooms at Aunt Ida's, only a few blocks from campus, will be much less than Evanston. Produce and meat can come from the farm, and Lester Stam delivers milk to Aunt Ida's house every day. Most importantly, Vera is pregnant. It's better that they remain in town, with all the family resources and support nearby.

Ronald sees Chemistry as a useful major for the farm, as well as a study

Ron and Vera honeymooning, homeward bound.

that interests him. Except for World History from Dickie Richardson, he takes all chemistry courses. He tries to make money by getting out a college blotter, as he did at Northwestern, but when the college president decides he should be paid a miniscule stipend for this and the college keep the profits, he abandons the project. Delta Upsilon is not among the fraternities at Beloit. Ronald organizes all the non-fraternity men into an independent group. The Independents carry off the scholarship prizes, the athletic prizes, and win the Homecoming Float trophy. The fraternities are left blinking.

Aunt Lillian, Grampa's unmarried sister, lives at Aunt Ida's, too. Every morning she comes down to breakfast and every morning she says, "I never slept a wink all night."

One morning in March she comes downstairs. "I never slept a wink all night," she says to Ronald and Aunt Ida.

"Then why aren't you congratulating me?" asks Ronald.

"Congratulate? What for?"

"Surely you heard all the commotion in the night," says Ronald. "Vera went to the hospital, and little Vera Joan was born at three o'clock!"

Aunt Lillian clamps her jaw shut and in spite of the good news is sulky for much of the morning.

In June Ronald graduates with top honors from Beloit College, and he and Vera and little Joan move out to the Big House. They live there with

Sleep Little Baby, the lullaby Vera wrote for Joan's first Christmas.

Grama and Grampa and Esther while the Little House is extended on its east side to include space at the end of the living room with built-in bookcases and a fireplace, and over this space, upstairs, a sleeping porch filled with windows. Then they move into the Little House.

Ronald goes to work for his father, which eventually becomes a partnership. He takes over most of the business end of the farm. He and Vera buy an upright piano so that Vera can play. Vera joins Treble Clef music club, and starts teaching ballet. She also, most days, does four hours secretarial work for Grampa, typing many of his letters.

Every morning Grama comes over to see Vera. She watches her work, and tells Vera how she has finished all her own housework and baked five pies and eight loaves of bread, all before nine o'clock. She plays with the baby, creeping up on Joan on her hands and knees, being a growling bear. Joan screams with delight and kicks her little legs.

At some time every day, Grampa also stops by to see Vera and the baby. One autumn day he takes a workday off and spends it entirely at the Little House. He follows Vera around, watching everything she does: bathing and nursing the baby, washing the clothes and diapers, putting Joan down for her nap, taking her outside. He watches Vera do her housework and make the meals. He watches her do her ballet exercises, using the back of a chair for a barre. He asks her to play the piano for him, and even though he can't hear with his ears, he puts his hand on the instrument and feels the vibrations. Vera plays and sings for him the lullaby she has written for Joan's first Christmas; he first reads the words, and then follows her lips as Vera sings:

> Sleep, little baby, the daylight is fading;
> Dim yellow stars the dark heavens adorn;
> Once, long ago, in a Bethlehem manger
> The Little Lord Jesus was born.
> Lulluby, lullaby, sleep, little baby, sleep.
>
> Sleep, little baby, my arms are about thee,
> A circle of love which enfolds thee secure;
> So Mary cradled the wee baby Jesus,
> The little Lord Jesus, so pure.
> Lullaby, lullaby, sleep, little baby, sleep.
>
> Sleep, little baby, thine eyelids are drooping,
> Thy warm, tender body relaxing to rest;
> Jesus thus slept in the arms of sweet Mary,
> His dear little head on her breast.
> Lullaby, lullaby, sleep, little baby, sleep.
> Lullaby, lullaby, sleep, little baby, sleep.

Grampa's eyes are moist when the song finishes. He says, "I can hear it, Vera."

He does nothing of farm work all that day. He talks to Vera about many concerns of his; he asks about hers. Vera writes back to him, or he reads her lips. He has specially requested that she not learn the hand language that Ronald and Grama use so rapidly. He wants to practice reading lips, and he wants to be able to look at Vera's face when they talk.

It's a happy day for Vera, for Joan, for Grampa. "You are a dear little mother," says Grampa in benediction when he leaves at evening to go over to the Big House. Vera feels blessed.

Grampa admires baby Joan in front of the Big House.

57 ⚔ PLAY

For Joan and Patsy, Jackie and Craig, the farm is one vast playground. Not that they think that; playgrounds mean school recess, or parks with slides and teeter-totters. But on the farm there's always a rope to swing on, a fence to scale, silo rungs to climb. Nails, hammers, planes are handy. The four can do things together or alone. Even if it seems there's nothing to do, if one wanders about, poking here and there, some item will provide inspiration. Jip accompanies any of them, leading the way with his tail awave. Butter, the goat, lags behind, snatching bites of greenery.

There are activities to watch. Today Mr. Griffiths is mixing cement in a long box; he uses a hoe. Tomorrow George is lowering the grid on a vat of clobbered milk for cottage cheese. In the barn udders are washed, in the Big House kitchen pie crust rolled out. Sometimes in the Big House living room, the Friendly Club sits around a huge frame and the women talk and laugh while they make a quilt, and tell gossip not meant for young ears. Once, in that living room, paper hangers slop paste on strips of paper, and cover the walls with new designs.

When Daddy was six he milked two cows. By twelve, his quota was eight, and four horses to curry before breakfast. Now barn hands do these chores. The four don't have regular jobs, but they search for eggs in the hay, or a nest of spitting kittens, which lets Grama know where the big cat has disappeared to. They carry in kindling for the wood stove, or hand clothespins to Josie hanging aprons on the Big House lawn.

They do have garden jobs—Grampa drags a furrow alongside a string he's tied to stakes at either end of a row, and directs their spacing of lumpy beet seeds in the trench. They pick peas, beans, strawberries, and later sit on Grama's cool front porch and shell peas into a basin—there's a special spot on the pod to press your thumb—or snap the ends off beans, or hull strawberries. These are good garden jobs. A loathsome one is picking potato bugs. One dairy job pays: when there's a special, such as chive cottage cheese, you

Mom costumed us for our own 4th of July parade around the farm.

stand at the end of the bottler and drop an advertising cuff over each capped bottle. This earns a dime.

The Little House has regular chores: drying dishes, making your bed, picking up your toys. When they are older they will detassel corn, pull suckers, help on the milk routes, tend a 4-H calf. For now, they mostly play.

Summer garb is barefoot. Shoes come off the last day of school, and don't go on again till after Labor Day. By then their thick, hard soles can scamper over anything.

One farm space doesn't have any specific use. It's a small grassy field between the milkhouse and the road. When the grass is mowed, the drying swatches are sweet smelling. That's the best time for building a village from the slatted wooden crates the new milk bottles come in. The four drag out five or six; each is a ready-made house. The extra ones are for second stories. Height is risky, however, and more for looks, for the piled crates are flimsy to climb into.

The fun of the dwellings is their embellishment. Mown grass makes thatch for the roofs; spread inside it's a soft carpet. The spaced slats allow a resident to look out, chat with neighbors, issue invitations to come drink chocolate milk.

There are other places for houses. Across Colley Road beyond the large garden is the orchard. Each apple tree becomes a house, and with the variety of trees, the larder in each is a different kind of apple. Crisp or tart, sweet or sour, even the mushy Snow apples, thrown away after a bite. In springtime the houses are fragrant with blossoms, dangerous with bees, and the garden yields new raw peas, raw asparagus, the last of the strawberries, and currants that pucker your lips.

The woodpile behind Grama's kitchen door is another play space. When a farmhand has split wood, he often builds a sturdy wall of unsplit logs, and inside its generous circumference are heaped the loose sticks. The four clamber up, claim spots, level floors, use logs for tables and chairs, and sticks for other necessities. The woodpile isn't comfortable, one gets slivers, and the sticks can slide — it's a dangerous place for a settlement. As for supplies, they can bring a lunch from the Little House, Grama's cookie jar is nearby, and bottles of chocolate milk and orange are omnipresent.

There is more to do than play house. The bottle crates make a vegetable stand beside the ditch, displaying a few potatoes and carrots. Nobody driving by ever stops so that tending the stand soon becomes boring. It's more fun in the old schoolhouse, the one Daddy went to school in. This takes four; the teacher needs pupils to order about and make sit in corners, and the pupils need other pupils to pass notes to, or throw spit balls at. The slatted corn crib, when empty, makes a jail, for locking up a captive from cops-and-robbers. Once Joan, Patsy, and Jackie forget that Craig is in jail, until they pass nearby and hear him shaking the corn crib door and howling.

There are other places yet to play — the slightly sloping roof of a single story building behind the Little House, behind the rabbit hutches, makes an excellent stage; the audience claps from the ground. The sidebarn, with its wide rafters and ropes that swing over the sawdust pile, is ideal for circuses. The tool shed is good for borrowing any sort of implement so long as it's put back. The four find a trunk in the rafters of this building, one filled with old fashioned lady's clothing, mostly black. No one knows whose trunk it was. Maybe Delcyetta's, Daddy's grandma? She lived on the farm when he was little.

The round barn loft, of course, is best for playing when it's filled with hay; they must watch out for the open chutes. And balanced on top of the broad wall that separates the hay from the overhead grain bins, is an old sleigh. They take trips over imaginary snow with pretend horses. The sleigh disappears one year. When Jackie is grown she asks what ever happened to it. Daddy says a neighbor, Milton Bumstead, borrowed it, a truck backed into it, and that was that. "Milton fixed it up, after a fashion," Daddy says, "and I never had the guts to ask for it back. I told him I hoped he wouldn't plant flowers in it."

Along the lane to the pasture several empty flatbed wagons are grouped amid rank smelling weeds; these make ships. The pirates leap from one to the next, stick-swords clenched between teeth, to do battle with the good sailors defending their cargo. The lane passes a fenced pig-field. Pigs busy leading pig lives are always worth a watch, especially when squealing and jostling over a full trough. Beyond is the pasture gate, with the crick to be waded in, or dammed to make a pond. They've tried fishing, with bent pins on strings, but nobody ever catches anything. Daddy says there were frogs and snapping turtles in the crick when he and Trever were damming it. The shallow stream is dangerous in spring spate, or in summer when a downpour causes it to overflow its banks. They then have to keep a respectful distance, watching the roiling waters, for in no way is a raft allowed.

Beyond the crick is the gravel pit, with a small wood bridge with a hole in it, ideal for Billy Goats Gruff. Joan is always the troll. When they're in need of gravel, they fill their wagon, careful not to overload. Daddy's much loved wagon (he and Trever even made a sail and tried to sail it on the railroad tracks) they one day piled so high with rocks that the front wheels went forward, the back wheels back—"Just like a little dog spreads out," recounts Daddy—and the wagon box fell to the ground.

It's pleasurable to follow the crick to the railroad underpass, where the cows go through to the back pasture, and crouch there when a train rumbles overhead. Then they can take another lane, the cows' lane, back up to the barnyard and the cowtank. Mother writes in a letter, "The youngsters are in the tank all the time," and they are, except when the cows come to drink. Cows take priority.

Jackie and Patsy share a tricycle.

All this is spring, summer, autumn activity. Winter brings different fun. Wind blows snow into giant drifts beside the snow fences. Long tunnels are dug, cathedral-size rooms hollowed out, with dim light filtering through.

Best, though, is when the snow is scant and Daddy runs a hose out onto the small front field. A pond spreads

Town kids ride out to play on Saturdays.

out, an inch or two deep, and freezes into a skating rink. The middle is glassy, but grass tufts poke through the ice near the edges. Everybody skates, Mother and Daddy, the hired men from the Big House, the four kids, an occasional kid living in the apartment over the milkhouse. Grampa and Grama come to watch and laugh. Skating is usually after supper, with a light rigged up on a pole. A milk can of hot chocolate milk melts a snowbank. As long as the season lasts, water is daily run over the surface to freeze and renew the smoothness. Jackie, Patsy, Joan, and Craig name the pond; it's an imaginary country. Indoors they draw maps, naming the inlets and small islands, and a long sliver of ice that runs along a path out toward the road. A couple times, when there is no pond, Grampa hitches a horse to the large bobsled and gives everyone rides. The can of hot chocolate is present there, too.

The young hired men living at the Big House don't just play in winter. In the other seasons they often come out after supper for a ball game in that same field. They are willing to let the Little House dwellers join in, too.

In all this play on the farm, here's an extraordinary thing. Jackie doesn't realize how extraordinary until she's grown with kids of her own. Yes, when Mother and Daddy go out at night, the four aren't left alone. Eloise Marston from the next farm comes, or Ernie Capps from the Big House good naturedly lets them examine his rotten ear, a skin discoloration. The term "baby sitter" has not yet been invented, though the function is an old one.

But outside there's no sense of adult hovering. They know there are places they mustn't play—the strawstack is forbidden, and the bull yard—but except when they're in the cowtank they are left to their own devices, whether it's riding their bikes and trikes on the circular sidewalk of the empty cow

A pause in snow play.

barn, or climbing to the swaying tops of the pine trees and hollering their heads off.

Jackie also realizes this, however. They are supervised all the time. Dozens of people are on the place, and while no one in particular is charged with watching them, the adults are all aware of where the kids are and what they're up to. It could not be a happier arrangement.

58 ❈ PHIL JOHNSON

Ron, having finished his business in Clinton, stops by to see two old employees, always favorites, Phil and Jeannie Johnson. "Remind me about your coming to the farm," says Ron.

———✦———

Well, my girlfriend Jeannie Higgins—you've known her since she was in three-cornered pants—she started to work in the house, up at your place, the seed farm, summer of '41, and your dad, we all called him Daddy—came in—and he of course was an old friend, knew all the Higginses, living up there beyond the Hill Farm, and he asked if Jeannie knew where he could hire a good man. Well, she recommended me, she knew I was out of work, and Daddy came over to the garage where I was helping out at Shopiere and asked if I wanted a job. So he took me over to your place, and there were 40 acres of oats lying on the ground, all in windrows waiting to be shocked, there were several guys shocking, and Daddy said, there it is. So I began shocking, like I always did, and Daddy watched, and Lee Holmbeck wrote to Daddy, how come we have to put the bundle under our arm to shock it and he does it that way—I could take a bundle in each hand and pull them together, they only did one at a time—well, Daddy just laughed, and Lee went back to shocking the way he did and I did it the way I did, and we got the field done in a day or so.

Then I did work around the farm. Daddy had bought a team of horses from Jeannie's dad, it was the best team on the farm, and I was driving Barney, the old blind horse with the moon eye, and one noon after dinner Daddy says, "Phil, you take the bay team, the Higgins horses, and you drive them from now on," and I was thinking, Oscar Skogan, he's been driving that team, he'll get teed off, which he did. I wasn't very popular around there.

Then it came corn husking time. I had one wagon and the bay team and the other wagon had Cliff Holmbeck and a guy named Brown. They husked two rows and I husked two rows. They started out ahead of me and I was right on their tail, I got up to the end of the field and went right around them and back down my rows until my wagon was full, and I got back to the barn and had my load shoveled off before they came in. I did this for two or three days and then I asked Daddy—I didn't ask him, I wrote a note, and asked if I wasn't entitled to a raise, I was doing as much work as those other two men and doing it faster. Daddy threw up his hands and cried, "NO! For that's a God-given GIFT!" So I went on husking, day after day. Jeannie said I was lucky to even have a job!

Her story about Daddy is that she'd be working at your place, and the phone would ring, Ruby from the office at the dairy, and Ruby'd say that Daddy had a group of men up there, some from the university, working with the seed corn, and he wanted them all to come in for noon dinner, so she'd have to hustle around and quick fix a big meal with what was on hand, sometimes even have to call the grocery store in town to send some stuff out. They delivered in those days, even into the country. And then she'd feed Daddy, and his crew of men, and Vera and you, Ron, it was all very jolly, and Daddy was appreciative. He always gave a heartfelt blessing before the meal, too, Jeannie says.

Well, it got into the fall, I was doing chore work, a lot of cropping, a lot of shelling corn, and I asked Daddy if I could get in the barn for the winter. Daddy and I got along real well—it meant he'd have to kick Cliff Holmbeck out of the barn, but he did it. I was not popular, but I done a lot of work. I followed the barn routine, with the cows and cleaning, very careful with cleaning the utensils, wearing the white aprons and so on. Griffiths was foreman, Red Richardson was herdsman. I got along fine with the higher ups, I got along real well with you too, Ron; the lower downs, the guys that were just there for the job, they resented me. I was there to work.

It's like this. When I was thirteen, Bill Nitz, he was a neighbor, came over and asked if I'd cultivate his corn. He had some scrubby horses, barely able to walk, he had them all hooked up, he said to me, cross the road, cross the fence, and start. He told me how to use the cultivator, I'd never done it. But before I left, my father said to me—he never lost his Norwegian accent— "Philip-killip, wherever you work, give them a good day's work and you'll always have a yob!"

So I've worked hard all my life, hard work never hurt me. I've always given a good day's work, and I've always had a 'yob'! I guess it's a God-given gift.

59 ✳ GRAMPA'S GLORIOUS DAY

I t's spring of 1948. Grampa has been working alone in a field all day, and has gone on home to Grama and Effie in the house on the edge of town. Ron has been out of the office, doing discouraging work on the milkhouse plumbing. Close to six o'clock he stops by his desk. Two little scraps of memo paper are laid across the day's work, so that he'll notice them. He recognizes Grampa's familiar pencil scrawl.

Ronald: I had a glorious
good time today.
The sky and clouds have
been grand.
The team responded to every
touch & were so strong
& willing.

The machines were good if
they are old. That wonderful
field of No. 1 grass is such
a satisfaction—we have been
preparing for that for the
past ten years.
     "Dad"

Ron reads his father's note twice, grins, sticks the little papers in his pocket to show Mother, straightens his shoulders, and heads for home.

Books by Jacqueline Jackson

Julie's Secret Sloth, 1953

The Paleface Redskins, 1958

The Taste of Spruce Gum, 1966

Missing Melinda, 1967

Chicken Ten Thousand, 1968

The Ghost Boat, 1969

Spring Song, 1969

The Orchestra Mice, 1970

The Endless Pavement (with William Perlmutter), 1973

Turn Not Pale, Beloved Snail, 1974

Stories from the Round Barn, 1997

More Stories from the Round Barn, 2002

The Round Barn,
A Biography of an American Farm
Volume One, 2011

Jacqueline Dougan Jackson (pictured here at about the time she promised she would some day write this book) grew up on a Wisconsin dairy farm amidst extended family and pet goats. Various accounts of her early years are included in this volume, and in two earlier Barn books. She majored in Classics at Beloit College, studying with poet Chad Walsh and artist Franklin Boggs. At the University of Michigan her writing tutor was Hopwood Director Roy Cowden. She began teaching at Kent State University, and continued at Sangamon State (now U of Illinois Springfield) where she was on the founding faculty. She led eight groups of students on hostelling trips to England. Studying children's lit one group climbed Watership Down with Richard Adams; on a mysteries trip, they spent a day with Colin Dexter.

At eight Jackie Jackson won a first in short stories at Beloit's city-wide hobby show; her first novel was serialized in *The Galesburg Post* when she was ten. As an adult she has twelve published books, two self-illustrated, has had plays and musicals performed, and her stories read over Wisconsin Public Radio. *The Taste of Spruce Gum* was the 1968 runner-up for the Newbery Award. For twenty years she hosted "Reading and Writing and Radio," listened to in classrooms throughout Wisconsin's School of the Air, and in central Illinois. Some of the programs are included in her writing book, *Turn Not Pale, Beloved Snail,* and are free on her website for classroom or personal use. She currently has a weekly poem in Springfield's *Illinois Times*.

Jackie Jackson's daughters are Damaris, Megan, Gillian, and Elspeth. She has six grandchildren, all (of course) above average.

Pasture

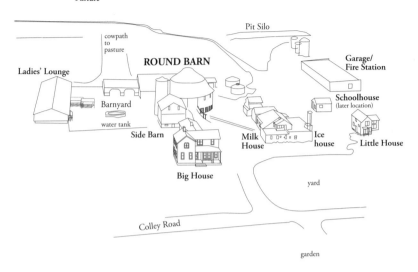

cowpath to pasture

ROUND BARN

Pit Silo

Garage/ Fire Station

Ladies' Lounge

Barnyard

water tank

Side Barn

Milk House

Ice house

Schoolhouse (later location)

Little House

Big House

yard

Colley Road

garden

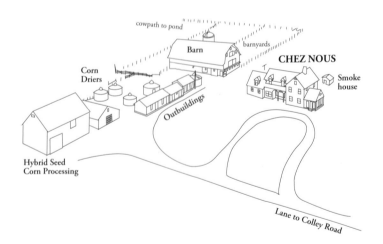

cowpath to pond

Barn

barnyards

CHEZ NOUS

Corn Driers

Outbuildings

Smoke house

Hybrid Seed Corn Processing

Lane to Colley Road